ASSESSING REGIONAL INTEGRATION IN AFRICA | ARI

NEXT STEPS FOR THE AFRICAN CONTINENTAL FREE TRADE AREA

G000113031

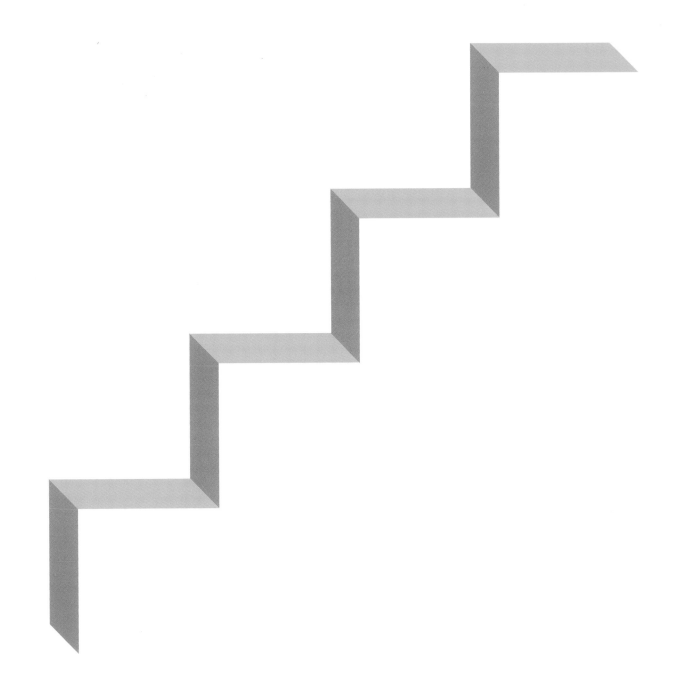

United Nations
Economic Commission for Africa

African
Union

UNITED NATIONS
UNCTAD

Ordering information

To order copies of this report, please contact:

Publications Section
Economic Commission for Africa
Menelik II Avenue
P.O. Box 3001
Addis Ababa, Ethiopia

Tel: +251 11 544-9900
Fax: +251 11 551-4416
E-mail: eca-info@un.org
Web: www.uneca.org

Addis Ababa, Ethiopia

Title:	Assessing Regional Integration in Africa IX
Language:	English
ISBN:	978-92-1-125137-1
eISBN:	978-92-1-004299-4
Sales No. :	E.19.II.K.3
Print ISSN:	2411-8192
eISSN:	2411-8206

Cover design and layout: Karen Knols, Ginnette Ng, Carolina Rodriguez and Tessa Schlechtriem.

Printed in Addis Ababa by the ECA Printing and Publishing Unit. ISO 14001:2015 certified. Printed on chlorine free paper.

Contents

Figures

Key Messages and Policy Recommendations

Key messages

- **The historic signing of the AfCFTA Agreement on 21 March 2018 marked a momentous milestone for regional integration in Africa.** The signing strongly indicated commitment by policy makers and African leaders to regional integration.

- **Regional integration faces challenges.** They include limited energy and infrastructure development, insecurity and conflicts, multiple and overlapping membership of RECs, poor sequencing of the regional integration arrangements and limited financial resources.

- **Monetary integration continues to be actively pursued by five of the eight regional economic communities.** These RECs have adopted macroeconomic convergence criteria, but their member countries have had mixed success in meeting these criteria.

- **Integration in services is important, given its contribution to African GDP growth.** In 2017, over 53 per cent of the continent's GDP came from services.

- **Gradual progress is being made towards the free movement of people.** Steps have included the launching of the Common Electronic Biometric African Passport in July 2016 and the adoption of the AU Protocol on Free Movement of Persons, Right of Residence and Right of Establishment in January 2018—the latter, however, has struggled to gain country ratifications.

- **A mismatch between available skills and the needs of Africa's labour markets slows the continent's economic integration and overall development.** Deepening of regional cooperation in education, including through the implementation of Africa's Higher Education Harmonization Strategy, can help.

- **Africa's large infrastructure deficit hinders intra-regional trade.** Infrastructure financing can be supported by maximizing the use of public–private partnerships, tapping into national resources and using regional and global infrastructure development funds and innovative financing tools.

- **Regional energy integration through power pools can attract considerable investment in energy.**

- **Africa's governance, peace and security challenges are inextricably linked and are prerequisites to establishing a continental-wide economic space.**

Policy recommendations

- **More economic and physical integration, including through important infrastructure projects, is needed.** It will require significant resources, including leveraging public–private partnerships and innovative financing tools.

- **Cross-border collaboration in energy trade should be strengthened.** Mechanisms include regional energy policy frameworks, gas and power pools and integrated regional energy markets.

- **African States at the level of both RECs and the African Union should strengthen and resource their existing instruments promoting good governance, peace and security.** These will create the right environment for the pursuit of regional integration

- **Monitoring the implementation of regional integration is critical.** The development of the African Regional Integration Index by ECA in collaboration with the African Union Commission and the African Development Bank is a powerful tool for monitoring integration.

- **African countries must address the crisis of implementation and translate promises at the continental and regional levels into action.** These include ratifying and implementing the AfCFTA, the Single African Air Transport Market, peace and security instruments, monetary integration commitments and the AU protocol on the movement of persons.

Chapter 2 The State of Play and Next Steps for the African Continental Free Trade Agreement

Key messages

- **Remarkable progress has been made in realizing the AfCFTA. Fifty-four of 55 AU member States have now signed the agreement.** As of July 2019, 27 have ratified and deposited ratification instruments with the AUC. Negotiators have concluded all four of the phase I protocols to the agreement and 10 of the 12 annexes (Trade in Goods annex 1 on Schedules of Commitments and annex 2 on Rules of Origin are to be concluded by July 2019), marking commendable progress since the launch of negotiations in June 2015.

- **Implementing the AfCFTA is about more than trade. It is about dispelling the "crisis of implementation" of AU decisions and initiatives and validating the African Union and its Agenda 2063.** It is a litmus test of the commitment of African countries to economic integration.

- **The AfCFTA aspires towards deepening the integration of the African continent beyond merely a free trade area.** It includes as objectives to "create a liberalized market [...] through successive rounds of negotiations," "lay the ground for the establishment of a Continental Customs Union" and "contribute to the movement of capital and natural persons."

- **African countries must take care that the AfCFTA not simply add an additional strand in the African spaghetti bowl of preferential trade regimes.** Instead, it must provide coher-

ence to the internal and external trade policy landscape in Africa.

Policy recommendations

- **The remaining African countries should ratify the AfCFTA without** delay and ensure that the continent moves together by greatly exceeding the minimum number of 22 ratifications required for entry into force.

- **Critical technical components that need to be finalized before the AfCFTA can be operationalized must be urgently concluded.** They include schedules of concessions for trade in goods, rules of origin and schedules of specific commitments for trade in services. These must be followed by the phase II negotiations on investment, competition policy and intellectual property rights.

- **Ratification of the AfCFTA must be followed through by effective implementation.** This requires creating the AfCFTA institutions, establishing the mechanisms envisaged in its operative provisions and incorporating AfCFTA obligations into the laws and regulations of each State party. And countries must strategically take advantage of the AfCFTA to achieve economic development and poverty alleviation.

- **The effectiveness of the AfCFTA committees will require many prompt decisions.** Certain perfunctory decisions could be delegated to the Secretariat, other decision-making authority delegated to REC representatives in the absence of State representation or permanent representatives accredited to the Committee of Senior Trade Officials, as is done in the WTO in Geneva.

- **Implementing of the AfCFTA will be more effective if national ministries responsible for trade create AfCFTA committees.** The committees can comprise persons focal for satisfying the commitments and interest of the AfCFTA and can harmonize their country's approach to implementation. These should ideally be framed within the structure of an AfCFTA national strategy.

- **Using the AfCFTA to realize the deeper forms of integration in Africa that have been called for by African Heads of State and Government.** This requires progressively deepening the liberalization achieved under the AfCFTA until it is sufficient to subsume the existing REC FTAs into a single, fully liberalized, African trade area.

- **Unilateral trading schemes of Africa's partners can reinforce African regional value chains if they are designed appropriately.** African countries should accordingly deploy their diplomatic capabilities towards influencing trading partners to promote regionalism as they design their unilateral trading schemes, including generalized systems of preferences.

Chapter 3 Taking Full Advantage of the AfCFTA

Key message

To take full advantage of the AfCFTA, countries must buttress its implementation with complementary measures in investment, production, trade facilitation, trade-related infrastructure and import defence.

Policy recommendations

- **Investment in the AfCFTA can be supported through:** (1) national investment plans that channel investment flows into sectors that benefit from AfCFTA market liberalization; (2) investment promotion agencies to attract and facilitate investment, including through "matchmaking" between international and domestic firms, one-stop shop centres for investors,

and measures detailed in the UNCTAD Global Action Menu for Investment Facilitation and (3) partnerships with other African countries to learn from their experiences and with UNCTAD and ECA for support with UNCTAD investment policy reviews and UNCTAD/ECA online investor guides.

- **A productive capacity development agenda can support a country in producing the goods demanded by the AfCFTA market through:** (1) an industrial policy to create a supportive and facilitative overarching enabling environment, (2) sector-specific strategies that take a regional approach to value chains development and (3) the AUC Service Sector Development Programme, which seeks to provide a blueprint for the development of competitive services sectors in Africa.

- **Trade facilitation measures can support AfCFTA trade opportunities through:** (1) an effectively designed AfCFTA non-tariff barrier mechanism, (2) investment in standards infrastructure and strategically harmonizing standards in sectors with high AfCFTA potential and (3) introduction of a continental simplified trade regime, to help small and informal traders gain from the AfCFTA.

- **Trade-related infrastructure for pursuing the opportunities of the AfCFTA can be supported through:** (1) effective implementation of the Programme for Infrastructure Development in Africa and (2) strategic logistics management to align trade facilitation with infrastructure development.

- **Import defence measures can help to manage import competition from the AfCFTA through:** (1) pooled resources to establish regional trade remedy institutions at the REC level, (2) competition institutions established or reinforced at the regional or continental levels, (3) ministries of trade focal persons assigned by the ministry of trade to proactively assess likely import implications of the AfCFTA and monitor customs data for changing import patterns and (4) platforms sponsored by the ministry of trade for private sector stakeholders to flag import stress.

- **National AfCFTA strategies can provide a coherent and strategic approach towards measures to complement the AfCFTA.** They should incorporate gender mainstreaming to ensure that the gains from the AfCFTA support gender equality.

Chapter 4 Intellectual Property Rights Protocol

Key messages

- **As private rights used in the industrial and commercial context, IP rights function as policy tools to promote entrepreneurship, investment, competition and innovation. At the same time, IP regimes are essential in maintaining certain public policy objectives that relate to the dissemination of knowledge and indigenous learning. The AfCFTA provides an opportunity to advance a continental approach to a balanced IP rights system that responds to the aspirations contained in Agenda 2063.**

- **Membership of the WTO by 44 African Union member States has a significant influence on how the IP rights protocol in the African Continental Free Trade Area can be designed:** the WTO TRIPS Agreement does not provide exceptions for regional preferential agreements, which means that, unlike other the protocols in the AfCFTA, the benefits of an IP rights protocol must be extended to all WTO member States. African countries also differ significantly in their use of TRIPS flexibilities.

- **African countries have different levels of obligations in IP treaties beyond WTO:** including participation in multilateral IP treaties and commitments arising from bilateral trade agreements.

- **African countries have undergone extensive reforms in IP laws and regulations:** nevertheless, the use of IP rights, as demonstrated by patents and trademarks, is very limited in Africa compared to other regions and most patents and trademarks registered in Africa belong to non-residents. Considerable innovation is tak-

ing place in Africa, but without receiving protection from IP rights.

- **Three options may be identified in regional economic integration in IP rights:** (a) arrangements for regional cooperation and sharing of experiences on IP rights in general; (b) regional filing systems, usually for patents, but also for trademarks and industrial designs; and (c) development of one substantial law or unification of laws for members of a regional organization. Different parts of Africa have experience with all three of these models.

- **Developing one substantive IP regime for 55 African Union member States would be challenging:** (a) it may well prove over-ambitious to negotiate; (b) it may undermine existing flexibilities that African countries enjoy in their multilateral and bilateral IP commitments; and (c) it may conflict with obligations that African countries have committed to in international and bilateral agreements.

- **An African Continental Free Trade Area protocol involving only a cooperative framework for IP rights would fail to take advantage of many opportunities,** including developing tools for promoting regional integration, ensuring non-discrimination between countries with different international treaty membership and advancing the objectives of industrial diversification and value chain integration.

Policy recommendations

- **A viable IP rights protocol in the African Continental Free Trade Area could do the following:**

  a Provide guiding principles for national IP law and policy, as well as for engagement of African countries in international IP treaties.

  b Provide for non-discrimination among nationals of States parties on matters of IP rights.

  c Develop norms to safeguard African interests, including non-discrimination among African countries on matters pertaining to IP rights.

d Establish a regional IP exhaustion system to prevent fragmentation of the AfCFTA market and encourage regional value chain development.

e Provide the minimum requirements for the protection of traditional knowledge, genetic resources, and cultural expressions, but with sufficient flexibility for domestic law and multilateral negotiations on these issues.

f Require the ratification of the Marrakesh Treaty, with the additional commitment to adhere to any other multilateral agreement that promotes access to work for persons with disabilities.

g Require the ratification of the protocol amending the TRIPS Agreement, 2005, in order to benefit from the facilitated production and exportation of pharmaceuticals for a regional trade agreement in which 50 per cent of the members are least developed countries.

h Oblige the protection of geographic indications through either a sui generis system or certification and collection marks.

i Develop minimum standards on plant variety protection, including on availability, scope of protection, and exceptions to plant breeders' rights and the protection of traditional and new farmers' varieties.

j Develop guidelines on procedures for the enforcement of IP rights.

- **African regional organizations specializing in IP already exist (ARIPO and OAPI):** a protocol on IP rights, in its institutional arrangements, should accord observer status to these organizations.

- **Phase 2 of the Tripartite negotiations intends to include IP;** in view of the imminent negotiations related to the IP rights protocol for the AfCFTA, it would be prudent to consolidate these negotiations to avoid duplication and proceed from a single undertaking approach.

- **As a highly controversial negotiating topic, it is especially important for IP negotiations to be open, transparent and inclusive:** this should involve broad public consultations and debates and iterative capacity building for key stakeholders, as well as training to ensure that negotiators are deeply engaged with subject-matter expertise and knowledgeable of available policy options.

Chapter 5. Competition Policy Protocol

Key messages

- **Africa's competition regime remains patchy.** Only 23 countries have both competition laws in force and competition authorities to enforce them, a further 10 have laws but no authority, 4 have competition legislation in an advanced stage of preparation and 17 have no competition law.

- **Competition policy is a key driver of the growth of competitive markets in Africa.** Cross-border anti-competitive practices prevalent in Africa—such as cartels and abuse of dominance—constrain the growth of competitive markets and harm consumers. National, regional and continental enforcement of competition law will boost the fight against them.

- **The proliferation of competition regimes in Africa calls for a harmonization.** To consolidate the efforts of regional economic communities—such as the East African Community, the Economic Community of West African States, the Common Market for Eastern and Southern Africa, the Economic and Monetary Community of Central Africa and the West African Economic and Monetary Union—a continent-wide competition regime would be a timely and necessary next step, and countries not belonging to these communities could be included under the AfCFTA framework.

- **The African Competition Forum is a springboard for cooperation on competition matters at continental level.** The forum is an informal network established in 2011, comprised of 31 members and five regional competition agencies, promoting the adoption of competition principles in African countries to alleviate poverty and enhance inclusive economic growth, development and consumer welfare, by fostering competition in markets.

- **Consumer protection can be addressed in the AfCFTA protocol on competition.** Consumer protection is related to competition, and the protocol can ensure that the advantages of an integrated African market extend to consumer welfare.

Policy recommendations

- **The AfCFTA protocol on competition must cover the main substantive competition issues.** These include cartels, merger control, abuse of dominance and anti-competitive agreements.

- **The protocol should embrace consumer protection in a dedicated chapter.**

- **The protocol can be enforced through three arrangements:** (1) a supranational AfCFTA competition authority, (2) a competition cooperation framework or (3) a sequential approach in which a supranational authority follows a competition network.

- **A continental procurement policy can complement the competition protocol.** This would ensure predictability, transparency and harmony in procurement policies and produce competitively tendered government procurement, while preserving policy space for legitimate public policy objectives.

- **The AfCFTA may be used to provide a framework for rules and guidelines on buyer power.** Excessive buyer power in corporate conduct has emerged as an important issue that could affect many industries in Africa.

- **The advancing digital economy raises competition challenges.** The capacity of competition authorities will require investment so they can better identify new developments in digital markets, players and business models.

Chapter 6 Investment Protocol

Key messages

- **To channel investment for sustainable development, the investment protocol should foster flexible and robust regulatory frameworks supporting an attractive investment environment.** Capital formation can promote sustainable development, regional integration, and faster socio-economic advancement for African countries by enabling trade diversification and the emergence of regional and global value chains, but investments can also threaten human rights and entail social, environmental and economic costs.

- **The African investment policy landscape is fragmented, marked by 854 bilateral investment treaties (512 in force), of which 169 are intra-African (44 in force).** Binding regional treaties add further complexity to this entangled and overlapping investment regime.

- **Traditional investment treaties predominate on the continent, with major repercussions for the policy and regulatory space available to policy makers, but the AfCFTA investment protocol represents an unparalleled opportunity for AU member States to revamp the investment policy landscape.** Up to now, vaguely defined (and therefore potentially far-reaching) standards of treatment, inconsistent jurisprudence and vulnerability to treaty shopping have fuelled uncertainty since investors may challenge legitimate State action in international arbitration.

- **The AfCFTA protocol on investment should be informed by the Pan-African Investment Code (PAIC).** Although the PAIC guides investment treaty negotiations, the 5th Meeting of the AfCFTA Negotiating Forum in March 2017 declined to annex the PAIC to the AfCFTA since it was "not a binding agreement but a framework of cooperation"; however, the protocol should build on the PAIC's innovations in a binding investment treaty.

Policy recommendations

- **The investment protocol should feature new-generation investment treaty innovations for predictable, forward-looking and transparent rules to pave the way for further economic integration.** Among the features would be substantive obligations and dispute settlement provisions, development-oriented investor obligations and mutual commitments among African countries to an equilibrium between business activity and sustainable development.

- **The investment protocol can be built on four pillars: investment promotion and facilitation, investment protection, investor obligations and State commitments.** However, investment promotion and facilitation ought to remain separate from investment protection so as not to create additional obligations towards investors or lower regulatory standards, while investor obligations and State commitments represent novel features intended to harness investment for sustainable development.

- **A cross-thematic dialogue among specialists and negotiators needs to be established to align the investment protocol with the other AfCFTA protocols.** Parallel negotiations of the phase II protocols provide a unique opportunity for complementarities and minimizing undesirable overlaps.

- **Policy makers can use the protocol on investment as a reference point for future negotiations and renegotiations of treaties with external partners.** Adopting a common African approach ensure coherence and provide greater negotiating leverage than bilateral negotiations.

Key messages

- **E-commerce is likely to be a significant driver and outcome of intra-African trade.** The public and private sectors are increasingly adopting e-commerce platforms—governments deliver services through them, electronic marketplaces aggregate consumer and producer demand as well as trade-related services, traditional businesses have incorporated e-commerce into their business models and operations and individual entrepreneurs and small businesses use social media platforms to engage with market opportunities.

- **Opportunities and challenges of e-commerce in Africa interplay with other policy issues.** These include the Boosting Intra-African Trade action plan, AfCFTA phase II issues and policy issues such as data, gender, inclusion, cybercrime, taxation, informal trade, consumer protection, the digital divide, digital identity and e-transaction laws.

- **The e-commerce policy landscape is evolving with policies and strategies at regional and national levels.** Cooperation between African countries can prevent barriers in digital space from being erected through varied regulatory approaches and can inhibit the fracturing of African countries by technology giants.

- **Consistent rules across the African continent could create an environment where firms (whether digital or not) can compete fairly and can simplify cross-border and national e-commerce.**

- **A gap in digital infrastructure and literacy and disparities in access to technologies and the cost of using them determine the extent to which e-commerce will be adopted and, by extension, enable intra-African trade.**

- **An important step for e-commerce development in Africa is the African Digital Trade and Digital Economy Strategy mandated by the AU Executive Council in January 2019.** This strategy seeks to enable AU member States to fully benefit from the fourth industrial revolution and facilitate the implementation of the African Continental Free Trade Area; it will be presented to the AU Assembly for adoption in February 2020.

Policy recommendations

Three policy options are identified for e-commerce in the AfCFTA:

- An e-commerce protocol as an instrument within the AfCFTA agreement.

- An African digital economy strategy covering the governance of cross-border e-commerce and related issues.

- E-commerce perspectives integrated into existing AU instruments.

Regardless of the approach taken for e-commerce in the AfCFTA, African countries can support the development of e-commerce through investing in digital policy capacities, e-readiness evaluations, research agendas for academics and researchers and technical assistance.

Acknowledgements

The ninth edition of *Assessing Regional Integration in Africa* (*ARIA IX*) is a joint publication of the Economic Commission for Africa (ECA), the United Nations Conference on Trade and Development (UNCTAD), the African Union Commission (AUC), and the African Development Bank (AfDB).

The report was prepared under the overall guidance of Vera Songwe, ECA Executive Secretary, with oversight by Stephen Karingi, Director, Regional Integration and Trade Division.

The core team preparing the report consisted of David Luke, Coordinator of ECA's African Trade Policy Centre (ATPC), Joy Kategekwa, Head of UNCTAD Regional Office for Africa, and Jamie MacLeod, ATPC Trade Policy Expert.

Chapter leads contributing to the report were: Francis Ikome (ECA), Guillaume Gérout (ECA), Melaku Desta (ECA), Martin Kohout (ECA), Hamed El Kady (UNCTAD), Ermias Biadgleng (UNCTAD), Caroline Ncube (University of Cape Town), Elizabeth Gachuiri (UNCTAD), Martine Julsaint-Kidane (UNCTAD) and Ifeyinwa Nwanneka Ogo (ECA). They received support from Emmanuel Chinyama (ECA), Jane Karonga (ECA), William Davis (ECA), Christian Knebel (UNCTAD), Robert Tama Lisinge (ECA), Nadira Bayat (ECA), Komi Tsowou (ECA), Maximiliano Mendez-Parra (ODI), Wafa Aidi (ECA), Simon Mevel (ECA), Lily Sommer (ECA), Mintewab Gebre Woldesenbet (ECA consultant), Leyou Tameru (I-ARB Africa), Marisella Ouma (ICTSD), Nozipho Freya Simelane (ECA), Lashea Howard-Clinton (ECA), Nathalie Bernasconi (IISD), Beatrice Chaytor (AUC) and Million Habte (AUC).

The core team would like to acknowledge the support of ATPC colleagues, in particular, Senait Afework, Haimanot Assefa, Eden Lakew, Batanai Chikwene, Souleymane Abdallah and Heini Suominen.

The core team is also grateful to the African Union Trade and Industry Commissioner Albert Muchanga for his oversight and direction. African Union Commission colleagues, including Prudence Sebahizi, Youssouf Hamid Takane, Halima Noor and Khauhelo Mawana, provided valuable inputs to the report. Inye Nathan Briggs of the AfDB anchored the AfDB's oversight of the report.

The following contributed to the consultations on the report concept note, technical inputs, peer review and validation of the report findings: Rosemina Nathoo (CTPL), Meaza Ashenafi (formerly ECA), Won Kidane (Seattle University), Peter Oluonye (ECOWAS), Ahmed Suliman (formerly ECA), Victor Konde (ECA), Pierre Runiga (ARIPO), Fernando dos Santos (ARIPO), Jonathan Aremu (consultant), Makane Mbengue (University of Geneva), Sarah Brewin (IISD), Suzy Nikièma (IISD), Falou Samb (Special Advisor to the President of Senegal), Rosebela Oiro (CAK), Adano Roba (CAK), Magui Angele Koubitobo Batisseck (OAPI), Mulalo Hardin Ratshisusu (ACF), Colette van der Ven (Sidley Austin LPP), Sandra Akite (UNCTAD), Sirack Kasshun (UNCTAD), Elisabeth Tuerk (UNCTAD), Pilar Fajarnes (UNCTAD), Luisa Rodriguez (UNCTAD), Torbjorn Fredriksson (UNCTAD), Laura Paez Heredia (ECA), Adeyinka Adeyemi (ECA), and Shamnaaz Begum Sufrauj (ECA).

A special mention goes to Bruce Ross-Larson and his team from Communications Development Incorporated for professional editing for the report, and to Carolina Rodriguez and her team from Dilucidar Pte Ltd for providing infographics. The Publication Section of ECA are thanked for the translation, design, printing and distribution of *ARIA IX*.

Finally, ATPC would like to acknowledge the support of Global Affairs Canada to its work programme through a partnership that stretches back to 2004.

Foreword

The signing of the African Continental Free Trade Agreement (AfCFTA) by 54 African Union member states marked a historic milestone for economic integration in Africa. By 1 April 2019, just over a year after the signing ceremony, the threshold of ratification by 22 countries required for the agreement's entry into force had been reached. The speed of this ratification process is unprecedented in AU history.

The significance of this achievement is not to be underestimated. The vision of African continental integration to which the AfCFTA contributes is more than 50 years old and, as demonstrated in this and previous editions of this report, embodies great opportunities for Africa's structural transformation, economic diversification and development.

The momentum behind the African Continental Free Trade Agreement initiative inspires the focus of this ninth edition of the flagship *Assessing Regional Integration in Africa (ARIA IX)* report, which asks, "What's next?".

With the phase I negotiations of the agreement now concluded, we must harness its operationalization and use it for further advancing Africa's economic integration. This will involve finalizing the remaining technical work of the phase I negotiations to promptly ensure that the goods of African businesses, traders and consumers flow freely and that service suppliers are unhindered. It will also involve enlarging the number of countries signing, ratifying and depositing ratification instruments. The impressive 27 countries that have ratified it as of July 2019, representing 50 per cent of African Union member States, should now be joined by the rest of the continent to move forward collectively, and meaningfully, in trade integration.

But it is not enough merely for the African Continental Free Trade Agreement to be operational and encompassing. It must also change lives, reduce poverty and contribute to economic development. For this, complementary measures are needed. This report considers a breadth of such measures within the context of AfCFTA national strategies for implementing the agreement.

Further, the main focus of this report—and of what's next for the African Continental Free Trade Agreement—concerns the phase II negotiations scheduled to commence later in 2019. This comprehensive and deep agreement goes beyond mere tariff liberalization to include investment, competition policy and intellectual property rights, far-reaching and transformative topics that are the subject of the phase II negotiations. Provisions on investment—its promotion, facilitation and protection—can allow the AfCFTA to galvanize the investments needed to restructure Africa's economies. Provisions on competition policy can enable fair competition and market outcomes that stimulate industrialization, competiveness and development. And provisions on intellectual property rights can incentivize increased innovation, ensure a level playing field and support trade, while protecting policy space for African governments. This report gives rich treatment to the substantive analyses of those topics.

Finally, the potential of the African Continental Free Trade Agreement after operationalization and after conclusion of the phase II negotiations requires attention. This report offers that, considering both how the agreement can help achieve the deeper forms of integration called for by African Heads of State and Government, and also how the modes and means of trade are changing in an increasingly digitizing world. The last chapter of the report deliberates how African countries can prepare for the digital economy. In doing so, it asks whether policy makers should consider e-commerce as a negotiating topic in the AfCFTA, following its prominence in other negotiating fora.

ARIA IX is buttressed with deep and ground-breaking research into topics of considerable interest for African policy makers, trade negotiators, partners and development stakeholders. For the first time in the *ARIA* series, the African Union Commission, Economic Commission for Africa, and African Development Bank are joined by the United Nations Conference on Trade and Development in preparing this edition. We believe that the rich and actionable research on the issues covered by the report can advance Africa's development, both in the context of the African Union Agenda 2063 and the United Nations Sustainable Development Goals. We commend it and its findings to those seeking to support Africa in its regional integration, economic transformation and development.

Moussa Faki Mahamat	**Vera Songwe**	**Akinwumi Adesina**	**Mukhisa Kituyi**
Chairperson	Under-Secretary-General	President	Secretary-General
African Union Commission	United Nations Executive Secretary Economic Commission for Africa	African Development Bank Group	United Nations Conference on Trade and Development

Chapter 1
The Status of Regional Integration in Africa

Regional integration remains an economic and political priority for African leaders and policy makers, as evidenced in their adoption and implementation of many regional integration programmes both at continental and regional levels. The regional economic communities (RECs) now play a key role in promoting Africa's regional integration agenda. In the long term, an African Economic Community (AEC) is envisaged. This vision arose during the formative years of the Organization of African Unity (OAU), took shape as a systematic political programme embodied in the 1980 Lagos Plan of Action and was given legal expression in the 1991 Abuja Treaty. Its importance was reaffirmed by various continental integration initiatives—the 2000 constitutive act of the African Union, the 2012 Boosting Intra-African Trade action plan and, most recently, the agreement establishing the African Continental Free Trade Area (AfCFTA), signed in 2018. The vision has evolved to reflect new approaches (such as Agenda 2063), while the pathway to it has been updated with new steps—the AfCFTA, for example, was not foreseen in the original stages set by the Abuja Treaty. The vision thus endures, upholding the idea that integration, by driving efficiency both within the continent and globally, enhances the continent's competitiveness.

The RECs have been building blocks for the African Economic Community throughout the history of integration in Africa. Although they have similar objectives, the RECs were established independently of each other and differ in both structure and activity. And their integration has proceeded unevenly. Some have achieved tangible outcomes in key areas of integration, as this chapter will show, while others struggle to meet even the basic objectives of the Abuja Treaty. Despite this mixed picture, monitoring the implementation of the provisions of the Abuja Treaty has remained a priority for many RECs, as well as the African Union Commission.

The historic signing of the African Continental Free Trade Area Agreement in Kigali, Rwanda, on 21 March 2018 represents the most remarkable progress in Africa's integration since the 2017 publication of the previous *Assessing Regional Integration in Africa* report *(ARIA VIII)*. Another continental-level achievement was African countries' endorsement of the Kigali Consensus on migration and mobility—which urges all the RECs to develop and implement protocols on the free movement of persons and recommends that a roadmap be developed for implementing the Joint Labour Migration Programme in Africa. Regional-level integration progress during the same period included the July 2018 expansion of COMESA from 19 to 21 members through the admission of Tunisia and Somalia and the implementation of ECOWAS's Common External Tariff by all its member States, except one.

But impediments to continental and regional integration linger, notably Africa's huge infrastructure deficit, limited macroeconomic convergence and ongoing peace and security threats. These challenges must be steadfastly addressed to reap the benefits of integration, including the AfCFTA.

This chapter updates and analyzes current trends in regional integration in Africa. It highlights the major shifts since the publication *ARIA VIII* in the areas of macroeconomic convergence; trade and market integration; migration and free movement of persons, goods and services; infrastructure integration and financing, including for landlocked countries; health; governance, peace and security and mining. The section on migration discusses enhancing labour mobility through cooperation in education and skills formation. The section on landlocked countries features the Vienna Program of Action.

SADC macroeconomic convergence targets, 2008–18

INDICATORS	2008	2012	2018
Inflation (% a year)	Single digits	5	3
Fiscal deficit (% of GDP)	5	3, with a range of 1%	3 as anchor, with a range of 1%
Public debt (% of GDP)	60	60	60
Current account deficit (% of GDP)	9	9	3

Source: SADC document—RISDP.

Macroeconomic convergence and monetary and financial integration

Macroeconomic policy convergence and financial and monetary integration promote efficiency, public accountability and economic growth and sustainable development. Macroeconomic convergence is defined as a reduction of disparities in economic indicators, such as inflation, growth levels and per capita income. The reason to pursue macroeconomic convergence is to prompt the members of economic groupings to react similarly to such economic variables as price stability, budget deficits and debt-to-GDP ratios—this benefits the whole region.

Regional groupings employ macroeconomic policy convergence mechanisms to prepare for monetary integration. The European Monetary Union, for example, used macroeconomic convergence criteria in preparation for the introduction of the euro. Regional groupings also benefit from the macroeconomic stability brought about by the "good'" macroeconomic behaviour rewarded by incentives for macroeconomic convergence criteria.

The 1991 Abuja Treaty set out the vision of African financial and monetary integration. In the sixth phase under the treaty, after an African common market was established, an African monetary union was to be realized through the creation of a single African central bank and a single African currency. The vision saw the continent moving as one from a common market to a monetary union. In practice, that has not happened. Several RECs have moved individually towards financial and monetary union, while others have not. RECs may later consolidate to achieve continental financial and monetary inte-gration, thereby re-aligning with the intentions of the Abuja Treaty, but in the meantime, several are achieving deeper integration through financial and monetary integration.

Three monetary unions are currently operating in Africa—the West African CFA franc, covering most francophone countries in West Africa; the Central African CFA franc, covering six countries of Central Africa, and the Common Monetary Area, linking Eswatini, Lesotho, Namibia and South Africa. None of the monetary unions is conterminous with any of the eight AU-recognized RECs—each is a distinct island of deeper integration within one of them. Nevertheless, future monetary unions are envisaged for the Common Market for Eastern and Southern Africa (COMESA), the East African Community (EAC), the Economic Community of Central African States (ECCAS), the Economic Community of West African States (ECOWAS) and the Southern African Development Community (SADC).

Five of the eight RECs have set macroeconomic and monetary convergence targets aimed at harmonizing economic indicators. However, the member countries within these RECs have not converged enough. Coordinating the endorsed programmes to facilitate meeting targets set by both the RECs themselves and the AU has proved challenging, resulting in a mixed picture with some countries progressing more than others.

Figure 1.1:
ECOWAS States meeting macroeconomic convergence targets, 2016–17

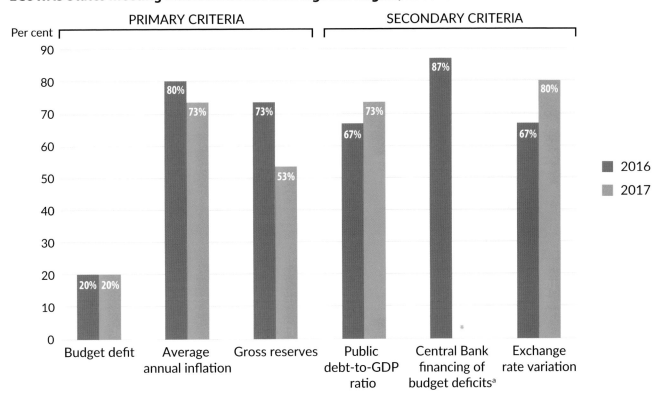

Source: Compiled from various sources (ECOWAS website, 2017; IMF database, 2018; AfDB website, 2018; and UNCTAD, 2019). *2017 data not yet available for central bank financing of budget deficits.

Macroeconomic convergence in RECs

The Southern African Development Community (SADC) aimed for a common market by 2015, a monetary union by 2016 and a single currency by 2018. These targets proved overly ambitious. Now policy makers face the challenge of seeing whether the macroeconomic convergence framework formulated in the 2004 Regional Indicative Strategic Development Plan[1] (RISDP) can still be achieved at a later date. Table 1.1 shows the macroeconomic variables selected by the SADC region as its priority indicators.

In 2017, SADC's average inflation decelerated to 9.4 per cent. It was expected to decline further to 7 per cent in 2018–19, as domestic food conditions improve due to a bumper harvest and exchange rates stabilize. By September 2018, the average had fallen to 8.4 per cent, 12 of 15 SADC members were achieving single-digit inflation and 7 of them were achieving the convergence target of less than 5 per cent. Only one member had achieved the conver-

gence target for 2017–2018 of less than 3 per cent inflation (Southern Africa Economic Outlook, 2018).

The Economic Community of West African States (ECOWAS) Heads of States and Governments realigned the ECOWAS convergence criteria in 2014 to pursue merging the West African Monetary Zone (WAMZ)[2] and West African Economic and Monetary Union (WAEMU)[3] countries into a single monetary zone by the start of 2020. The new primary criteria require member countries' budget deficits not to exceed 3 per cent of GDP, average annual inflation not to be more than 5 per cent by 2019 and gross reserves not to be less than 3 months of imports. The secondary criteria require the public debt-to-GDP ratio not to exceed 70 per cent, central bank financing of budget deficits not to exceed 10 per cent of the previous year's tax revenue and nominal exchange rate variation to stay within +/– 10 per cent (Business News Staff, 2014; ECOWAS, 2017). Despite progress, challenges remain, particularly in the choice of an exchange rate regime, the monetary policy framework and the choice of the central bank model for the future common monetary

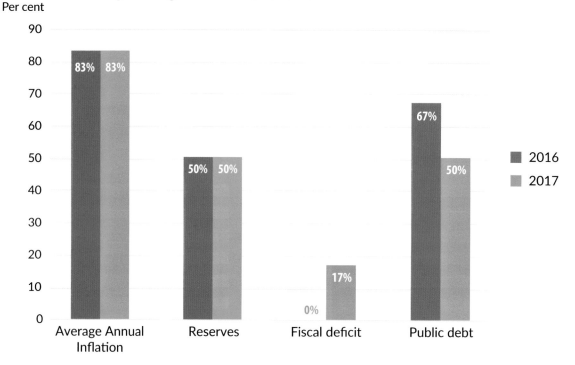

Figure 1.2:

EAC States meeting convergence criteria, 2016–17
Per cent

Source: Compiled from various sources (EAC website, 2017; IMF database, 2018; AfDB website, 2018; and UNCTAD, 2019).

Note: The assessment for the public debt criterion is based on gross debt-to-GDP ratio for general government. Due to a lack of up-to-date data, some assessments (Burundi for both years and Rwanda, Tanzania and Uganda for 2017) are based on estimates published by IMF.

area. The number of ECOWAS countries achieving the primary criteria on the average inflation rate and gross external reserves fell in 2017, while the number of countries satisfying the secondary criteria on ratio of public debt and exchange rate variation rose (2017 data on central bank financing of budget deficits was not yet available) (Figure 1.1).

The East African Community (EAC) anticipates introducing a common currency to replace the national currencies of member countries by 2024. Progress includes: harmonizing monetary policy frameworks and exchange rate operations, rules and practices governing bank supervision and integrating the payment systems, financial markets and financial reporting. The convergence criteria adopted by the EAC are a headline inflation ceiling of 8 per cent, a reserve cover of 4.5 months of imports, a 3 per cent of GDP fiscal deficit ceiling, including grants and a 50 per cent of GDP (net present value) ceiling on gross public debt (Trademark East Africa, 2017). Member States also need to manage fiscal deficits to meet the convergence criterion and to ensure the stability of the future

monetary union (EAC, n.d.). In both 2016 and 2017, the EAC members did fairly well in meeting the inflation target and least well in meeting the fiscal deficit target—only 17 per cent in 2017 (Figure 1.2).

The Economic Community of Central African States (ECCAS) region has made little progress in macroeconomic convergence. Although the existing Economic and Monetary Community of Central Africa[4] (CEMAC) has been merged into the ECCAS configuration, efforts to expand the CEMAC monetary union to the rest of the ECCAS member States have been slow, partly because ECCAS has no formal mechanism for macroeconomic policy convergence. CEMAC's macroeconomic convergence mechanisms are expected to be broadened to the wider ECCAS membership. Within CEMAC, member countries performed well on convergence on the public debt ratio, but less well on the three other criteria: maintaining a positive or zero-based budget balance; annual inflation ceiling of 3 per cent and no accumulation of domestic or external arrears. ECCAS should develop a dashboard for extending the CEMAC convergence framework to all ECCAS countries.

The Common Market for Eastern and Southern Africa (COMESA) pursues a cooperation programme adopted in 1992 that aims at monetary union by 2025. COMESA's financial integration achievements include a regional payment and settlement system (REPSS) providing end-of-day settlement in a single currency and a single gateway for central banks within the region to effect payment in a multi-currency environment. Importers and exporters are therefore able to pay and receive payments for goods and services through an efficient and cost-effective platform. As of March 2017, nine countries were implementing REPSS.

The Community of Sahel-Saharan States (CEN-SAD) members did not include an objective for financial and macroeconomic convergence or monetary integration in the 2013 revision of their underlying treaty. Ten CEN-SAD member States are, however, party to either the WEAMU or CEMAC monetary union,[5] whose West African CFA franc and Central African CFA franc, both pegged to the euro, have always been at parity and are effectively interchangeable. Six other CEN-SAD countries[6] are members of COMESA and pursue its macroeconomic convergence goals.

Intergovernmental Authority on Development (IGAD) countries agreed in its founding treaty to "cooperate in the gradual harmonization of their fiscal and monetary policies."[7] It has yet to estab-

lish a macroeconomic convergence mechanism. Still, seven of the eight IGAD countries are party to the COMESA macroeconomic convergence goals,[8] given that the aims and objectives of the IGAD treaty provide that its members shall "promote and realize the objectives of the Common Market for Eastern and Southern Africa (COMESA)."[9]

The Arab Maghreb Union (AMU) aims to establish a Maghreb economic union (AMU website, 2019), but financial and macroeconomic convergence and the creation of a single currency are not articulated in its founding treaty. Of the five AMU countries, Libya and Tunisia are members of COMESA.[10]

Trade and investment integration

Trade integration

Trade is envisaged as the foundational area for integration in many regional groupings. Expressed in the form of free trade areas, trade integration removes tariffs and non-tariff barriers between members. It can advance from a free trade area to a customs union through the adoption of common external tariffs. Trade integration is included in the African Union's 2009 Minimum Integration Programme and Agenda 2063. The third phase of the Abuja Treaty tasked RECs with establishing free trade areas and customs unions before consolidating them into a continent-wide customs union in

Table 1.2:

Export trade of the regional economic communities by partner, 2010–17 average

Per cent

REC	INTRA-COMMUNITY	CHINA	UNITED STATES	EUROPEAN UNION	AFRICA	REST OF THE WORLD
ECCAS	2	34	15	20	4	25
SADC	19	20	8	20	3	30
UMA	3	5	8	63	2	19
ECOWAS	9	3	12	29	7	40
COMESA	9	12	4	37	8	30
IGAD	14	21	3	16	12	34
CEN-SAD	7	5	9	40	5	34
EAC	20	5	4	19	18	34
Africa average	10	13	8	31	7	30

Source: ECA, compiled from UNCTAD data base.

Import trade of the regional economic communities by partner, 2000–17 average

Per cent

REC	INTRA-COMMUNITY	CHINA	UNITED STATES	EUROPEAN UNION	AFRICA	REST OF THE WORLD
ECCAS	3	34	13	19	5	26
SADC	16	27	8	21	3	25
UMA	3	5	8	64	2	18
ECOWAS	8	4	13	31	6	38
COMESA	9	13	5	38	5	29
IGAD	14	21	3	16	12	34
CEN-SAD	6	5	11	41	4	33
EAC	17	14	5	19	14	31
Africa average	9	17	8	31	6	28

Source: ECA, compiled from UNCTAD data base

its fourth phase. In practice, however, this has not happened, since most RECs have not advanced to customs unions.

Meanwhile, the AfCFTA offers a new approach. The signing of the Agreement Establishing the African Continental Free Trade Area by African Heads of State and Government in Kigali on 21 March 2018 marked a milestone in continental trade integration. The AfCFTA has the potential to promote employment, industrial linkages, economic diversification and structural transformation in Africa (ECA, AfDB and AUC, 2018). Long-term gains are forecast to include a boost to intra-African trade of more than 50 per cent and welfare gains amounting to $16 billion (ECA, 2017; Depetris-Chauvin, et al. 2016; Saygili, et al. 2018). If trade facilitation reforms take place at the same time, the forecast economic benefits are even larger (Mevel and Karingi, 2013; Chauvin, et al. 2016; Jensen and Sandrey, 2016). (Chapter 2 of this report gives an update of the AfCFTA.)

Intra-African trade accounted for only a small share of Africa's total exports and imports over 2010–17 (Tables 1.2, 1.3). The continent traded more with the outside world than internally, with the European Union taking the largest share of Africa's exports—an average of more than 30 per cent. China's share increased, and that country will soon

be compete favourably with the European Union. Of the RECs, SADC and EAC traded the most internally, with SADC registering 19 per cent of exports as intra-community, and EAC 20 per cent.

All RECs import more from the EU than from Africa (see Table 1.3). During 2010–17, EAC's intra-community imports were 17 per cent of imports, and SADC's were 16 per cent.

The **EAC** is the most advanced REC in regional integration, establishing a common market in January 2010 that provides for the free movement of goods, services, capital, labour and persons, plus rights of establishment and residence. It made steady progress in implementing common standards, rules of origin and a common external tariff and completely eliminated internal tariffs. All EAC partner States except Burundi had Logistics Performance Indices higher than other African countries, except countries in North Africa and near the East Asia and the Pacific average (UNCTAD 2018). The introduction of common documentation, single windows at intra-EAC customs ports and the development of the Northern Corridor scheme have also improved integration (Gasiorek et al., 2016). Another success in EAC is cross-border mobile telephone services through cuts in roaming charges and the use of mobile phones for cross-border financial transactions.

EAC member States' intra-African imports as a share of total imports from all sources, and sub-share of sources for African imports, 2017

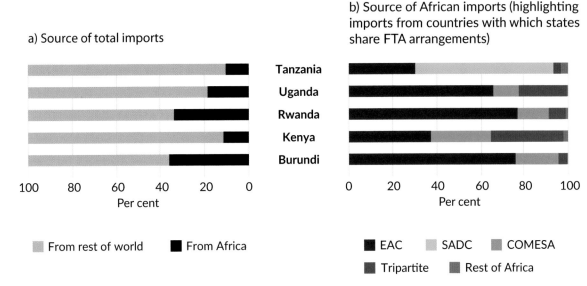

a) Source of total imports

b) Source of African imports (highlighting imports from countries with which states share FTA arrangements)

Tanzania
Uganda
Rwanda
Kenya
Burundi

Per cent

Per cent

From rest of world ■ From Africa

■ EAC　SADC　■ COMESA
■ Tripartite　■ Rest of Africa

Source: Authors' calculations based on UNCTADStat, 2019.

Note: Panel a shows the share of imports that are from Africa and the rest of world, including intra-EAC imports. Panel b shows where the sub-set of African imports came from, highlighting those from countries that are party to the same FTAs as the EAC countries. To prevent double counting, COMESA is considered only to cover those imports not already covered by EAC or SADC arrangements. The grey bars show the additional share of imports in 2017 that would have flowed from additional Tripartite FTA countries, were the TFTA in force. All EAC countries, except Tanzania, are party to the COMESA FTA. All are party to the Tripartite Free Trade Area negotiations. Tanzania is the only EAC member to additionally be member of the SADC. Data were not available for imports into South Sudan.

Nevertheless, according to the most recent data available (for 2017), only 14 per cent of the imports into EAC countries were from African countries (Figure 1.3a). Of these, 78 per cent flowed from countries with which the EAC States share FTA arrangements, including the EAC FTA (49 per cent), the COMESA FTA (16 per cent) and, in the case of Tanzania, which is also a SADC member, the SADC FTA (13 per cent) (Figure 1.3b). Though much of the intra-African imports into EAC countries came from countries that shared FTA arrangements, some of these imports would not have used FTA preferences, for instance by not satisfying rules of origin requirements.

If the COMESA–EAC–SADC Tripartite Free Trade Area (TFTA) had been in force, it could have covered additional countries from which a further 19 per cent of the EAC countries' intra-African imports flowed in 2017. The grey bars in Figure 1.3b show the share of imports flowing from these additional countries. Tanzania, however, already a member of SADC and EAC, would cover only a very small share of additional imports through the tripartite configuration.

Most African imports flowing into EAC countries are from countries with which those EAC countries already share REC FTAs—or would be covered by the Tripartite Free Trade Area when it enters into force. Imports from elsewhere in Africa accounted for only 2 per cent of African imports into EAC countries in 2017 (see the green bars in Figure 1.3b), suggesting that, if trade flows continue, the AfCFTA could only liberalize an additional 2 per cent of intra-African imports into EAC countries. This would account for only 0.3 per cent of total imports into EAC countries from all sources. So, the AfCFTA will have a very limited impact on imports into EAC countries unless it stimulates much new trade from central, western and northern Africa.

In ECOWAS, trade integration is governed by the ECOWAS Trade Liberalization Scheme (ETLS). As of November 2018, the 15 member States had approved 1,708 products and 642 enterprises to benefit from the ETLS.[11]

ECOWAS member States' intra-African imports as a share of total imports from all sources, and share of their intra-African imports that were intra-ECOWAS, 2017

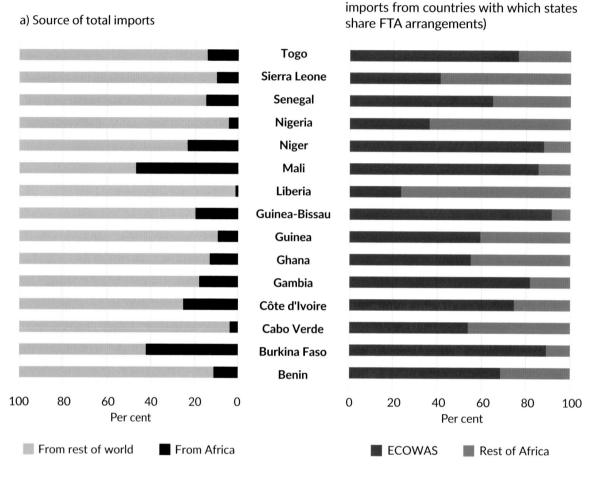

a) Source of total imports

b) Source of African imports (highlighting imports from countries with which states share FTA arrangements)

From rest of world ▇ From Africa ▇ ECOWAS ▇ Rest of Africa

Source: Authors' calculations based on UNCTADStat, 2019.

Note: Panel a shows the share of imports that are from Africa and the rest of world. Panel b shows where the African imports came from, highlighting the imports that flowed from within ECOWAS.

All members of ECOWAS except Cabo Verde have implemented the ECOWAS common external tariff, moving ECOWAS towards being a customs union. Other trade integration programmes include a task force for enhanced implementation of the ETLS, the single currency programme and the protocol on free movement of persons.

In 2017, only 13 per cent of the total imports into ECOWAS countries were from African countries (Figure 1.5a). Of these, 68 per cent were intra-ECOWAS imports to which the ETLS arrangements would have been available (Figure 1.4b).

No ECOWAS country is a party to any other African FTA (except WAEMU, which is entirely a sub-set

of ECOWAS). The 32 per cent of African imports into ECOWAS countries not covered under the ETLS would thus be liberalized under the AfCFTA. Although that liberalization would be a relatively large jump, it would still account for only 9 per cent of ECOWAS countries' total imports from all sources.

SADC has increased both intra-regional and international trade as it implements its Industrialization Strategy and Roadmap 2015–2063. Enhancing SADC competitiveness in industrial and other productive activities is viewed as a priority to increase both regional and international trade.

In 2018, SADC, Germany and the European Union launched a €18.7 million programme support-

SADC member States' intra-African imports as a share of total imports from all sources, and share of their intra-African imports by free trade area, 2017

a) Source of total imports

b) Source of African imports (highlighting imports from countries with which states share FTA arrangements)

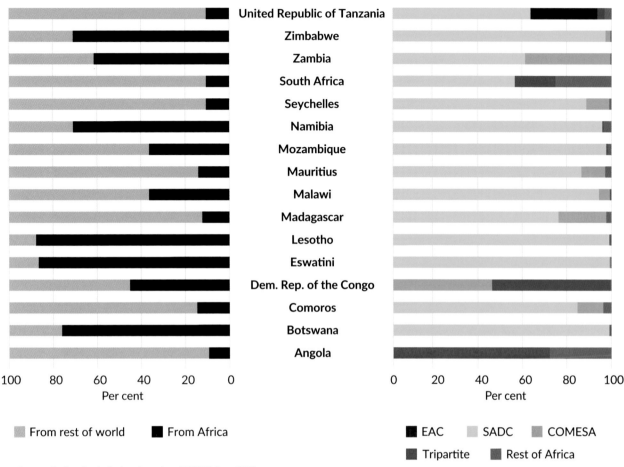

Source: Authors' calculations based on UNCTADStat, 2019.

Note: Panel a shows the share of imports that are from Africa and the rest of world. Panel b shows where the sub-set of African imports were from, highlighting the imports that flowed from FTAs to which each country is a party. To prevent double counting, COMESA is considered only to cover those imports not already covered by EAC or SADC arrangements. The grey bars show the additional share of imports in 2017 that would have flowed through the Tripartite FTA were it in force.

ing the capacity of the SADC secretariat and the national structures of SADC member States to facilitate and co-ordinate regional programmes identified in the SADC Revised Regional Indicative Strategic Development Plan (SADC, 2018). The national structures will be key in accelerating regional integration programmes.

In 2017, 24 per cent of the imports into SADC countries were from African countries (Figure 1.5a). Of these, 82 per cent flowed from countries with which the SADC countries shared FTAs, including the SADC FTA, the COMESA FTA and, in the case of Tanzania, the EAC FTA (Figure 1.5b). Some 72

per cent of African imports into SADC countries were from other SADC countries that are party to the SADC FTA. An additional 9 per cent of imports were from other COMESA countries into SADC members that were also part of COMESA, while 0.8 per cent were EAC imports into Tanzania covered by Tanzania's membership in the EAC.[12] The and Democratic Republic of the Congo and Angola, though members of SADC, do not currently implement the SADC FTA, yet the Democratic Republic of the Congo receives 78 of its intra-African imports from SADC countries, and Angola receives 68 per cent. Angola is in an advanced stage of acceding to the SADC FTA.

If the AfCFTA had been in force in addition to the TFTA, it could have covered the remaining 8 per cent of intra-African imports into SADC countries in 2017 (see the green bars in Figure 1.5b), equivalent to 2 per cent of total imports into SADC from all sources. As with the EAC region, most intra-African imports into SADC are already covered by existing FTA arrangements or would be covered by the TFTA, meaning that the AfCFTA will have a limited impact on SADC imports unless it stimulates much new trade from central, western and northern Africa.

COMESA membership increased from 19 to 21 States with the admission of Tunisia and Somalia in July 2018, making it the largest REC in the continent with a combined gross domestic product of $769 billion and a population of 560 million. COMESA has recently benefited from a €15 million cross-border trade programme (CBTP) signed in May 2018 to facilitate small-scale cross-border trade flows. The CBTP is an instrument of the Tripartite Transport and Transit Facilitation Programme meant to harmonize regulations, standards and systems in East and Southern Africa. In 2018, the region marked the 24th anniversary of its 1994 transformation from the Preferential Trade Area for Eastern and Southern Africa in December to COMESA.

Recent COMESA achievements include resolving 98 per cent of reported non-tariff barriers; removing foreign exchange restrictions, taxes on foreign exchange and import and export quotas; removing road blocks and easing of customs formalities and extending border post open times and creating one-stop border posts.

The region is also pursuing a digital free trade area expected to boost intra-COMESA exports by an estimated $17.5 billion (COMESA, 2019). Many of COMESA's flagship trade support programmes are now operational, including the COMESA Yellow Card Insurance Scheme and a regional Third-Party Motor Vehicle Insurance Scheme, which provides legal liability cover and compensation for medical expenses resulting from road traffic accidents. Uniform road user charges and a simplified trade regime for small cross-border traders are also in operation in all COMESA member States. These

instruments have helped to propel intra-COMESA trade from $3 billion in 2000 to more than $21 billion in 2017 (COMESA website, December 2018).

In 2017, 34 per cent of the total imports into COMESA countries were from African countries (Figure 1.6a). Of this, 79 per cent flowed from countries that the COMESA countries shared FTAs with (Figure 1.6b), so, most intra-African trade into COMESA countries is already liberalized. As COMESA overlaps widely with the EAC and SADC, much trade within the COMESA region is already covered by the EAC and SADC FTA arrangements.[13] Ethiopia, while a member of the COMESA, does not fully implement the COMESA FTA.

If the Tripartite Free Trade Area had been in force, it would have covered additional countries that a further 10 per cent of the COMESA countries' intra-African imports flowed from in 2017 (see grey bars in Figure 1.6b). A further 10 per cent of African imports could be liberalized by the AfCFTA, equivalent to 1.4 per cent of total imports into COMESA from all sources. As in the EAC and SADC regions, the AfCFTA would have a limited impact on imports into COMESA if trade flows remain as they were in 2017, because most intra-African trade in this region is already liberalized.

In **ECCAS,** leaders from the public and private sectors in the Central African Republic, the Democratic Republic of the Congo and Gabon have been mobilized to support including their national industrial products in the ECCAS–CEMAC harmonized preferential tariff regime. This will help these countries to participate to a greater extent in intra-ECCAS trade and to benefit from the regime (ECA, 2018a, 2018b and 2019a).

In 2017, 26 per cent of imports into ECCAS countries were from African countries (Figure 1.7a). This high share is mostly accounted for by the Democratic Republic of the Congo, which sources 45 per cent of its imports from African countries, as well as Burundi, Congo and Rwanda, which each source more than 30 per cent of their imports from African countries. Some 62 per cent of the African imports into ECCAS countries flowed from countries with which the ECCAS countries share FTAs

COMESA member States' intra-African imports as a share of total imports, and share of their intra-African imports by free trade area, 2017

a) Source of total imports

b) Source of African imports (highlighting imports from countries with which states share FTA arrangements)

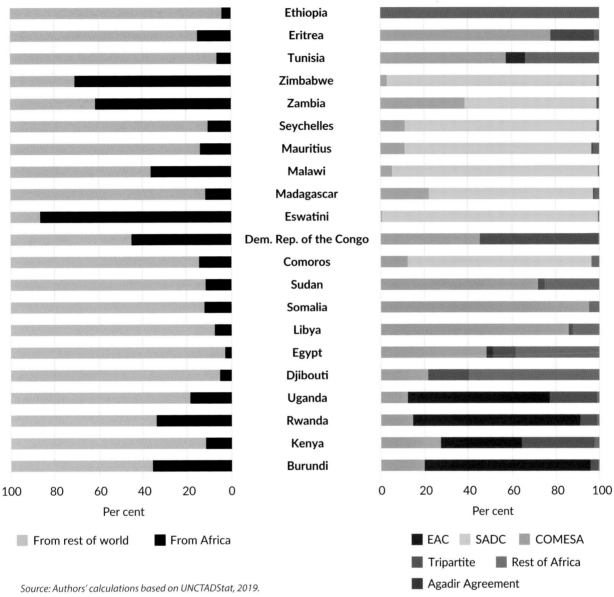

Source: Authors' calculations based on UNCTADStat, 2019.

Note: Panel a shows the share of imports that are from Africa and the rest of world. Panel b shows where the sub-set of African imports were from, highlighting the imports that flowed from FTAs to which each country is a party. To prevent double counting, COMESA is considered only to cover those imports not already covered by EAC or SADC arrangements. The grey bars show the additional share of imports in 2017 that would have flowed through the Tripartite FTA if it were in force. Tunisia and Somalia have been included as COMESA countries to simulate their effective FTA coverage of imports, but in 2017 they were not yet members of the COMESA FTA.

arrangements (Figure 1.7b). In particular, trade within the CEMAC customs union (see the blue bars in Figure 1.7b) accounted for 18 per cent of African imports into ECCAS countries. However, Burundi and Rwanda are significantly more integrated into the rest of Africa, given their overlapping mem-bership of EAC and COMESA (see the orange and brown bars in Figure 1.7b).

ECCAS currently has the legal architecture in place for its own REC FTA, yet this is currently not in force. In Figure 1.7b the dark blue bars show the addi-tional share of each country's imports that would

Figure 1.7:

ECCAS member States' intra-African imports as a share of imports from all sources, and share of their intra-African imports by free trade area, 2017

a) Source of total imports

b) Source of African imports (highlighting imports from countries with which states share FTA arrangements)

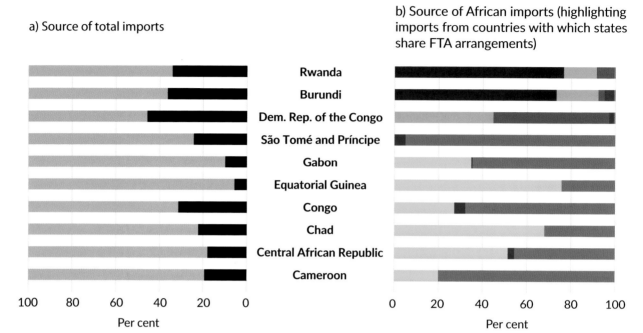

Source: Authors' calculations based on UNCTADStat, 2019.

Note: Panel a shows the share of imports that are from Africa and the rest of world. Panel b shows where the sub-set of African imports were sourced, highlighting the imports that flowed from FTAs to which each country is a party. The grey bars show the additional share of imports in 2017 that would have flowed through the Tripartite FTA were it in force. Two ECCAS countries are party to the EAC, these members are also party to COMESA and the Tripartite Free Trade Area negotiations. Six other ECCAS members are members of CEMAC.

be covered by the ECCAS FTA, were it to have been in force in 2017. Because most ECCAS trade is already covered by existing FTAs, the ECCAS FTA would have only covered an additional 2 per cent of the ECCAS countries' intra-African imports in 2017, most notably imports into Burundi, Central African Republic, Congo and São Tomé and Príncipe, and the rest from other ECCAS countries. Assuming the ECCAS FTA soon enters into force, the AfCFTA would be expected to liberalize the remaining 36 per cent of African imports into the ECCAS region, equivalent to 9 per cent of total ECCAS imports from all sources.

The remaining RECs—AMU, CEN-SAD and IGAD— lag behind in trade integration. However, due to memberships in multiple RECs, many AMU, CEN-SAD and IGAD member States are making progress

in trade integration initiatives through the better performing RECs, as demonstrated above. However, Algeria, Ethiopia, Mauritania and Morocco are not party to any existing REC FTA. Morocco's intra-African imports from Egypt and Tunisia are liberalized through the Agadir Agreement (Figure 1.8). Ethiopia is a member of COMESA but does not fully implement the COMESA FTA, and Mauritania is an associate member of ECOWAS but does not implement the ECOWAS FTA. The coming into force of the AfCFTA will extend the coverage of trade integration to include these countries. Because they are starting with little or no liberalization of intra-African trade, the AfCFTA amounts to a far larger leap for them. Since intra-African trade currently amounts to only 3 per cent of the imports into these countries from all sources, the appreciable effect on total imports should be manageable.

Intra-African imports of Ethiopia, Morocco, Mauritania, and Algeria as a share of imports from all sources, and sub-share of sources for African imports, 2017

a) Source of total imports

b) Source of African imports (highlighting imports from countries with which states share FTA arrangements)

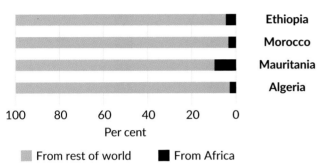

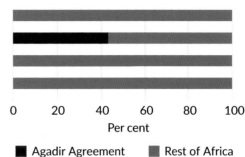

Source: Authors' calculations based on UNCTADStat, 2019.

Note: Panel a shows the share of imports that are from Africa and the rest of world. Panel b shows from where the sub-set of African imports were sourced from, highlighting the imports that flowed from FTAs to which each country is a party.

Tripartite Free Trade Area negotiations for the COMESA–SADC–EAC Tripartite Free Trade Area (TFTA) were launched in 2011 and culminated in the 2015 signing of the TFTA agreement on trade in goods. As of December 2018, 22 Tripartite member States had signed the agreement, but only four had ratified it (Egypt, Kenya, South Africa and Uganda). Once a threshold of 14 ratifications is achieved, implementation will commence. However, several operative elements of the agreement are still being negotiated. The tariff negotiations between EAC and Egypt are complete, while those between SACU/Egypt and SACU/EAC are nearing completion. Negotiations on the Tripartite rules of origin are advanced. A number of instruments are ready for use, including the Tripartite non-tariff barrier mechanism, guidelines on implementation of trade remedies, export and import declaration forms and an agreement on the movement of business persons.

Though the TFTA consolidates trade liberalization across the COMESA, EAC and SADC RECs, much of that trade has already been liberalized by the multiple and overlapping membership of countries across the three RECs. If the TFTA had been in force in 2017, it would have covered only an additional 8 per cent of the intra-African imports that flowed into the 26 TFTA countries. Thus, the TFTA amounts to an incremental step, and a rationalization, of the liberalization of intra-African trade in the eastern side of the continent.

Trade in services integration

In 2017, over 53 per cent of Africa's GDP came from services, and in most African countries, services accounted for at least 49 per cent. Some 16 per cent of Africa's GDP came from wholesale, retail trade, restaurants and hotels, while 9 per cent came from transport, communications and storage services (UNCTAD, 2019).

Although data on intra-African trade in services are unavailable, the potential benefits of such trade can be assessed by looking at the continent's imports of commercial services, which approximate the size of its market. Africa's imports of commercial services grew in real terms from $140 billion in 2016 to $150 billion in 2017, indicating a substantial potential market for African suppliers if the continent can reduce barriers. In individual sectors, the continent imported $1 billion in goods-related services in 2017 (up 6 per cent from 2016), $59 billion in transport services (up 4 per cent), $24 billion in travel services (up 15 per cent) and $76 billion in "other services" (up 9 per cent) (authors' analysis of UNCTAD, 2019).

Figure 1.9:

Africa and EAC's service trade deficits in five categories, 2017

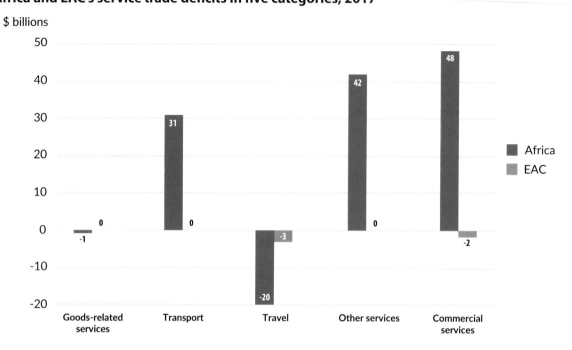

Source: authors' analysis of UNCTAD (2019).

Note: The deficits in transport and other services exceed the sum of the deficits in the other categories. This may be because the other categories include a component of government, that is, non-commercial services. Since government services include services supplied between governments and their diplomats and military staff abroad, they may not reflect efforts to facilitate trade in services within the region and are therefore not considered here (UNCTAD, 2019).

In addition, the level of services that Africa is importing from *outside* the continent can be estimated to show the additional business that could potentially be captured by integrating intra-African trade in services. The continent's services trade deficit for a given type of service must be filled from outside Africa (any service imports in excess of the continent's service exports must be imported from outside the continent, otherwise they would be matched by a corresponding intra-regional export and be captured in the export statistics).[14]

Africa imported an estimated $48 billion in commercial services from the rest of the world in 2017, with large deficits in transport and other services (Figure 1.9). EAC can be examined, as well, since it is the only REC with a formal trade in services agreement that exceeds its commitments under the WTO's General Agreement in Trade and Services. EAC had a surplus, rather than a deficit, in all service categories, so it is not possible to estimate a minimum level of services it imported from outside EAC.

Although trade in services presents African countries with growth opportunities, it also presents challenges. According to a World Bank report, domestic regulatory hurdles and trade barriers fragment service markets on the continent, making the cost of trading in services high. For instance, education and health services in East Africa are hindered by restrictions on using telemedicine or e-learning, while medical tourism is restricted by the non-portability of insurance policies. Legal restrictions on hospitals entering the market in countries such as Tanzania and Uganda and limits on repatriating earnings in Kenya and Uganda constrain the establishment of foreign hospitals. Finally, the high cost of visa and work permits in many countries stringently restrict the movement of health and education professionals to provide services abroad (World Bank 2016). At the other end of the spectrum, informal services ranging from hairdressing, construction and housekeeping to education, health and finance are widespread in Africa—those flows seem to flourish despite many barriers to the movement of service providers.

14

Factors driving intra-African investment

"A study on factors spurring intra-FDI indicates that trade openness, infrastructure and the performance of the logistics and business environment influence the attraction of investment within Africa. Furthermore, improvements in logistics, the business environment and trade cost can enhance intra-African investment, in addition to trade openness.

"The international legal framework governing FDI flows in Africa is complex, consisting of bilateral investment treaties and regional investment agreements. Since the 1960s, African countries have signed 853 bilateral investment treaties, out of which 173 are intra-African. In line with global trends, the pace of concluding bilateral investment treaties picked up around the turn of the century, but it has slowed significantly in recent years. Many of the existing African bilateral investment treaties belong to the old generation marked by broad standards of treatment. Those unreformed treaties can make African countries vulnerable to costly investor disputes."

Source: Assessing the Status of Regional Integration in Africa (E/ECA/COE/38/3ECA, 2018).

Intra-African investment

African countries are pursuing measures for greater intra-African investment. Preparations are currently under way to negotiate a pan-African investment agreement as a protocol to the AfCFTA.

At the same time, African countries are concluding fewer new bilateral intra-African investment agreements. This accompanies a general reduction in the number of bilateral investment treaties. The reason for the decline may be evidence that bilateral investment agreements have not led to increased investment in African countries and have facilitated tax avoidance by multinational corporations (ECA, 2016 and 2018c). The planned investment protocol to the AfCFTA should avoid creating loopholes for multinational tax avoidance (see Chapter 6).

Intra-African foreign direct investment (FDI) has fallen recently. Greenfield intra-African FDI projects (an indicator of future FDI trends) fell substantially from around $8.6 billion in 2016 to around $1.9 billion in 2017 (World Investment Report, 2018). Net intra-African mergers and acquisitions rose from $400 million in 2016 to $796 million in 2017, though this was much smaller than the decline in the abovementioned intra-African greenfield FDI projects. This came in an overall context of falling announced greenfield investment projects in Africa (from $94.0 billion in 2016 to $85.3 billion in 2017) and falling net foreign merger and acqui-

sition sales in African countries (from $9.7 billion in 2016 to $3.5 billion in 2017) (World Investment Report, 2018). According to the World Investment Report 2018 the overall decline in FDI to Africa can be explained in part by "weak oil prices and harmful ongoing macroeconomic effects from the commodity bust," which may also explain the decrease in intra-African FDI. In addition, the decline in indicators of intra-African FDI came when Africa's total *outward* announced greenfield FDI projects rose— indicating that African firms invested more abroad but shifted new investments away from Africa— while worldwide announced greenfield FDI projects in Africa fell by much less (only 10 per cent) than the fall in intra-African announced greenfield FDI projects (World Investment Report, 2018).

The decline in intra-African FDI does not appear to be due to new barriers—this report could not identify any. Moreover, Africa's propensity to invest in Africa was still much higher than that of the rest of the world, as 34 per cent of African countries' outgoing announced greenfield investment projects went to Africa in 2017, while only 12 per cent of such projects worldwide went to Africa. Similarly, 40 per cent of African countries' international net mergers and acquisitions were purchased from other African countries in 2017, while only 4 per cent of world net mergers and acquisitions were purchased from Africa (authors' calculations based on World Investment Report 2018). Thus, African countries still have a stronger propensity to direct FDI to Africa than does the rest of the world.

Migration and free movement of persons

Migration

Migration is both a means of economic mobility and a survival strategy. About two-thirds African migrants are economically motivated, searching for better opportunities, including education and employment. Africa's growing and increasingly educated youthful population constitutes a driver of migration. Growth of employment in Africa has not kept pace with the growing numbers of entrants into the labour force. In the past 10 years, Africa created over 37 million wage-paying jobs, but approximately 110 million people joined the workforce in this period (McKinsey, 2014).

With the failure of economically active persons to enter their countries' economies, migration offers a coping mechanism. Intra- and inter-country movement both feature in Africa. The bulk of African migrants stay within the continent. The proportion moving within the same sub-region is close to 90 per cent in West Africa, 65 per cent in Southern Africa, 50 per cent in Central Africa, 47 per cent in East Africa and 20 per cent in North Africa.[15] Africans are underrepresented in the world migrant population, and Africa has the lowest intercontinental emigration rate of any world region (AUC-ECA-ILO Report, 2017).

The drivers of migration include conflict and civil unrest, political instability and market failures causing unemployment and increasing living costs. A vision is needed that embraces migration as an intrinsic and inevitable part of development rather than treating it as a problem to be solved. With the labour supply in Africa projected to increase by 198 million by 2030 (ILO, 2018), more African governments are embracing migration as an opportunity for development and regional integration (AUC-ECA-ILO Report, 2017).

Free movement of persons

Africa is making gradual progress towards the free movement of people across borders. Economic growth will follow, through tourism, trade and investment, human capital mobility, and labour skill gap and mismatch solutions. Free movement lets firms find talent and skills more easily, in turn driving productivity. But it also brings challenges. Recipient countries fear foreigners competing with locals, while source countries fear brain drain and the loss of working-age individuals.

The milestone African Union Protocol on Free Movement of Persons, Right of Residence and Right of Establishment was adopted by the 30th Ordinary Session of the African Union Assembly in Addis Ababa, Ethiopia, on 29 January 2018. Yet it has struggled to gather country ratifications. The initiative promotes the free movement of persons across Africa through rights of entry, visa-free entry for short visits, rights of residence and rights of establishment, as well as the ability to establish a business.

Visa openness varies widely in Africa from country to country and from region to region. The AfDB and AU Visa Openness Index Report 2018 showed progress in liberalizing visa regimes for other Africans. The average African can now travel to 25 per cent of other African countries without a visa (up from 22 per cent in 2017, and from 20 per cent in 2016), while a steady 24 per cent of African countries offer a visa on arrival to the average African. Benin, Kenya, Rwanda, Senegal and Zimbabwe have liberalized entry rules for Africans from other countries. Beginning 2018, Namibia has decided to allow visas on arrival for travellers from other African countries, and Ethiopia has allowed online visa applications for citizens of all countries. Of the 20 top-performing countries on visa openness towards other African countries in 2018, 40 per cent were in East Africa, 35 per cent in West Africa, 20 per cent in Southern Africa and 5 per cent in North Africa, while none were in Central Africa, which lags the most in free movement (AfDB and AU, 2018).

RECs also achieved progress, particularly ECOWAS, EAC and AMU. The ECOWAS region remains the best-performing REC in offering free movement to its citizens with no visa requirement, thus achieving a 100 per cent performance rate, followed by EAC with 90 per cent, AMU with 60 per cent, SADC with 56 per cent, CEN-SAD with 33 per cent, ECCAS with 25 per cent, COMESA with 19 per cent and IGAD with 11 per cent in IGAD (AfDB and AU, 2018).

The ECOWAS region has implemented right of residence and establishment, allowing citizens to move freely for work and start businesses in its member States without applying for permits. Citizens are free to travel among member States visa-free and can use an ECOWAS passport, viewed as a key achievement of regional mobility and identity. Seven West African countries—Burkina Faso, Cabo Verde, Gambia, Ghana, Mauritania, Senegal and Togo, are among the 20 most visa-open countries in Africa. Togo is the best-ranked West African country and third overall on the Africa Visa Openness Index (AfDB, 2016). The region also recorded the highest score (0.8) on the Africa Regional Integration Index (ECA, 2016). The ECOWAS National Biometric Identity Card replaces the handwritten ECOWAS Travel Certificate to facilitate intra-regional mobility and enhance security in the region (adopted in December 2014 by the Authority of ECOWAS Heads of State and Government by Decision A/DEC.01/12/14).

The EAC adopted a protocol on movement and labour. But eight years after the coming into force of the East African Community (EAC) Common Market Protocol in 2010, and despite advocacy by the East African Employers Organization and the East African Trade Unions Confederation, free movement of labour remains contentious. Nevertheless, successes include Tanzania reducing its residence permit fee, which was more than $500, by 50 per cent in 2017.

SADC made progress in implementing its protocol on the movement of people, originally drafted in 1995. However, that protocol does not reach as far as the ECOWAS and EAC versions, mandating only visa-free entry for up to 90 days in a year and leaving rules on residence and establishment to the discretion of individual member States. To date, nine countries have signed the protocol. South Africa has ratified it and implemented visa waiv-

ers in line with the spirit of the agreement, so that nationals of almost all 15 SADC countries may visit South Africa visa-free.

A further SADC protocol on employment and labour (2014) calls for member States to ensure fundamental rights regarding labour, employment and social protection for migrant workers and their families. A 2014 Regional Labour Migration Policy Framework and SADC Labour Migration Action Plan for 2016–19 has assisted SADC member States in these identified priority areas.

Though free movement of persons is a core objective of **AMU, CEN-SAD**, **COMESA**, **ECCAS** and **IGAD**, they have made less progress. Free movement exists only within the CEMAC subset of countries in ECCAS, only to Tunisia in AMU, and only through bilateral arrangements in IGAD (Ethiopia–Djibouti, Kenya–Ethiopia and Kenya–Uganda) (ECA, 2019b). Only Burundi has ratified the COMESA Free Movement Protocol, but Mauritius, Rwanda and Seychelles waive visas to all COMESA citizens, and Zambia waives visas for COMESA nationals on official business (ECA, 2019b). Free movement between CEN-SAD States is accounted for mostly by the member countries that are part of ECOWAS.

REC implementation of free movement has been hampered lack of information on the pros and cons and faced such challenges as:

- More developed member States worrying about being flooded with job seekers from less developed ones.

- Less developed nations worry about losing talent to leading regional economies due to brain drain.

- Overlapping and contradictory requirements as African countries join multiple RECs.

Enhanced labour mobility through education and skills development

The non-recognition, non-compatibility and non-comparability of skills, educational qualifications and experiences in Africa have impeded labour mobility. The mismatch between skills and the needs of labour markets has slowed the continent's economic integration and overall development. Efforts over the years towards cooperation and integration in Africa's educational sector, particularly in higher education, have had mixed results. The Arusha Convention, adopted in 1981, laid the legal foundation for cooperation in higher education. Although only 19 of the then 54 AU member States ratified the convention, it formed the basis for the African Higher Education Harmonization Strategy (HEHS), adopted by the Conference of Ministers of Education of the African Union in 2007. The African HEHS facilitates the mutual recognition of academic qualifications and enhances intra-African academic mobility, as well as assuring quality, competitiveness and the relevance of qualifications for the knowledge economy. It currently employs four main instruments: the Nyerere Mobility Programme, the African Quality Rating Mechanism and Accreditation, the Pan-African University and the Tuning Africa (Woldegiorgis et al., 2015, 244–46).

Initiated by the AU in 2007 and launched in 2011, the Mwalimu Nyerere Mobility Programme facilitates the mobility of African students in science and technology among African universities to promote the intra-African mobility of students and the retention of high-level African human resources. The African Regional Quality Rating Mechanism and Accreditation, established by the African Union Commission (AUC) in 2012, facilitates benchmarking quality development in higher education and research to achieve international standards for greater competitiveness in the global knowledge market.

The third instrument for higher education cooperation in Africa is the Pan-African post-graduate training and research network of university nodes within the framework of the Pan-African University, established by a 2010 AU Executive Council Decision. It consists of 55 universities spread across the five sub-regions of the continent and aims to enhance Africa's research and innovation capacity in science and technology and produce world-class human resources at the master's and doctoral levels. The programme started in 2012 with 100 students and by 2015 had enrolled 1,500. On 6 April 2018, the AU granted the government of Cameroon the hosting of the rectorate of the Pan-African University.

The fourth instrument is "programme tuning," which in the Africa context means programme-level harmonization through specific curriculum integration methods, credit accumulation mechanisms and transfer systems. The Tuning Africa pilot involved 60 higher education institutions, divided into five subject groups of 12 universities each. The effectiveness of the African regional quality assurance mechanism depends on establishing and operationalizing national-level quality assurance structures.

The AU has issued a ten-year Continental Education Strategy for Africa (CESA 2016–2025), which seeks to establish a system of educating and training human resources capable of achieving the AU's vision and ambitions. It plans, through reorienting and harmonizing Africa's education and training systems, to meet the knowledge, competence and skill innovation and creativity required to nurture African core values and promote sustainable development at the national, regional and continental levels.

Infrastructure integration

Adequate infrastructure is the key missing driver of economic growth and sustainable development across the African continent. Infrastructure enables export-oriented firms to access international markets quickly, cheaply and efficiently. It underpins the competitiveness of manufacturing exports and the ability of agricultural exporters to comply with sanitary and phytosanitary requirements in international markets. Insufficient investment in infrastructure constrains African countries' ability to fully capitalize on the growth and job creation opportunities of the AfCFTA.

Africa has forgone an estimated 25 per cent of cumulative economic growth in the past two decades due to inadequate Infrastructure investment accounts for more than half the recent improvement in African economic growth yet remains insufficient (Figure 1.10) (AfDB, 2018). The AfDB has estimated Africa's infrastructure requirements at

Figure 1.10:
Quality of overall infrastructure, world rankings, 2018

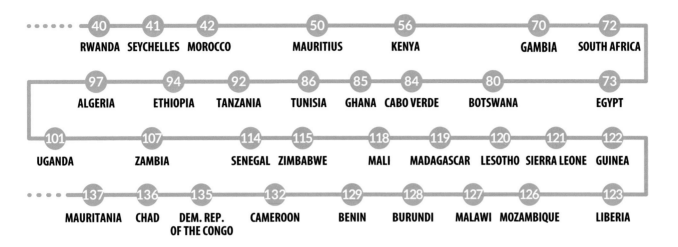

Source: World Economic Forum (2018).

Note. Data only available for selection of countries.

$130–170 billion a year, with a financing gap in the range of $68–$108 billion (AfDB, 2018). The deficit hinders intra-regional trade by reducing connectivity between countries (AEO, 2018). Improving infrastructure enables African countries to engage more fully in trade and reap the benefits of economic regionalization.

African leaders are pursuing key regional and continental infrastructure initiatives, including those under the eye of the AU's Programme for Infrastructure Development in Africa (PIDA) Steering Committee—which is mandated to monitor progress on infrastructure developments in the context of Agenda 2063.[16] The notable Trans African Highway initiative, with nine highways adding up to 56,683 kilometres, is about 60 per cent complete. Table 1.4 summarizes the top 5 transport projects under PIDA according to the World Bank.

Table 1.4:
Top five priority Programme for Infrastructure Development in Africa transport projects in advanced stages of preparation or ready for funding and implementation

PROJECT	DESCRIPTION	COST ($ MILLIONS)	COVERAGE
Yamoussoukro Decision—SAATM	Accelerate its implementation across the continent	5	All African countries
Abidjan–Lagos Coastal Corridor	To modernize heavily travelled ARTIN corridor in West Africa	290	Benin, Côte d'Ivoire, Ghana, Nigeria and Togo
North–South Multimodal Corridor	To modernize highest priority ARTIN corridor in Southern Africa	2,325	Dem. Rep. of the Congo, Mozambique, South Africa, Zambia and Zimbabwe
Central Corridor	To modernize the third priority ARTIN corridor in Eastern Africa	840	Burundi, Dem. Rep. of the Congo, Rwanda, Tanzania and Uganda
Trans-Maghreb Highway	To improve the movement of goods and services across the Maghreb region	75	Algeria, Egypt, Libya, Morocco and Tunisia

Source: World Bank, 2014.

Note: ARTIN is African Regional Transport Infrastructure Network. SAATM is Single African Air Transport Market.

Road Transport

Road density in Africa is a quarter of the world average (Mafusire and others, 2010; African Energy Forum, 2016). Only 25 per cent of the continent's road network is paved, while the world average exceeds 50 per cent (Figure 1.11).

Rail transport

Pan-African continental high-speed rail, foreseen in Agenda 2063, aims at connecting Africa's cap-ital cities and megacities, including (but not only) commercial hubs, economic zones and tourist destinations (Figure 1.12, Box 1.3). Developing and delivering this network requires heightened and sustained political leadership. Currently, the New Partnership for Africa's Development (NEPAD) procurement division is reviewing the technical and financial proposals received from seven engineering consulting firms (of eight shortlisted) in response to a 2017 request for proposals.

Figure 1.11:
Quality of railroad infrastructure, world rankings, 2018

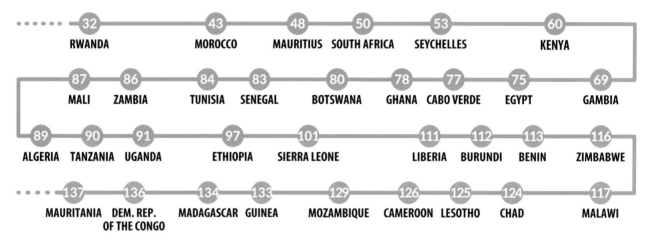

Source: World Economic Forum (2018).

Note. Data only available for selection of countries..

Box 1.2:
The LAPSSET Corridor programme

The Lamu Port–South Sudan–Ethiopia Transport (LAPSSET Corridor programme) is East Africa's largest and most ambitious infrastructure project, bringing together Ethiopia, Kenya and South Sudan. This mega-project consists of seven key infrastructure projects: a new 32-berth port at Lamu (Kenya), inter-regional highways connecting Ethiopia, Kenya and South Sudan, a crude oil pipeline across the three countries, a product oil pipeline from Kenya to Ethiopia, 1,500 kilometres of interregional standard gauge railway lines through the three countries, three international airports and resort cities (one in each country) and the multipurpose High Grand Falls Dam along the Tana River. According to the LAPSSET Corridor Development Authority, over 5,000 jobs have been created since construction started in 2012. The standard gauge railway was launched in Kenya in 2017. The overall cost is estimated to be more than $25.5 billion.

The $449 million contract for the first three berths at Lamu was awarded to China Communications Construction Company Limited in 2015. These developments reflect completed supportive infrastructure, such as the modern LAPSSET building, police station, Lamu power sub-station and power supply, steel pipe manufacturing plant and water reticulation system. The new Lamu port will be able to handle the largest ships in the world with its 500-metre-wide channel and 18-metre depth (in comparison, the port of Durban has a 220-metre-wide channel with a 16 metre-depth).

Figure 1.12:
Quality of road infrastructure, world rankings, 2018

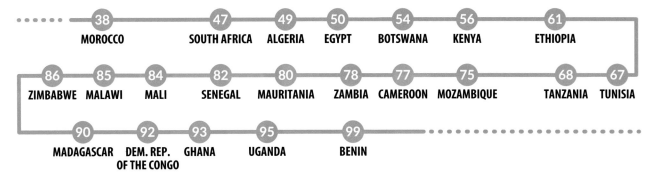

Source: World Economic Forum (2018).

Note. Data only available for selection of countries..

Box 1.3:
National rail development

The Egyptian National Railways signed a five-year contract worth more than €1 billion for 1,300 passenger car trains with the Transmashholding-Hungary Kft consortium in September 2018. Upgrading and expanding railway road networks in Egypt requires approximately $10 billion over a 10-year period, and a further $8 billion for the following 5 to 10 years (British Expertise, 2015).

In Uganda, an agreement to fund rehabilitation of the 375-kilometre Northern Line between Tororo and Gulu has been signed by the European Union, which will provide a €21.5 million grant alongside €13.1 million contributed by the government of Uganda. Reviving the railway is intended to reduce transport costs in northern Uganda, South Sudan and eastern Democratic Republic of the Congo and to transport freight currently traveling by road.

In Kenya, the upgraded and modernized SGR railway system was launched in March 2017.

In Senegal, the government intends to revamp the country's highly degraded and almost abandoned railway network. A programme to build 1,520 kilometres of new lines connecting Dakar to the main cities and regional markets has been developed for the next five years (ECA, 2019a). In January 2019, the first section of the Dakar Regional Express Train (TER) was completed. The 55-kilometre TER connects central Dakar with Blaise Diagne International Airport.

Under a tripartite agreement signed in 2017, the Société Nationale des Chemins de Fer français and the French government development agency Agence Française de Développement agreed to provide suburban passenger operator Passenger Rail Agency of South Africa (PRASA) technical and financial assistance worth 6.2 million South African rand. The 12-month partnership, which commenced in December 2017, provided technical expertise, skills training and exchanges of best practice with PRASA as the operator and upgraded the 1,067-millimetre-gauge commuter networks around Cape Town, Durban and Johannesburg. These steps contributed to the broader PRASA renewal programme of procuring 7,224 new passenger trains over 2015–30, costing about 123.5 billion rand ($10 billion). More than 5,256 coaches will be brought into operation by 2020, and a further 456 by 2030 (ECA, 2019).

Air transport

Intra-African air connectivity received a major boost in January 2018, when the Single African Air Transport Market (SAATM), a flagship project under Agenda 2063 for liberalizing and unifying the African skies, was launched during the African Union Heads of State and Government Summit in Addis Ababa. The SAATM facilitate free movement of people and goods, enhances the continent's integration and connectivity and fosters the aviation sector, tourism and trade. It is expected to support the Action Plan for Boosting Intra-African Trade (BIAT) and the AfCFTA. The AUC estimates that the SAATM will translate into 300,000 direct and up to 2 million indirect jobs. Other forecast benefits include improved air service connectivity, a 25 per cent reduction in airfares, increased convenience, saved time and a cushion for the survival of African airlines.

Twenty-eight AU member States belong to SAATM, covering more than 700 million persons. The States are harmonizing their bilateral air service agreements, with 16 countries signing a memorandum of implementation to remove all restrictions in their agreements and comply with the Yamoussoukro decision on the liberalization of air transport markets in Africa (AFCAC, 2019).

Maritime and waterway transport

Demographic growth and regional integration can nurture Africa's maritime trade if shipping, ports and hinterland access are boosted. Africa relies heavily on ships and ports to service its intercontinental trade. While Africa accounts for approximately 2.7 per cent of global trade by value, the continent contributes higher shares to global seaborne trade—7 per cent of maritime exports and 5 per cent of imports by volume (UNCTAD 2018). Africa's shipping and ports do not always match global trends and standards. Besides the four container terminals in Egypt, Morocco and South Africa, no African port was featured in the 2016 global list of the 100 top container ports. Most of Africa's container ports and hinterland transport networks need upgrading. Enhancing crane productivity is required: on average, cranes make around 20 moves per hour in West Africa and 25

to 30 in South Africa, compared with 35 to 40 in Asia (Maritime Executive, 2019). Employing technology and digital solutions, cutting inefficiency, improving processes, enhancing transparency and promoting security and resilience of transport systems is critical. Implementing the AfCFTA will also improve containerized trade and port traffic volumes by increasing integration into regional and global value chains.

Maritime trade in Africa is shaped by the continent's limited trade diversification. Forty per cent of Africa's sea exports in 2017 were crude oil, while over two-thirds of imports were dry cargoes (dry bulk and containerized goods) and almost 20 per cent were gas and petroleum products (UNCTAD, 2018b). Geography shapes African countries' shipping connectivity: the best-connected countries are at the continent's corners, hub ports connect to international shipping routes, notably in Egypt, Morocco and South Africa, followed by sub-regional load centres in Djibouti, Mauritius and Togo. These countries become leaders in African container shipping connectivity with help from public and private investments, port reforms and improved transit to connect to neighbouring landlocked countries (African Economic Outlook, 2018).

Energy

The energy sector drives growth and development across Africa. Investment in energy infrastructure at both the national and regional level is needed for future economic growth, poverty reduction and access to affordable energy for all. Frequent power outages in Africa directly harm industrial performance and, consequently, the economy. Reliable and affordable power supply is required for African firms to produce goods and services for exchange within the continent to take advantage of the AfCFTA.

The average effective cost of electricity to manufacturing enterprises in Africa is close to 20 cents per kilowatt-hour, around four times higher than industrial rates elsewhere in the world. This reflects both high-cost utility power (10 cents per kilowatt-hour) and heavy reliance on emergency back-up generation during frequent power outages (around 40 cents) (African Economic Outlook 2018).

The power sector represents Africa's largest infrastructure deficit: insufficient generation capacity, insecure supply and low and inefficient electricity consumption. More than 607 million people in Africa did not have access to electricity in 2016, the year for which the most recent data is available (World Bank, 2019). Insufficient energy generation often exacerbated the situation. Over 2010–15, just three countries had 66 per cent of Africa's electricity capacity—Algeria, Egypt and South Africa (British Petroleum, 2016). The Programme for Infrastructure Development in Africa (PIDA) estimates that demand for power will grow annually by 6 per cent until 2040. Installed generation capacity in Africa, around 191 gigawatts in 2016, will have to increase to 446 gigawatts by 2040 to meet demand (U.S. Energy Information Administration, 2019).

Regional energy integration through power pools is a prerequisite for the "Africa We Want" (as Agenda 2063 puts it). Given the smallness of many African economies, regional energy integration can attract investment, ensure the security of energy supply and mix and, through economies of scale, reduce costs to businesses and consumers. It provides an optimal economic solution by generating energy where it is most economical and providing it where it is most needed. The Ethiopia–Sudan transmission interconnector provides an exemplary regional model. This project promoted power system stability and encouraged energy connectivity by integrating the networks of Ethiopia and Sudan and thereby developing the scope for building larger power projects to meet larger regional markets. Other notable initiatives include the 400 megawatt Batoka Gorge hydroelectric power project between Zambia and Zimbabwe, and the Zambia–Tanzania–Kenya transmission interconnector, which facilitates regional electricity trading and promotes power system stability by connecting the Southern African Power Pool with the East African Power Pool.

Ongoing initiatives are establishing renewable energy projects across Africa with the support of the AfDB, which has approved an equity investment of up to $25 million in ARCH Africa Renewable Power Fund (ARPF). A $250 million private equity fund for ARPF will provide for the development and construction of 10 to 15 greenfield renewable energy projects in Africa, adding about 533 megawatts of installed generation capacity. These projects will focus on mature technologies including wind, solar photovoltaic, small to medium hydro, geothermal and biomass.

Information and communications technology

Mobile and internet telephone charges in Africa are about four times higher than those in South Asia, and international call prices are more than twice as high (AfDB, African Economic Outlook, 2018). Connectivity of African countries to international broadband networks is nearly complete, but continues to restrain adoption. In Africa, 1 gigabyte (GB) of data cost nearly 18 per cent of average monthly income in 2016, compared with only 3 per cent in Asia (Alliance for Affordable Internet, 2017). Anti-competitive pricing policies of mobile telephone operators, such as charging more for calls to competitor networks, contributes to making information and communications technology (ICT) expensive. However, some African countries are making progress in upgrading their telephone infrastructures (Box 1.4).

Infrastructure financing

Channelling financing into infrastructure development in Africa is a top priority for African policy makers. The Dakar Financing Summit of June 2014 and the Addis Ababa Action Agenda of the Third International Conference on Financing for Development in July 2015 both recognized the importance of scaling up infrastructure investments in Africa.

Infrastructure development in Africa reached $81.6 billion in 2017, an increase of 22 per cent from 2016 (ICA, 2018). According to the Infrastructure Consortium of Africa, the single biggest factor driving the higher level of commitments in 2017 was an increase in identifiable Chinese investments, from $6.4 billion in 2016 to $19.4 billion in 2017 (Figure 1.13). In addition, internally funded African

> **Box 1.4:**
> ## National information and communications technology developments
>
> Egypt was among the leading countries in outsourcing and information technology service exports in 2016 and 2017, bringing Egypt's treasury around 94.6 billion Egyptian pounds ($5.34 billion), more than 3.5 per cent of GDP.
>
> Phase two of Kenya's National Optic Fibre Backbone Infrastructure Extension Project is being supported by $107 million in Chinese financing (Infrastructure Consortium for Africa, 2018). The project will provide 1,600 kilometres of fibre linking all 47 counties and 500 kilometres dedicated to military use. Phase two adds to the existing 4,300 kilometres of cable completed in 2009, connecting 58 towns in 35 counties.
>
> Zimbabwe's TelOne signed a $98 million loan facility with Eximbank of China to finance its network modernization programme, with Huawei as the project contractor.
>
> Eximbank of China is financing the second stage of the National Telecommunications Broadband Network project in Cameroon, worth $338 million.
>
> In Togo, 500 administrative buildings will be connected by a $22 million fibre optic network built by Huawei and funded by China Eximbank.
>
> In Niger, China Eximbank provided a $99 million preferential loan for establishing a fibre optic backbone. In Benin, China Eximbank provided a preferential loan to the telecommunications sector, part of which will be used to develop the broadband network (ICA, 2018).
>
> Burundi has formulated a Regional Communications Infrastructure Programme with support from the World Bank.

national and sub-national government budget allocations for infrastructure development rose from $30.7 billion in 2016 to $34.4 billion in 2017. Total commitments to Africa's ICT sector stood at $2.3 billion in 2017, a 37 per cent increase from $1.7 billion in 2016, with China making most of the investments (ICA, 2018).

The value of projects with private sector participation in 2017 reached $5.2 billion, an increase from $3.6 billion reported in 2016. Of this, $2.3 billion (44.8 per cent) was privately financed (ICA, 2018). The transport sector, with commitments of $34 billion, continued to be the largest beneficiary of infrastructure commitments in 2017, accounting for nearly 42 per cent of all funding. The energy sector, which recorded $24.8 billion of investments in 2017, accounted for 30.4 per cent, and the water sector, $13.2 billion or 16.2 per cent. Multi-sector investments followed, with $5.1 billion or 6.3 per cent.

West Africa received $22 billion of the $81.6 billion committed to Africa's infrastructure development in 2017, followed by North Africa with $15.9 billion and East Africa with $15.8 billion. Southern Africa (excluding South Africa) received $12.2 billion, South Africa $8.7 billion and Central Africa $6 billion (ICA, 2018).

Several infrastructure road maps with clearly identified projects and timeframes at the country level have also developed. For instance, Gabon needs about $34 billion for the infrastructure to achieve its industrialization goals for 2025 (Gabon, 2013). The cost of South Africa's infrastructure is estimated at $191 billion up to 2025 (Leke, 2015).

Africa must rely on a mix of mechanisms and financing instruments to overcome its financing gaps for infrastructure. Maximizing the potential of public–private partnerships (PPPs) and tapping into national resources, regional and global infrastructure development funds and innovative financing tools are all required. Pooling resources using the AfCFTA framework and PPP promotion are critical. Although PPPs are not the only means to increase private sector involvement in infrastruc-

Africa's infrastructure funding trends, 2013–17

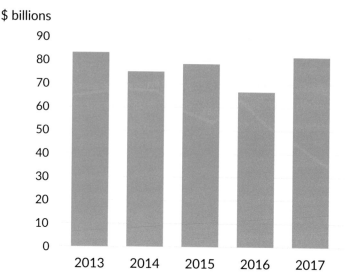

Source: Infrastructure Consortium for Africa (2018).

ture projects, most private sector–funded projects across the continent are initiated through them (International Finance Corporation, 2016; UNCTAD, 2016). PPPs in the infrastructure sector are hampered by lack of sound regulatory frameworks for transparency in contractual arrangements and inconsistency in the terms of reference for projects, political interference and limited capacity of government officials (International Finance Corporation, 2016). Implementing the AfCFTA can address regulatory and policy discord within the continent and provide safeguards required by development finance institutions and the private sector.

Infrastructure for Africa's landlocked countries

Africa's 16 landlocked countries have built-in geographic disadvantages that contribute to economic, social and even political performance. Improving their competiveness, industrialization and access to seaports requires developing and maintaining quality infrastructure systems, especially multimodal transport and transport corridors. High freight costs and unpredictable transit times hinder their integration into regional and global value chains, which relies on the import and export of components, and de-links their economies from regional and world markets. The 2014 Vienna Programme of Action aims to respond to

the specific needs and problems of landlocked developing countries (LLDCs) resulting from their remoteness and geographical constraints.

Regional and national infrastructure projects can support the continent's integration and link landlocked countries to coastal countries. Examples include the North–South Corridor Programme in Eastern and Southern Africa; the Walvis Bay Corridor in Southern Africa; the navigation line project linking Lake Victoria to the Mediterranean Sea through the Nile and the Africa Clean Energy Corridor, expected to facilitate cross-border trade in green and renewable energy in a network from Cape Town to Cairo. Other projects include the West African rail network to connect Benin, Burkina Faso, Côte D'Ivoire, Ghana, Niger, Nigeria and Togo; the Grand Ethiopian Renaissance Dam; the Mombasa–Kigali Railway Project; the Grand Inga Dam in the Democratic Republic of the Congo and the Bagamoyo Port in Tanzania.

In an emerging trend in countries such as Ethiopia, public-funded infrastructure aims to encourage the movement of goods and people. Ethiopia spends more than 50 per cent of its federal budget on infrastructure and skills development (Ethiopia Industrial Policy Document, 2016). This includes the building of the Grand Ethiopian Renaissance Dam and an electric railway system that connects Addis Ababa to Djibouti.

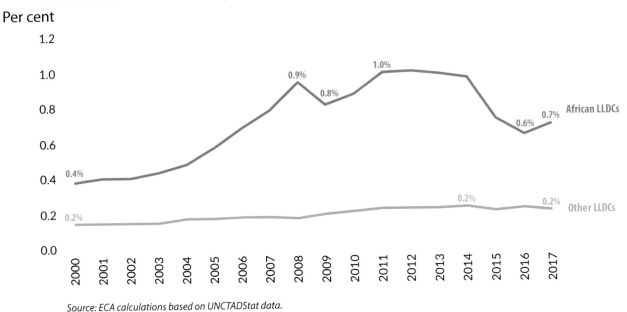

Figure 1.14:
Landlocked developing country merchandise exports
Per cent of world merchandise exports

Source: ECA calculations based on UNCTADStat data.

Table 1.5:
African country ratifications and notifications for the WTO Trade Facilitation Agreement

STATUS	AFRICA	OF WHICH LLDCS	TOTAL
Ratification	28	10	135
Category A	35	12	112
Category B	17	7	61
Category C	16	7	51

Source: https://www.tfadatabase.org, accessed 6 November 2018.
Note: LLDCs are landlocked developing countries.

In trade, African LLDCs have maintained a fairly steady share of world merchandise exports since the late 2000s (Figure 1.14). In 2017, they contributed around 0.21 per cent of world exports, a small decrease from the 0.22 per cent of 2016. They trailed behind the performance of non-African LLDCs, which reached 1 per cent in 2012, then decreased to 0.7 per cent by 2017, still more than three times the African LLDC performance.

The WTO Trade Facilitation Agreement entered into force in 22 February 2017. Most African LLDCs that are WTO members have already ratified it, with the exception of Burkina Faso, Burundi, Uganda and Zimbabwe.[17] Those four countries have, however,

submitted their category A notifications,[18] signalling their commitment to the agreement. In addition, 17 African countries—including 7 LLDCs—have submitted their category B notifications,[19] indicating the need for transition time before entry into force. And 16—also including 7 LLDCs—have submitted their category C notifications,[20] indicating the need for additional support for such areas as single windows, customs risk management and test procedures. The commitment shown in the fairly high notification rate by African LLDCs is encouraging, because the agreement is expected to benefit most the countries that are further behind.

Health integration

The free movement of persons, where public health is concerned, translates into free movement of diseases. In Africa, this is particularly worrisome because of limited national and cross-border health monitoring systems.[21]

Health security challenges the continent due to its high disease burden, the prevalence of poor and inadequate healthcare systems, weak pharmaceutical manufacturing facilities, a paucity of qualified health personnel and low investment in health-related research and development. African countries need to establish institutions—with early warning mechanisms—for maintaining reliable public health data, including that of migrants, and enhancing government health agency capacities to prevent and respond to acute public health risks, such as Ebola virus disease, that have the potential to cross borders.

The African Medicines Agency, which was adopted by African health ministers on 19 May 2018, intends to establish common standards and guidelines for public health emergencies and for the provision of affordable, safe and effective medicines. In addition, the AU Pharmaceutical Manufacturing Plan for Africa supports the African Medicines Regulatory Harmonization Programme, which since its launch in 2012 has encouraged Africa's economic regions to collaborate on regulating and registering medicines.

Experiences from the RECs can inform at the continental level. The AfCFTA can promote health integration approaches that use information communication technologies accompanied by coordination and advocacy.

The EAC has paired nations with well-functioning regulators with others that do not for training and assistance. Kenya has helped Zanzibar, Uganda has helped Rwanda and Tanzania has helped Burundi (NEPAD 2017). A successful framework for promoting safe medicines on the African market was piloted in EAC five member States, and it is hoped that the experiences can be transferred to other regional economic communities.

ECOWAS's West African Health Organization is charged with safeguarding the health of the sub-region's peoples by initiating and harmonizing health policies across all 15 member States, pooling resources and fostering cooperation. A framework for tracking, monitoring and reporting by the manufacturer, importer, exporter and distribution of medicines was developed and formally endorsed in September 2017.

Africa's research and development capacities for collaborative regional health work have been enhanced by the Regulatory Centres of Research Excellence (RCOREs). To date, 11 RCOREs provide research and development and practical hands-on professional learning in different medical disciplines.

Mining sector integration

The mining sector contributes to Africa's regional integration regime through strategies that realize regionally based linkages across the mineral value chain. Given most African countries' small markets, regional approaches are crucial to maximize regional economies of scale and minimize allowing mines to wreck the environment. But most mineral rich countries in Africa have not taken advantage of the collective economic opportunities that would be boosted by a regional minerals development strategy.

The African Mining Vision (AMV) adopted by the African Union Heads of State and Government in 2009 provides an opportunity to change this narrative. The AMV recognizes that regional integration in Africa offers many advantages for developing the mineral sector. It is anchored on the notion that closer trading links between countries would strengthen African countries' competitive advantage in world trade. Regional integration would support developing common mineral-specific taxation instruments, harmonizing regional mineral-based feedstocks for manufacturing, infrastructure and agriculture and pursuing regional content targets and policies that cater for variable geometry—the differences in countries' speed of change since low-capacity, low-income countries proceed more slowly. These steps would enable many countries to overcome the obstacles posed by their relatively small domestic markets.

For example, the Southern African region is a home to more than 700 mines and mineral development projects. Approximately 367 mines are operating—58 per cent in South Africa, 14 per cent in Zimbabwe, 7 per cent in Zambia and 7 per cent in Democratic Republic of the Congo, among others. The region has more than 339 mineral development projects—194 conceptual, 48 at a prefeasibility stage, 45 at a feasibility stage, 14 under construction, 30 suspended with restart-up plans and 7 mines closed with reopening plans.[22] Thus, the SADC region represents a larger market for mining sector inputs than China or the European Union. But the small individual economies of SADC countries have not been able to take advantage.

Four of Africa's eight RECs—SADC, ECOWAS, COMESA and EAC—with technical and advisory support from the Economic Commission for Africa, are moving towards harmonized regional approaches to mining development through Regional Mining Vision initiatives. In the SADC and COMESA regions, studies led to draft regional strategies for anchoring mining projects or clusters by identifying related upstream and downstream investment opportunities and building integrated approaches to financing the projects. The strategies are expected to support the development of trunk infrastructure (ports, gas, power, water, and rail and road transport), open related investment opportunities and promote other high-impact sectors, such as agriculture and agro-processing. Further, a Geological and Mineral Information Systems Strategy has been developed to coordinate and strategically support AU member States, RECs and their geological survey organizations in tracking, aligning, linking, engaging and facilitating geological initiatives across borders.

By integrating different aspects of the mining sector through a regional approach, while factoring in the regional variable geometry, divergent mining trajectories and national political economies, countries in Africa stand to optimize the developmental impact of mineral resources extraction.

Governance, peace and security

Africa's governance, peace and security challenges are inextricably linked and seriously affect the continent's development efforts, including its drive to establish a continent-wide economic space. Achieving meaningful regional integration in poorly governed settings is difficult, partly because they are usually vulnerable to considerable conflict and insecurity (Ikome & Kode, 2018). Peace and security create conducive environments for pursuing regional integration processes and initiatives, including the AfCFTA, and attaining broader development objectives, such as those embodied in the 2030 Agenda on Sustainable Development and Africa's Agenda 2063.

The AU discusses and champions continent-wide norms and instruments for good governance and of peace and security on the continent. Its two most important frameworks are the African Governance Architecture (AGA) and the African Peace and Security Architecture (APSA). AGA seeks to foster operational linkages by coordinating and harmonizing existing governance institutions and mechanisms, such as the African Peer Review Mechanism; the New Partnership for Africa's Development; the African Charter on Democracy, Elections and Governance; the Pan-African Parliament; the African Court of Justice and Human Rights and the Economic, Social and Cultural Council. APSA, a core component of the AU Peace and Security Council, is AU's central institution for preventing, managing and resolving conflicts. APSA is envisaged as working in tandem with AGA to strengthen the nexus between democratic governance, peace and security and development (Khadiagala, 2018, 5).

The APSA Roadmap 2016–2020 places a premium on collaboration between the AU and the RECs. RECs not only constitute key building blocks for economic integration in Africa, but also, by virtue of their proximity to local realities, lead in interventions to uphold democratic norms and principles and to resolve conflicts. REC performance on these tasks has not been uniform. ECOWAS, SADC and EAC have made greater strides in institutionalizing democratic norms and peace and security, as well as in economic integration, than AMU, ECCAS, IGAD and COMESA. Similarly, ECOWAS, IGAD and

SADC have set the pace in peacekeeping, mediation and early warning (specifically regarding pastoralist conflicts) (Khadiagala, 2018).

In 2016, ECOWAS strengthened its long-standing presence in Guinea-Bissau by deploying additional personnel to the ECOWAS Peace Mission in Bissau—ECOMIB—and fielding mediators when a leadership conflict reopened between the president and the prime minister. ECOWAS oversaw the signing of the October 2016 Conakry Accord, which was, however, overlooked by the major protagonists. Amid a persisting impasse, ECOWAS in June 2017 threatened targeted sanctions against the country's leadership with a view toward steering the country to stability. In 2017 in Gambia, ECOWAS also championed mediation efforts in the post-election crisis. ECOWAS deployed a 7,000-man peace mission to Gambia, led by Senegal, and applied intense regional diplomatic pressure.

SADC was afflicted by Lesotho's protracted political instability, which arose in part from the politicization of the military forces and subsequent politically motivated assassinations of high-profile military leaders. SADC deployed a contingent force of military and civilian experts to Lesotho after the September 2017 assassination of the head of the Lesotho Defence Force (Khadiagala, 2018). Meanwhile, Zimbabwe and the Democratic Republic of the Congo continued to present SADC with severe governance and peace and security challenges. In Zimbabwe, SADC was unable to mediate in the November 2017 events that culminated in the peaceful replacement of long-serving president Robert Mugabe.

In the Democratic Republic of the Congo, the main threat to democratic governance, peace and security revolved around President Joseph Kabila's designs to extend his stay in power beyond the expiration of his term in December 2016. President Kabila subsequently yielded to pressure from various internal and external actors to agree to organize elections at the end of 2018, where he was not to be a candidate. However, SADC has not been the main influence in this outcome, partly because of an apparent democratic recession in the region. The emergence of new leadership in Angola, South

Africa and Zimbabwe constitute positive developments, with the potential to revive SADC's alignment to a democratic ethos, as well as the promotion of peace and security, which have the potential to boost regional integration efforts.

The EAC and IGAD, with the support of the AU and the UN, have continued to jointly lead efforts to resolve the wars in Somalia and South Sudan and the conflict in Darfur. In December 2017, Uganda began to pull troops back from the Somalia mission. In East Africa, the highly contested 2017 general elections in Kenya had the potential to create regional instability. Although the election outcomes were followed by violence, the EAC, in partnership with various actors, including the AU and the UN, mediated and forestalled escalation.

Despite the commendable efforts of both the AU and RECs, Africa's governance and peace and security landscape in 2017–18 shows minimal change. In governance, for example, although the continent's overall trajectory has been positive, the pace of improvement has slowed. Between 2007 and 2016, 40 African countries improved governance overall, and between 2012 and 2016, 18 of these countries (including Côte d'Ivoire, Morocco, Namibia, Nigeria and Senegal) accelerated their progress. Over the same period, however, Africa' annual average rate of progress slowed—with more than half of the 40 African countries that improved their governance during the past decade either doing so more slowly (Ethiopia and Rwanda), or actually deteriorating (Angola, Cameroon and Mauritius) (IIAG, 2018). In peace and security in 2017, Africa (excluding North Africa) witnessed only a slight increase in the total number of conflicts, from 93 in 2015 to 94 in 2016 and 95 cases in 2017.[23] For the entire continent, the aggregate number of armed conflict and violent events in Africa in 2017 stood at 17,105, representing a slight drop of 2.5 per cent from the total recorded during the two previous years—17,539 in 2016 and 17,537 in 2015 (ICLED, 2018:7).[24]

Both the AU and RECs need to be strengthened through better financing and through restructured and strengthened partnerships with other organizations, such as the European Union and the UN. The AU Heads of State and Government during their January and June 2015 summits agreed to contribute up to 25 per cent of the costs of AU peace and security efforts, including peace support operations, by the year 2020. This step is part of the AU commitment to "Silence the Guns" by 2020 within the larger Agenda 2063. In July 2016, the AU summit adopted the recommendations of the High Level Panel for the Peace Fund, to introduce a 0.2 per cent levy on defined imports by AU member States to increase the funding of the AU. The levy is expected to fund 100 per cent of running costs and 75 per cent of programmes of the AU and 25 per cent of AU/REC-led peace support operations. It is expected to endow the Peace Fund with $325 million in 2017, rising to $400 million by 2020, against an estimated overall Peace Fund budget of $302 million in 2020.

The African Union and RECs have continued nurturing partnerships with actors outside the continent in their efforts to promote good governance and peace and security. A recent initiative, the 2017 Joint UN–AU Framework for Enhanced Partnership in Peace and Security, details the principles, themes and modalities for the partnership and covers the peace, security and development nexus. It further builds upon the recommendations and analysis outlined in the report of the High-Level Independent Panel on UN Peace Operations and the Independent Review of the UN Peacebuilding Architecture; resolutions of the Security Council and AU Peace and Security Council and annual reports of the organizations. The joint framework will support peace and security initiatives in the continent, bolster Africa's regional integration and support the AfCFTA.

In 2018 African collaboration with the UN, African countries continued, as in previous years, as leading contributors of police, military experts, staff officers and troops to UN peace missions. Ethiopia and Rwanda occupying the first and second rungs, with Ethiopia deploying 8,335 staff and Rwanda deploying 7,112 staff. Other African countries in the top 20 contributors to UN peace missions in 2018 include Burkina Faso, Cameroon, Chad, Egypt, Ghana, Morocco, Senegal, South Africa, Tanzania, Togo and Zambia (ACLED in IPSS, 2018, 7).

Key messages and policy recommendations

Key messages

- **The historic signing of the AfCFTA Agreement on 21 March 2018 marked a momentous milestone for regional integration in Africa.** The signing strongly indicated commitment by policy makers and African leaders to regional integration.

- **Regional integration faces challenges.** They include limited energy and infrastructure development, insecurity and conflicts, multiple and overlapping membership of RECs, poor sequencing of the regional integration arrangements and limited financial resources.

- **Monetary integration continues to be actively pursued by five of the eight regional economic communities.** These RECs have adopted macroeconomic convergence criteria, but their member countries have had mixed success in meeting these criteria.

- **Integration in services is important, given its contribution to African GDP growth.** In 2017, over 53 per cent of the continent's GDP came from services.

- **Gradual progress is being made towards the free movement of people.** Steps have included the launching of the Common Electronic Biometric African Passport in July 2016 and the adoption of the AU Protocol on Free Movement of Persons, Right of Residence and Right of Establishment in January 2018—the latter, however, has struggled to gain country ratifications.

- **A mismatch between available skills and the needs of Africa's labour markets slows the continent's economic integration and overall development.** Deepening of regional cooperation in education, including through the implementation of Africa's Higher Education Harmonization Strategy, can help.

- **Africa's large infrastructure deficit hinders intra-regional trade.** Infrastructure financing can be supported by maximizing the use of public–private partnerships, tapping into national resources and using regional and global infrastructure development funds and innovative financing tools.

- **Regional energy integration through power pools can attract considerable investment in energy.**

- **Africa's governance, peace and security challenges are inextricably linked and are prerequisites to establishing a continental-wide economic space.**

Policy recommendations

- **More economic and physical integration, including through important infrastructure projects, is needed.** It will require significant resources, including leveraging public–private partnerships and innovative financing tools.

- **Cross-border collaboration in energy trade should be strengthened.** Mechanisms include regional energy policy frameworks, gas and power pools and integrated regional energy markets.

- **African States at the level of both RECs and the African Union should strengthen and resource their existing instruments promoting good governance, peace and security.** These will create the right environment for the pursuit of regional integration

- **Monitoring the implementation of regional integration is critical.** The development of the African Regional Integration Index by ECA in collaboration with the African Union Commission and the African Development Bank is a powerful tool for monitoring integration.

- **African countries must address the crisis of implementation and translate promises at the continental and regional levels into action.** These include ratifying and implementing the AfCFTA, the Single African Air Transport Market, peace and security instruments, monetary integration commitments and the AU protocol on the movement of persons.

References

Alliance for Affordable Internet. 2017. *2017 Affordability Report*. Available at: https://1e8q3q 16vyc81g8l3h3md6q5f5e-wpengine.netdna-ssl. com/wp-content/uploads/2017/02/A4AI-2017-Affordability-Report.pdf

AfDB (African Development Bank). 2018. *Africa Economic Outlook*. Abidjan, Côte d'Ivoire: AfDB.

AfDB (African Development Bank) and AU (African Union). 2018. *Africa Visa Openness Report 2018*. Abidjan, Côte d'Ivoire: AfDB.

Africa Energy Forum. 2016. *Road Infrastructure in Africa*. Available at: https://www.ashurst. com/en/news-and-insights/insights/ road-infrastructure-in-africa/.

AMU (Arab Maghreb Union). 2019. "Objectives and tasks" [website]. Available at: http://www. umaghrebarabe.org/?q=en/Objectives_and_tasks.

AU (African Union). 2009. "Status of Integration in Africa (SIA)." Addis Ababa, Ethiopia: AU.

———. 2012. "Decisions on Boosting Intra-African Trade and Fast Tracking the CFTA." Addis Ababa, Ethiopia: AU.

AUC (African Union Commission). 2004. *The Mission, Vision and Strategic Framework of the African Union Commission (2004–07)*. Addis Ababa, Ethiopia: AUC.

AUC (African Union Commission) and ECA (United Nations Economic Commission for Africa). 2009. *African Mining Vision*. Addis Ababa, Ethiopia: AUC and ECA.

ECA. Assessing Regional Integration in Africa (Series: III, IV, V, VI, VII, and VIII), Addis Ababa, Ethiopia.

COMESA (Common Market for Eastern and Southern Africa). 2018. "COMESA in Brief," 3rd ed. Lusaka, Zambia: COMESA Secretariat.

———. 2019. "COMESA Turns 24" [website]. Available at: https://www.comesa.int/2018/12/08/ comesa-turns-24/.

ECA (United Nations Economic Commission for Africa). 2016. *Investment Policies and Bilateral Investment Treaties in Africa Implications for Regional Integration*. Addis Ababa, Ethiopia: ECA.

———. 2017. "An Empirical Assessment of the African Continental Free Trade Area Modalities on Goods." Available at: https://www.uneca.org/sites/ default/files/PublicationFiles/brief_assessment_ of_afcfta_modalities_eng_nov18.pdf.

———. 2018a. "Central Africa's free trade instruments gaining traction in DR Congo." Press Release. Yaounde, Cameroon: ECA. Available at: https://www.uneca.org/stories/central-africas-free-trade-instruments-gaining-traction-dr-congo.

———. 2018b. "Free Trade: Gabonese experts trained on the ECCAS-CEMAC Preferential Tariff." Press Release. Yaounde, Cameroon: ECA. Available at: https://www.uneca.org/stories/free-trade-gabonese-experts-trained-eccas-cemac-preferential-tariff.

———. 2018c. *Base Erosion and Profit Shifting in Africa: Reforms to Facilitate Improved Taxation of Multinational Enterprises*. Addis Ababa, Ethiopia: ECA.

———. 2019a. *Promoting Infrastructure Development for Africa's Industrialization*. Addis Ababa, Ethiopia: ECA.

———. 2019b. "Regional Economic Communities" [website]. Available at: https://www.uneca.org/ oria/pages/regional-economic-communities.

ECA (United Nations Economic Commission for Africa), AfDB (African Development Bank) and AUC (African Union Commission). 2018. *African Statistical Yearbook 2018*. Addis Ababa, Ethiopia and Abidjan Côte d'Ivoire: ECA, AfDB and AUC.

ECOWAS (Economic Community of West African States). 2007. *ECOWAS Annual Report: Consolidation of the Restructured Community Intuitions for the Effectiveness and Accelerated Regional Integration and Development*. Abuja, Nigeria: ECOWAS.

———. 2017. *2016 ECOWAS Convergence Report*. Abuja, Nigeria: ECOWAS. Available at: http://www. ecowas.int/wp-content/uploads/2017/11/2016-Convergence-report_Clean-final-final.pdf.

IEA (International Energy Agency). 2014. *Africa Energy Outlook: A Focus on Energy Prospects in Sub Saharan Africa*. Paris: IEA.

Ikome, Francis, and David Kode. 2018. "West African Integration: Participatory Democracy and the Role of Civil Society in ECAOWAS." In *Building Regionalism from Below: The Role of Parliaments and Civil Society in Regional Integration in Africa*, edited by Korwa G. Adar, Giovanni Finizio and Angela Meyer. Brussels: Peter Lang.

ILO (International Labour Organization). 2018. *World Employment Social Outlook 2018*. Geneva: ILO.

IMF (International Monetary Fund). 2018. World Economic Outlook [database]. Washington, DC: IMF. Accessed October 2018.

Jensen, Hans Grinstead, and Ron Sandrey. 2016. "Continental Wide Service Liberalization within Africa." Working Paper S16WP20/2016, TRALAC (Trade Law Centre), Stellenbosch, South Africa.

Karingi, Stephen, and Simon Mevel. 2013. "Towards a Continental Free Trade Area in Africa: A CGE Modelling Assessment with a Focus on Agricultur.e. In *Shared Harvests: Agriculture, Trade, and Employment*, edited by David Cheong, Marion Jansen and Ralf Peters. Geneva: ILO and United Nations.

The Maritime Executive. 2019. "Fulfilling Africa's Maritime Trade Potential." Available at: https://www.maritime-executive.com/article/fulfilling-africa-s-maritime-trade-potential.

Mafusire Albert, John Anyanwu, Zuzana Brixiova and Maurice Mubila. 2010. "Infrastructure deficit and opportunities in Africa." *African Development Bank Economic Brief* 1 (September): 1–15.

McKinsey Global Institute. 2014. "Global Flows in a Digital Age: How Trade, Finance, People, and Data Connect the World Economy." McKinsey & Company.

NEPAD (New Partnership for Africa's Development). 2017. *Annual Results Based Report (2017): Fast-Tracking the Implementation of Africa's Development Agenda*. Mirand, South Africa: NEPAD.

OAU (Organization of African Unity). 1980. *Lagos Plan of Action*. Addis Ababa, Ethiopia: OAU.

———. 2000. *Constitutive Act of the African Union*. Addis Ababa, Ethiopia: OAU.

Shayanowako, Petros. 2011. "Towards a COMESA, EAC, and SADC Tripartite Free Trade Area." Trade and Development Studies Issue 40, Trades Centre, Harare, Zimbabwe.

SADC (Southern African Development Community). n.d. "Free Trade Area" [website]. Available at https://www.sadc.int/about-sadc/integration-milestones/free-trade-area/.

———. 2018[a]. "EU, Germany and SADC Secretariat launch a €18.7 Million Programme to support SADC Member States and Secretariat in implementing Regional Integration." Press Release.

———. 2018[b]. "SADC Harmonised Consumer Price Indices (HCPI)." Press Release, News Release Issue 85, September 2018. Available at: https://www.sadc.int/files/2115/4280/8951/SADC_HCPI_-_September_2018_ff.pdf.

TRALAC (Trade Law Centre). 2018. "Tripartite FTA Update: COMESA Welcomes South Africa's Ratification." Stellenbosch, South Africa: TRALAC.

Trademark East Africa. 2017. "EAC Eyes Single Currency by 202." Available at: https://www.trademarkea.com/news/eac-eyes-single-currency-by-2024/.

UNCTAD (United Nations Conference on Trade and Development). 2018a. UNCTADStat [database]. Available at: http://unctadstat.unctad.org/EN/.

———. 2018b. *Review of Maritime Transport 2018*. Geneva: UNCTAD.

———. 2018[c]. World Investment Report 2018: Investment and New Industrial Policies. Geneva: UNCTAD. Available at: https://unctad.org/en/PublicationsLibrary/wir2018_en.pdf.

———. 2018[d]. *East African Community Regional Integration: Trade and Gender Implications*. Geneva: UNCTAD: Available at: https://unctad.org/en/PublicationsLibrary/ditc2017d2_en.pdf.

———. 2019. UNCTADStat [database]. Available at: http://unctadstat.unctad.org/EN/.

U.S. Energy Information Administration. 2019. Total Electricity Installed Capacity, Africa, Annual.

World Bank. 2014. "Regional Infrastructure in Sub-Saharan Africa: Challenges and Opportunities." Background note for the 1818 Society presentation, 20 February 2014. Washington, DC: World Bank.

———. 2019. World Development Indicators [database]. Washington, DC: World Bank.

———. World Economic Forum. 2018. The Global Competitiveness Report 2018. Geneva, Switzerland: World Economic Forum.

Endnotes

1 The RISDP is a development and implementation framework detailing the regional integration strategy of SADC for the period 2005 to 2018 and sets out convergence criteria for the region.

2 WAMZ comprises Gambia, Ghana, Guinea, Nigeria, Liberia and Sierra Leone.

3 WAEMU comprises Benin, Burkina Faso, Côte d'Ivoire, Mali, Niger, Senegal and Togo.

4 CEMAC comprises Cameroon, Congo, Gabon, Equatorial Guinea, the Central African Republic and Chad.

5 Benin, Burkina Faso, Côte d'Ivoire, Guinea-Bissau, Mali, Niger, Senegal and Togo are members of WAEMU while Central African Republic and Chad are members of CEMAC.

6 These are Comoros, Djibouti, Eritrea, Libya, Somalia, Sudan and Tunisia.

7 Article 13.k of the Agreement Establishing the Inter-Governmental Authorty on Development (IGAD).

8 These are Djibouti, Eritrea, Ethiopia, Kenya, Somalia, Sudan and Uganda. Only South Sudan is a member of IGAD but not COMESA.

9 Article 13.k of the Agreement Establishing the Inter-Governmental Authorty on Development (IGAD).

10 The members of the AMU are Algeria, Libya, Mauritania, Morocco and Tunisia.

11 Mauritania is negotiating to re-join ECOWAS, having left in 2000.

12 Eleven SADC members are also members of COMESA. All SADC members are party to the Tripartite Free Trade Area negotiations. Tanzania alone is a member to both the SADC and the EAC.

13 Ten COMESA members are also members of SADC, four are members of EAC and two are party to the Agadir Agreement. All COMESA members are party to the Tripartite Free Trade Area negotiations. Note that not all trade between parties of each of the included RECs may be fully liberalized.

14 Due to challenges in reconciling mirror services trade statistics, this should be considered as an estimate of services imports from the rest of the world (See Markhonko, 2014).

15 Calculations based on UNDESA 2017.

16 The PIDA Steering Committee is composed of NEPAD, AUC, African Development Bank (AfDB) and the Regional Economic Communities (RECs). It is responsible for evaluating the current status of implementation, identifying challenges and recommending ways to improve working processes within PIDA and to oversee its work and activities.

17 Ethiopia and South Sudan are not WTO members.

18 Provisions that the member will implement by the time the Agreement enters into force (or in the case of a least-developed country member within one year after entry into force).

19 Provisions that the member will implement after a transitional period following the entry into force of the Agreement.

20 Provisions that the member will implement on a date after a transitional period following the entry into force of the Agreement and requiring the acquisition of assistance and support for capacity building.

21 IOM Regional Office for Southern Africa, "Migration in Southern Africa", 2016. Available from www.europarl.europa.eu/intcoop/ acp/2016_botswana/pdf/warn-en.pdf. Accessed October 18 2018.

22 Department of Mineral Resource (2018), Annual Report, Republic of South Africa.

23 HCB cited in IPSS, 2018: 7.

24 ACLED, cited in IPSS, 2018: 7.

Chapter 2
Status and Next Steps for the AfCFTA

The African Continental Free Trade Area (AfCFTA) is among the most interesting and momentous developments in trade. Signed by 54 African countries, the agreement creating it is, by the number of participating countries, the largest trade agreement since the formation of the WTO. This chapter takes stock of the state of play in the AfCFTA negotiations.

It is not enough for the AfCFTA to be negotiated, concluded and ratified. It must also change lives, reduce poverty and contribute to economic development. To consider this, the chapter looks ahead and asks, "What next?". In doing so, it considers what the AfCFTA means for internal and external trade policy coherence in Africa. It also looks at the next six steps to take the AfCFTA from operationalization, through effective implementation, towards a single market in Africa.

Status of the AfCFTA negotiations

The signing of the African Continental Free Trade Area agreement by 44 African Union member States at the 10th Extraordinary Summit in Kigali, Rwanda, on 21 March 2018, marked a momentous milestone for economic integration in Africa. A year and a half later, in July 2019, a further ten African Union member States signed, leaving only one of the 55 African Union member States (Figure 2.1).

This achievement should not be underestimated. The vision of African continental integration to which the AfCFTA contributes is over 50 years old (Gerout, MacLeod, & Desta, 2019). It originated in an appreciation that the political independence achieved with decolonization would not lead to a better life for the people of Africa unless consummated with economic independence (Nkrumah, 1957). Like political independence, this "economic

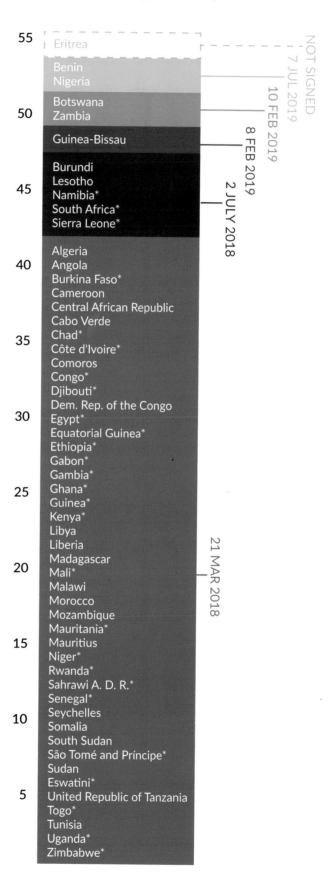

Figure 2.1:
AfCFTA agreement signatories by date

* Countries which have ratified the AfCFTA
Source: African Union Commission.

Figure 2.2:

Phases of African continental economic integration

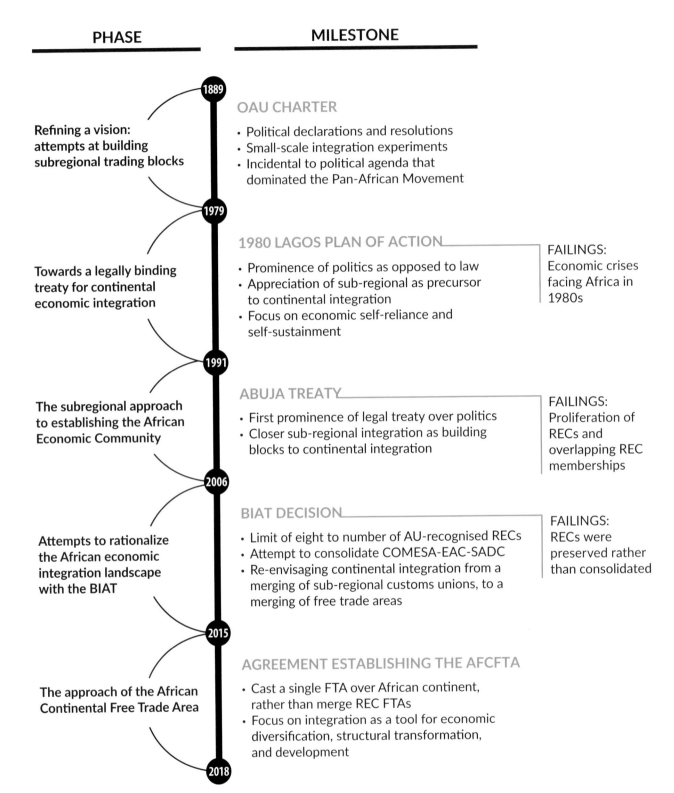

PHASE	MILESTONE

1889

OAU CHARTER

Refining a vision: attempts at building subregional trading blocks

- Political declarations and resolutions
- Small-scale integration experiments
- Incidental to political agenda that dominated the Pan-African Movement

1979

1980 LAGOS PLAN OF ACTION

Towards a legally binding treaty for continental economic integration

- Prominence of politics as opposed to law
- Appreciation of sub-regional as precursor to continental integration
- Focus on economic self-reliance and self-sustainment

FAILINGS: Economic crises facing Africa in 1980s

1991

ABUJA TREATY

The subregional approach to establishing the African Economic Community

- First prominence of legal treaty over politics
- Closer sub-regional integration as building blocks to continental integration

FAILINGS: Proliferation of RECs and overlapping REC memberships

2006

BIAT DECISION

Attempts to rationalize the African economic integration landscape with the BIAT

- Limit of eight to number of AU-recognised RECs
- Attempt to consolidate COMESA-EAC-SADC
- Re-envisaging continental integration from a merging of sub-regional customs unions, to a merging of free trade areas

FAILINGS: RECs were preserved rather than consolidated

2015

AGREEMENT ESTABLISHING THE AFCFTA

The approach of the African Continental Free Trade Area

- Cast a single FTA over African continent, rather than merge REC FTAs
- Focus on integration as a tool for economic diversification, structural transformation, and development

2018

Source: Adapted from Gerout, MacLeod and Desta, 2019.

decolonization" was thought to be best leveraged through a regional approach (Adedeji, 1984). The vision of economic integration has persisted. Though its expression has evolved and the methods of attaining it have developed, it has held fast as an instrument of economic prosperity for Africa (Figure 2.2).

AfCFTA negotiators surpassed expectations with the pace of the negotiations. Launched on 15 June 2015 at the 25th Ordinary Summit of the African Union Heads of State and Government, the texts of the AfCFTA Agreement and its protocols on trade in goods, trade in services and on rules and procedures on the settlement of disputes were concluded in less than three years (Figure 2.4). By the June 2018 Summit of the African Union Assembly,

most of the annexes to the agreement had been negotiated and added.

The speed is remarkable, showing appetite and commitment from all parties to reach an agreement in an area where negotiations typically drag out, consume much time and often languish without ever entering into force (Figure 2.3). Free trade area negotiations between the European Union and Canada took eight years. Those between a number of Asian countries in the Regional and Comprehensive Economic Partnership have been ongoing for more than six years. Negotiations between the United States and Europe on the Transatlantic Trade and Investment Partnership waned after four years, and those between 34 countries under the Free Trade Area of the Americas

Figure 2.3:
Status of selected trade negotiations

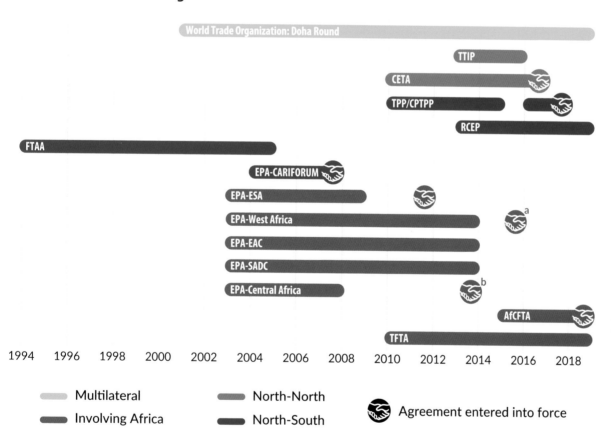

Note: Bold shows that the agreement entered into force. Agreements: CARIFORUM, Caribbean ACP States; CETA, EU–Canada Comprehensive Economic and Trade Agreement; EAC, East Africa Community; EP, Economic Partnership Agreement; ESA, Eastern and Southern Africa; FTAA, Free Trade Area of the Americas; RCEP, Regional Comprehensive Economic Partnership; SADC, Southern African Development Community; TFTA, Tripartite Free Trade Area; TPP, Trans-Pacific Partnership, which evolved in to CPTPP Comprehensive and Progressive Agreement for Trans-Pacific Partnership; TTIP, Transatlantic Trade and Investment Partnership.

a. Interim EPAs in west Africa entered into force in 2016 for only Côte d' Ivoire and Ghana.

b. The EPA-Central Africa entered into force with only Cameroon from Central Africa, with the intention that other Central African States would eventually join.

Figure 2.4: **Technical timeline of the AfCFTA negotiations**

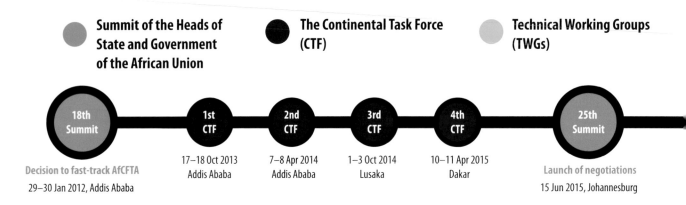

Summit of the Heads of State and Government of the African Union

The Continental Task Force (CTF)

Technical Working Groups (TWGs)

18th Summit

Decision to fast-track AfCFTA
29–30 Jan 2012, Addis Ababa

1st CTF
17–18 Oct 2013
Addis Ababa

2nd CTF
7–8 Apr 2014
Addis Ababa

3rd CTF
1–3 Oct 2014
Lusaka

4th CTF
10–11 Apr 2015
Dakar

25th Summit
Launch of negotiations
15 Jun 2015, Johannesburg

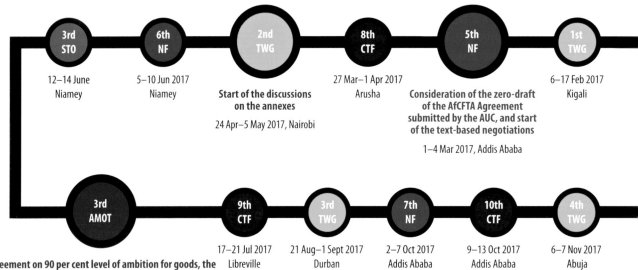

3rd STO
12–14 June
Niamey

6th NF
5–10 Jun 2017
Niamey

2nd TWG
Start of the discussions on the annexes
24 Apr–5 May 2017, Nairobi

8th CTF
27 Mar–1 Apr 2017
Arusha

5th NF
Consideration of the zero-draft of the AfCFTA Agreement submitted by the AUC, and start of the text-based negotiations
1–4 Mar 2017, Addis Ababa

1st TWG
6–17 Feb 2017
Kigali

3rd AMOT
Agreement on 90 per cent level of ambition for goods, the timeframe for liberalization, qualifications for sensitive products, a procedure for reviewing excluded products, the scope for special and differential treatment to support LDCs, and a common approach for progressive services liberalization
15–16 Jun 2017, Niamey

9th CTF
17–21 Jul 2017
Libreville

3rd TWG
21 Aug–1 Sept 2017
Durban

7th NF
2–7 Oct 2017
Addis Ababa

10th CTF
9–13 Oct 2017
Addis Ababa

4th TWG
6–7 Nov 2017
Abuja

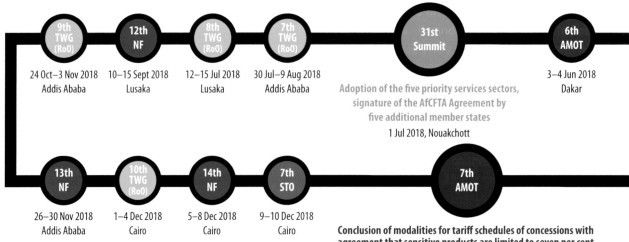

9th TWG (RoO)
24 Oct–3 Nov 2018
Addis Ababa

12th NF
10–15 Sept 2018
Lusaka

8th TWG (RoO)
12–15 Jul 2018
Lusaka

7th TWG (RoO)
30 Jul–9 Aug 2018
Addis Ababa

31st Summit
Adoption of the five priority services sectors, signature of the AfCFTA Agreement by five additional member states
1 Jul 2018, Nouakchott

6th AMOT
3–4 Jun 2018
Dakar

13th NF
26–30 Nov 2018
Addis Ababa

10th TWG (RoO)
1–4 Dec 2018
Cairo

14th NF
5–8 Dec 2018
Cairo

7th STO
9–10 Dec 2018
Cairo

7th AMOT
Conclusion of modalities for tariff schedules of concessions with agreement that sensitive products are limited to seven per cent and excluded prodcuts to three per cent, roadmap adopted for the conclusion of rules of origin and tariff concessions by June 2019
12–13 Dec 2018, Cairo

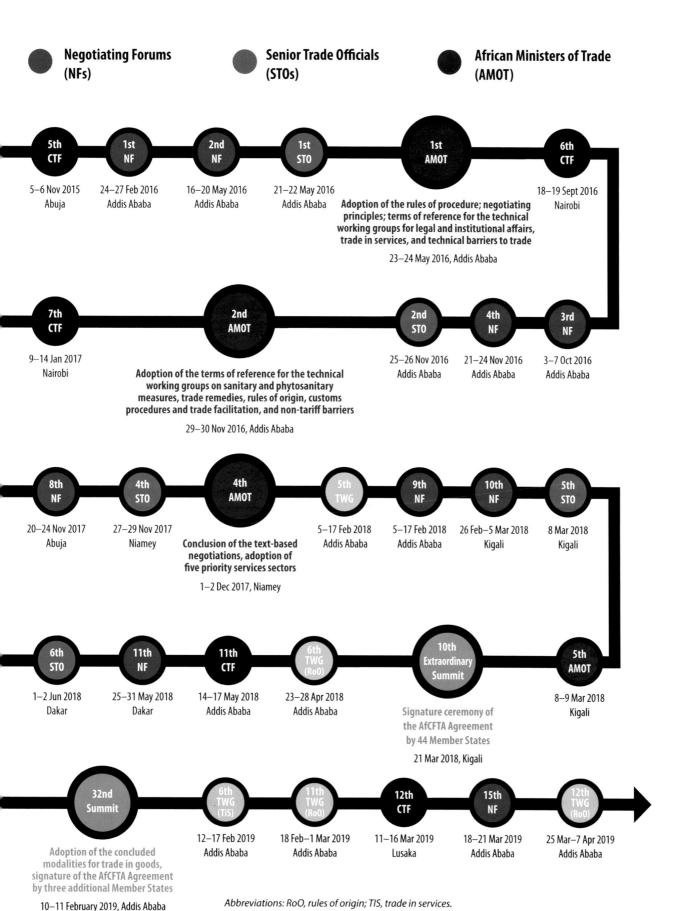

Negotiating Forums (NFs)

Senior Trade Officials (STOs)

African Ministers of Trade (AMOT)

5th CTF
5–6 Nov 2015
Abuja

1st NF
24–27 Feb 2016
Addis Ababa

2nd NF
16–20 May 2016
Addis Ababa

1st STO
21–22 May 2016
Addis Ababa

1st AMOT
Adoption of the rules of procedure; negotiating principles; terms of reference for the technical working groups for legal and institutional affairs, trade in services, and technical barriers to trade
23–24 May 2016, Addis Ababa

6th CTF
18–19 Sept 2016
Nairobi

7th CTF
9–14 Jan 2017
Nairobi

2nd AMOT
Adoption of the terms of reference for the technical working groups on sanitary and phytosanitary measures, trade remedies, rules of origin, customs procedures and trade facilitation, and non-tariff barriers
29–30 Nov 2016, Addis Ababa

2nd STO
25–26 Nov 2016
Addis Ababa

4th NF
21–24 Nov 2016
Addis Ababa

3rd NF
3–7 Oct 2016
Addis Ababa

8th NF
20–24 Nov 2017
Abuja

4th STO
27–29 Nov 2017
Niamey

4th AMOT
Conclusion of the text-based negotiations, adoption of five priority services sectors
1–2 Dec 2017, Niamey

5th TWG
5–17 Feb 2018
Addis Ababa

9th NF
5–17 Feb 2018
Addis Ababa

10th NF
26 Feb–5 Mar 2018
Kigali

5th STO
8 Mar 2018
Kigali

6th STO
1–2 Jun 2018
Dakar

11th NF
25–31 May 2018
Dakar

11th CTF
14–17 May 2018
Addis Ababa

6th TWG (RoO)
23–28 Apr 2018
Addis Ababa

10th Extraordinary Summit
Signature ceremony of the AfCFTA Agreement by 44 Member States
21 Mar 2018, Kigali

5th AMOT
8–9 Mar 2018
Kigali

32nd Summit
Adoption of the concluded modalities for trade in goods, signature of the AfCFTA Agreement by three additional Member States
10–11 February 2019, Addis Ababa

6th TWG (TiS)
12–17 Feb 2019
Addis Ababa

11th TWG (RoO)
18 Feb–1 Mar 2019
Addis Ababa

12th CTF
11–16 Mar 2019
Lusaka

15th NF
18–21 Mar 2019
Addis Ababa

12th TWG (RoO)
25 Mar–7 Apr 2019
Addis Ababa

Abbreviations: RoO, rules of origin; TIS, trade in services.

Negotiating institutions: The Technical Working Groups report to the Negotiating Forums, which in turn report to the Senior Trade Officials, African Ministers of Trade, and the Summit of the Heads of State and Government. The Continental Task Force prepares documentation for the negotiating institutions.

after 12 years. The multilateral Doha Development Round negotiations at the WTO have dwindled over 17 years without conclusion. In Africa, several Economic Partnership Agreement negotiations between regional groupings of African countries and the European Union have not yielded tangible results more than 14 years after their launch.

The pace of AfCFTA ratifications is also remarkable. By 1 April 2019, only one year and ten days after the signature, the threshold of 22 countries required for entry into force of the agreement had been reached. As of July 2019, 27 countries had ratified. The speed of this ratification process is unprecedented in AU history.

Despite obvious political commitment, several important technical steps remain before the AfCFTA agreement can become operative.

All the more impressive is the diversity of countries brought together under the AfCFTA. The economic size ranged from less than $1 billion in GDP in São Tomé and Príncipe to more than $350 billion in Nigeria and South Africa in 2017 (Figure 2.5). The largest population, Nigeria's, was 190 million in 2017, while the smallest, Seychelles's, was 94,000 (Figure 2.6). GDP per capita ranges from over $20,000 in Equatorial Guinea to under $250 in South Sudan. There are 15 landlocked countries and six small island developing economies (ECA, AUC, & AfDB, 2017). Several countries have sizeable manufacturing sectors, while many have largely undiversified economies, dominated by a small number of agricultural, mineral or fuel commodities (ECA, AUC, & AfDB, 2017). Most economies in Africa remain poor compared with the rest of the world—with Africa including almost 70 per cent of the world's least-developed countries.

Figure 2.5:
Relative size of African economies, GDP 2017

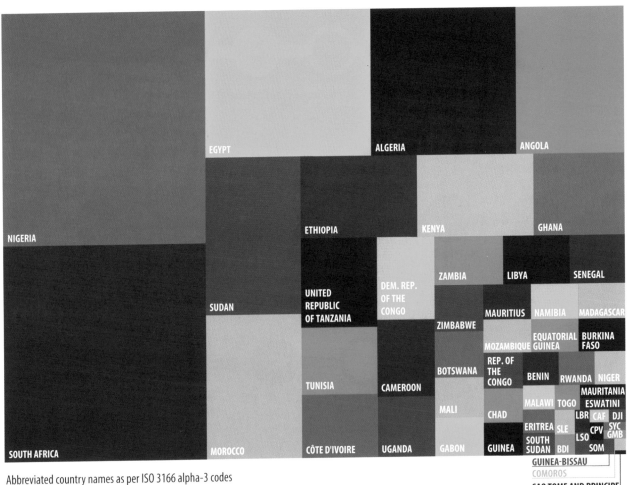

Abbreviated country names as per ISO 3166 alpha-3 codes

Source: UNSD 2019, available unstats.un.org/.

Figure 2.6:
Relative size of African populations, 2017

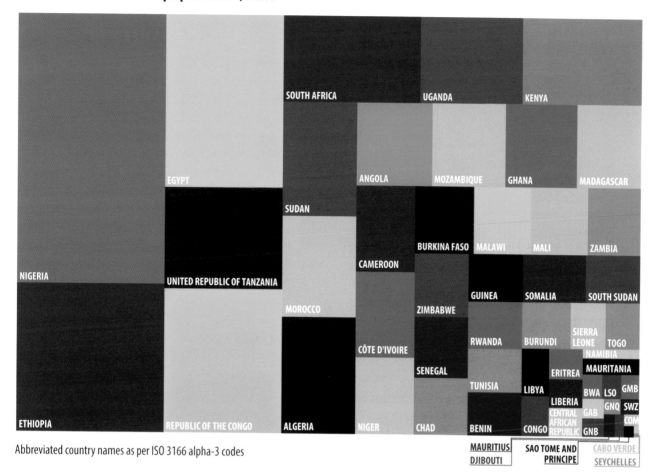

Abbreviated country names as per ISO 3166 alpha-3 codes

Source: UNSD 2019, available unstats.un.org/.

What is in the agreement?

Structure of the agreement

The AfCFTA agreement has three layers (Figure 2.7). First is a framework agreement that defines, in general terms, the purposes and intentions of the agreement, establishes its primary definitions and outlines its scope. The framework agreement also creates the institutional framework for implementing the AfCFTA and outlines procedures for administering it. This layer also provides overarching guidelines on the principles of transparency and relates the agreement to other relevant international and regional instruments.

The second layer comprises the protocols to the agreement, which cover trade in goods, trade in services, rules and procedures on the settlement of disputes, investment, competition policy and intel-

lectual property rights. The protocols constitute the main substantive and operative components of the agreement, including its obligations, intentions, objectives, exceptions and institutional provisions. The first three protocols were the subject of the first phase of AfCFTA negotiations, with the three others postponed to the second phase scheduled to commence in the second half of 2019.

The third layer contains the annexes, guidelines, lists and schedules to the protocols. These articulate the provisions of the protocols in detail. For instance, while articles 7 and 8 of the protocol on trade in goods oblige State parties to progressively eliminate import duties, annex 1 details the exact tariff schedules to be used for such liberalization. In some instances, this third layer goes deeper by appending additional documents, such as appendices to the annex on rules of origin, or guidelines to the annex on trade remedies. The annexes

PROTOCOL ON TRADE IN GOODS

Annex 1 Schedules of Tariff Concessions
Annex 2 Rules of Origin
Annex 3 Customs Cooperation and Mutual
Administrative Assistance
Annex 4 Trade Facilitation
Annex 5 Non-Tariff Barriers
Annex 6 Technical Barriers to Trade
Annex 7 Sanitary and Phytosanitary Measures
Annex 8 Transit
Annex 9 Trade Remedies

PROTOCOL ON TRADE IN SERVICES

- Schedules of Specific Commitments
- MFN Exemption
- Air Transport Services
- List of Priority Sectors
- Framework document on Regulatory Cooperation

PROTOCOL ON **INVESTMENT**
PROTOCOL ON **COMPETITION POLICY**
PROTOCOL ON **INTELLECTUAL PROPERTY RIGHTS**

Phase II Negotiations

PROTOCOL ON RULES AND PROCEDURES ON THE SETTLEMENT OF DISPUTES

Annex 1 Working Procedures of the Panel
Annex 2 Expert Review
Annex 3 Code of Conduct for Arbitrators and Panelists

may establish further institutional arrangements, including sub-committees, dedicated to administration and implementation.

The three layers create a balance of rights and obligations designed to reduce or eliminate barriers to trade and investment between State parties and create common grounds for addressing trade-related issues. They create a rules-based legal system for governing the practices of preferential trade between the State parties to the AfCFTA.

Institutional framework for implementation of the AfCFTA

Too frequently, pan-African initiatives remain unimplemented and fail to live up to expectations. The same could be feared for the AfCFTA, as explained in one op-ed: "There is much to celebrate with the conclusion of the [Af]CFTA negotiations, but this is just the first step. Matching ambition with implementation is now the challenge" (Issoufou & Songwe, 2018). Central to implementation are the AfCFTA institutional framework, set out in arti-

cles 9 to 13 of the framework agreement, and further sub-structures detailed in the protocols and annexes charged with implementing the AfCFTA and its protocols, annexes and appendices (Figure 2.8).

The African Union Assembly of Heads of State and Government ("the Assembly") is at the apex of the implementing institutions. It acts as the oversight body, providing political and strategic guidance.

The Assembly pre-exists the AfCFTA agreement: it is the highest decision-making authority of the African Union, comprising the heads of state of all the African Union member States. The Assembly's membership may extend beyond the AfCFTA membership, since it may include African Union members not yet party to the AfCFTA agreement. This inclusion reflects the centrality of the AfCFTA to the African Union's integration agenda, ensuring that the project maintains the political commitment of all member States of the African Union and the intention that all African Union member States will eventually be part of the AfCFTA. It also ensures

Institutional framework for implementing the AfCFTA

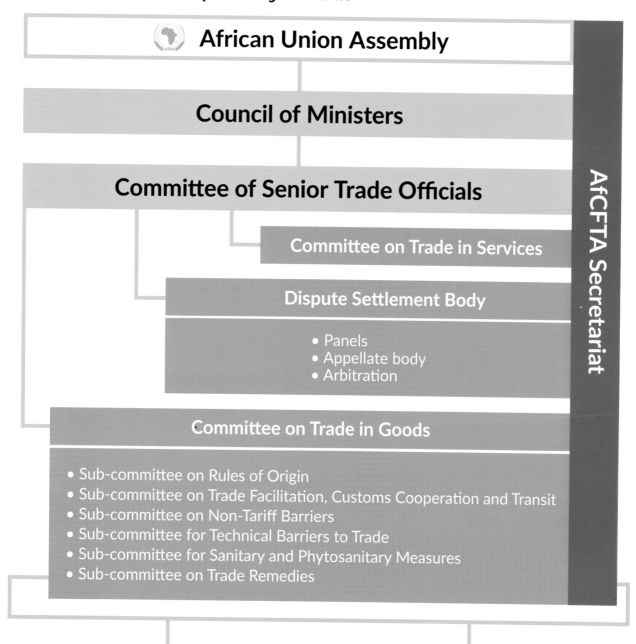

that AfCFTA institutions are firmly rooted within and aligned with the African Union's institutions.

Underneath the Assembly, the Council of Ministers is the main decision-making institution for the AfCFTA. Its mandate is to establish and supervise the AfCFTA Secretariat and committees, issue directives and regulations related to the agreement and consider and propose legal, financial and structural decisions for adoption by the Assembly. Unlike the Assembly, it includes only the State parties to the agreement, ensuring that the AfCFTA is administered only by the States that have signed and ratified the agreement. This structure, it is argued, puts pressure on the remaining African Union member States to ratify and become State parties to the agreement so they are not left out of important technical decisions (Sodipo, 2019). The Council of Ministers is expected to also promote broader trade policy harmonization beyond the AfCFTA. Such broadening has a precedent: these ministers, in their meetings under the African Ministers of Trade (AMOT) configuration for the AfCFTA negotiations, also devoted time to other trade issues, such as Africa's positions in the WTO negotiations.

The Committee of Senior Officials reports to the Council of Ministers. It has two functions: acting as a clearing house for technical decisions submitted to the council and ensuring the implementation of Council decisions by supervising relevant sub-committees. Reporting in turn to the Committee of Senior Officials are the committees for the protocols on trade in goods, trade in services and, upon their conclusion, the institutions established by the phase II protocols. Beneath the committees are sub-committees, which assist the committees in their functions related to the various annexes to the protocols.

To service these bodies, the agreement provides for a secretariat to be established by the Assembly. Until it is established, the African Union Commission (AUC) is directed to serve as the interim secretariat. The secretariat is to be a functionally autonomous institution within the African Union system with a budget derived from the African Union budget. It is to have an 'independent legal personality'. This status is equivalent to that of other African Union organs, such as the Pan African Parliament, NEPAD and the African Court. Being functionally autonomous, the secretariat will have the power to make administrative and operational decisions, including its own recruitment and human resources activities, without seeking approval from the African Union headquarters. But, since it is financed from the African Union budget, it will follow the African Union's financial and procurement rules. It is estimated that the AfCFTA secretariat could have 50 to 70 professional and administrative staff and an indicative annual cost of between $5 and 7 million, to effectively support the institutions and committees of the AfCFTA institutional framework (Sodipo, 2019).

The secretariat remains an intergovernmental institution, so decision-making powers are held by the hierarchy of committees, ensuring that State parties retain ownership and sovereignty over the agreement's execution. Since those committees might be called upon to make a considerable number of decisions promptly, they must function effectively. To do so, they could delegate certain perfunctory decisions to the secretariat, delegate decision-making authority to REC representatives in the absence of State representation, or accredit permanent representatives to the Committee of Senior Trade Officials, as is done in the WTO in Geneva.

In certain instances, the AfCFTA agreement explicitly requires implementation through regional or national committees, including national committees on trade facilitation and non-tariff barriers. In practice, effective implementation is more likely if trade ministries create AfCFTA committees or institutions comprising people focused on satisfying the commitments and interests of the AfCFTA and harmonizing their country's approach to implementation. Such national implementation mechanisms, ideally within the structure of an AfCFTA National Strategy (see Chapter 3), will promote effective national domestication of the AfCFTA.

Substance of the AfCFTA and linkages with its African Union ecosystem

The protocol on trade in goods establishes a free trade area (FTA) and an economic integration agreement (EIA), in the sense of the WTO.[1] AfCFTA State parties that are also WTO members will need to abide by certain WTO rules for the AfCFTA agreement to be compatible with WTO law. These notably include disciplines on the scope and coverage of the AfCFTA.

The core of the protocol on trade in goods is the elimination of import duties and taxes of equivalent effect. To ensure that the tariff preferences derived from the AfCFTA benefit only goods made in member States, the rules of origin specify the criteria and conditions for a product to be considered "made in" an AfCFTA party. Rules of origin are first of all designed to prevent tariff circumvention by non-AfCFTA State parties. However, they are also designed to: deepen regional and continental market integration, boost intra-Africa trade, promote regional and continental value chains and foster economic transformation of the continent through industrialization. The rules of origin thus require close cooperation between the State parties, so an annex focused on customs cooperation and mutual administrative assistance addresses origin verification.

Non-tariff barriers (NTBs) are generally considered to inhibit intra-African trade more than tariffs (ECA, AUC and AfDB, 2017b; IMF, 2019). Accordingly, the agreement pays considerable attention to eliminating NTBs, as well as to common disciplines that affect trade such as sanitary and phytosanitary measures and technical regulations. Annexes on trade facilitation and transit require State parties to cooperate on simplifying and harmonizing trade procedures and giving fair treatment to goods in transit. An annex on NTBs provides for reporting, monitoring, categorizing and eliminating them by creating an NTB mechanism. Provisions on technical regulations and sanitary and phytosanitary measures seek to reduce the burden of diverging norms by promoting cooperation between State parties' standards bodies, encouraging the mutual recognition of different standards and the harmonization of norms and standards.

Finally, provisions on trade remedies set out the means and procedures available for State parties to apply remedial import duties, for instance to respond to damaging import surges or unfair competition causing material injuries to the importing economy.

One-third of African employment is in the service sector (UNSD, 2019). The protocol on trade in services seeks to "create a single liberalized market for trade in services"[2] through two channels: a framework for the progressive liberalization of service sectors and a framework of common disciplines. To do so, the protocol provides for detailed commitments by countries in each service sector and for each mode of service delivery. Beyond these commitments, countries have also agreed to complement their commitments in all sectors with common sectoral regulatory cooperation frameworks.

Air transport will be included in the protocol on trade in services. But negotiators will need to pay attention to preserving the *acquis* of the 2018 Single African Air Transport Market (SAATM). Preserving the acquis is a principle that AfCFTA negotiations "not reverse or be inconsistent with the Acquis of the Union including but not limited to the Constitutive Act, the Abuja Treaty and other relevant legal instruments of the Union."[3]

Many other AU instruments similarly call for trade liberalization reforms, monitoring and evaluation mechanisms relevant to the AfCFTA and cooperation frameworks overlapping with those established under the AfCFTA agreement. A whole ecosystem can thus be identified where other AU instruments that constitute part of the acquis bear on negotiating and implementing the AfCFTA. The AfCFTA thus complements existing AU instruments towards achieving an African single market (Figure 2.9).

For instance, at the 2018 March Summit, another instrument, the protocol to the Abuja Treaty on the movement of persons, right of residence and right of establishment, was also opened for signature. Its provisions laying the groundwork for an integrated labour market to complement the objectives of the AfCFTA. The movement of persons protocol, by providing a legal basis for a continental qualifications framework, complements the AfCFTA's encouragement to members to negotiate mutual recognition agreements.[4] Going further, the protocol envisages at a later stage the rights of free residence and establishment. Those rights contribute to the freedom of movement of labour and capital, which are essential to a single market (AUC & ECA, 2006, p. 34).

Various other AU instruments provide for sectoral liberalization, including the SAATM in air transport, the Maritime Transport Charter and the Convention on African Energy Commission, policy governance cooperation statutes such as the Pan-African Intellectual Property Organization Statute and the Convention on Nature Protection and institutions such as the African Organisation for Standardisation and Pan African Quality Infrastructure. So, numerous AU instruments contribute to a regulatory

Ecosystem of African Union instruments

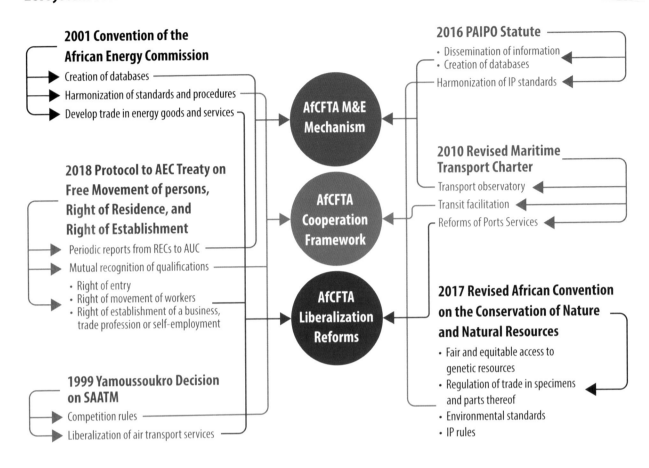

2001 Convention of the African Energy Commission
- Creation of databases
- Harmonization of standards and procedures
- Develop trade in energy goods and services

2018 Protocol to AEC Treaty on Free Movement of persons, Right of Residence, and Right of Establishment
- Periodic reports from RECs to AUC
- Mutual recognition of qualifications
  - Right of entry
  - Right of movement of workers
  - Right of establishment of a business, trade profession or self-employment

1999 Yamoussoukro Decision on SAATM
- Competition rules
- Liberalization of air transport services

AfCFTA M&E Mechanism

AfCFTA Cooperation Framework

AfCFTA Liberalization Reforms

2016 PAIPO Statute
- Dissemination of information
- Creation of databases
- Harmonization of IP standards

2010 Revised Maritime Transport Charter
- Transport observatory
- Transit facilitation
- Reforms of Ports Services

2017 Revised African Convention on the Conservation of Nature and Natural Resources
- Fair and equitable access to genetic resources
- Regulation of trade in specimens and parts thereof
- Environmental standards
- IP rules

Instrument adopted ▮▮▮   Instrument adopted into force ▮▮▮

environment that would complement the AfCFTA. Those instruments, implemented synergetically, bolster cross-sectoral realization of the AfCFTA's objective to "create a single market."[5]

The AfCFTA and RECs: Ensuring internal trade policy coherence

Role of the RECs in the negotiating process

The Abuja Treaty envisioned the establishment of an African Economic Community through six stages over 34 years, entailing the creation of a common market with the RECs as building blocks. The Treaty assumed that RECs would all conduct economic integration programs to become customs unions within 23 years of the entry into force of the treaty—that is, by 2017. That did not happen (see Chapter 1). The AfCFTA was originally con-

ceived to address these shortcoming by consolidating pre-existing FTAs into a single pan-African FTA (Figure 2.10).

The first AfCFTA negotiating guiding principle determined that AfCFTA would be a "Member State / REC / Customs Territories-driven process."[6] But since it was left to the member States to define the negotiating parties, the AfCFTA became a forum where the expression of national interests prevailed, sometimes even over REC-level commitments, even though the REC FTAs were to be the building blocks of the AfCFTA (see Box 2.1 for an example of conflicting negotiating principles). In the negotiations, the RECs and customs territories were given only observer-like status, with the right to attend and eventually make written or oral presentations upon request of the negotiating institutions.[7] Consequently, the REC secre-

Continental integration under the 2012 Boosting Intra-African Trade Action Plan

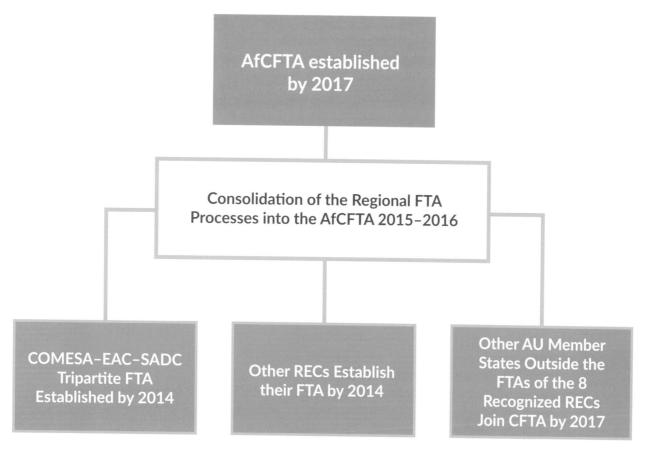

Source: (AU & ECA, 2012).

tariats—custodians of their respective community instruments—had only a secondary role (Kotcho, 2017, p. 22), contributing their voice only through the AfCFTA Continental Taskforce (the continental advisory body to the negotiating institutions) or through regional consultations on the side of the negotiations.

The second AfCFTA negotiating guiding principle prescribed the "REC FTAs as building blocks of the [Af]CFTA," and the third required the "preservation of the acquis" so that the negotiations "build on and improve the acquis of the existing REC FTAs" and not reverse what had been agreed previously. These negotiating guiding principles explain the results of the negotiations: negotiators were conscious from the start that the AfCFTA should not unravel the progress made in the RECs, yet the AfCFTA was driven by the individual interests of State parties, rather than those of the collective RECs.

The RECs and Africa's internal trade coherence

Only 12 African countries belong to a single REC; 33 belong to 2 RECs, 8 to 3 RECs and 1 to 4 RECs (AfDB, AU and ECA, 2016). Four RECs operate free trade areas. Some have islets of deeper integration, including customs and monetary unions. Others have free trade arrangements entirely alongside and above the REC groupings.

Figure 2.11 demonstrates the results of this by showing the share of intra-African imports in 2017 that flowed into each country through existing intra-African FTAs (grey bars), the share that could have been covered by the TFTA (orange bars) and the share that could have been covered by the AfCFTA (blue bars). The multiple and overlapping membership of countries across RECs and trading arrangements means that more than half of intra-African trade in 39 African countries is already covered by existing FTA arrangements.

Box 2.1:
The vessels definition issue

When the 31st Ordinary Assembly considered the draft annex on rules of origin, contending proposals for the definition of vessel were as follows:

Proposal 1

The terms "their vessels" and "their factory ships" in paragraph 1(h) and 1(i) shall apply only to vessels, leased vessels, bare boat and factory ships which are registered in a State Party in accordance with the national laws of a State Party and carry the flag of the State Party and, in addition, meet one of the following conditions:

(a) at least, 50 per centum of the officers of the vessel or factory ship are nationals of the State Party or State Parties; or

(b) at least, 50 per centum of the crew of the vessel or factory ship are nationals of the State Party or State Parties; or

(c) at least, [50 / 51] per centum of the equity holding in respect of the vessel or factory ship are held by nationals of the State Party or State Parties or institutions, agency, enterprise or corporation of the government of the State Party or State Parties.

Proposal 2

The terms "their vessels" and "their factory ships" in paragraph 1(h) and 1(i) shall apply only to vessels, leased vessels, bare boat and factory ships which are registered in a State Party in accordance with the national laws of a State Party and meet one of the following conditions:

(a) the vessel sails under the flag of a State Party; or

(b) at least, 50 per centum of the officers of the vessel or factory ship are nationals of the State Party or State Parties; or

(c) at least, 50 per centum of the crew of the vessel or factory ship are nationals of the State Party or States Parties; or

(d) at least, [50/51] per centum of the equity holding in respect of the vessel or factory ship are held by nationals of the State Party or State Parties or institutions, agency, enterprise or corporation of the government of the State Party or State Parties.

The main difference lies in the fact that Proposal 1 requires the vessels to register in the State Party and to sail under its flag of a State Party as mandatory criteria, in addition to one of the three additional criteria, whereas Proposal 2 requires the vessels only to register in a State Party as a mandatory criterion, in addition to one of four additional criteria.

Proponents of Proposal 2 argued that this approach is consistent with the SADC FTA acquis. Main opponents of Proposal 2 included SADC FTA members. Some SADC countries argued that the principle of preserving the SADC FTA acquis should guide the negotiations. Other SADC countries, including members of the SADC FTA, considered that approach to be contrary to the best practices adopted at the REC or international level, such as the UN Convention on the Law of the Sea—which left it to member States to the Convention to fix the conditions for granting rights of nationality, registering and flying the flag, provided that "ships have the nationality of the State whose flag they are entitled to fly" and that "there must exist a genuine link between the State and the ship."

Belongs to Figure 2.11:

Source: Authors' calculations based on UNCTADStat, 2019.

Note: Existing FTAs considered here are the Agadir Agreement, CEMAC customs union, COMESA FTA, EAC FTA, ECOWAS FTA and SADC FTA. It is assumed that the TFTA takes precedence over the AfCFTA in covering trade between TFTA member countries.

Figure 2.11:

Intra-African imports covered by existing FTAs, and that which could have been covered by the TFTA or AfCFTA, by importing country, 2017

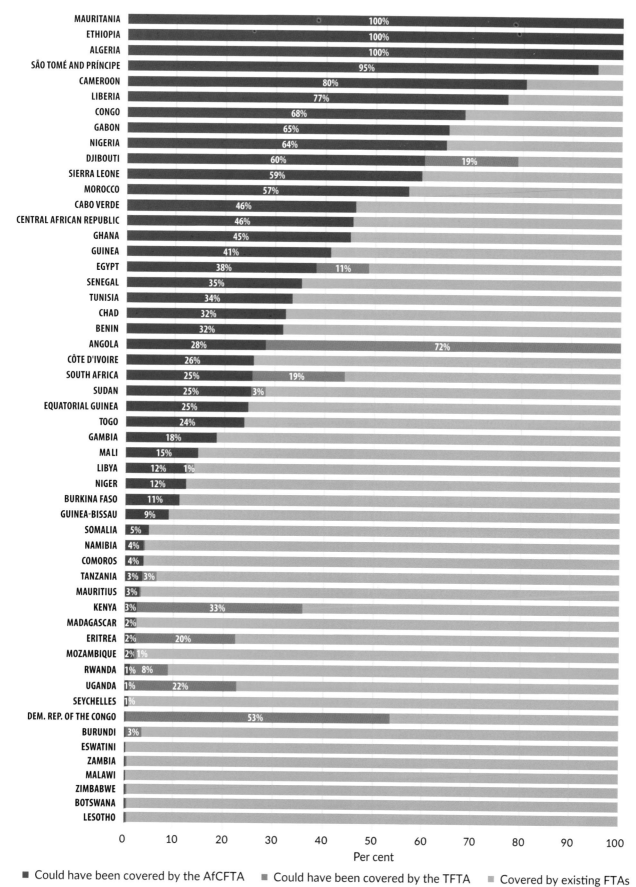

Country		
MAURITANIA	100%	
ETHIOPIA	100%	
ALGERIA	100%	
SÃO TOMÉ AND PRÍNCIPE	95%	
CAMEROON	80%	
LIBERIA	77%	
CONGO	68%	
GABON	65%	
NIGERIA	64%	
DJIBOUTI	60%	19%
SIERRA LEONE	59%	
MOROCCO	57%	
CABO VERDE	46%	
CENTRAL AFRICAN REPUBLIC	46%	
GHANA	45%	
GUINEA	41%	
EGYPT	38%	11%
SENEGAL	35%	
TUNISIA	34%	
CHAD	32%	
BENIN	32%	
ANGOLA	28%	72%
CÔTE D'IVOIRE	26%	
SOUTH AFRICA	25%	19%
SUDAN	25%	3%
EQUATORIAL GUINEA	25%	
TOGO	24%	
GAMBIA	18%	
MALI	15%	
LIBYA	12%	1%
NIGER	12%	
BURKINA FASO	11%	
GUINEA-BISSAU	9%	
SOMALIA	5%	
NAMIBIA	4%	
COMOROS	4%	
TANZANIA	3%	3%
MAURITIUS	3%	
KENYA	3%	33%
MADAGASCAR	2%	
ERITREA	2%	20%
MOZAMBIQUE	2%	1%
RWANDA	1%	8%
UGANDA	1%	22%
SEYCHELLES	1%	
DEM. REP. OF THE CONGO	53%	
BURUNDI	3%	
ESWATINI		
ZAMBIA		
MALAWI		
ZIMBABWE		
BOTSWANA		
LESOTHO		

Per cent (0 10 20 30 40 50 60 70 80 90 100)

■ Could have been covered by the AfCFTA   ■ Could have been covered by the TFTA   ■ Covered by existing FTAs

51

Still, the AfCFTA has an important role in bringing forward in intra-African trade liberalization those countries, particularly in northern, central and western Africa, that lag behind. The agreement, were it in force, could have covered 21 per cent of the intra-African imports in 2017 that were not covered by existing intra-African FTAs or would have been covered by the TFTA. But the AfCFTA is likely to have a far smaller impact in several countries, particularly in eastern and southern Africa, that currently import only a small share of their imports from African countries that do not share FTA arrangements with them.

The overlap and duplication of trading arrangements in Africa complicates customs procedures for customs administrators, traders and producers, allows forum shopping, frustrates the creation or functioning of customs unions and complicates the advancement of deeper continental economic integration. For these reasons and others, an explicit objective of the AfCFTA is to "resolve the challenges of multiple and overlapping memberships and expedite the regional and continental integration processes." Achieving this requires amalgamating and consolidating trading arrangements in Africa.

Article 19 of the AfCFTA agreement guides the relationship between the AfCFTA and Africa's pre-existing FTAs by providing for the resolution of incompatibilities or inconsistencies between the AfCFTA and other intra-African trade instruments. In such cases, the AfCFTA is to prevail, but with one crucial caveat: RECs that have achieved "among themselves higher levels of regional integration" are to persist as islets of such higher integration (Box 2.2). This ensures the preservation of the acquis, in line with the third principle of the AfCFTA negotiations.

All four African Union–recognized RECs with FTAs have achieved higher levels of integration than the AfCFTA will when it enters into force. EAC and ECOWAS have customs unions with fully liberalized trade,[8] COMESA and the FTA established by the Agadir Agreement have achieved a fully liberalized FTA, and SADC has achieved an FTA with some exclusions from liberalization. In comparison, the AfCFTA Agreement requires a threshold of liberalization of 97 per cent of tariff lines representing no less than 90 per cent of trade volume. Article 19 allows the REC trading arrangements to persist as islets of deeper integration within the AfCFTA system. Thus the AfCFTA does not, in the short term, consolidate the REC FTAs.

This coexistence poses the question of how treatment between REC FTA members and other AfCFTA parties will differ. Provisions in the AfCFTA agreement on "continental preferences" and most favoured nation (MFN) treatment counter a free rider problem, yet risk creating multiple sets of market access conditions depending on the ability of the other State parties to reciprocate (Box 2.3).

Due to overlapping trade regimes and the particular crafting of the AfCFTA MFN clause, where preferential trade links already existed, better preferences than those offered under the AfCFTA will not be unconditionally and automatically extended to

Box 2.2:
Agreement Establishing the African Continental Free Trade Area, Article 19

Conflict and Inconsistency with Regional Agreements

1 In the event of any conflict and inconsistency between this Agreement and any regional agreement, this Agreement shall prevail to the extent of the specific inconsistency, except as otherwise provided in this Agreement.

2 Notwithstanding the provisions of Paragraph 1 of this Article, State Parties that are members of other regional economic communities, regional trading arrangements and custom unions, which have attained among themselves higher levels of regional integration than under this Agreement, shall maintain such higher levels among themselves.

AfCFTA provisions on continental preferences and most favoured nation treatment

MFN in trade agreements

Protection from discrimination is the prize for membership in trade agreements. To achieve this, agreements include MFN clauses, requiring parties to grant, immediately and unconditionally, to all parties thereto, treatment no less favourable than that accorded to any other country. This gives parties to an agreement, as a matter of right, access to the best treatment that may be on offer in any of the countries that are parties to the agreement.

MFN clauses play two main roles in a trade agreement:

1. They make the trade liberalizing instrument the platform of choice—as the collector of all the best treatment. The MFN principle has been the basis of the success of the WTO.

2. They force countries to select carefully what they leave out of agreements with third countries—knowing that if and when they eventually choose to share that with any country, they would, by virtue of the MFN obligation, have to grant it to all parties to their existing agreements.

MFN clauses therefore put a premium on membership, encouraging parties to do any additional liberalization within the agreement. When crafted well, MFN clauses foster equality in treatment between and among all countries that are party to an agreement with respect to customs duties and charges of any kind imposed on or in connection with importation/exportation of goods or with any measures covered under service trade agreements.

But an MFN clause in a regional trade agreement (RTA) plays a further role by ensuring that any more favourable treatment given to large trading partners (typically defined by thresholds of their participation in international trade within a given period) must also be granted, immediately and unconditionally, to the parties to the RTA. Although it can be legally argued that such access would have been granted by virtue of a general MFN clause, RTAs single out large traders to ensure that trade is not deflected from the RTA in capitulation those with stronger trading muscle. Examples of include provisions in several Economic Partnership Agreements between the EU and regional groupings requiring that any preferable treatment accorded a large trader, such as China, also be extended to the EU.

MFN obligations can deter countries from pursing ambitious liberalization for fear of having to extend it to all, harming their domestic economies.

The AfCFTA MFN clause and its implications

The AfCFTA takes a unique approach to matters concerning MFN. The Agreement Establishing the AfCFTA Article 18 on Continental Preferences provides for MFN principles that are then elaborated in the protocols on trade in goods and services.

AfCFTA protocol on trade in goods, Article 4

Most-Favoured-Nation Treatment

1. State Parties shall accord Most-Favoured-Nation Treatment to one another in accordance with Article 18 of the Agreement.1

2. Nothing in this Protocol shall prevent a State Party from concluding or maintaining preferential trade arrangements with Third Parties, provided that such trade arrangements do not impede or frustrate the objectives of this Protocol, and that any advantage, concession or privilege granted to a Third Party under such arrangements is extended to other State Parties on a reciprocal basis.

3. Nothing in this Protocol shall prevent two or more State Parties from extending to one another preferences which aim at achieving the objectives of this Protocol among themselves, provided that such preferences are extended to the other State Parties on a reciprocal basis.

4   Notwithstanding the provisions of paragraphs 2 and 3 of this Article, a State Party shall not be obliged to extend to another State Party, trade preferences extended to other State Parties or Third Parties before the entry into force of the Agreement. A State Party shall afford opportunity to the other State Parties to negotiate the preferences granted therein on a reciprocal basis, taking into account levels of development of State Parties.

The MFN clause of the AfCFTA does two things:

1   It recognizes that the AfCFTA will not catch up right away with some faster liberalizations on the continent. So, it preserves continental preferences—allowing the RECs to continue giving each other better-than-AfCFTA treatment. This is the import of article 18, paragraph 1 of the AfCFTA agreement. So, as a starting point, the AfCFTA creates no MFN obligation in the standard sense. State parties may maintain more favourable treatment with AfCFTA and non-AfCFTA parties without according them to all AfCFTA parties. Strictly speaking, such a provision should not be couched as MFN because it is not granting MFN rights to any party. It is more an exception to MFN than an expression of the principle.

2   It does not provide for MFN in the traditional sense—by incorporating conditionality in access by referring to reciprocity and, in the case of the protocol on trade in services, to non-discrimination. Because of the unique approach, the definition of a third country within the AfCFTA is obscure—it could be one AfCFTA party alongside others (a continental preference) or, more typically, a country that is not party to the AfCFTA. It remains unclear how a provision aimed at creating equality in treatment between parties to an agreement can have conditions that, if unmet, result in discrimination. The approach also creates various classes of AfCFTA parties with various levels of rights within the AfCFTA—most of whom would be discriminated against, if they cannot reciprocate the better treatment accorded to third countries. So although this provision was clearly seeking to ward off free riders, it potentially complicates the AfCFTA market place, rather than streamlining and consolidating it.

It is contradictory to require that access to such better treatment be granted only on the basis of reciprocity, yet at the same time be non-discriminatory. It is possible that in the near future, AfCFTA parties could give third parties more favourable treatment than they are granting in the AfCFTA (at best rising to 97 per cent within 15 years), including on so-called sensitive or excluded tariff lines—effectively putting the third parties in a better position than African exporters. In such a case, African exporters will risk being spectators to the promise of the AfCFTA—watching a boost, not in intra-African trade as promised by the agreement, but in AfCFTA-facilitated African trade with third countries.

all State Parties, but will be subject to negotiations and reciprocity.[9] Where islets of deeper regional integration exist, those islets will coexist with the AfCFTA. The AfCFTA thus fosters liberalization across the continent but does not conclusively address the issues posed by membership in overlapping trading regimes. The AfCFTA does not fully consolidate Africa's fragmented markets into a single regime, but instead leaves a web of better connected but distinct trade regimes. Nevertheless, by liberalizing trade between these regimes, the AfCFTA functions as an intermediate step towards their later consolidation.

Merging the AfCFTA and REC FTAs: A way forward

The objectives of the AfCFTA include, as discussed earlier, "lay[ing] the foundation for the establishment of a Continental Customs Union at a later stage" and the "creat[ion] of a single market."

A customs union incorporates free trade among the members and a common external tariff (though residual tariffs are possible in a customs union; see Box 2.4). A common market adds the free movement of capital, labour and services. A single market subsequently removes nearly all frictions, to the point where all market factors circulate as freely in the single market as they do in the domestic one.

This requires harmonized economic and fiscal rules and portability of social security benefits, among other aspects. In the AfCFTA, the single market is to be reached incrementally through "successive rounds" of liberalizing negotiations.[10] Through these successive rounds, the AfCFTA can more fully consolidate Africa's fragmented trading regimes into a coherent continental regime.

The AfCFTA must now take six steps to establish a continental customs union and evolve into a unified single African market, consolidating the REC FTAs (Table 2.1). This roadmap mirrors the six stages proposed in the Abuja Treaty but addresses the delay in achieving customs unions in several RECs. Instead of waiting for each REC to achieve a customs union—the approach of the Abuja Treaty—the roadmap divides the continental customs union into its two constituent parts—a free trade area and a common external tariff. In step 2, the liberalization achieved by the AfCFTA deepens through successive rounds until it reaches the level of the most liberal preferential trade schemes in Africa. In step 3, the AfCFTA is used to consolidate a unified free trade area in Africa. Only then, in step 4, is a common external tariff cast around the continent to form the African continental customs union (residual tariffs remain—see Box 2.4). As freedom of capital, labour and services are achieved (processes that started with the AfCFTA), an African common market is created, and with further harmonization of economic policies, the African single market arrives.

Table 2.1:

A six-step roadmap from the AfCFTA to the African single market

1	2	3	4	5	6
AfCFTA with REC FTAs as islets of deeper integration	Fully liberalized AfCFTA	Merger of all African FTAs	African continental customs union	African common market	African single market
Achieved by the AfCFTA in its current form	Liberalization under the AfCFTA is deepened until all trade is liberalized	REC FTAs are subsumed as the AfCFTA reaches 100% liberalization. Competing tariff concessions and rules of origin are phased out. REC customs unions are maintained	REC customs unions are subsumed with a continental common external tariff	Freedom of capital, labour and services are achieved, building on the AfCFTA	Deep economic harmonization

Box 2.4:

Residual tariffs within customs unions

Difficulties may arise if, in the longer term, the AfCFTA is complemented by a common external tariff (CET) but some tariffs in intra-African trade persist. Though article 24 of the GATT provides for eliminating tariffs on substantially all trade in a customs union, lessons may be drawn from outside Africa. From a WTO law perspective, a customs union according to the GATT requires only a CET and for substantially all trade within the union to be liberalized. In this light, an African continental customs union can include internal duties and barriers. The case of Turkey and the EU is a classic example, because Turkey and the EU hold a customs union but Turkey retains tariffs on certain agricultural products.

However, the administration of those residual tariff may become a headache in the context of the free movement of goods. And since the AfCFTA already comprises elements of a common market, there may be a need to think beyond a mere FTA to embrace AfCFTA rules that overflow GATT article 24 or GATS article 5.

The risk, were this not to happen, is that the AfCFTA remains merely a platform for multiple bilateral and regional FTAs with a single set of disciplines within Africa. Though this would still liberalize intra-African trade, it would mark a failure to take advantage of far greater opportunities for integration in Africa.

The AfCFTA and external trade policy coherence

Continental solidarity in international negotiations

Since 1963, the OAU and then the AU have called for cohesion and solidarity among African countries in international trade meetings and negotiations. The inaugural meeting of the OAU called for "all States concerned to conduct negotiations, in concert."[11] OAU and AU summits made many appeals for solidarity in negotiating in international economic and trade fora.[12]

During the latest 7th AMOT meeting on 12-13 December 2018, the AUC drew attention to the 2018 Nouakchott Summit decision on the AfCFTA—specifically, to the decision's paragraph 9, which calls on the AU member States to refrain from signing new FTAs for trade in goods, economic integration agreements (EIAs) for trade in services and Bilateral Investment Treaties (BITs) with third parties until the AfCFTA enters into effect. This appeal aimed to highlight the AfCFTA's status as the first step in creating a continental common space with a common external trade policy. This common policy depends on harmonized—if not unified—instruments that preserve the coherence of continental trade architecture.

Member States may face a trade-off between the long-term objectives of pursuing policy coherence and the short-term objectives of preserving or pursuing preferential market access with external trade partners, which still represent a substantial share of their trade. For instance, the prospective impact of Brexit on African producers exporting to the United Kingdom forced African governments to take proactive measures, such as negotiating a post-Brexit SACU–UK FTA, to maintain their preferential market. Similarly, African governments are considering new FTAs to preserve preferential access to the US

market after the likely 2025 expiry of the US African Growth and Opportunity Act (AGOA) (ECA, AUC and AfDB, 2017b).

The individual economic interests of African countries have led them to conclude no fewer than 18 FTAs with third parties, as well as several partial scope agreements. Negotiations or discussions are ongoing for several further agreements, among them a Mauritius–India FTA, a Mauritius–China FTA, a post-AGOA Mauritius–USA FTA and a post-Brexit SACU–UK FTA or post-Brexit Eastern and Southern Africa economic partnership agreement (ESA EPA)–UK FTA.

Left unaddressed, this situation is likely to impede the objectives of the AfCFTA agreement and the broader African integration agenda because (Desta, Gerout and MacLeod, 2019):

- By prying open inlets into Africa's tariff structure, such external agreements widen the divide between the tariff schedules of African countries and prevent the creation of an African Common External Tariff (CET), which is itself a prerequisite for the Continental Customs Union envisaged not just in Article 3.(d) of the AfCFTA Agreement, but in the aspirations of the 1991 Abuja Treaty, the 2000 Constitutive Act of the African Union and the 2012 Boosting Intra-African Trade (BIAT) Action Plan. A Common External Tariff is no longer common if some of the countries party to it have FTAs in place with external countries. This challenge has precedents Africa—both the ECOWAS and CEMAC regional groupings face existential challenges to their own common external tariff systems from bilateral agreements between the EU and Cameroon, Côte d'Ivoire and Ghana.

- Such external agreements threaten the intent of the AfCFTA that African countries should "accord each other […] preferences no less favourable than those given to Third Parties."[13] Article 18, "Continental Preferences," which invokes this language, is designed to ensure that the preferences shared among African countries are the deepest. Yet, because article 18 qualifies such treatment on reciprocity—so as to prevent a free rider problem—it becomes toothless, doing very little to actually prevent

AU Summit decisions on external trade policy coherence, since 2012

Since the 2012 decision on boosting intra-African trade and fast-tracking the AfCFTA, no fewer than five AU Summit decisions supported coherence between the trade-oriented African integration programs and trade negotiations involving third parties, whether bilateral or multilateral. The emphasis shows the importance given to the matter by the policy organs of the AU.

- The 22nd Ordinary Summit (Jan. 2014), called upon AU member States for caution when negotiating with third partners not to "fatally compromise the African trade integration process and undermine the vision and scope of the Abuja Treaty." Thus, when member States pursued those negotiations, they were requested to "not further constrain the policy space and flexibilities they need for effective intra-African trade, industrialization, regional integration, value addition and employment creation" and to "speak with a single voice in order to be heard in the global arena."

- The 23rd Ordinary Summit (June 2014), "[c]ognizant of the impact of the negotiations of bilateral, multilateral and megatrade agreements on the African integration agenda," called upon member States and RECs "once more" to ensure not compromising African trade integration efforts when engaging in bilateral or multilateral trade negotiations.

- The 24th Ordinary Summit (Feb. 2015), addressing WTO negotiations, recalled "the importance of African countries speaking in one voice" to reflect common African positions in multilateral trade negotiations.

- The 27th Ordinary Summit (July 2016) requested all "Member States to speak with one voice on all issues related to trade negotiations with third parties."

- The 31st Ordinary Summit (June 2018) committed to "engage external partners·as one block speaking with one voice" and asked member States to "abstain from entering into bilateral trading arrangements until the entry into force of the Agreement establishing the AfCFTA."

These appeals for coordination in trade negotiations with the rest of the world stress coherent, sequential implementation of commitments to preserve the integrity of the African approach to regional integration, whether internally, to bolster efforts to deepen African integration, or externally, to strengthen harmonious participation by an integrated African economic space in the global economy. In this light, the AU decisions suggest implementing the AfCFTA as a step towards deeper integration before making further commitments with the rest of the world. As a common trade policy tool, the AfCFTA would thus set a benchmark for new or deeper AfCFTA-compatible trade agreements with third partners. Moreover, to respect the ambition of the AfCFTA, FTAs, EIAs and BITs with third partners will take into account the evolutionary dimension of the African integration process, thus providing the necessary space the AfCFTA to evolve into an African single market.

third countries from enjoying greater access than other African countries to parts of the African market.

- Such external agreements challenge the long-held idea that, to use the language of the AU Agenda 2063, Africa can achieve more if it will "speak with one voice and act collectively to promote our common interests and positions in the international arena" and of the importance of "unity and solidarity in the face of continued external interference." With a single voice, Africa can negotiate trade deals better than can 55 AU member States with smaller disunited voices. Together Africa is an economic giant, as large as India in population and economic output. Yet without a common external tariff and, ultimately, a continental customs union, Africa's divided voice will be at risk of being picked apart by larger external interests.

When external agreements are concluded without coherence, there may be costs to intra-African trade. ECA (2015) research suggests that implementing EPAs may come at the cost of intra-African trade unless the AfCFTA reforms are implemented before the EPAs (Box 2.6). And the EPAs create asymmetrical sourcing opportunities, while they maintaining preferential access to the EU market for the exported goods. Since such provisions are expected to enhance intra-regional trade and foster regional value chains, if sourcing opportunities were facilitated across the AfCFTA for exporting to the EU under the EPA, that would both enhance predictability under the EPA and boost intra-African trade in raw materials and intermediaries, the ECA study concludes.

To this end, the AU Summit has called for solidarity and requested African States to refrain from taking any new commitments to the rest of the world that would impede the AfCFTA.[14] This request notably includes demonstrating that the commitments taken shall be in contradiction or creating obligations that undermine the contracting State Party to abide to the vision of establishing an African single market.

Engaging with the rest of the world as a coherent regional grouping

The regional approach to external trade negotiations

African countries will continue to face, on the one hand, a desire to cohere a common African position and on the other, pressure to maintain or pursue legitimate but individual national interests in external trade negotiations. Without action, these pressures will further unravel and impede a coherent African external trade policy. Several steps can be taken to enforce a coherent and unified external trade policy (Desta, Gerout, & MacLeod, 2019):

- Empower the African Union Commission with genuine trade policy powers so it can serve as the single African voice on trade negotiations with external countries. Though this could frustrate some African countries that take pride in holding the reins to their own trade policy, the benefits are worth it. Such is

the EU model, which wields considerable trade negotiating clout, as many African countries might unhappily attest. We can look, too, to less-developed regional groupings: the ASEAN configuration of south and southeast Asian countries has exercised considerably more power as a consolidated negotiating bloc in the Comprehensive and Progressive Agreement for Trans-Pacific Partnership (CPTPP) and Regional Comprehensive Economic Partnership (RCEP) negotiations than any of their constituent countries could have done (Mikic & Shang, 2019).

- Ensure effective institutional mechanisms for referring national level trade policy interests up to the AUC and ensuring that the AUC remains accountable to the AU member States on issues of trade policy. The seeds are in place. The African Ministers of Trade (AMOT) have met eight times so far during the AfCFTA negotiations, regularly discussing policy towards external trade issues such as the WTO.[15] The AfCFTA agreement strengthens these institutions, formalizing a Council of Ministers to meet biannually in ordinary session and under express AfCFTA decision-making disciplines to ensure effectiveness.

- Rationalize Africa's existing external trade arrangements. This can take time. The EU, for example, has only since 2010 begun gradually harmonizing the various BITs historically held between different EU and external countries.[16] In doing so, it has resorted to establishing transitional conditions for the continued application of BITs currently in force, as well as conditions for EU member States to modify existing agreements and negotiate or conclude new or similar ones, while at the same time delegating authority to the European Commission for negotiating new EU-wide investment agreements.[17] Similarly, Africa can establish conditions to impose order on existing trade agreements while defining the parameters through which the competency is gradually delegated to the AUC for negotiating trade and investment agreements with external partners.

- Subsume problematic bilateral treaties within broader alternatives. The SADC EPA offers a valuable lesson. Before it, South Africa and the EU

Experiences of the economic partnership agreements

Economic partnership agreements (EPAs) have encountered much resistance in African countries because they are seen as disruptive of the regional integration efforts. But some agreements were concluded by non-LDC countries to preserve their preferential access to the EU market.

For those non-LDCs, preferential access to the EU market was deemed necessary to avoid the consequences of the expiration of unilateral preferences by 1 October 2014 due to an EU decision. This EU decision goes back to the 2000 version of the African, Caribbean and Pacific¬–EU Partnership Agreement (CPA) which, under economics and trade, provided that WTO-compatible trade agreements were to be concluded between African, Caribbean and Pacific¬ (ACP) States and the EU to ensure the continuity of preferential trade between the historical partners. To that end, the CPA provided for a transition until 31 December 2007, during which the EU would continue granting unilateral preferences to ACP countries, pending the entry into force of the new agreements. This transition arrangement was formalized in annex V of the CPA.

On 1 January 2008, negotiations were ongoing. Accordingly, the EU adopted a new law replace previous regulations that became obsolete with the expiry of annex V. The new regulation, Regulation (EC) No. 1528/2007, became the new market access regulation (MAR) that governed preferential market access conditions for ACP countries pending the entry into effect of the EPAs. But in 2011, the European Commission noted unsatisfactory progress by some countries and suggested that "these countries no longer met the conditions of the Market Access Regulation for advance provisional application of trade preferences which were extended to them as of 1 January 2008 in anticipation of the steps towards ratification of an EPA" (European Commission, 2011, 2). This observation was embedded in a proposal for amending the list of the beneficiaries of the MAR.

After more than a year and half of legislative process, Regulation (EU) No 527/2013 amending annex I of the MAR was adopted. It provided that countries that did not complete the "necessary steps" towards an EPA would lose benefit of the MAR and be subjected to ordinary trading conditions, falling under MFN or GSP in accordance with their respective level of development by 1 October 2014.

The entry into force of this new regulation forced negotiations to accelerate, with the level of urgency varying among countries. LDCs would fall under the everything but arms (EBA) sub-scheme of the GSP, which offers duty-free and quota-free access to the EU market for all products except weapons and ammunition—that is, very similar market access to that under the MAR. But non-LDCs could fall back only to the less generous preferences—if any—under the normal sub-scheme of the GSP. In this context, non-LDCs in Central Africa, the East African Community, Southern Africa and West African rushed to conclude and implement regional EPAs.

LDCs in the EAC region did not suffer major disruption after Regulation (EU) No 527/2013 entered into effect. But non-LDC Kenya was severely affected, and by December 2014 negotiations were concluded and Kenya readmitted under the MAR benefit. Kenya then ratified the EPA to signal its good will, but pending ratification by the rest of the region, the agreement cannot enter into force.

Similarly, in 2016, two ECOWAS non-LDC countries, Côte d'Ivoire and Ghana, broke away from the regional configuration to implement "stepping stone" agreements to maintain their preferential access to the EU market.

To date, three non-LDCs belonging to customs unions have decided to implement EPAs, while the rest of the membership of their customs unions are not participating. These countries (Côte d'Ivoire and Ghana in ECOWAS, and Cameroon in CEMAC) represent serious challenges to the implementation of their respective common external tariff and movement of goods in the customs union.

Additionally, the situation in EAC puts Kenya in a precarious position, though preferential access of Kenya-originating products is still granted to the EU market.

already had a free trade area under their Trade, Development and Cooperation Agreement (TDCA). This undermined the SACU CET by applying different tariff structures within its customs union, posing the exact same problem as the interim EPAs in ECOWAS and CEMAC. The SADC EPA restored coherence by replacing TDCA with an alternative that encompassed the whole SADC region, such that it "now harmonises the SACU tariffs imposed on imports originating in the EU and consequently improves the functioning of the customs union [...]. In this way, the SADC EPA strengthens regional integration."[18] In the context of the AfCFTA, continental agreements between Africa and respective trading partners can be used to subsume and replace conflicting older ones.

What happens if the AfCFTA fails? Latin America offers a precedent. After the 34-country Free Trade Area of the Americas (FTAA) initiative failed in 2005, the United States chose individual "can do" Latin American countries for bilateral negotiations (Hereros, 2019; ECA, AUC, & AfDB, 2017). Many resulting FTAs were concluded and have entered into force. But they split Latin America into countries that had trade agreements with the United States and those that did not and did not want one.[19] The split continues to this day, evidenced by division between the MERCOSUR countries in the east of South America and those in western South America, many of which were aiming to strengthen links with the United States through the TPP negotiations, before the Trump administration withdrew the United States from them.

What effect would such a divide have in the context of an aspiring African customs union? The risk of precipitately complicating Africa's external trading arrangements under further FTAs is clear: if the AU vision is disregarded, incompatible trade agreements will erode the policy space needed to create an African single market. Customs unions risk being Balkanized, as seen in the destabilization of the ECOWAS and CEMAC customs unions due to interim EPAs, as well as the political split in the EAC over the EPA.

But positive developments are afoot. The EU, Africa's single biggest trading partner, is itself changing its approach, recently considering a "continent-to-continent agreement [that] would use as a stepping stone the African Continental Free Trade Area."[20] This would reconcile not just the divergent EPAs but also the association agreements between the EU and North Africa, and it would contribute to a harmonized, coordinated European approach to African trade. Africa could pursue this method with other regions, as well. It would unite Africa's external trade policy and provide external partners a direct pathway to negotiating with 55 African Union member States.

The regional approach in unilateral preferential trade schemes

African economies rely on unilateral preferences granted by third partners but have been unable to use such schemes to diversify their export base (ECA, 2015). The AfCFTA may offer a way for State parties to leverage continental value chains to better benefit from unilateral schemes.

A number of countries or customs territories grant unilateral preferences to LDCs or to developing countries under various schemes.[21] Some or all African countries—depending on the preference-granting country and the applicable scheme—receive unilateral preferences from:

- Under GSPs, Armenia, Australia, Canada, European Union, Iceland, Japan, Kazakhstan, New Zealand, Norway, Russia (Eurasian Economic Commission), Switzerland, Turkey and the United States.[22]

- Under LDC-specific schemes, Chile, China, Chinese Taipei, India, Korea, Kyrgyz Republic, Morocco, Montenegro, Tajikistan and Thailand.

Those preferences are not negotiated, so their conditions are dictated at the discretion of the granting countries. It is up to the granting countries to create schemes that support regional integration in Africa. Several schemes consider regional value chains and pre-existing regional groupings. For instance, the Norwegian GSP allows cumulation of origin between LDCs and also within a coherent regional grouping. This is granted upon request by the regional grouping and examination by the Norwegian government.[23] So far, Norway recognizes two groupings: ASEAN and SAARC. The Swiss GSP allows countries to request regional cumulation under conditions like those accepted in the Norwegian GSP.[24]

Another example occurs under the Chinese LDC scheme, which also provides for regional cumulation. So far, it recognizes two groupings: ASEAN and ECOWAS.

Under the EU GSP, regional cumulation does not cover Africa; however, extended cumulation covers EPA countries, so African GSP beneficiaries (whether under GSP, GSP+ or Everything But Arms) can cumulate with EPA countries, but not with other GSP beneficiaries.[25]

These schemes also usually provide platforms for beneficiaries to comment. They may also offer periodic review schemes. Partners that consider the AfCFTA a credible regional integration and value chain–oriented instrument able to contribute to the pursuit their respective schemes might be persuaded to incorporate all AfCFTA State parties in their GSP.

African countries should thus consider using diplomatic means to press for the recognition of the AfCFTA in future unilateral preference schemes. There is good justification: the AfCFTA helps African countries diversify their exports and so better use such unilateral preferences. With regards to the EU GSP, this discussion fits into the ongoing post-Cotonou negotiations, which entail a trade and economic pillar.

Next steps for the AfCFTA

The Phase I negotiations of AfCFTA are concluded, 54 African Union member States signed on, and, as of April 2019, the 22 ratifications received that are the required threshold for entry into force. The agreement has considerable momentum to be used to operationalize it. But the momentum can also deepen African economic integration by realizing the trade and welfare gains forecast for the AfCFTA (ECA, AUC, & AfDB, 2017) and legitimizing the AU, dispelling what President Kagame of Rwanda, who led AU reform efforts, called the

"crisis of implementation" of AU decisions and initiatives (Kagame, 2017). The AfCFTA is about more than trade; it is about commitment to the AU and its Agenda 2063 and to translating that commitment into action.

Step 1: Operationalize the AfCFTA

On 2 April 2019, Gambia's parliament approved the AfCFTA agreement, becoming the 22nd country to ratify it, so that the agreement reached the threshold for entry into force. An AU Summit is being organized for the start of July, in Niamey, to launch the entry into force and operationalise the AfCFTA. Upon entry into force, the AfCFTA will immediately supersede any national laws in State parties with contrary provisions. Yet, critical technical components need to be finalized before goods can flow duty-free and service suppliers unhindered. These include: schedules of concessions for trade in goods, rules of origin and schedules of specific commitments for trade in services.

The African Ministers of Trade, in the report of their 7th meeting in Cairo in December 2018, targeted the end of June for concluding schedules of concessions for trade in goods. This target, however, was not met. They must do so rapidly, or else fail to establish the AfCFTA as a meaningful instrument.

Technical work on the rules of origin was, as of April 2019, advanced and yet likewise failed to meet the same end-of-June deadline. As a fall-back, annex 2 to the rules of origin article 42 provides for "Transitional Arrangements." The operative clause dictates that, "Pending the adoption of the outstanding provisions, State Parties agree that the Rules of Origin in existing trade regimes shall be applicable."[26] So, the existing regional FTAs will constitute the fall-back measure. Trade between State parties that did not have pre-existing FTAs will be dealt on an MFN basis, until adoption of the rule of origin for the traded product.

Other secondary technical work remains on components of the AfCFTA that are not critical to its operationalization but will ease its implementation and interpretation. They include guidelines on infant industries, guidelines and a manual on rules of origin, regulations for goods produced under special economic zones and guidelines on the implementation of trade remedies.

Africa's trade negotiators and technocrats must conclude the remaining technical components of the AfCFTA without delay and prevent them from hindering continental trade integration that has been repeatedly envisioned by the Heads of State and Government.

In the medium term, negotiations of the schedules of specific commitments for trade in services are scheduled to be completed by January 2020 for the launch of the AfCFTA EIA.

Step 2: Enlarge the group of State parties

Twenty-seven country ratifications in one year and a half since the agreement was concluded is an impressive show of political will and commitment in the AfCFTA, representing 50 per cent of the African Union member States. More impressive still is the 54 countries that have now signed the agree-

ment. For the AfCFTA to deliver its transformative economic potential, the countries that have not yet signed the agreement must do so, and the remaining signatory countries must ratify it to ensure that the continent moves together en masse.

It is particularly important that the collective membership of Africa's four customs unions (CEMAC, EAC, ECOWAS and SACU) ratify and begin implementing the agreement (Box 2.7). As customs unions, these groupings have common external tariffs, and sub-sets of them cannot move ahead with tariff reductions without undermining the commonality of their external tariffs and consequently the integrity of the customs union.

Joining the agreement early is in each country's individual interest at entry into force, only those that are party to the agreement will have decision making power at the technical and ministerial levels. Early joiners to the agreement will affect the shape, structure and operation of the agreement to which late-comers will be subject.

Box 2.7:
Options for customs unions in the AfCFTA

The AfCFTA negotiating principles call for customs unions to submit a single offer. But faced with the imminent entry into force of the AfCFTA, membership in customs unions has been challenging.

- In CEMAC, Chad and Congo have ratified, leaving four out.
- In EAC, Kenya, Rwanda and Uganda have ratified, leaving three out.
- In ECOWAS, Côte d'Ivoire, Gambia, Ghana, Guinea, Mali, Niger, Senegal, Sierra Leone and Togo have ratified, leaving six out.
- In SACU, Eswatini, Namibia and South Africa have ratified, leaving two out.

At least two possible options are conceivable:

- Should priority be put on the integrity of the CET, a delay implementing the AfCFTA in a customs union may be considered until all are members of the AfCFTA. But this option is suboptimal, since it will mean that even with 22 participating countries, the AfCFTA does not have the critical mass for entry into force.
- Should priority be put on implementing the AfCFTA, State parties could offer preferential treatment, and in case of re-exportation to another member of the customs union which is not a State party, the unpaid tariff may be reclaimed. But this will mean that the free movement of goods within the customs union is no longer assured.

So, both choices are suboptimal. The ideal way forward is to ensure that all customs union members also be AfCFTA State parties and with common market access.

The African Union intends for all its member States to join the AfCFTA. For this reason, the Assembly is the highest decision-making body of the AfCFTA institutions, providing political and strategic guidance. As a flagship initiative of the African Union's Agenda 2063, the AfCFTA is not merely a project of a small sub-set of African Union members. An enlarged group of State parties, greatly exceeding the minimum 22 required for entry into force, is necessary for the continent to move forward collectively and meaningfully in trade integration.

Step 3: Effectively implement the AfCFTA

Making the AfCFTA work effectively requires creating institutional structures for implementing it as discussed earlier, establishing the mechanisms envisaged in its operative provisions and introducing the obligations it imposes into the laws and regulations of each State party.

Besides the main AfCFTA institutional bodies—the Council of Ministers and the Committee of Senior Officials—committees on each of the protocols and dedicated sub-committees must be created. Focal points at the national level responsible for substantive areas of the agreement, such as non-tariff barriers, must be identified. National and regional AfCFTA committees are required for coordination. The AfCFTA secretariat must be established by the assembly to support the council and committees.

The AfCFTA also envisages a number of mechanisms. Most notably, a dispute settlement mechanism is to be established in accordance with the protocol on rules and procedures on the settlement of disputes. A non-tariff barrier mechanism is to be instituted for identifying, categorizing and progressively eliminating NTBs within the AfCFTA. State parties are also to decide on a mechanism for exchanging information on subsidies related to trade in services and for cooperating on technical assistance and capacity building to address standards, metrology, accreditation, technical regulations and conformity assessment.

Finally, State parties incorporate the AfCFTA into their respective laws and regulations. Most fundamentally, this requires changing their tariff sched-ules and service regulations to reflect their trade in goods and services commitments.

Step 4: Undertake complementary measures to take advantage of the agreement

It is not enough for the AfCFTA to be operational. State parties must strategically take advantage of it to derive its full benefits. That requires designing and implementing national AfCFTA strategies to identify opportunity export sectors and value chains that can benefit from the AfCFTA market access openings, and the measures needed to support them. Chapter 3 of this report delves into exactly this issue, identifying along the export pathway complementary measures in investment, productive capacities, trade facilitation, trade-related infrastructure and import defence.

Such steps will prove that continental initiatives are not just abstract declarations but actions that affect the lives of individuals and foster poverty alleviation and economic development.

Step 5: Conclude phase II negotiations on investment, competition policy and intellectual property rights

When the African Union Heads of State and Government launched the AfCFTA negotiations in 2015, they established a mandate beyond negotiations on trade in goods and services to deeper levels of integration in investment, competition policy and intellectual property rights. They envisaged not just a traditional free trade area agreement, but one that could integrate these further areas of policy.

The AfCFTA negotiations apportioned phase I to focus on a framework agreement establishing the AfCFTA and negotiations on protocols on trade in goods and services and dispute settlement. A second phase was dedicated to negotiations on investment, competition policy and intellectual property rights.

As the phase I negotiating issues draw to a conclusion, phase II negotiations are expected to begin after the July 2019 African Union Summit that will operationalize the AfCFTA. The 7th meeting of the AMOT meeting, in Cairo in December 2018, set a deadline of December 2020 for concluding the phase II negotiations. (The phase II topics—critical issues to be addressed and options—are the subject of Chapters 4, 5 and 6 of this report.) African policy makers must also consider how, or whether, to address the new issue of e-commerce within the framework of AfCFTA negotiations (the subject of Chapter 7).

Step 6: Use the AfCFTA as a vehicle for achieving an African single market

The AfCFTA is not just a free trade area but a tool for achieving the deeper forms of integration in Africa called for by the African Heads of State and Government in their Assembly declarations since the Abuja Treaty. Moving towards such deeper forms of integration will require conjoining internal and external trade policy as steps towards an African single market.

The AfCFTA does not fully consolidate internal trade policy within Africa but retains the REC FTAs and customs unions as deeper islets of integration within the AfCFTA market. In doing so, it does not fully resolve the challenges of multiple and overlapping trade regime memberships. Instead, it leaves a web of better connected, but distinct, trade regimes in Africa. This important step in African economic integration must be taken further.

According to the objectives of the AfCFTA, it "lay[s] the foundation for the establishment of a Continental Customs Union." Building upon this foundation will require progressively deepening the integration under the AfCFTA until it can subsume the existing REC FTAs into a single, fully liberalized, African trade area. Doing so allows a common external tariff across Africa and a continental customs union.

At the same time, Africa must consolidate its external trade policy. Delegating trade policy powers to the African Union Commission, ensuring that the Commission remains accountable to its membership and rationalizing existing external agreements

to be consistent with Africa's integration vision are key steps.

The AfCFTA exists within a constellation that includes the AU Protocol on the Free Movement of Persons, Right of Residence and Right of Establishment; the Single African Air Transport Market; the Convention on the Conservation of Nature and Natural Resources and the Convention of the African Energy Commission, among others. The march towards an African single market will involve consolidating and deepening these other integration instruments.

Key messages and policy recommendations

Key messages

- **Remarkable progress has been made in realizing the AfCFTA. Fifty-four of 55 AU member States have now signed the agreement.** As of July 2019, 27 have ratified and deposited ratification instruments with the AUC. Negotiators have concluded all four of the phase I protocols to the agreement and 10 of the 12 annexes (Trade in Goods annex 1 on Schedules of Commitments and annex 2 on Rules of Origin are to be concluded by July 2019), marking commendable progress since the launch of negotiations in June 2015.

- **Implementing the AfCFTA is about more than trade. It is about dispelling the "crisis of implementation" of AU decisions and initiatives and validating the African Union and its Agenda 2063.** It is a litmus test of the commitment of African countries to economic integration.

- **The AfCFTA aspires towards deepening the integration of the African continent beyond merely a free trade area.** It includes as objectives to "create a liberalized market […] through successive rounds of negotiations," "lay the ground for the establishment of a Continental Customs Union" and "contribute to the movement of capital and natural persons."

- **African countries must take care that the AfCFTA not simply add an additional strand in the African spaghetti bowl of preferential trade regimes.** Instead, it must provide coherence to the internal and external trade policy landscape in Africa.

Policy recommendations

- **The remaining African countries should ratify the AfCFTA without** delay and ensure that the continent moves together by greatly exceeding the minimum number of 22 ratifications required for entry into force.

- **Critical technical components that need to be finalized before the AfCFTA can be operationalized must be urgently concluded.** They include schedules of concessions for trade in goods, rules of origin and schedules of specific commitments for trade in services. These must be followed by the phase II negotiations on investment, competition policy and intellectual property rights.

- **Ratification of the AfCFTA must be followed through by effective implementation.** This requires creating the AfCFTA institutions, establishing the mechanisms envisaged in its operative provisions and incorporating AfCFTA obligations into the laws and regulations of each State party. And countries must strategically take advantage of the AfCFTA to achieve economic development and poverty alleviation.

- **The effectiveness of the AfCFTA committees will require many prompt decisions.** Certain perfunctory decisions could be delegated to the Secretariat, other decision-making authority delegated to REC representatives in the absence of State representation or permanent representatives accredited to the Committee of Senior Trade Officials, as is done in the WTO in Geneva.

- **Implementing of the AfCFTA will be more effective if national ministries responsible for trade create AfCFTA committees.** The committees can comprise persons focal for satisfying the commitments and interest of the AfCFTA and can harmonize their country's approach to implementation. These should ideally be framed within the structure of an AfCFTA national strategy.

- **Using the AfCFTA to realize the deeper forms of integration in Africa that have been called for by African Heads of State and Government.** This requires progressively deepening the liberalization achieved under the AfCFTA until it is sufficient to subsume the existing REC FTAs into a single, fully liberalized, African trade area.

- **Unilateral trading schemes of Africa's partners can reinforce African regional value chains if they are designed appropriately.** African countries should accordingly deploy their diplomatic capabilities towards influencing trading partners to promote regionalism as they design their unilateral trading schemes, including generalized systems of preferences.

References

Adedeji, A. 1984. "The Monrovia Strategy and the Lagos Plan of Action for African Development— Five Years After". Presented at the ECA/Dalhousie University Conference on the Lagos Plan of Action and Africa's Future International Relations: Projections and Implications for Policy-Makers, Halifax, NS, 2–4 November.

AfDB (African Development Bank), AU (African Union) and ECA (United Nations Economic Commission for Africa). 2016. *Africa Regional Integration Index Report 2016*. Addis Ababa, Ethiopia: ECA.

AUC (African Union Commission). 2009. "Minimum Integration Programme (MIP)". Addis Ababa, Ethiopia: AUC.

AUC (African Union Commission) and ECA (United Nations Economic Commission for Africa). 2006. *Assessing Regional Integration in Africa II: Rationalizing Regional Economic Communities in Africa*. Addis Ababa, Ethiopia: AUC and ECA.

AUC (African Union Commission) and ECA (United Nations Economic Commission for Africa). 2012. *Boosting Intra-African Trade. Issues Affecting Intra-African Trade, Proposed Action Plan for Boosting Intra-African Trade and Framework for the Fast Tracking of a Continental Free Trade Area*. Addis Ababa, Ethiopia: AUC and ECA.

AUC (African Union Commission), ECA (United Nations Economic Commission for Africa) and AfDB (African Development Bank). 2012. *Assessing Regional Integration in Africa V: Towards an African Continental Free Trade Area*. Addis Ababa, Ethiopia: AUC, ECA and AfDB.

Bhagwati, J. 1995. *US Trade Policy: The Infatuation with FTAs*. New York: Columbia University.

COMESA, EAC and SADC. 2008. "Final Communique of the COMESA-EAC-SADC Tripartite Summit of Heads of State and Government". Kampala: COMESA, EAC and SADC.

Desta, M., G. Gerout and J. MacLeod. 2019. "Safeguarding the African Continental Free Trade Area from Externally Imposed Threats of Fragementation". Retrieved from Afronomics Law: http://www.afronomicslaw.org/2019/03/14/safeguarding-the-african-continental-free-trade-area-from-externally-imposed-threats-of-fragmentation/

ECA (United Nations Economic Commission for Africa). 2015. *Economic Report on Africa 2015: Industrializing through Trade*. Addis Ababa, Ethiopia: ECA.

———. Forthcoming. *Economic Report on Africa 2018: Development Thinking and Practice in Africa*. Addis Ababa, Ethiopia: ECA.

ECA (United Nations Economic Commission for Africa), AUC (African Union Commission) and AfDB (African Development Bank). 2017a. Assessing Regional Integration in Africa VIII: Bringing the Continental Free Trade Area About. Addis Ababa: ECA.

ECA (United Nations Economic Commission for Africa), AUC (African Union Commission) and AfDB (African Development Bank). 2017b. *Assessing Regional Integration in Africa VIII: Bringing the CFTA About*. Addis Ababa, Ethiopia: ECA, AUC and AfDB.

Erasmus, G. 2015. "The Continental FTA Should Develop Its' Own REC Acquis". Available at: http://www.truckandbus.co.za/the-continental-fta-should-develop-its-own-rec-acquis/

Estevadeordal, A., K. Suominen and C. Volpe. 2013. *Regional Trade Agreements: Development Challenges and Policy Options*. Geneva: ICTSD and WEF.

European Commission. 2011. "Proposal for a Regulation of the European Parliament and of the Council amending Annex I to Council Regulation (EC) No 1528/2007/* COM/2011/598". Brussels: European Commission.

Gerout, G., J. MacLeod and M. Desta. 2019. "The AfCFTA as Yet Another Experiment towards Continental Integration: Retrospect and Prospect". In I*nclusive Trade in Africa: The African Continental Free Trade Area in Comparative Perspective*, edited by D. Luke and J. MacLeod. London: Routledge.

Hereros, S. 2019. "The Failure of the Free Trade Agreement of the Americas: A Cautionary Tale for the African Continental Free Trade Area". In *Inclusive Trade in Africa: The African Continental Free Trade Area in Comparative Perspective*, edited by D. Luke and J. MacLeod. London: Routledge.

IMF (International Monetary Fund). 2019. *Regional Economic Outlook Sub-Saharan Africa: Recovery amid Elevated Uncertainty*. Washington, DC: IMF.

Issoufou, M., and V. Songwe. 2018. Africa's Continental FTA, Boost to Growth, Development. Fortune.

Kagame, P. 2017. *The Imperative to Strengthen our Union: Report on the Proposed Recommendations for the Institutional Reform of the African Union*.

Kotcho, J. 2017. "The CFTA Negotiations and the Issue of Coherence". *Bridges Africa* 6 (6): 20–23.

Mikic, M., and W. Shang. 2019. "ASEAN at 50 and Beyond". In *Inclusive Trade in Africa: The African Continental Free Trade Area in Comparative Perspective*, edited by D. Luke and J. MacLeod. London: Routledge.

Nkrumah, K. 1957. *Ghana: The Autobiography of Kwame Nkrumah*. Edinburgh: Thomas Nelson.

OAU (Organisation of African Unity). 1963. "Resolutions Adopted by the First Conference of the Independent African Heads of State and Government (CIAS/Plen.2/Rev.2)". Addis Ababa, Ethiopia: OAU.

Sandrey, R. 2015. *Rules of Origin: Looking Outside the Box*. Stellenbosch, South Africa: TRALAC.

Sodipo, B. 2019. "Governance for an effective AfCFTA". In *Inclusive Trade in Africa: The African Continental Free Trade Area in Comparative Perspective,* edited by D. Luke and J. MacLeod. London: Routledge.

UNSD. 2019. UNData [database]. Available at: http://data.un.org/en/reg/g2.html.

WTO (World Trade Organization). 2014. *Challenges Faced by LDCs in Complying with Preferential Rules of Origin under Unilateral Preference Schemes*. Geneva: WTO.

Zamfir, I. 2015. *The Tripartite Free Trade Area Project. Integration in Southern and Eastern Africa*. Brussels: European Parliament Research Service.

Endnotes

1   It is still to be determined whether the AfCFTA will be notified under article 24 of the GATT or under the enabling clause for the trade in goods component.

2   Article 3, Protocol on Trade in Services, Agreement Establishing the African Continental Free Trade Area.

3   Paragraph 3 of Annex III to the Report of the 1st AfCFTA-AMOT, held in May 2016.

4   Article 18 of Protocol on Free Movement…

5   Article 3(a) of the Agreement Establishing the African Continental Free Trade Area.

6   Report of the 1st Meeting of African Union Ministers of Trade, 24 May 2016, Annex III 'Definitions for the Continental Free Trade Area (CFTA) Negotiating Guiding Principles'.

7   Rule 15.4, Annex II, 1st AMOT report.

8   See paragraph 54 of the 2013 Revised Report by the Secretariat of the WTO Trade Policy Review of EAC; and, paragraph 3.55 of the 2018 report by the Secretariat of the WTO Trade Policy Review of Guinea.

9   Article 4.5 of the goods protocol and article. 4.4 of the services protocol complement article. 18 of the Framework Agreement with the aim of covering holistically the sets of preferences given to state parties in the context of MFN to other state parties.

10   Article 3(b) AfCFTA.

11   1963 Resolutions of OAU Summit, CIAS/Plen.2/Rev.2.

12   For example, the 1966 Ordinary Resolution on UNCTAD II; 1980 Extraordinary Resolution on African participation in international negotiations; 1983 Resolution on UNCTAD VI; 1984 and 1985 Declarations on the critical economic situation in Africa; 1987 Resolution on commodities; 1991 Declaration and 1994 Resolution on the Uruguay Round of Multilateral Trjade Negotiations; 1998 Decisions on ACP-EU relationships, on TICAD II and on WTO; 2003 Declaration on EPA negotiations; 2006 Declarations on WTO; 2007 Declarations on EPA negotiations and on WTO; 2008 Declaration and Decision on EPAs; 2015 Decision on WTO and 2017 and 2018 Decisions on the AfCFTA.

13   Article 18. Agreement Establishing the African Continental Free Trade Area.

14   Paragraph 7, Decision on the AfCFTA (Assembly/AU/Dec.714(XXXII)), 10-11 February 2019.

15   See, for instance, the report of the Seventh Meeting of the African Union Ministers of Trade (TI/AfCFTA/AMOT/7/FINAL/REPORT).

16   See Article 207(1). 2009 Treaty on the Functioning of the EU.

17   See Regulation No. 1219/2012 establishing transitional arrangements for bilateral investment agreements between Member States and third countries (http://trade.ec.europa.eu/doclib/docs/2013/february/tradoc_150494.pdf) for examples of agreements negotiated by the European Commission under its new investment competency see the EU-Singapore FTA (as the first example of the EU's new competence as expanded post-Lisbon) (http://trade.ec.europa.eu/doclib/press/index.cfm?id=961) , the 2016 EU-Canada Comprehensive Economic and Trade Agreement ("CETA") (http://ec.europa.eu/trade/policy/in-focus/ceta/ceta-chapter-by-chapter/), the agreement in principle for the EU-Mexico Agreement in April 2018 (http://trade.ec.europa.eu/doclib/press/index.cfm?id=1833) and the EU-Vietnam investment agreement in August 2018 (http://trade.ec.europa.eu/doclib/press/index.cfm?id=1437).

18   See http://trade.ec.europa.eu/doclib/docs/2014/october/tradoc_152818.pdf.

19   See Herreros, S. *The failure of the Free Trade Area of the Americas: a cautionary tale for the African Continental Free Trade Area*, in Eds. Luke, D. and MacLeod, J. 'Inclusive Trade in Africa: The African Continental Free Trade Area in Comparative Perspective', forthcoming.

20   See https://www.ictsd.org/bridges-news/bridges/news/eu%E2%80%99s-juncker-calls-for-advancing-suite-of-trade-economic-goals-as-bloc and https://ec.europa.eu/commission/sites/beta-political/files/soteu2018-speech_en_0.pdf.

21   Except as otherwise mentioned, all the information under the present sub-section has been sourced from the WTO PTADB.

22   Deeper preferences are also granted by the United States to some African countries under the AGOA. African GSP beneficiaries are not necessarily AGOA beneficiaries and vice versa. For instance, Botswana and South Africa are eligible for AGOA preferences but not GSP, and Democratic Republic of the Congo and South Sudan are GSP beneficiaries but are not eligible for AGOA. Source: WTO PTABD, updated 30/06/2017.

23 Paragraph (3), section 8-4-32 of Regulations to the Act on Customs Duties and Movement of Goods (Customs Regulations).

24 Article 13 of 946.39 Ordonnance du 30 mars 2011 relative aux règles d'origine régissant l'octroi de préférences tarifaires aux pays en développement (Ordonnance relative aux règles d'origine, OROPD).

25 Article 53—56 of Commission Delegated Regulation (EU) 2015/2446.

26 Article 42.3, Annex 2 of the Protocol on Trade in Goods, of the Agreement Establishing the African Continental Free Trade Area.

Chapter 3
Taking full advantage of the AfCFTA

The AfCFTA provides considerable opportunities for economic development in Africa. Yet to fulfil them, it must be buttressed with complementary measures, including prioritizing AfCFTA-potential sectors in national investment plans, establishing simplified trading regimes and investing in trade-related infrastructure.

In framing such measures, this chapter considers five steps along an export path: investment, production, export compliance, transport logistics and importation. For each step, the reforms obligated by the AfCFTA and complementary measures are presented.

Complementary measures also prepare governments to react to adverse trade events. Sudden import surges or product dumping can damage local producers, while changes in market dynamics can pose anti-competitive threats. Measures to develop trade defence and competition institutions and effective trade monitoring and evaluation can help governments prepare for challenges resulting from trade liberalization.

This chapter walks through the five steps of the export path, identifying the complementary measures at each that can get the most out of the AfCFTA. While each complementary measure has value, a strategic approach to coordinating them is important. The chapter concludes in calling for national AfCFTA strategies to take full advantage of the AfCFTA, and it includes an appendix on guidelines for the development of such strategies.

Complementary measures to take advantage of the AfCFTA

The AfCFTA embodies reforms that liberalize and facilitate trade along the export path. They include reducing tariffs, the traditional heart of free trade

agreements, but also liberalizing service sectors, supporting customs cooperation and addressing non-tariff barriers. Figure 3.1 links the key reforms of the AfCFTA agreement to the export path, showing the great range of reforms beyond tariff reductions through which the AfCFTA can support trade in Africa.

These reforms open opportunities. But taking advantage of them requires further deliberate steps from government. For instance, for boosting investment, governments can ease investors through a streamlined one-stop shop investment centre, buttressed by a national investment legal framework and supported by investment promotion authorities. When it comes to production, a productive capacities development agenda can target national production towards AfCFTA trade opportunities through industrial policy, enhancing productive infrastructure and sector-specific policies. Other complementary measures can assist firms with AfCFTA export compliance and transport logistics.

Investment measures

Investment is the first step in building capacity to take advantage of the AfCFTA. In fact, such investment interventions as export promotion or short-term tax holidays for new investors can be even more appealing to investors than reduced external tariffs (UNCDP, 2016).

The AfCFTA directly treats investment through two channels. First is the protocol on services, involving ongoing negotiations to open designated service sectors to other African countries' commercial presence (known as "mode 3" in negotiating parlance).[1] AfCFTA State parties will thus exchange offers that allow their investors better access to each other's sectors. The second channel is a dedicated protocol on investment, one of the topics of the phase

Figure 3.1:
Complementary measures along the export path

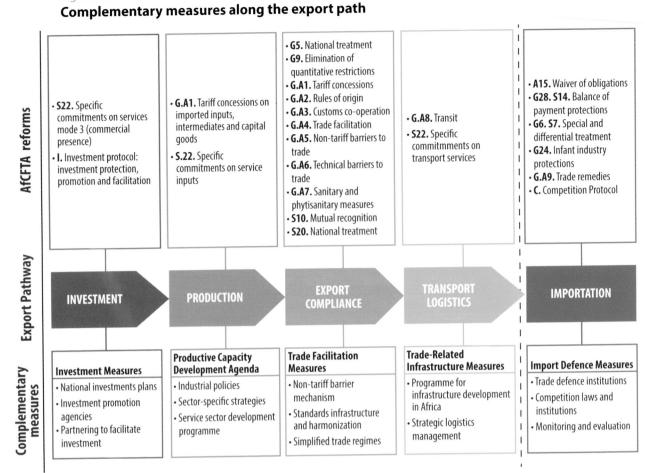

Source: Authors.

Reforms: A: AfCFTA agreement. C: Protocol on competition. G: Protocol on trade in goods. I Protocol on investment. IP: Protocol on intellectual property rights. Numbers indicate articles, so "A15" indicates article 15 of the AfCFTA agreement. Subsequent "A" numbers indicate annexes, so "G.A2" indicates annex 2 of the protocol on trade in goods.

II AfCFTA negotiations. Though its exact form and content will depend on the outcome of negotiations, it will likely include protections for investors across African countries, as well as provisions on investment promotion and facilitation.

National investment plans

National investment plans can support grasping the opportunities provided by the AfCFTA by promoting investment flows into sectors that benefit from AfCFTA market liberalization. They can also contain measures to facilitate outward investments. National investment plans typically include investment promotion measures (such as incentives) and investment facilitation (for example, through single windows for investors). They may also include efforts to improve the business environment to influence operating conditions for investors. Investment plans maximize positive spillovers from the affiliates of foreign firms through technology and know-how dissemination and linkages with domestic suppliers. They minimize negative effects through social and environmental safeguards.

Implementing national investment plans can require legal and institutional changes. National policies governing investment should be aligned with the AfCFTA protocols to enhance complementarities and foster clarity and predictability for investors, while also reflecting national development plans.

Investment promotion agencies

Investment promotion agencies attract and facilitate investments (UNCTAD, 2017a). They may host or empower physical or digital one-stop shops for investment so that investors can register their companies with all the necessary authorities in one place. Such centres, reducing the transaction and time costs of investment, already exist in several African countries, including Ethiopia, Nigeria and Rwanda.

Investment policy tools

UNCTAD investment policy reviews

Investment policy reviews provide developing countries with concrete recommendations to improve policies, strategies and institutions for attracting foreign direct investment (FDI) and deriving greater benefits from investment for sustainable development.

Investment policy reviews address a single country. They include:

- A review of the policy, regulatory and institutional environment for investment.
- The identification of strategic investment priorities consistent with the Sustainable Development Goals (SDGs) and with the national development objectives.
- A set of concrete recommendations.

Follow-up support is provided to bring the investment policy review recommendations into the country's reform agenda and implement them.

As of February 2019, investment policy reviews had been conducted in 26 African countries: Algeria, Benin, Botswana, Burkina Faso, Burundi, Cabo Verde, Congo, Djibouti, Egypt, Ethiopia, Gambia, Ghana, Kenya, Lesotho, Madagascar, Mauritania, Mauritius, Morocco, Mozambique, Nigeria, Rwanda, Sierra Leone, Sudan, Tanzania, Uganda and Zambia.

Online investor guides

Online investor guides (iGuides) provide prospective investors with information that they need to invest in a country. They are produced and updated by governments with support available from UNCTAD, ECA and the International Chamber of Commerce.

iGuides typically provide investors with:

- Locally available data, costs and prices for taxes, transport, rent values, utility prices, termination indemnities, and wages across different job categories and non-wage labour costs. The data, comparable across countries, enable investors to build a basic business model before going further in choosing a location.
- Relevant rules and licensing requirements, timelines and useful contacts. The iGuides explain which licenses are required, how long they take to get and who in government can facilitate the process or provide more information. They also provide a realistic view of procedures such as customs clearance, obtaining work permits and repatriation of funds.
- Experiences of established investors. Whether on paying taxes, hiring labour or obtaining electricity, iGuides summarize the experiences of established investors and provide case studies of their investment history. Though UNCTAD and ECA canvass the candid views of investors, governments also have the opportunity to explain how they are addressing investors' concerns.

As of February 2019, iGuides were available for 15 African countries: Benin, Burkina Faso, Burundi, Comoros, Ethiopia, Kenya, Mali, Morocco, Mauritania, Mozambique, Nigeria, Rwanda, Tanzania, Uganda and Zambia, as well as the East African Community.

Source: For more information on investment policy review, see https://unctad.org/en/Pages/DIAE/Investment%20 Policy%20Reviews/Investment-Policy-Reviews.aspx; for more information on iGuides see https://www.theiguides.org/.

Investment promotion agencies can serve as matchmakers between domestic firms and international or continental market leaders seeking to utilize AfCFTA opportunities. They identify and target leading international, continental and sub-regional firms in priority industries. They can be instrumental in concluding cooperation contracts between local and foreign firms and in forming research and development consortiums with foreign participation.

Greater investment facilitation will be needed across African economies to take advantage of the AfCFTA. Bureaucratic difficulties in obtaining required permits and approvals, accessing land or office space or bringing in qualified personnel can discourage investors, delay or derail projects and tarnish the business reputation of the investment promotion agency and the country. For more information, UNCTAD's *Global Action Menu for Investment Facilitation* details measures that agencies can take as well as recommendations for national and international investment policies.[2]

Partnering to facilitate investment

Learning from other African countries' strides in attracting investment will strengthen productive capacity in light of the accepted role that investment can play in the AfCFTA. The African Union Commission can facilitate intra-African dialogues to develop a blueprint of African best practices in investment promotion. Development partners, such as ECA and UNCTAD offer investment policy tools, including UNCTAD investment policy reviews and UNCTAD/ECA Online Investor Guides (Box 3.1).

A productive capacity development agenda

What a country produces determines what it trades. Though the AfCFTA entails considerable export opportunities, including access to a consolidated market of over 1.2 billion consumers, only countries that can produce the goods desired by that market can use the opportunities. Productive capacity, according to UNCTAD, includes productive resources (natural, human, physical and financial); entrepreneurial and institutional capabilities

Figure 3.2:
Elements of productive capacities

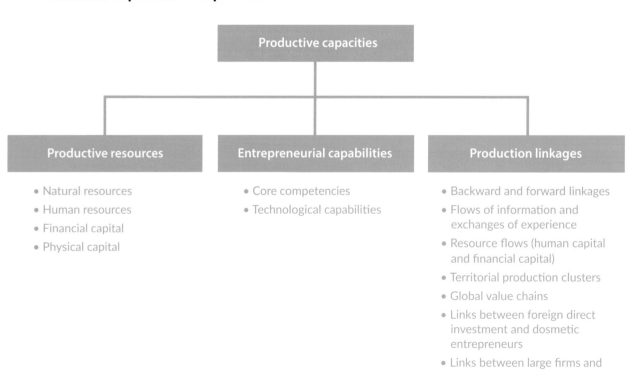

Source: UNCTAD, 2016a.

10 agricultural products in intra-African trade, 2017

HS GROUP	PRODUCT	EXPORT VALUE ($ BILLIONS)
15	Animal or vegetable fats and oils and their cleavage products; prepared edible fats; animal or vegetable waxes	1.7
33	Essential oils and resinoids; perfumery, cosmetic or toilet preparations	1.7
17	Sugars and sugar confectionery	1.4
10	Cereals	1.4
22	Beverages, spirits and vinegar	1.0
03	Fish and crustaceans, molluscs and other aquatic invertebrates	0.9
24	Tobacco and manufactured tobacco substitutes	0.9
07	Edible vegetables and certain roots and tubers	0.8
09	Coffee, tea, maté and spices	0.7
04	Dairy produce; birds' eggs; natural honey; edible products of animal origin, not elsewhere specified or included	0.5

Source: Trade map, accessed on 6 November 2018.

Note: HS is the Harmonized System commodity classification.

and production linkages. Together, they determine a country's capacity to increase production, diversify its economy towards higher productivity sectors and produce faster growth and sustainable development (Figure 3.2) (UNCTAD, 2006). For many countries in Africa, improving productive capacities is a prerequisite for taking advantage of the AfCFTA's opportunities.

The AfCFTA liberalizes both goods and service sectors. This change expands the options for African businesses to import productive resources from partner African countries into their production (ECA, AUC and AfDB, 2017). The AfCFTA thus directly affects African countries' productive capacity. However, AfCFTA's indirect effect on productive capacity is the main one: by opening potential trade opportunities, AfCFTA stimulates new export-oriented production.

Structural change is central in developing productive capacity and moving economies into the right development trajectory (UNDESA, 2017). Increased productive capacities raise value addition in natural resource–based industries and diversify local products and exports, especially in services, agriculture and manufacturing. Greater productive capacities can thus increase African countries' developmental potential due to the trade they gain through the AfCFTA.

Because agriculture, manufacturing and services gain new trade opportunities through the AfCFTA, they must focus on adding value in various chains of production so as to increase intra-African exports. This in turn calls for strengthening productive capacity.

Strengthening productive capacities requires two layers of intervention. One focuses on creating a supportive and facilitative overarching enabling environment, often through developing industrial policy, enhancing infrastructure enhancement and aligning these instruments with investment policy. The other provides sector-specific support in line with national and subregional priorities.

The role of industrial policy

Industrial policy is a strategy that focuses implicit or explicit policy instruments selectively on specific industrial sectors to shape structural change in pursuit of a broader national vision and strategy (Oqubay, 2015). Its package of interactive strategies and measures aims at building enabling industrial systems—such as infrastructure and financial systems—and productive capacity—with such assets as skills, capital and technology and supporting the development of internal and export markets (UNCTAD, 2018a).

A sector-specific value chain in agriculture: Tea in intra-African trade

The potential to boost value added is high in the tea sector. Currently, most tea from Eastern Africa is exported in bulk, but several regional opportunities exist:

- In packaging, more processing could lead to exporting smaller, branded retail packages or to packing tea into tea bags, instant tea and ready-to-drink beverages.

- In product diversification, producing more green tea, flavoured tea or tea with health benefits, such as Zimbabwe's Makoni or South Africa's Rooibos, could supply niche markets.

- In certification and standards, organic tea and Fair trade–labelled tea is getting growing interest among domestic consumers ready to pay a higher price.

Current drawbacks are:

- Heavy tariffs imposed by some important continental buyers.

- Unstable international demand, which can be compensated by a faster development of continental sales.

- High costs of production, especially due to insufficient energy infrastructure.

- Climate change threats, which will soon require redesigning the tea growing map in Eastern Africa.

Upgraded trajectories for commodity value chains can be organized around four blocks:

- **Processes.** Increase the efficiency of internal processes, which could be improved and scaled up at the regional levels within the AfCFTA. A strong regional institutional mechanism could design a marketing strategy for boosting regional consumption and promoting the sector at the continental level, for example, by campaigning for an early eradication of high tariffs in importing markets.

- **Products.** Introduce new products or improve existing ones. Seeking standards and certification opportunities at the continental level can be help identify best practices for producing economies of scale.

- **Functions:** Change the mix of activities, or move to different links in the value chain.

- **Chains:** Move to a new value chain.

Source: Adapted from UNCTAD (2016b).

Developing a proactive industrial policy within the AfCFTA to adopt skills and technology, improve public–private partnerships and expand industrial knowledge is key. The policy must also recognize the resources and the context in which firms operate. It should focus primarily on structural features related to trade, industry and labour market transformation.

Agriculture, a major contributor to intra-African trade, should be embraced in industrial policy in the context of building productive capacity. The main agricultural commodities and agri-food products exported within Africa (Table 3.1) should receive new regional policy attention, increased investment and technological and industrial upgrading.

A new generation of agricultural policies should improve agricultural production, agribusiness and value chain advancement and aligned with AfCFTA opportunities. For instance, cotton may serve the textile industry, while palm oil can be incorporated into agri-food products (UNCTAD, 2016b).

Promoting FDI is integral to industrial policy because FDI is more than a flow of capital that can stimulate economic growth. It comprises assets that include long-term capital, technology, market access, skills and know-how, all of which are crucial for industrial development. Aligning investment policy and industry policy is therefore valuable and natural.

Industrial policy is a continuous work in progress for countries at all levels of development. Its configuration evolves with a country's level of development and productive capabilities, as well as with the adoption of new technologies in industrial value chains.

Sector-specific considerations to build productive capacity for structural transformation

Trade is increasingly organized through value chains. So, strengthening productive capacities along these chains is important.

A value chain is the full range of activities required through different phases of production to bring a product or service from conception to delivery to the final consumer and final disposal after use. It therefore includes input sourcing, primary production, transformation, marketing and final consumption (Figure 3.3) (UNCTAD, 2016b).

Most methodologies for prioritizing value chains take a national perspective or pursue national integration into a global value chain. But the AfCFTA encourages adapting to the regional context and maximizing regional effects, for example by creating regional innovation centres. By pooling resources in regional configurations, African countries can share technical skills and training capacities, standard certification capabilities, research and development expertise, processing facilities and intermediate inputs. Regional value chains also take account of economic, social, environmental and regional integration (UNCTAD, 2016b).

Realizing the promise of the AfCFTA requires developing both overarching and sector-specific capacity, focusing on enablers and fostering country sectoral initiatives that create and strengthen regional value chains. Tea and textiles provide two examples (Box 3.2, 3.3).

Figure 3.3:

A model value chain model for food production and consumption

PRODUCERS OF PRODUCTION INPUTS

FARMERS & GROWERS

PROCESSORS & TRADERS

RETAILERS

CONSUMERS

Source: BASF (n.d.).

A product-specific value chain in industry: Textiles

The textile industry value chain begins with the production of cotton. It goes on to spinning and twisting the fibre into yarn, weaving and knitting yarn into fabric and bleaching, dying and printing fabric. The value chain from cotton farming to textile processing and apparel manufacturing is important to the economies of Botswana, Eswatini, Lesotho, Malawi, Mozambique, South Africa, Tanzania, Zambia and Zimbabwe in Africa.

Africa is still at the early stage of the value chain—farming and exporting cotton. African countries can also take advantage of manufacturing opportunities in the value chain, including in yarns, fabrics, zippers and buttons, among others, and in services such as training, export marketing and brokerage services.

How productive capacities can be strengthened.

The cotton-to-textiles industry in Africa is characterized by much higher cotton yields in Western Africa than in Eastern and Southern Africa. But some dynamic and internationally competitive textile companies are located in Eastern and Southern Africa. To build on these different competitive advantages in the context of scarce public funds, governments could pool resources and raise private financing for regional centres of excellence for training creative technology- and innovation-oriented workforces.

Source: UNCTAD (2018a).

The Services Sector Development Programme

The Services Sector Development Programme (SSDP) is an African Union blueprint for member States, regional economic communities (RECs) and the African Union Commission (AUC) to jointly develop efficient and internationally competitive service sectors in Africa. SSDP will increase exports of services, boost employment in the service sector and improve Africa's attractiveness to foreign direct investment. The SSDP, led by the AUC Department of Trade and Industry, will shape a crucial policy for developing service trade in Africa through the AfCFTA. The programme's five-year time frame is designed to allow for continuity, monitoring, evaluation and follow-through of its various activities.

The SSDP aims to provide a strategic approach to service sector development. The general absence in national development strategies of service trade policy frameworks, services export strategies and attention to service sectors other than tourism, financial services and information and communications technology (ICT) underscores this problem. Export promotion and investment promotion strategies have not focused on service trade despite its growing contribution to GDP. For African Union member States to boost intra-African trade, alleviate poverty and achieve higher levels of economic growth and sustainable development, as well as to achieve the trade policy objectives set out in the BIAT Action Plan, more attention to the services sector and the achievement of more efficient services are vital.

The SSDP has six steps to help AU member States liberalize services—either unilaterally, through the RECs or within the AfCFTA negotiations—and strengthen regulatory frameworks for key service sectors. The programme additionally includes elements to strengthen the capacity of AU officials helping member States negotiate service trade, and to promote active private sector engagement in discussing and designing service policy and negotiating services at the regional, continental and multilateral levels. To better coordinate the work, the SSDP outlines steps allowing the AUC Department of Trade and Industry to liaise more effectively with the RECs. The programme also sets out a communication strategy to improve the available information and knowledge on services.

The service sector in Africa

In most African countries, the service sector constitutes the largest segment of the economy. During 2000–12, it contributed an increasing share of GDP, trade and employment. Efficient and competitive service economies and trade in services, especially in finance, transport, energy, telecommunications and other infrastructure services, could improve the African economic outlook considerably (UNCTAD, 2015b).

Many African economies are shifting from agriculture to services without developing manufacturing that would entail productivity improvements, formal job creation, exports of sophisticated goods and the application of technology to the wider economy).

Box figure 3.4.1:
Sectoral shares of real gross domestic product by percentage and value, 2000–12

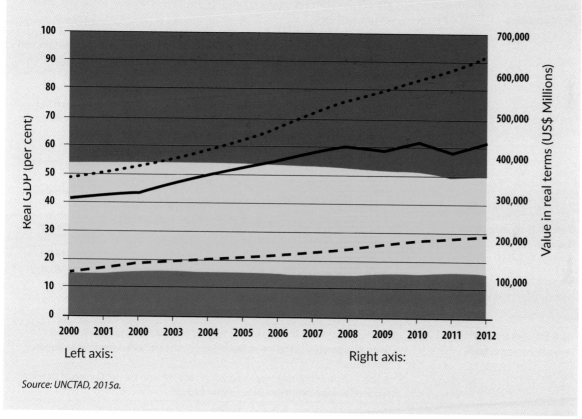

Left axis: Right axis:

Source: UNCTAD, 2015a.

Trade facilitation measures

Trade facilitation simplifies, harmonizes and automates import and export procedures to reduce the costs businesses face complying with trade requirements. It can include modernizing border procedures, improving transparency and predictability and eliminating procedural inefficiencies, while ensuring that trade complies with legitimate public policy objectives, such as consumer welfare, health and safety standards and environmental sustainability.

Trade facilitation addresses non-tariff barriers (NTBs) that can burden businesses even more than traditional tariffs. The gains from tariff reductions could be dwarfed by gains from eliminating NTBs and increasing regulatory collaboration (Vanzetti, Peters and Knebel, 2018). So, the AfCFTA has many provisions to ease compliance with import and export procedures for African businesses (Table 3.2). The provisions are to be implemented through a system of national focal persons in coordination with committees and sub-committees established under the institutions of the AfCFTA.

Table 3.2:

AfCFTA agreement trade facilitation reforms

AFCFTA PROVISIONS	CORE REFORMS
Trade in Goods annex 1: Schedules of tariff concessions	• Specifies schedules for the gradual elimination of tariffs on goods for each State party
Trade in Goods annex 2: Rules of origin	• Clarifies the rules to be satisfied by businesses in order to qualify for the preferential tariffs, as specified in annex 1
Trade in Goods annex 3: Customs cooperation and mutual administrative assistance	• Articles 3 and 4. Adopt harmonized customs nomenclature and non-discriminatory and transparent customs valuation systems • Article 5. Simplify and use harmonized customs procedures • Article 6. Use automated customs processing systems • Articles 9 and 12. Exchange customs information • Article 8. Identify contact points for investigating customs offenses through which to cooperate over the prevention, investigation and suppression of customs offenses
Trade in Goods annex 4: Trade facilitation	• Article 4. Transparency, including publication of trade compliance procedures, duties and relevant laws • Article 5. Identify country enquiry points for trade facilitation • Articles 6, 7 and 9. Provide pre-arrival processing and advanced rulings on imports, and release of goods prior to the final determination of duties if such a determination is not done prior to arrival • Article 8. Provide for electronic payment of duties, fees and charges • Article 10 and 11. Adopt risk management systems to focus customs checks on high-risk consignments, avoid arbitrary discrimination and conduct post-clearance audits • Article 12. Publish average release times for customs • Article 13. Use "authorised operator regimes" to ease customs compliance • Article 14 and 15. Provide for expedited shipments regimes, especially for air cargo and perishable goods • Article 16, 17, 18 and 20. Use international standards, ICT and uniform documentation, and endeavour to establish single windows
Trade in Goods annex 5: Non-tariff barriers	• Article 3. Encourages use of a common categorization system for NTBs to improve transparency over NTBs • Articles 4, 5, 6, 7, 8, 9, 10 and 14. Establishes national monitoring committees and country focal persons for identifying, resolving and monitoring NTBs, in coordination with a continental committee on NTBs and REC NTB monitoring mechanisms • Articles 12 and 13. Creates a mechanism for identifying, reporting and monitoring NTBs to facilitate the elimination of NTBs within the AfCFTA
Trade in Goods annex 6: Technical barriers to trade	• Articles 6, 7, 8, 9 and 10. Cooperate in the field of standardization, development and implementation of technical regulations, conformity assessment, accreditation, metrology • Article 11. Ensure transparency and predictability through the notification of technical regulations and conformity assessment procedures
Trade in Goods annex 7: Sanitary and phytosanitary measures	• Article 5. Obliges State parties to use sanitary and phytosanitary (SPS) measure protections for legitimate reasons and not to frustrate trade • Article 6. Base SPS measures on regional conditions, including pest- or disease-free areas and areas of low pest or disease prevalence • Article 7. SPS measures of exporting State parties to be judged as equivalent to those of the importing State party after demonstration of appropriate risk assessment measures • Article 8. Cooperate to harmonize SPS measures based on international standards • Article 11. Cooperate to improve transparency in the application of SPS measures through the identification of national focal persons
Trade in Goods annex 8: Transit	• Articles 4, 5, 6 and 9. Provide for the licencing of transit carriers with approved AfCFTA transit documentation and procedures
Trade in services	• Article 10. Encourages the mutual recognition of standards or criteria for the authorization, licencing or certification of services suppliers

Source: ECA analysis of the Agreement Establishing the AfCFTA.

The AfCFTA trade facilitation provisions are closely related to those in the WTO Trade Facilitation Agreement, so countries can align their efforts to abide by commitments in both the AfCFTA and the Trade Facilitation Agreement. In particular, countries may use aid for trade support committed through the WTO Trade Facilitation Agreement Facility to help finance required trade facilitation improvements.

African countries can take complementary and reinforcing trade facilitation measures in the context of the AfCFTA: implementing an AfCFTA NTB reporting, monitoring and elimination mechanism; investing in standards infrastructure and harmonization and introducing an AfCFTA simplified trade regime.

AfCFTA non-tariff barrier mechanisms

Low levels of intra-African trade are in large part caused by proliferating and persistent non-tariff barriers (NTBs), diverging sanitary and phytosanitary (SPS) measures and technical barriers to trade (TBT).

NTBs—such as licences, quotas and fees and charges—are usually considered instruments of commercial policy and procedural obstacles. TBT and SPS measures are primarily implemented for legitimate and important reasons of food safety and environmental protection. They have considerable restrictive and distorting effects on international trade (Box 3.5). Although eliminating such measures is generally not an option, regulatory cooperation and transparency can alleviate their cost-raising effects.

The AfCFTA Trade in Goods annex 5 on NTBs establishes a reporting, monitoring and elimination mechanism so that private sector operators and State parties can file complaints on specific trade obstacles and governments can then try to resolve them. The annex foresees the establishment of national focal points, national monitoring committees, an NTB sub-committee and an AUC NTB coordination unit. The annex defines eight categories of NTBs: TBT; SPS measures; charges on imports; clearing and forwarding; specific limitations; other

procedural problems and transport; customs administrative entry procedures and government participation in trade and restrictive practices tolerated by governments.

The categorization thus acknowledges that TBT and SPS measures can turn into NTBs. In addition, the AfCFTA has annexes dedicated to TBT (annex 6) and SPS measures (annex 7). They are not redundant with the NTB annex but complementary to it. The NTB annex aims at the resolution of specific existing barriers, whereas the SPS and TBT annexes more systematically address regulatory cooperation to prevent the emergence of new barriers. The TBT and SPS annexes build on international best practices of promoting international standards, good regulatory practice, regulatory cooperation and transparency.

Annex 5 on NTBs builds upon the existing NTB reporting, monitoring and elimination mechanism in the COMESA–EAC– SADC Tripartite Free Trade Area, which has been implemented through the online portal *tradebarriers.org*. The Tripartite NTB mechanism allows private sector operators to report any NTBs they encounter in the region via the website, email, fax, telephone and even SMS. The system administrator forwards the complaint to national focal points, who work with national monitoring committees to resolve the issue.

As of October 2018, 532 of 616 complaints in the Tripartite area had been resolved.[3] This is a major success, even though some long-standing NTBs persist. The mechanism proves that consultative and collaborative approaches can succeed and that formal dispute settlement can usually be avoided. The online system has broken down bureaucratic barriers through a real-time NTB network connecting government officials (Hove, 2015). The online mechanism has also increased awareness and transparency. It has given the private sector, especially small and medium-sized enterprises, a voice that is heard.[4] Much can be learned from the experience of the Tripartite, and it deserves to be scaled up to the continental level through the mandate established for this in the AfCFTA annexes.

How burdensome are non-tariff barriers?

Although the aggregate price-raising effect of SPS measures, TBT and NTBs tends to be lower in Africa than in the rest of the world, the prevalence of NTBs is higher (Box Figure 1) (Cadot et al., 2015). And the costs of NTBs and TBT are high in manufacturing sectors. Barriers in manufacturing sectors are a particularly important impediment to structural transformation, industrialization and the creation of regional value chains (Saygili, Peters and Knebel, 2018).

Box figure 3.5.1:
Average price-raising effects of non-tariff measures in the world (left) and Africa (right)

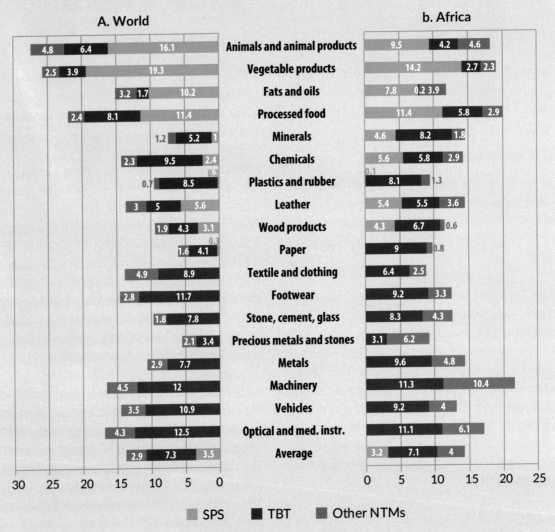

Source: Cadot et al. (2015)
Note: Non-Tariff Measures (NTMs) are policy measures other than ordinary customs tariffs that can potentially have an economic effect on imports, and include NTBs.

TBT and SPS measures impose proportionately higher costs on less advanced African countries that are less able to comply with technical requirements at a low cost and may be more likely to rely on agricultural exports, which face higher ad valorem tariff equivalents). Moreover, according to an International Trade Centre survey, more than half of African exporting and importing firms were affected by non-tariff measures, the most affected being small companies and companies in the agro-food sector (ITC, 2015).

The effective implementation of NTB reporting, monitoring and elimination mechanisms in other RECs and across RECs could have a major impact for intra-regional trade. It could make or break the AfCFTA, because without the reduction of NTBs, the impact of tariff reductions is likely to be marginal.

The NTB annex should not be implemented in isolation. Policy makers should reinforce its complementarities and synergies with the TBT and SPS annexes, for example through regular meetings of the sub-committees to be established for NTBs, SPS measures and TBT. Many NTBs could be avoided through good regulatory practice and cooperation on SPS measures and TBT.

The AfCFTA annexes provide all the right mandates and tools to reduce intra-African trade costs and deliver progress towards structural transformation, but execution will be critical. It requires a high level of sustained commitment from the political and technical levels.

Standards infrastructure and harmonization

Trade in Goods annexes 6 (TBT) and 7 (SPS) encourage cooperation on standards, which can be supported with improved infrastructure, including metrology, standardization, accreditation, quality management and conformity assessment. Compliance with standards and technical regulations signals and guarantees the quality of traded goods. This encourages trade and industrialization through (ECA, 2017):

- Protecting consumers and creating confidence in traded goods.

- Enhancing trade capacity and competitiveness.

- Facilitating mutually beneficial trade (particularly in industrial products) and the integration of firms into regional and global value chains.

- Improving the efficiency of production and trade.

- Contributing to technology upgrading and absorption.

Harmonizing standards is a mechanism the TBT and SPS annexes recommend to eliminate unnec-

essary and unjustifiable trade barriers. It is, however, expensive, requiring extensive, costly and lengthy negotiations. So, not all standards will be able to be harmonized at once, and a well-informed and appropriate prioritization strategy is needed. Due to the diverse sizes and capacities of member States' national standards bureaus, sharing best practice and regional capacity building programmes will be key to the inclusiveness of AfCFTA outcomes.

Since agricultural goods face the most stringent TBT and SPS measures, harmonizing standards can especially boost under-exploited intra-African trade in agricultural products and support agricultural employment, agro–regional value chain development and food security in Africa. At the REC level, for example, standards for nine priority staple foods—maize (grain), wheat, milled rice, dry beans, dry soybeans, maize flour, wheat flour, sorghum flour and millet flour—were launched in May 2018 by the Eastern Africa Grain Council, in partnership with the USAID East Africa Trade and Investment Hub. The standards aim to give East African farmers access better and greater markets within the region, while providing consumers with safe and high-quality food grain products. They will also reduce the risk of food shortage in the region by allowing easy movement of grains across States.

Simplified trading regimes

The EAC and COMESA simplified trading regimes (STRs) simplify the procedures required for small and informal cross-border traders to import and export (Box 3.6). The traders receive simplified certificates of origin from customs officials. And they receive a list of qualified goods, simplified customs documents and assistance in completing customs documents, clearing procedures and answering trade-related queries from the trade information desk officers at the borders. The STR addressed some of the challenges the traders face, brought them into the formal trading system and extended to them the benefits of freer trade. Informal cross-border traders interviewed in COMESA are confident their businesses will succeed and formalize just as former colleagues have "who were once 'small' like them but had graduated into 'big peo-

Informal cross-border trade in Africa

Informal cross border trade (ICBT) is an important dimension of intra-African trade. ICBT contributes about 30-40 per cent of total intra-regional trade in the Southern African Development Community (SADC) region and 40 per cent in the Common Market for Eastern and Southern Africa (COMESA) region (Nshimbi and Moyo, 2017).

In the absence of sufficient formal opportunities, ICBT is crucial to income generation, job creation and food security, particularly for Africa's most vulnerable people such as women and youth, who usually constitute the majority of informal cross-border traders. In West and Central Africa, women represent nearly 60 per cent of informal traders, and in Southern Africa, about 70 per cent (Afrika and Ajumbo, 2012). ICBT has proven more responsive to food crises than formal trade. Because it is largely practised by the officially unemployed and micro, small and medium enterprises (MSMEs), it is important for strategies of inclusion.

Challenges to traders, however, prevent the full developmental potential of ICBT. They include a lack of trade facilitation, inadequate border infrastructure, limited access to finance, a lack of market information, corruption and insecurity and limited knowledge, education and business management skills (Afrika and Ajumbo, 2012).

Although ICBT is not explicitly addressed in the AfCFTA agreement or the separate AU protocol on the free movement of people, the AfCFTA indirectly benefits informal cross-border traders. In addition, there is still time for AfCFTA implementation to incorporate ICBT issues. In particular, African countries could consider establishing a continental simplified trade regime building upon the experiences of the East African Community (EAC) and COMESA.

ple' (formalized traders) because they had successfully taken advantage of the STR" (Nshimbi, 2017). According to a recent study by COMESA, more than 75 per cent of those who had tried the STR reported quick clearance as a main benefit, more than 70 per cent said it offered an attractive tax regime and 60 per cent thought the system protected traders (Njiwa, 2013).

Introducing a continental STR under the AfCFTA would bring informal traders into the formal trading system, provide them greater protection and support their participating in the new export opportunities the AfCFTA creates. To resolve the perception of illegality, the COMESA STR officials refer to those using the scheme as *small-scale* rather than *informal* traders. The COMESA STR improves the understanding of ICBT's contribution to trade, since the STR form captures data for the UNCTAD-created Automated System for Customs Data. Improving data collection on ICBT is crucial to assessing its magnitude and ensuring that the challenges informal traders face more adequately influence national and regional trade policy.

The AfCFTA has openings to introducing a continental STR. Article 5, "Simplification and Harmonisation of Customs Procedure,'" of annex 3 on customs cooperation encourages State parties to cooperate on trade procedures. Article 28 of annex 2 on rules of origin, which currently allows small consignments of goods to be admitted as originating products without proof of origin, gives scope for simplified rules of origin for MSMEs. But they are limited to small parcels not exceeding $500 sent between private individuals or small parcels or personal luggage not exceeding $1,200, meaning that they cannot currently be used by micro, small and medium enterprises.

Designing and implementing a continental STR would best be handled at the level of the RECs and at the level of a given REC's neighbouring member States working bilaterally, since economic and market conditions are not uniform across the continent. The AfCFTA could establish an STR platform over which RECs and member States could negotiate on exchanging specific goods and services under a common list as dictated by local conditions. Such lists should aim to extend further than the common lists of the COMESA and EAC STRs (including to manufactured goods) and should reach a reasonably high threshold. Investing in outreach and knowledge dissemination on both the contents of the AfCFTA agreement and a Continental STR will also be key so as to empower cross border traders to use the STR.

Trade-related infrastructure measures

Infrastructure quality strongly influences not only export levels, but even the likelihood that exports between country pairs takes place at all (Francois and Manchin, 2007). Recent analysis has suggested that "trade logistics is the most important direct impediment to intra-regional trade," greatly exceeding the impact of tariffs in frustrating trade in Africa (IMF, 2019). To take full advantage of the AfCFTA, policy makers in Africa must complement it with trade-related infrastructure development.

Programme for Infrastructure Development in Africa

Infrastructure in Africa is weak—limiting its critical role in bringing to fruition the promise of the AfCFTA. For example, a poor road network and electricity supply shortages are among the key impediments to deploying agro-processing industries (AfDB, 2014; UNCTAD, 2018b)).

The Programme for Infrastructure Development in Africa (PIDA) comprises projects focused on a more interconnected and integrated Africa with substantially improved power generation, transport logistics, information and communications technology infrastructure and water resources. PIDA offers a vision and strategic framework for developing regional and continental infrastructure in all those areas.

The total estimated cost of all the projects identified in PIDA to address infrastructure needs projected by 2040 is $360 billion. The PIDA Priority Action Plan includes 51 priority "backbone" projects and programmes requiring $68 billion by 2020. Seeing the implementation of PIDA through

can ensure that Africa has the right infrastructure in place to take advantage of the AfCFTA.

Strategic logistics management

Strong cross-border infrastructure must be complemented with efficient transport services for their full effectiveness to be utilized. Investments in transport corridor infrastructure are necessary but not sufficient to ensure a smooth flow of goods. All too often, investments in physical infrastructure are undermined by non-physical barriers.

Such non-physical barriers include high port dwell times, road stops (including at weighbridges and police checkpoints) and cumbersome border-crossing procedures. For instance, the dwell time at the Port of Dar es Salaam was more than twice the time that goods spend on the road, while that of imports to Burundi was 75 per cent of the total time between cargo discharge at Dar es Salaam and arrival at final destination in Bujumbura (Lisinge, 2017). In another example, more than 10 weighbridges in Tanzania delay transit transport by operating only with limited working hours—some closing at 6 p.m.—while road routes include numerous police checkpoints (Lisinge, 2017).

Strategic logistics management can help overcome non-physical barriers by aligning trade facilitation efforts with new, and existing, physical infrastructure. For instance, one-stop border posts can ensure that the benefit of new road infrastructure is not undermined by customs clearance bottlenecks, while pre-arrival processing and customs risk management systems can reduce documentation delays in upgraded port facilities. Electronic cargo management, including cargo-tracking systems, can improve clearance times for transiting cargo at police and customs checkpoints. Harmonized or mutually recognized standards on vehicle load and dimension controls, carrier licences and transit plates and third-party motor insurance schemes can also ease trade flowing through new road connections.

Strategic logistics management takes a deliberate and considerate approach to aligning infrastructure development and trade facilitation. It selects appropriate transport modes for different trade volumes and composition and different product origins and destination. For instance, air transport is appropriate for transporting perishable goods over long distances, while railways and ocean freight are ideal for transporting heavy goods. Increased diversification of Africa's trade also suggests the need for countries on the continent to improve different modes of transport as appropriate—road, rail, air and maritime. Reducing transaction costs and time through sound decisions on infrastructure and service development will increase the competitiveness of African countries. Incorporating strategic logistics management into the workings of the AfCFTA committees on transit, trade facilitation and customs cooperation can ensure full use of the benefits of investments in African infrastructure, such as those made through the PIDA.

Import defence measures

Trade liberalization can impose adjustment costs on an economy as some sectors expand to take advantage of new export opportunities and other sectors react to import competition. Over the longer term, such adjustments are necessary to improve economic efficiency as resources move to where they are used most effectively. But in the short run, liberalization must be managed to defend appropriately against import competition.

Several mechanisms in the AfCFTA agreement help ease short-run adjustment shocks. Trade is liberalized only gradually—over 10 years for least-de-

Table 3.3:
Import flexibilities in the AfCFTA

GENERAL FLEXIBILITIES IN THE AGREEMENT ESTABLISHING THE AFCFTA	
Article 15. Waiver of obligations	A legal basis for a State party to request a waiver from any obligations held under the agreement and the conditions under which such a waiver will be considered
TRADE IN GOODS FLEXIBILITIES	
Article 11. Modification of schedules of tariff concessions	Flexibility for State parties in "exceptional circumstances" to request modifications to their tariff liberalization concessions and the detailed procedures to be followed therein.
Articles 17-19. Anti-dumping and countervailing measures, global safeguard measures and preferential safeguards	A scope for using trade remedies and guidelines for implementing such measures, as detailed in annex 9 on trade remedies.
Article 24 Infant industries	A basis for taking "measures for protecting" infant industries deemed to have "strategic importance at the national level" with guidelines to be adopted for implementation the article.
Article 26. General exceptions	General Agreement on Tariffs and Trade (GATT)–inspired general exceptions
Article 27. Security exceptions	GATT-inspired security exceptions
Article 28. Balance of payments	Flexibility for State parties in critical balance-of-payments difficulties, or under imminent threat of them, to take restrictive measures to remedy such circumstances.
TRADE IN SERVICES FLEXIBILITIES	
Article 14. Restrictions to safeguard the balance of payments	Flexibility for State parties in critical balance-of-payments difficulties, or under imminent threat of them, to take restrictive measures, including on payments or transfers, to remedy such circumstances
Article 15. General exceptions	GATS-inspired general exceptions
Article 16. Security exceptions	GATS-inspired security exceptions
Article 23. Modification of schedules of specific commitments	Flexibility for State parties to request modifications to their services liberalization concessions and the detailed procedures to be followed therein, including for the provision of compensatory adjustments

Source: Adapted from Sommer & MacLeod, 2019.

veloped countries (LDCs) and 5 years for non-LDCs. Countries may designate 7 per cent of their imports as "sensitive products" accorded a longer liberalization period—13 years for LDCs and 10 years for non-LDCs. A country may exclude a final 3 per cent of products from liberalization entirely, to be reviewed only at a later point. And provisions on flexibilities in the AfCFTA agreement allow State Parties to temporarily halt liberalization (Table 3.3), including annex 9 on trade remedies.

The structure of intra-African trade also helps reduce short-run adjustment costs. Intra-African trade is currently relatively small, with imports from other African countries accounting for only 15 per cent of total African imports (see Chapter 1). Of these imports, about two-thirds are intra-community, meaning that many are already liberalized through regional community free trade arrangements (ECA, AUC and AfDB, 2017). This implies that the AfCFTA will amount to relatively modest liberalization of African countries total trade. Nevertheless, measures can be taken to ensure that African countries are well prepared to monitor and react to any adverse trade flows emanating from the AfCFTA.

Trade defence remedies

Trade remedies are an important fail-safe for trade liberalization, allowing countries to take remedial action against imports that are causing, or threatening to cause, material injury to a domestic industry.

Members of the WTO would normally seek recourse to trade remedies under substantive and procedural conditions outlined in the GATT from 1994. However, 11 African Union member States are not WTO members (Algeria, Comoros, Eritrea, Equatorial Guinea, Ethiopia, Libya, São Tomé & Príncipe, Somalia, South Sudan, Sudan and Sahrawi Republic). For them, annex 9 of the AfCFTA protocol on trade in goods determines conditions for trade remedies.

The AfCFTA annex 9 on trade remedies will provide guidelines on implementing trade remedies, but they have not yet been finished. In the meantime,

"pending the adoption of the AfCFTA Guidelines, the relevant provisions of the WTO Agreements, national legislation and regional economic communities' agreements relating to trade remedies may apply, where applicable."[5]

Most African countries have little experience in satisfying the procedural conditions (which require complex investigations) for implementing trade remedies. Trade remedy institutions demand specialized legal and economic expertise that is expensive to train and retain for any but the most advanced African countries (ECA, AUC and AfDB, 2017). In preparing for the implementation of the AfCFTA, African countries should therefore pool their resources at the REC level to establish trade remedy institutions (ECA, AUC and AfDB, 2017). Doing so would extend coverage to Africa's small and less developed countries, which would otherwise not have these capacities, so that all African countries can participate in a system that enables them to protect themselves from imports from more advanced competitors outside the AfCFTA.

Competition laws and institutions

The AfCFTA helps to establish a larger and more integrated African economy. Alongside many benefits, this gives scope for cross-border anti-competitive practices. Currently, only 23 African countries have both competition laws in force and an operational competition authority to enforce them. Other African countries are not sufficiently prepared to identify, monitor and react to the presence of cross-border anti-competitive practices in their economies.

Establishing competition institutions is important to protect the benefits from liberalization in the AfCFTA from being undermined by anti-competitive practices (see Chapter 5). Like trade remedy institutions, competition institutions need expertise that can be expensive to train and retain, and so, similarly, a regional or continental approach to supporting competition institutions can prove economical (see Chapter 5).

Table 3.4:

Key elements of AfCFTA national strategies

COMPONENTS	BRIEF DESCRIPTION AND KEY ELEMENTS	CROSS-CUTTING ISSUES
Macroeconomic framework, production systems and trade patterns review	• Analysis of macroeconomic context and overview of enabling conditions for structural transformation • Identification of key macroeconomic challenges and risks • Reviews of production and trade for goods and services (including sectoral analysis)	
AfCFTA situational analysis	• Analysis of existing policy, regulatory and institutional frameworks at national and regional levels and assessment of their alignment with the AfCFTA • Assessment of capacity needs to effectively implement the AfCFTA Agreement • Review of instruments provided by the AfCFTA relevant to the national strategies, including NTB mechanism, trade facilitation arrangements, trade remedy requirements, composition of the technical committees of the AfCFTA, market access offers	
AfCFTA related risks and mitigation actions review	• Identification of potential risks and cost adjustments resulting from AfCFTA implementation • National capacity assessment to identify threatening import competition, monitor sensitive sectors, take remedial actions should such sectors experience any adverse effect • Development and enactment of required mitigation actions, covering the wide spectrum of identified potential risks and cost adjustments, if any	
Identification and prioritization of production and trade opportunities	• Identification of market opportunities and prioritization of sectors or products for value addition, trade and regional value chain development, taking into account: competitiveness, trade facilitation measures, potential for sectoral linkages, economic risks and market size, existing revealed comparative advantages, degree of market concentration or specialization, alignment with national and regional policy priorities and others	The national strategies should account for the following cross-cutting issues among others: inclusivity, gender equality, youth employment, environment and climate change, as well as digital technologies
Identification of constraints to overcome and strategic actions required	• Identification of current constraints and potential impediments, especially non-tariff barriers that would undermine competitiveness and the ability to make the most of the AfCFTA, with regards to the priority sectors and products • Identification of actions to address identified constraints • Identification of institutional and policy weaknesses and skills gaps in priority sectors • Identification of actions required to address existing and potential constraints, enhance productive capabilities, foster enabling macroeconomic environment, boost competitiveness, promote RVCs, accelerate value addition and industrialization and others	
Strategic objectives, action plan and monitoring and evaluation framework	• Mapping strategic objectives to increased trade performance, in particular in intra-African trade for both goods and services • Development of indicators for achievements, baselines and targets under each strategic objective • Development of a robust monitoring and evaluation framework, with appropriate tools and instruments to support making decisions and taking corrective actions • Establishment of AfCFTA national implementation committee	
Financing the AfCFTA implementation	• Review and identification of potential sources of funding to support effective AfCFTA implementation	
Communication and visibility plan	• Awareness raising mechanism for a better understanding of the AfCFTA agreement among all stakeholders • Designation of AfCFTA ambassadors to champion national AfCFTA implementation	

Monitoring and evaluation

The first step that African countries can take to manage the impact of intra-African trade liberalization is to ensure that effective mechanisms are in place for monitoring and evaluating the effect of the AfCFTA.

The new AU Trade Observatory, part of the AfCFTA architecture, will be the main repository of qualitative and quantitative African trade data and information. It will bridge the current trade information gap across Africa, a major impediment to intra-African trade. One of the observatory's purposes is to "monitor and evaluate the implementation process and impact of the AfCFTA" (AU, 2019).

National trade ministries should assess the likely impact of the AfCFTA to identify susceptible import sectors. Then they should assign focal persons to assess customs data (usually available monthly) to proactively analyze import patterns. And they should complement this research with platforms for private sector stakeholders to flag deleterious import stress. Such arrangements will monitor trade both within Africa under the AfCFTA and with competitors outside Africa.

National AfCFTA strategies: A coherent approach to complementary measures

This chapter has identified complementary measures along the export path that countries can take to fully use the AfCFTA. National AfCFTA strategies ensure a coherent and strategic approach towards those measures.

The Conference of African Ministers of Finance, Planning and Economic Development recognized and clearly articulated the need for national AfCFTA strategies during their May 2018 meeting in Addis Ababa, and the July 2018 AU Summit in Nouakchott reiterated it. Through national AfCFTA Strategies, countries identify their comparative advantages within the scope of the AfCFTA agreement and target complementary measures towards those sectors. AfCFTA national strategies complement each State party's broader trade policy to the agreement and identify the key trade opportunities, current

constraints and steps required to take full advantage of the AfCFTA.

The cross-cutting issues of gender equality, environment and climate change should receive attention in national strategies (see Appendix 3A for guidelines on mainstreaming gender into AfCFTA national strategies). These issues are critical if African countries are to maximize their economic diversification and trade potential. Women are key players across all economic sectors in Africa, particularly trade. They constitute more than 70 per cent of small and medium enterprises in Africa and are known to invest their profits into bringing the family out of poverty. Yet, they are often marginalized owing to gender-related constraints, including legal and social norms in many countries. Mainstreaming gender with special consideration for the needs and interests of women is essential in implementing the AfCFTA. Addressing environmental issues and climate change is also necessary to promote environmentally friendly development and ensure sustainability.

For the AfCFTA national strategies to be effective, their development—from design to implementation and monitoring—should follow integrated and participatory approaches. The agreement's multi-dimensional and cross-cutting nature compels such an approach. Participation, often through multi-stakeholder consultations, allows the consideration of different actors' needs and interests and the interrelationships among them. The resulting environment will promote mutually reinforcing interests and actions from different entities, including small players—especially the micro, small and medium enterprises that are the backbone of many African economies. The multi-stakeholder process leads to synergies towards common objectives while tapping into the comparative advantages of each group of stakeholders. The results will build consensus around the key pillars of the AfCFTA national strategies and strengthen stakeholder buy-in.

During 2019, the Economic Commission for Africa (ECA) is providing support to 15 African countries to develop AfCFTA national strategies in accordance with seven key elements. (See Appendix

3B for guidelines that expand on each of these components.)

Key message and policy recommendations

Key message

To take full advantage of the AfCFTA, countries must buttress its implementation with complementary measures in investment, production, trade facilitation, trade-related infrastructure and import defence.

Policy recommendations

- **Investment in the AfCFTA can be supported through:** (1) national investment plans that channel investment flows into sectors that benefit from AfCFTA market liberalization; (2) investment promotion agencies to attract and facilitate investment, including through "matchmaking" between international and domestic firms, one-stop shop centres for investors, and measures detailed in the UNCTAD Global Action Menu for Investment Facilitation and (3) partnerships with other African countries to learn from their experiences and with UNCTAD and ECA for support with UNCTAD investment policy reviews and UNCTAD/ECA online investor guides.

- **A productive capacity development agenda can support a country in producing the goods demanded by the AfCFTA market through:** (1) an industrial policy to create a supportive and facilitative overarching enabling environment, (2) sector-specific strategies that take a regional approach to value chains development and (3) the AUC Service Sector Development Programme, which seeks to provide a blueprint for the development of competitive services sectors in Africa.

- **Trade facilitation measures can support AfCFTA trade opportunities through:** (1) an effectively designed AfCFTA non-tariff barrier mechanism, (2) investment in standards infrastructure and strategically harmonizing standards in sectors with high AfCFTA potential and

(3) introduction of a continental simplified trade regime, to help small and informal traders gain from the AfCFTA.

- **Trade-related infrastructure for pursuing the opportunities of the AfCFTA can be supported through:** (1) effective implementation of the Programme for Infrastructure Development in Africa and (2) strategic logistics management to align trade facilitation with infrastructure development.

- **Import defence measures can help to manage import competition from the AfCFTA through:** (1) pooled resources to establish regional trade remedy institutions at the REC level, (2) competition institutions established or reinforced at the regional or continental levels, (3) ministries of trade focal persons assigned by the ministry of trade to proactively assess likely import implications of the AfCFTA and monitor customs data for changing import patterns and (4) platforms sponsored by the ministry of trade for private sector stakeholders to flag import stress.

- **National AfCFTA strategies can provide a coherent and strategic approach towards measures to complement the AfCFTA.** They should incorporate gender mainstreaming to ensure that the gains from the AfCFTA support gender equality.

Appendix 3A
Methodology for gender mainstreaming in AfCFTA national strategies

Introduction

The importance of gender equality for the development of international trade and economic cooperation is recognized in the preamble of the Agreement Establishing the African Continental Free Trade Area (AfCFTA), while article 3(e) of the agreement emphasizes the promotion of gender equality as one of the general objectives of the AfCFTA. Gender mainstreaming in AfCFTA national strategies is key to achieving gender equality and women's empowerment within the context of the AfCFTA, Agenda 2063 and the 2030 Agenda for Sustainable Development. Gender mainstreaming is defined as

the process of assessing the implications for women and men of any planned action, including legislation, policies or programmes, in all areas and at all levels, . . . a strategy for making women's as well as men's concerns and experiences an integral dimension of the design, implementation, monitoring and evaluation of policies and programmes in all political, economic and societal spheres so that women and men benefit equally and inequality is not perpetrated. The ultimate goal is to achieve gender equality.

The AfCFTA provides an opportunity to champion gender and trade issues important to the continent's development agenda, but gaps will persist in the absence of complementary policy measures to maximize the benefits from trade liberalization and ensure an equitable distribution of these benefits.

As African Union member States craft implementation strategies to harness the opportunities of the AfCFTA, they must give further consideration to the potential differential impact of AfCFTA provisions and identify measures to ensure that the AfCFTA does not exacerbate existing gender gaps but contributes to greater equality of opportunities in an integrated continental market. To minimize negative effects, gender mainstreaming will be applied to AfCFTA national implementation strategies. This process will guide member States on policy measures and interventions to enhance women's economic opportunities under the AfCFTA, as an intrinsic component of gender equality and women's empowerment. The following discussion presents a methodological approach and framework for mainstreaming gender in the development of AfCFTA national strategies.

A methodological framework for mainstreaming gender in AfCFTA national strategies

Developing a methodological framework for gender mainstreaming in AfCFTA national strategies includes the following three stages:

Stage 1: Literature review

This literature review aims to highlight key gender and trade issues in specific sectors and occupations where women are concentrated in African economies. Special attention will be paid to the participation of African women in: (a) agriculture, (b) informal and cross-border trade and (c) export sectors as a major source of economic activity and employment, and to other channels of impact, including in non-trade sectors. The literature review, in providing a broad overview of priority issues, opportunities and constraints facing women in priority sectors of African economies, will inform requirements for gender-related data that must be collected at the country level.

Stage 2: Data collection

Gender mainstreaming in the development of AfCFTA national strategies requires an accurate understanding of the country context and existing gender relations in key industrial and trade sectors. Mapping is required to better understand the gender dimension in trade and industrial sectors that member States want national trade and investment strategies to prioritize and in priority sectors where women are concentrated. Gender-related data and information—both quantitative and qualitative—must be collected to inform this process. Among potential data sources are:

- Population census.

- Labour force surveys.

- Household-based sample surveys.

- National development plans, national or global surveys and research studies.

Given the limited data on gender and trade, a more specific gender diagnostic will require identifying key informants and conducting primary research in country through surveys, interviews and focus group discussions.

Stage 3: Gender analysis

The collected gender-disaggregated information will inform a gender analysis. A targeted gender analysis will ensure that the concerns and experiences of African women and men are integral to the design and implementation of AfCFTA national strategies, so that both benefit equally and existing gaps and patterns of inequality are not exacerbated by the AfCFTA. Such analysis will highlight:

- Economic sectors where women are concentrated and most actively involved, highlighting key gender issues, opportunities and distribution of benefits.

- Gender-based constraints that limit women's productivity and full inclusion in key sectors.

- Opportunities for women under the AfCFTA in identified sectors, and potential negative effects.

- Policy measures, interventions and support from governments towards gender equality and women's economic empowerment under the AfCFTA.

Stage 4: Gender mainstreaming in AfCFTA national strategies

The analysis of gender mainstreaming will culminate in a separate gender and trade chapter in AfCFTA national strategies. Gender mainstreaming must be undertaken in close collaboration with ministries of gender and trade and other relevant line ministries, as well as with regional economic communities. That collaboration will ensure that the integration of gender considerations in AfCFTA

national strategies is realistic and practical and that strategies build upon and complement existing national and regional gender frameworks and meet countries' needs and requests. Gender ministries and gender focal points in other ministries should play a central role in monitoring the implementation of commitments, actions and measures to ensure that women benefit equally from an integrated and growing continental market under the AfCFTA.

Conclusion

It is vital that gender be mainstreamed in AfCFTA national strategies for the AfCFTA and trade to contribute to industrialization and sustainable development. A systematic approach to gender-specific outcomes in the design of these strategies will support African women entrepreneurs, traders and producers in accessing new economic opportunities, thereby making intra-African trade under the AfCFTA a driver for inclusive and sustainable development. In this way, gender mainstreaming will further advance national development goals, gender equality and women's economic empowerment, within the context of Agenda 2063 and the 2030 Agenda.

Appendix 3B
Components of AfCFTA national strategies

Macroeconomic framework, production systems and trade patterns review

National strategies should be placed within a review of the country's macroeconomic framework, production systems and trade patterns for both goods and services. A review may include the following sub-components:

- *Macroeconomic framework:* The macroeconomic framework outlines recent developments in the country and its sub-region, depicts enabling conditions for structural transformation and identifies key macroeconomic challenges and risks. It may include the main economic and social development trends (economic growth and value added by sectors, fiscal and monetary indicators, debt sustainability, demography, education, employment, poverty and inequality and gender profiles); the level and structure of public and private investment, including foreign direct investment; technological progress and research and development; energy intensity and environmental sustainability.

- *Production systems and trade patterns for goods and services:* This review appraises the national production systems and trade patterns for both goods and services in national, regional, continental and global contexts.[6] It may analyze the sectoral growth of the economy and identify the most important sub-sectors for GDP and employment. It should identify the leading firms and services providers in key sub-sectors and describe, where possible, their main economic characteristics (capital employed, trading patterns, net sales, profitability, employment and research and development). The review carefully analyzes current patterns of intra-regional trade, by sector and destination and identifies opportunities for increased trade.[7] It can include analysis of existing regional value chains for goods and services, identifying constraints and opportunities. The review should cover transport and infrastructure networks and other trade facilitation measures. It should look at gender dimensions, examining female participation in the country's economic activities and identifying critical sectors for women in order to determine how the AfCFTA can advance gender equality and women's economic empowerment.

AfCFTA situational analysis

This component of the national strategy thoroughly analyzes national institutional frameworks and identifies capacity gaps and needs that must be filled to effectively implement the AfCFTA and other trade agreements. Such analysis may systematically screen the AfCFTA agreement's provisions and map them against relevant capacity needs.

The situational analysis should thoroughly examine policy, regulatory and institutional frameworks at national and regional levels and assess their coherence.[8] It should consider national development plans and specific policies and strategies for industry, trade, education, human rights, social policy, and other areas.[9] It must assess coherence among the national policies and their alignment with regional and continental frameworks, in particular the AfCFTA, identifying gaps or potential conflicts.

The situational analysis should also review particular instruments provided by the AfCFTA. They include AfCFTA provisions for a non-tariff barrier mechanism, trade remedy requirements, the technical committees of the AfCFTA and the products being liberalized under the agreement. The analysis should include the issues addressed in the AfCFTA phase II negotiations—investment, competition policy and intellectual property rights.

AfCFTA related risks and mitigation actions review

This component contributes to designing a compensatory mechanism for member States affected negatively by implementing the AfCFTA. It identifies risks and any cost adjustments that would result. The potential costs might be due to reallocated resources—possibly lost tariff revenues—that bring challenges to the government and shrinkage to economic sectors, temporarily increasing unemployment.

The review should specifically identify the possibility of adverse import competition resulting from the AfCFTA implementation. It will assess the national capacity to identify threatening import competition, monitor sensitive sectors and take remedial actions (including through trade remedies and safeguards) should such sectors experience any adverse effect.

This component should pay specific attention to vulnerable groups. Human rights, gender mainstreaming, environmental concerns and food security are among the issues to examine.

Mitigation actions should be developed and enacted to cover the spectrum of identified risks and possible cost adjustments.

Identification and prioritization of production and trade opportunities Maximizing the benefits of the AfCFTA implies carefully identifying market opportunities and prioritizing sectors and products for trade, value addition and regional value chain development under the agreement. A statistical analysis considering various scenarios of tariff liberalization can be used to make these identifications. Systematic screenings to identify promising export markets within the context of the AfCFTA are needed. Key indicators could include existing revealed comparative advantages; assessed economic risks; market size for trade; trade facilitation measures; market concentration and specialization; the prevalence of non-tariff barriers, sanitary and phytosanitary measures and technical barriers to trade; potential sectoral linkages with micro, small and medium-sized enterprises and alignment with national and regional policy priorities.[10] Gender-specific outcomes in industrial and trade opportunities must be examined closely.

Priority sectors should also identified in line with the key decisions of the African Union on sensitive product and exclusion lists, anti-concentration clauses and double qualification: 90 per cent of tariff lines are to be classified as non-sensitive, 7 per cent as sensitive and 3 per cent as excluded,

but in a way that 90 per cent of import value is non-sensitive.

The Economic Commission for Africa's (ECA) analysis finds that African countries should keep their exclusion lists to a minimum in order to maximize the trade-related gains. [11] ECA's empirical work further indicates that a 100 per cent liberalization would still generate greater benefits for African countries than a liberalization with exclusions and sensitive imports, so that the absence of excluded lists is ultimately preferred and should be a long-term objective under the AfCFTA. These results are corroborated by similar United Nations Conference on Trade and Development (UNCTAD) analysis (Saygili, Peters and Knebel, 2018).

Beyond being limited as much as possible, any excluded list must differ as little as possible between countries to avoid creating market access distortion. This is particularly important for a continental customs union that will require harmonization of African countries' external tariff structures towards the rest of the world. So, sensitive and excluded lists should be determined by regional groupings rather than individual countries as much as possible, and their determination in this way should be required for existing customs unions (the East African Community, Economic Community of West African States, and Southern African Customs Union).

The criteria for sensitive and excluded products will affect trade-related outcomes for African countries. An ECA toolkit suggests simple and easily implementable options to determine such criteria.[12] They relate to delaying tariff revenue losses and favouring industrialization, including green industrialization. For instance, liberalizing intermediates early on (keeping them off excluded lists) is critical to ensuring that intra-African trade in industrial products will be strongly stimulated by the AfCFTA reform.

Identification of constraints to overcome and strategic actions required for priority sectors

This component of the national strategy identifies current constraints and potential impediments that, if not addressed, would undermine a country's competitiveness and ability to make the most of the AfCFTA. Attention focuses on constraints that impede the country's ability to position itself on strategic segments of regional value chains, tap into new market opportunities and boost priority sectors identified under the strategy. Impediments to businesses, including difficulties in accessing such inputs as capital, labour and land, should be identified. The strategic actions needed to address constraints should also be determined.

Among impediments, non-tariffs barriers (NTBs) should receive particular attention, including infrastructure gaps (both soft and hard) confronting businesses, undermining their competitiveness in production and trade and inhibiting their ability to develop or integrate value chains in priority sectors at the national, regional and global level. UNCTAD analysis shows that eliminating NTBs and addressing regulatory non-tariff measures (NTMs)—as covered under the AfCFTA annexes on sanitary and phytosanitary measures and technical barriers to trade—would increase the benefits of the AfCFTA (Vanzetti, Peters and Knebel, 2018). Import- and export-related challenges can be raised to NTBs and regulatory measures. When applied to imports, they increase consumer prices or the prices of intermediate goods, which could hinder the development of value chains. When applied by other AfCFTA member States, they create a challenge to exporters in the exporting country. Both perspectives are important.

UNCTAD and the African Union Commission are implementing a project to build a continental NTB reporting, monitoring and eliminating mechanism. Private sector operators will have the opportunity to report NTBs that they experience in their day-to-day operations. To negotiate and resolve barriers, member State governments need to establish functioning institutions, as stipulated in the AfCFTA annex on NTBs.

UNCTAD's comprehensive data collection on NTMs can help to identify and assess potential obstacles to trade opportunities, both imports and exports. Data collection will build on past and ongoing initiatives in several regional economic communities

(RECs).[13] In some countries, NTM data is already available, in others, NTM data collection can be incorporated into the development of the AfCFTA national strategies.

The analysis under this component should stratify businesses into categories by cluster and size to the extent possible. Challenges faced by small and medium-sized enterprises, especially women-owned businesses, must be identified and recommendations proposed to improve productivity, enhance trade and move towards achieving the right to work and reaching other human rights indicators, including poverty reduction and gender equality.

Capacity and skill gaps at all levels in both the public and private sector must be identified. They include institutional weaknesses and policy gaps impairing AfCFTA implementation and skill gaps diminishing businesses opportunities. Lessons from *Guiding Principles on Business and Human Rights* could be incorporated.[14]

Once the constraints are identified, this component of the national strategy maps out actions to address gaps and boost the identified priority sectors to their highest potential within the AfCFTA context. Actions will address existing and potential constraints and enhance productive capabilities, foster an enabling macroeconomic environment, boost competitiveness, promote regional value chains and accelerate value addition and industrialization. Complementary activities will attract and increase sectoral investments, and develop or promote infrastructure and quality systems. Other strategic actions will advance the integration of digital economy tools to enhance trade facilitation, trade information and trade monitoring.

Strategic objectives in an action plan with effective monitoring and evaluation

The national strategies should include key objectives for increasing trade performance, particularly intra-African trade in goods and services. Key issues include capacities, regional context, country priority sectors, AfCFTA-related risks and opportunities under the AfCFTA for regional and global value chain integration. Indicators are to be developed under each strategic objective for baselines, targets and achievements. These elements will form the basis of the national strategy's action plan and an effective monitoring and evaluation (M&E) framework that provides timely and accurate data for decision making and corrective actions. The M&E should utilize a results-based management approach, incorporating the "PANEL" principles—participation, accountability, non-discrimination, empowerment and legality. The action plan and its M&E framework should be overseen by an AfCFTA national implementation committee, consonant with the AU general assembly decision in Nouakchott in July 2018.[15]

The M&E framework should identify tools and indicators to assess the implementation of the national strategy. They could include the trade observatory led by AUC and the International Trade Centre and the AfCFTA Country Business Index proposed by ECA. These indicators should include accurate gender-disaggregated data to measure the overall impact of the AfCFTA on men and women and allow gender analysis of specific interventions. To develop adequate data collection and consultative and monitoring processes, international assistance and other forms of cooperation should be sought through human rights channels and the World Trade Organization's Aid for Trade initiative.

Cross-cutting issues

The national strategy must account for such cross-cutting issues as inclusivity, gender equality, youth employment, environment, climate change and technology. These issues are critical to Africa maximizing its economic diversification and trade potential.

Examining inclusivity is important to ensuring that the AfCFTA implementation does not impair government abilities to fulfil human rights obligations and to pursue sustainable development policies regardless of trade challenges.

Gender equality is central to creating more sustainable and inclusive African economies and societies. Women are key players in the African economic sector, particularly in trade, whether formal or informal. Women do more than half of the informal cross-border trading in Africa. Informal cross-border traders stand to benefit from reduced import duties and simplified trade regimes if member States address some of the key challenges facing them, such as a lack of trade facilitation, inadequate border infrastructure, limited access to finance, a lack of market information, corruption and insecurity, gender-based violence and limited knowledge, education and business management skills.[16] The priority needs and concerns of women cross-border traders should be explicitly considered in implementing the AfCFTA, which has the potential to advance their entrepreneurship and to enhance their rights.

Addressing environmental and technology issues is also necessary to promote environmentally friendly development while realizing the full potential of digitalization. Environmental impacts could follow greater economic and trade engagement under the AfCFTA. So, requirements to sustain the environment in the AfCFTA context are to be examined. The opportunities and challenges of the fourth industrial revolution also warrant attention, especially the digital economy, which incorporates Internet-based changes leading to advanced robotics and factory automation (advanced manufacturing), the Internet of things, cloud computing, big data analytics and artificial intelligence (UNCTAD, 2017b). Specific attention should be given within the digital divide to the gender divide. The proportion of women using the Internet on the continent is 25 per cent lower than the proportion of men—a considerable challenge in harnessing the technology-driven fourth industrial revolution for inclusive and sustainable development.

The national strategy analysis of cross-cutting issues should focus on how these opportunities could reduce costs and increase efficiencies in priority sectors under the AfCFTA. The ability and readiness of countries to embrace the digital economy, in particular e-commerce, with its potential to offer equality of opportunity to women as entrepreneurs and traders, should be thoroughly examined.

Financing the AfCFTA implementation

The national strategy document should review and identify all the potential sources of funding to support AfCFTA implementation. This component should develop mechanisms to seek and mobilize financial resources from governments, the private sector and development partners to support implementation of the national strategies.

Communication and visibility plan

The AfCFTA national strategies should incorporate a strong mechanism for communication, advocacy and outreach. The communication and visibility plan should aim to raise awareness and understanding of the AfCFTA and leverage benefits of the agreement for stakeholders, including government, the private sector and civil society. A number of communication activities could be undertaken, including development of communications instruments (video and audio materials, among others) and the organization of awareness events around AfCFTA.

The communication strategy for the AfCFTA could seek designation of ambassadors, preferably from the private sector, to deliver key messages. The AfCFTA brand should be also widely promoted through all communication activities.

References

AfDB (African Development Bank). 2014. "Tracking Africa's Progress in Figures." Tunis: African Development Bank.

Afrika J., and G. Ajumbo. 2012. "Informal Cross Border Trade in Africa: Implications and Policy Recommendations." Africa Economic Brief 3 (10), African Development Bank, Tunis, Tunisia.

Afreximbank (African Export–Import Bank). 2018. *Africa Trade Report 2018. Boosting Intra-African Trade: Implications of the African Continental Free Trade Area Agreement.* Cairo: Afreximbank.

AU (African Union). 2019. "Signing of the Joint Letter of Intent between the African Union Commission, the European Union Commission, the International Trade Centre and Regional Economic Communities for the implementation of the African Union Trade Observatory Project." Addis Ababa, Ethiopia: AU. Available at: https://au.int/en/newsevents/20190209/signing-joint-letter-intent-between-african-union-commission-european-union.

BASF. n.d. "Food Value Chain Collaborations for Smarter Crop Production." Available at: https://agriculture.basf.com/en/Crop-Protection/Food-Value-Chain.html.

Cadot, O., A. Asprilla, J. Gourdon, C. Knebel and R. Peters. 2015. "Deep Regional Integration and Non-tariff Measures: A Methodology for Data Analysis." Policy Issues in International Trade and Commodities Study Series 69, UNCTAD (United Nations Conference on Trade and Development), Geneva.

ECA (United Nations Economic Commission for Africa). 2017. *Transforming African Economies Through Smart Trade and Industrial Policy.* Addis Ababa, Ethiopia: ECA.

ECA, AUC (African Union Commission) and AfDB. 2017. *Assessing Regional Integration in Africa VIII: Bringing the AfCFTA About.* Addis Ababa, Ethiopia: ECA.

Francois, J., and M. Manchin. 2007. "Institutions, Infrastructure and Trade." Policy Research Working Paper 4152. World Bank, Washington, DC.

IMF (International Monetary Fund). 2019. "Is the African Continental Free Trade Area a Game Changer for the Continent?" In *Sub-Saharan Africa Regional Economic Outlook 2019.* Washington, DC: International Monetary Fund.

Hove, V. S. 2015. "An Analysis of How the Online Non-Tariff Barriers Mechanism Facilitates Reporting, Monitoring and Elimination of NTBs in the COMESA, EAC and SADC Region." Research Report, Graduate School of Business, University of Cape Town.

International Trade Centre. 2015. "The Invisible Barriers to Trade: How Businesses Experience Non-Tariff Measures." Geneva: International Trade Centre. Available at: http://www.intracen.org/uploadedFiles/intracenorg/invisiblebarriers.pdf.

Lisinge, R. T. 2017. "Managing Africa's Regional Transport Infrastructure Programmes: Partnerships and Performance." Doctoral dissertation, Maastricht School of Management.

Njiwa, D. 2013. "Tackling Informal Cross-border Trade in Southern Africa." *Bridges Africa* 2 (1).

Nshimbi, C. C. 2017. "The Human Side of Regions: Informal Cross-border Traders in the Zambia–Malawi–Mozambique Growth Triangle and Prospects for Integrating Southern Africa." *Journal of Borderlands Studies.* DOI: 10.1080/08865655.2017.1390689.

Nshimbi C. C., and I. Moyo (eds.). 2017. *Migration, Cross-Border Trade and Development in Africa: Exploring the Role of Non-state Actors in the SADC Region.* Palgrave Studies of Sustainable Business in Africa. Cham, Switzerland: Palgrave Macmillan.

Oqubay, Arkebe. 2015. *Made in Africa: Industrial Policy in Ethiopia.* Oxford, UK: Oxford University Press.

Saygili, M., R. Peters and C. Knebel. 2018. "African Continental Free Trade Area: Challenges and Opportunities of Tariff Reductions." Research Paper 15, UNCTAD (United Nations Conference on Trade and Development), Geneva.

Sommer, L., and J. MacLeod. 2019. "How Important is Special and Differential Treatment for an Inclusive AfCFTA?" In *Inclusive Trade in Africa: The African Continental Free Trade Area in Comparative Perspective*, edited by D. Luke and J. MacLeod. Routledge.

UNCDP (United Nations Committee for Development Policy). 2016. "Expanding Productive Capacity for Achieving the Sustainable Development Goals." New York: UNCDP. Available at: http://www.un.org/en/development/desa/policy/cdp/cdp_news_archive/2016_ecosoc%20report_ch2.pdf.

UNCTAD (United Nations Conference on Trade and Development). 2006. *The Least Developed Countries Report: Developing Productive Capacities.* Geneva: UNCTAD.

———. 2015a. *Economic Development in Africa Report: Unlocking the potential of Africa's Services Trade for Growth and Development*. Geneva: UNCTAD.

———. 2015b. "Non-Tariff Measures and Regional Integration in the Southern African Development Community." Research Paper 5 (UNCTAD/DITC/TAB/2014/5), UNCTAD, Geneva.

———. 2016a. *African Continental Free Trade Area: Developing and Strengthening Regional Value Chains in Agricultural Commodities and Processed Food Products*. Geneva: UNCTAD.

———. 2016b. "Trading into Sustainable Development: Trade, Market Access, and the Sustainable Development Goals." Developing Countries in International Trade Studies. Geneva: UNCTAD.

———. 2017a. *Investment Facilitation: The Perfect Match for Investment Promotion*. Geneva: UNCTAD. Available at: https://unctad.org/en/PublicationsLibrary/webdiaepcb2017d4_en.pdf.

———. 2017b. *The New Digital Economy and Development*. Geneva: UNCTAD.

———. 2018a. *World Investment Report 2018: Investment and New Industrial Policies*. Geneva: UNCTAD.

———. 2018b. *Economic Development in Africa Report 2018: Migration for Structural Transformation*. Geneva: UNCTAD.

UNDESA (United Nations Department of Economic and Social Affairs). 2017. *Expanding Productive Capacity: Lessons Learned from Graduating Least Developed Countries*. New York: UNDESA.

Vanzetti, D., R. Peters and C. Knebel. 2018. "Non-tariff Measures: Lifting CFTA and ACP Trade to the Next Level." Research Paper 14 (UNCTAD/SER.RP/2017/14), UNCTAD (United Nations Conference on Trade and Development), Geneva.

Endnotes

1 The five priority sectors for negotiations in trade in services are: transport, communications, tourism, financial and business services.

2 For more, see http://investmentpolicyhub.unc-tad.org/Publications/Details/148. Accessed on 9 November 2018.

3 Statistics shown on www.tradebarriers.org, accessed on 23 October 2018.

4 While a similar mechanism was developed by a private sector-led coalition in ECOWAS, its success was limited due to a lack of government mandates and institutions to resolve NTB complaints (Hove, 2015). See Borderless Alliance website: http://www.borderlesswa.com/ .

5 Art 13, Annex 9 Trade Remedies, Protocol on Trade in Goods of the Agreement Establishing the AfCFTA.

6 There are a number of existing profiles on which the analysis can be based, such as UNIDO and UNCTAD country profiles, WTO tariff profiles and ECA country profiles.

7 National data should be used wherever possible, but can be complimented by use of international sources.

8 Relevant regulatory policies, such as competition policies, phytosanitary and safety standards, government procurement rules should all be considered in depth.

9 Relevant regulation to trade and business include national and international proclamation on Children's Rights (CRC), the Rights of All Migrant Workers (ICMW), Economic, Social and Cultural Rights (ICESCR), Discrimination against Women (CEDAW), Persons with disabilities (CRPD), Corruption (Guidelines on corruption and human rights:https://www.ohchr.org/Documents/Issues/Development/GoodGovernance/Corruption/HRCaseAgainstCorruption.pdf), Indigenous peoples' rights:

(https://documents-dds-ny.un.org/doc/UNDOC/GEN/N06/512/07/PDF/N0651207.pdf?OpenElement) the Environment (https://www2.ohchr.org/english/bodies/hrcouncil/docs/16session/A.HRC.RES.16.11_en.pdf) and relevant national legislation on internet and digital rights.

10 A number of tools and instruments exist to undertake this exercise. These include Revealed comparative advantage indicators; Decision Support Model Approach for export promotion; UNIDO's Assessment Framework; OECD's Production Transformation Policy Reviews; Product Space Analysis, to cite a few.

11 See https://www.uneca.org/publications/empirical-assessment-african-continental-free-trade-area-modalities-goods for greater details.

12 See https://www.uneca.org/publications/african-continental-free-trade-area-towards-finalization-modalities-goods.

13 UNCTAD has conducted data collection in 13 ECOWAS countries and will soon update data in some of them. In the EAC–COMESA–SADC Tripartite, UNCTAD is also currently assisting the RECs in data collection and dissemination efforts. The ITC has collected data in several North African countries.

14 See https://www.ohchr.org/documents/publications/GuidingprinciplesBusinesshr_eN.pdf.

15 See Assembly/AU/Dec. 692/(XXXI).

16 See https://www.ictsd.org/bridges-news/bridges-africa/news/the-african-continental-free-trade-area-an-opportunity-for-informal.

Chapter 4
Intellectual property rights protocol

The chapter begins by introducing intellectual property (IP) rights and discussing their interface with investment and entrepreneurship and the objectives under Agenda 2063, the international minimum standard established by the World Trade Organization (WTO) under the Agreement on Trade Related Aspects of Intellectual Property Rights (TRIPS) and subsequent norm-setting processes. This is followed by an extensive review of experiences at the regional level, including the initiatives of the African Union, regional economic communities, the African Regional Intellectual Property Organization (ARIPO), the Organisation Africaine de la Propriété Intellectuelle (OAPI) and the Pan-African Intellectual Property Organization (PAIPO). Next there are complementary lessons drawn from several case studies on the adoption and use of IP rights among African countries, the experience of regional cooperation among developing countries and the common positions advanced by African countries in multilateral processes. The chapter is concluded with an analysis of the potential elements of, and possible approach to, the development of an IP rights protocol in the African Continental Free Trade Area (AfCFTA).

Background to intellectual property rights

IP refers to creations of the mind, such as technological inventions, literary and artistic works and symbols, names and images used in commerce.[1] In principle, IP rights confer the right to prevent others from using, making and selling the subject of the protection. Box 4.1 contains a description of various categories of IP rights. Although the term IP rights appears to identify certain common characteristics, such as exclusivity and transferability, each category of IP rights has its own distinct legal approach and specific industrial and commercial application.

The African Union's Agenda 2063: The Africa We Want prioritizes science and innovation-driven manufacturing, industrialization and value addition, economic diversification and sustainable use of biodiversity.[2] As private rights utilized in the industrial and commercial context, IP rights function as policy tools to promote private investment and entrepreneurship, as well as competition and innovation, which are key to realizing these objectives. As illustrated in the United Nations Conference on Trade and Development (UNCTAD) *World Investment Report, 2011* on non-equity modes of international production and development, IP rights and other intangible assets have started to dominate global value chains.[3] A balanced IP regime, which creates private sector incentives while maintaining public policy objectives provides some of the essential tools for Agenda 2063. The AfCFTA provides an opportunity to advance an IP rights system that corresponds to the aspiration in Agenda 2063.

National IP laws determine eligibility for protection, scope of exclusive rights of the IP right holders, duration of protection, conditions for acquisition and maintenance, and rules on enforcement of IP rights. Right holders benefit from exclusive rights in the subject matter of protection, which enables them to provide a licence or transfer the IP right to others for the same purpose. IP law also determines the specific circumstances enabling third parties to use or make the subject matter protected by IP rights without the consent of the right holder. For example, patent laws may authorize researchers to undertake freely research on a protected subject matter, such as a pharmaceutical compound, without seeking authorization from the patent holder. Outside IP law, competition law and private practices have developed rules aimed at encouraging licensing of IP rights in certain circumstances, such as fair, reasonable and non-discriminatory licensing terms for patents relating to products to be made under product standards[4] or creative common licences for copyright over literary works and computer programs.[5]

Although historically there have been instances where IP rights were promoted as an extension of property rights, especially in cases of copyright, current systems of IP rights are largely developed as an incentive mechanism to promote innovation and facilitate disclosure of knowledge and the transfer of technology and know-how.[6] The TRIPS Agreement, administered by the World Trade Organization (WTO), determines, under Article 7, that the system of IP rights is an incentive mechanism and a tool to balance competing interests (TRIPS, Art. 7):

Box 4.1:
Descriptions of types of Intellectual property rights

Patents	A patent is an exclusive right granted for an invention, a product or process that provides a new way of doing something, or that offers a new technical solution to a problem.
Trademarks	A trademark is a distinctive sign that identifies goods or services of one enterprise as different from those of another.
Industrial designs	An industrial design refers to the ornamental or aesthetic aspects of an article, such as those applied to electric appliances, watches, jewellery, handicraft and textile goods.
Geographical indication	A geographical indication is a sign used on goods that have a specific geographical origin and possess qualities or a reputation due to that place of origin. Agricultural products typically have qualities that derive from their place of production and are influenced by specific local geographical factors, such as climate and soil.
Copyright and related rights.	Copyright laws grant authors, artists and other creators protection for their literary and artistic creations, generally referred to as "works".

A closely associated field is "related rights" or rights related to copyright that encompass rights similar or identical to those of copyright, although sometimes more limited and of shorter duration. The beneficiaries of related rights are performers, such as actors and musicians, in their performances; producers of phonograms, for example, compact discs, in their sound recordings and broadcasting organizations in their radio and television programmes |
| Plant variety protection | Plant variety protection, also called a "plant breeder's right", is granted to the breeder of a new plant variety. Rights extend to the propagating material and seeds. |
| Utility models | A utility model is similar to a patent but, depending on the country, limited to composition of materials and devices that represent an incremental invention. Taking a hospital bed as an example, the aesthetic aspect of the bed can be protected by an industrial design patent, whereas a utility model would protect the functional aspect of the bed. |

Source: World Intellectual Property Organization (WIPO). What is Intellectual Property? 2004.
International Union for the Protection of New Varieties of Plants (UPOV); WIPO Utility Models

The protection and enforcement of intellectual property rights should contribute to the promotion of technological innovation and to the transfer and dissemination of technology, to the mutual advantage of producers and users of technological knowledge and in a manner conducive to social and economic welfare and to a balance of rights and obligations.

The TRIPS Agreement also acknowledges the underlying public policy objectives of national systems for the protection of IP, including developmental and technological objectives, and advances principles to promote the supportiveness of IP protection and other socioeconomic objectives, such as environmental protection and public health.[7] Box 4.2 shows the case study of Safaricom in Kenya in which IP rights helped to support local innovation to address local problems.

IP rights are territorial, meaning that they apply and are enforced only within the country in which they are granted. The territorial aspect of IP rights has inspired international cooperation to harmonize the laws and administration of IP rights beginning in the nineteenth century when the Paris Convention for the Protection of Industrial Property Rights was adopted in 1883, followed by the Berne Convention for the Protection of Literary and Artistic Works in 1886. Several more treaties were negotiated thereafter.

The TRIPS Agreement came into existence in 1994 under the auspices of the World Trade Organization (WTO) as a trade-off to the demands of developing countries for an agreement on trade in agriculture and the phasing out of quotas and other restrictions on textile exports.[8] The multilateralization of IP rights may be said to have truly begun with the TRIPS Agreement, for three reasons. First, the Agreement established what is called "the interna-

Box 4.2:
Innovation and intellectual Property: the case of Safaricom

Safaricom is the largest mobile phone company in Kenya with more than 29.5 million subscribers, representing 67 per cent of the market share as of March 2018 (Communications Authority of Kenya, 2017). Safaricom has developed several products that ensure that it remains the market leader. The most successful product is the M-PESA mobile money transfer system.

M-PESA is a mobile money transfer platform that was introduced into Kenya by Safaricom. "Pesa" is the Kiswahili word for money/cash while "M" connotes mobile. The M-PESA platform offers a fast and secure means of transferring money using a mobile phone. It initially targeted the "unbankable" as a bank account is not needed for the transfer. The service has become very popular. From an initial subscription base of 20,000, numbers reached 23.6 million subscribers by March 2018 (Communications Authority of Kenya, 2017). The service is now used for payment of bills and the purchase of goods and services, including point of sale payments in all establishments, as well as online payments. Subscribers can withdraw money from their bank accounts and use it on the M-PESA platform, which functions as a mobile wallet. Safaricom has introduced the service into some neighbouring African countries.

The M-PESA system and other related software can be protected by IP regimes, such as copyright and patents. The issue of ownership of M-PESA specifically has twice been the subject of litigation, although in both cases the claim has been in relation to ownership of the idea or concept. It is important to note that an idea or concept is not protected by IP, a principle that in most jurisdictions is extended to methods of doing business. No software patent has been granted by the Kenya Industrial Property Institute for M-PESA, but it is protected under copyright. The most successful aspect of M-PESA, however, is the registered trademark that has been successfully used to brand and market the product, both nationally and regionally.

tional minimum standard" with which every WTO member should comply. Second, under TRIPS the substantive provisions of several World Intellectual Property Organization (WIPO) treaties were incorporated. Third, unlike the General Agreement on Tariffs and Trades and the General Agreement on Trade in Services, the TRIPS Agreement does not exempt regional preferential trade agreements established after it had come into force[9] (such as the AfCFTA) from providing better treatment to the nationals of the members of those agreements. In other words, agreements made by countries in the context of the AfCFTA, for example, must be extended to nationals of all WTO member States.

Beginning with the TRIPS Agreement, bilateral and regional trade agreements led by developed countries have been the main driving force behind the internationalization of IP rights. A recent study by UNCTAD indicates that many free trade agreements between developed and developing countries include mandatory obligations to agree to international treaties, particularly the International Convention for the Protection of New Varieties of Plants ("UPOV Convention"), last revised in 1991.[10] Until 1995, the 1991 UPOV Convention was accepted mainly by developed countries, but later gained acceptance by Eastern European and Central Asian countries that were acceding to the European Union or to the WTO. A number of devel-

---

Box 4.3:

From traditional knowledge to innovative applications: the case of Hoodia gordonii

Based on traditional knowledge passed from generation to generation, the indigenous San people of the Kalahari used the Hoodia gordonii as a natural appetite suppressant. The South African Council for Scientific and Industrial Research (CSIR), basing its study on the practice of the San people, undertook research on the plant that culminated in the isolation of a substance it named "P57" and that it identified as an active ingredient for a chemical product with a potential appetite-suppressant property and use as anti-obesity drug. The Council filed a patent application for production, use and related processes in South Africa in 1997, followed by an international patent application in April 1998 (WIPO, 2008) but because its capacity and specialization was in basic research and identification of potential products, it transferred the results thereof to Phytopharm (a company based in the United Kingdom focusing on plant extracts as functional foods and veterinary products) for further development and commercialization, through an IP licence.

Following initial criticism, the Council signed an access and benefit-sharing regime with the San communities. Accordingly, the San will obtain 8 per cent of all milestone payments received from the licensee by the Council as well as 6 per cent of any royalties it receives on sales of the final product (WIPO, 2008).

Although to date no product has been registered with food and medicine regulatory authorities for medicinal or supplementary use based on Hoodia gordonii, the case demonstrates the untapped potential of African traditional knowledge and genetic resources. The Nagoya Protocol on Access to Genetic Resources and the Fair and Equitable Sharing of Benefits Arising from their Utilization to the Convention on Biological Diversity that entered into force in 2014 settled the international debate and established the legal framework that many countries have incorporated under their domestic law. The dissemination of information about the traditional usage and the claims of the Council, however, triggered a hasty harvest of Hoodia gordonii for preparation of a weight loss herbal composition that endangered its survival in the wild. Consequently, although collaboration between public research organizations, the private sector and traditional communities could create a bridge between traditional and scientific knowledge for the development of innovative products, there is a need to consider the challenges of conservation.

Source: UNCTAD/Economic Commission for Africa (ECA) 2018 based on WIPO, 2008.

oping countries, including Costa Rica, Dominican Republic, Jordan, Morocco, Oman, Panama, Peru, Tunisia and Viet Nam, joined the 1991 UPOV Convention in connection with their obligations under free trade agreements which they had signed with developed countries.[11] Recent trends also show the treatment of IP rights as investment assets subject to protection under investment agreements, as discussed under section (see Chapter 6 of this report on Investment).

Developing countries have been promoting their development agenda at various forums. Within WIPO, under the development agenda sponsored by the African countries, a work programme for realigning IP rights with sustainable development objectives was agreed.[12] In the WTO, the African Group of countries led several initiatives including the Doha Declaration on TRIPS and Public Health in 2001.[13] Currently, African countries are promoting an agenda to ensure the protection of genetic resources and associated traditional knowledge in the context of the TRIPS Agreement. In exchange, the African Group of negotiators at the WTO and other developing countries offered to expand the protection of geographical indications as requested by the European Union.[14] The case of *Hoodia gordonii* (box 4.3) which was used as a natural product by the San people of the Kalahari but was later incorporated into patent claims, demonstrates the complex issues at play in the alignment of the protection of "traditional knowledge" IP rights with the development aspirations of the African peoples.

Intellectual property policy and regulatory frameworks: regional experiences in Africa

Initiatives for regional economic integration in the area of IP rights utilize three different models, as follows (Ncube, 2016):

- Arrangements for regional cooperation and sharing of experience on IP rights in general.

- Regional filing systems, usually for patents, but also for trademark and industrial designs.

- Development of one substantive law or unification of laws for members of the regional trade organization.

All these models are implemented in Africa by the African Union, regional economic communities and regional IP organizations, including ARIPO, OAPI and PAIPO.

The initiatives at the African Union and in the regional economic communities largely reflect efforts for cooperation over regional aspects of IP rights. ARIPO permits regional administration of IP rights while OAPI provides for the unification of laws of its member States.

African Union instruments

The African Union has adopted several instruments that are aimed at regulating IP rights. The most recent of these is the Continental Strategy on Geographical Indications, which was endorsed by the Second Ordinary Session of the Specialized Technical Committee on Agriculture, Rural Development, Water and Environment (Ministers' Session) in October 2017 (African Union, STC2/ARDWE/MIN, 2017). The strategy identified geographical indications as a tool for use in sustainable rural development and food security and, consequently, a legal framework should be developed at national and regional levels for their protection. Based on the study, it is recommended that a pilot project be established for registration of geographical indications, market development and raising awareness of stakeholders.

In 2000, the African Union also developed the African Model Legislation for the Protection of the Rights of Local Communities and Breeders and for Regulations of Access to Biological Resources. The Model Legislation was developed as an alternative to the 1991 UPOV Convention and to ensure the uniform implementation of the Convention on Biological Diversity.[15] The legislation provides rules and procedures for access to biological resources and arrangements for sharing benefits arising from the utilization of such biological resources, recognition of the rights of local and indigenous communities and the rights of farmers and plant breeders.

African regional economic communities

Common Market for Eastern and Southern Africa (COMESA)

Comprising 21 countries, including most members of the Southern African Development Community (SADC) and the East African Community (EAC), the Common Market for Eastern and Southern Africa (COMESA) is one of the largest African regional trading blocs. Article 104(1) (d) of the COMESA Treaty provides for information sharing on "legislation on patents, trademarks and designs". Article 128 (e) further provides as follows:

> In order to promote cooperation in science and technology development, the member States agree to jointly develop and implement suitable patent laws and industrial licensing systems for the protection of industrial property rights and encourage the effective use of technological information contained in patents.

In 2011, COMESA adopted a Policy on Intellectual Property Rights and Cultural Industries (COMESA IP Policy), which provides for the common understanding of member States on key measures to address the relationship of IP rights with development, trade, cultural industries, traditional knowledge, cultural expressions and information and communication technology, whereby member States agreed to utilize and exploit to the full the flexibilities provided in IP treaties such as the Doha Declaration on the TRIPS Agreement and Public Health and to "promote harmonization of industrial property legislation within COMESA".[16] In order to

advance national implementation of the regional policy, COMESA is developing guidelines for preparing a national IP policy.

East African Community (EAC)

The Community partners are Burundi, Kenya, Rwanda, the United Republic of Tanzania, South Sudan and Uganda. The East African Community Treaty provides for IP under Article 103 (1) (i) as follows:

> Recognizing the fundamental importance of science and technology in economic development, the Partner States undertake to promote cooperation in the development of science and technology within the Community through the harmonization of policies on commercialization of technologies and promotion and protection of intellectual property rights.

The Community Treaty further provides under Article 112.2 (n) as follows:

> [....], the Partner States undertake to adopt common policies for conservation of biodiversity and common regulations for access to management and equitable utilization of genetic resources.

Currently, the only instrument that implements the Community Treaty is the Regional Intellectual Property Policy on the Utilization of Public Health-Related WTO-TRIPS Flexibilities and the Approximation of National IP Legislation (East African Community IP Policy). The regional policy is based on the analysis of East African Community member States' national legislation designed to prompt the incorporation of TRIPS flexibilities under national laws. Under the policy, the utilization of the least developed countries' transition period for implementation of the TRIPS Agreement, extended until 2021,[17] and the transition period for the implementation of the TRIPS provision on pharmaceutical product patents and undisclosed pharmaceutical test data, which is extended until 2033,[18] are encouraged

For developing country members, the East African Community IP Policy encourages the adoption of flexibilities concerning the subject matter of protection, application of patentability criteria, exceptions to the rights conferred by patent to facilitate research and development and early release of generic medicines and an international exhaustion regime for patents, copyrights and trademarks. In terms of patent administration, the Policy recommends incorporation of pre-grant and post-grant patent opposition procedures, disclosure of the best method for implementing an invention and enforcement of competition policy.

In the Policy, member States are called upon to ratify the 2005 Protocol Amending the TRIPS Agreement which came into force on 23 January 2017, resulting in the first-ever amendment of the TRIPS Agreement, its new Article 31bis[19] The policy is designed to facilitate the export of pharmaceutical products produced in one country under compulsory licence to another developing country with no or limited pharmaceutical manufacturing capacity or to any least developed country. Article 31 further provides flexibility for re-exportation under regional trade agreements in which 50 per cent or more of its members are among the least developed countries.

The East African Community also published a draft policy on anti-counterfeiting, anti-piracy and other IP rights violations and a draft anti-counterfeit bill, 2010, neither of which has been adopted.[20]

Southern African Development Community

Article 24 of the SADC Protocol on Trade requires its 17 member States[21] to adopt policies and implement measures for the protection of IP rights, in accordance with the TRIPS Agreement. Other Southern African Development Community (SADC) instruments that buttress its IP efforts include the following:

- SADC Industrialization Strategy and Road Map (2015-2063);

- Objective (m) of Article 2 of the SADC Protocol on Science, Technology and Innovation, to "enhance and strengthen the protection of intellectual property rights" and the aspirations set out in Article 4 (k) to increase spending on

research and development as a percentage of GDP to "at least 1 per cent".

- SADC Revised Regional Indicative Strategic Development Plan (RISDP 2015-2020).

The Southern African Development Community has been developing a regional framework and guidelines on IP rights. The draft framework was endorsed during the meetings of ministers of SADC member States for science, technology and innovation in June 2018 and trade and industry in July 2018. The Protocol for the Protection of New Varieties of Plants (Plant Breeders' Rights) in SADC (referred to as "the SADC Plant Variety Protocol") adopted in August 2017, is the main substantive IP instrument that has yet to enter into force.

Tripartite free trade area

The Sharm El Sheikh Declaration launching the COMESA-EAC-SADC Tripartite free trade area (TFTA) was signed on 10 June 2015.[22] The Agreement requires 14 ratifications to enter into force. Article 9 of the TFTA Agreement states that member States shall do the following:

- Protect IP rights in a balanced manner that promotes the social and economic welfare of society through ensuring that the people of the region meaningfully benefit from and participate in advancements in the arts and science and technology.

- Adopt policies on IP rights, including the protection and promotion of cultural industries, in accordance with international agreements and cooperation.

- Cooperate and develop capacity to implement and utilize the flexibilities in all relevant international agreements on IP rights.

Phase 2 of the tripartite negotiations is intended to include IP and generate consolidated positions that will be taken forward to the negotiations related to an IP rights protocol in the AfCFTA. In view of the imminence of these negotiations, however, it would be prudent to consolidate them to avoid duplication and proceed from a single undertaking approach. The following have been suggested as key points for consideration in the TFTA negotiations:[23]

A Adoption of a regional IP exhaustion regime in order to prevent fragmentation of the market.

B Enforced ratification of the Protocol amending the TRIPS Agreement, 2005 to benefit from the facilitation of production and exportation of pharmaceuticals for a regional trade agreement in which 50 per cent or more of its members are least developed countries. (The AfCFTA will also qualify under the Protocol).

C Adoption of a tripartite regional policy on IP rights and public health based on the East African Community Regional IP Policy on the Utilization of Public Health-Related WTO-TRIPS Flexibilities and the Approximation of National IP Legislation.

D Endorsement of the Nairobi Statement on Investment in Access to Medicines[24] or adoption of a similar commitment.

E Adoption of an in-built agenda to develop a plant breeders' rights regime tailored to the interests of the region, based on the needs of the local seed industry and publicly funded agricultural research centres.

F Enforced ratification of the Marrakesh Treaty to Facilitate Access to Published Works for Persons who are Blind, Visually Impaired or Otherwise Print Disabled (2013).

G Adoption of mandatory disclosure requirements in patent laws and in plant variety protection laws, except for partner States that are members of the 1991 UPOV Convention.

H Consideration of the adoption of a tripartite agreement. which ascertains that measures in accordance with the WHO Framework Convention on Tobacco Control do not constitute an expropriation of IP assets or an infringement of IP rights.

I Adoption of measures for cooperation on patent examination, including for the sharing of patent examination results.

African regional intellectual property organizations

African Regional Intellectual Property Organization (ARIPO)

ARIPO was established in 1976 and currently has 19 member States[25]. It is designed to consolidate resources for the regional administration of IP rights and to provide a forum for negotiations. It has adopted four Protocols: the Harare Protocol (1982) for the Protection of Patents, Industrial Designs and Utility Models; the Banjul Protocol (1993) for the Protection of Trademarks; the Swakopmund Protocol (2010) for the Protection of Traditional Knowledge and Folklore; and the Arusha Protocol (2015) for the Protection of New Varieties of Plants. In addition, it adopted the African Agenda on Copyright and Related Rights in 2017. The organization is currently working towards the establishment of a regional voluntary copyright registration and notification system and is also assisting member States to establish collective management offices with enhanced operations.

The main aim of creating ARIPO was to promote, develop and harmonize IP laws and policies. Its objectives include the integration of IP into development programmes and policies, IP administration (registration, exploitation and enforcement), undertaking IP awareness initiatives, promoting capacity building and development of human resources in IP and promoting the dissemination of technological information and transfer of technology.

ARIPO is not a unitary system for the registration of IP rights but a two-tier system in which its member States retain their national IP laws and operational IP offices. However, an application for the protection of IP rights may designate some or all of the member States in which it wants to protect its rights.

The African Intellectual Property Organization (OAPI)

OAPI was created in 1962 and currently operates under the Bangui Agreement, which was adopted in 1999 and came into force in 2002. The Bangui Agreement established the substantive laws and procedures for acquisition, maintenance and enforcement of patents, utility models, trademarks, industrial designs, trade names, geographical indications and layout designs of integrated circuits. Annex 10 of the revised Bangui Agreement, which provides for plant variety protection, is considered compliant with the 1991 UPOV Convention and came into force in 2006. The organization has 17 member States,[26] with a unitary system with a uniform legislation, a common office and centralized procedures, which grant IP rights over its entire territory.

The organization pursues the following objectives: ensuring the protection and publication of industrial property titles; encouraging creativity and technology transfer using industrial property networks; and making its territory attractive to private investment through the creation of an enabling environment for the effective application of IP principles. Other objectives include establishing efficient training programmes and creating an enabling environment for the exploitation of technological innovations.

OAPI has cooperation programmes with some African national IP offices and ARIPO. The two organizations hold an annual joint commission, which is intended to facilitate a common recognition of the protection procedures in both areas and the protection of industrial property rights in Africa, thereby making the continent an attractive place for foreign investors.

Pan-African Intellectual Property Organization (PAIPO)

PAIPO, whose statute was adopted in January 2018 by 17 African Union member States[27], has some 18 functions summarized as follows in the African Union Handbook (2017):

The Pan-African Intellectual Property Organization will be responsible for promoting effective use of the intellectual property system as a tool for economic, cultural, social and technological development of the continent as well as setting intellectual property standards that reflect the needs of the African Union, its member States and regional economic communities, ARIPO and OAPI (Statute,

article 3). Membership will be open to all African Union member States (article 5), and the organization will be based in Tunisia (article 8). The Organization will be composed of a Conference of States Parties, Council of Ministers, Secretariat and Board of Appeal (article 9).

As of September 2018, only three countries have signed the Pan-African organization's Statute, namely Sierra Leone (14 July 2016), Ghana (4 July 2017) and the Comoros (29 January 2018) (African Union 2018). There are no ratifications to date.

The World Intellectual Property Organization (WIPO), ARIPO and OAPI Tripartite Committee

In 2018, WIPO, ARIPO and OAPI signed a memorandum of understanding establishing a tripartite cooperation framework between them. Pursuant to the memorandum, the Tripartite Committee:

- Coordinates and conducts joint studies on regional and international developments on the IP landscape, organizing joint seminars and workshops to build capacity of stakeholders and address topical IP rights issues, including on management and administration of IP rights;

- Collaborates in providing technical assistance for development of national IP policies and strategies, skills development for small- and medium-sized enterprises, access to and utilization of technological and scientific information for innovation, including institutional capacity building for the IP Offices of member States.[28]

Preferential trade agreements between African countries and regions and non-African partners with intellectual property provisions

The European Union concluded Euro-Mediterranean Association Agreements between 1998 and 2005 with countries in the southern Mediterranean, including Algeria, Egypt, Morocco and Tunisia from Africa. These agreements required the African partners to join the UPOV Convention and the Budapest Treaty on the International Recognition of the Deposit of Microorganisms for the Purposes of Patent Procedure. Consequently, Morocco and Tunisia joined the 1991 UPOV Convention. In addition, in 2004, Morocco entered into a free trade agreement with the United States of America, which contains IP provisions (Fink and Reichenmiller, 2006).

The economic partnership agreement between the European Union and SADC was signed on 10 June 2016 and became fully operational in April 2017. From SADC, Botswana, Lesotho, Mozambique, Namibia, South Africa and Swaziland are partners to the Agreement, which is considered in the present report in detail because it is the first such agreement between the European Union and Africa to be ratified and consequently has great significance for future partnership agreements with other African subregions.

Article 16 of the European Union-SADC Economic Partnership Agreement provides for cooperation on the protection of IP rights and reaffirms the rights, obligations and flexibilities set out in the TRIPS Agreement. It commits the parties to grant and ensure adequate, effective and non-discriminatory protection of IP rights and provide for measures to enforce such rights in accordance with the provisions of the international agreements to which they are a party. The partners agree that they "may cooperate" in matters related to geographical indications and recognize "the importance of geographical indications and origin-linked products for sustainable agriculture and rural development". In the meantime, parties should respond to reasonable requests by other parties to provide information and clarification to each other on geographical indications and other IP rights-related matters. Article 16 also notes the option for conducting future negotiations on the protection of IP rights and traditional knowledge. The approach to geographical indications and traditional knowledge under the European Union-SADC economic partnership agreement mirrors the approach within the WTO where African countries have agreed to consider the European Union agenda on geographical indications in exchange for the latter's commitment on genetic resources and associated traditional knowledge.

Intellectual property policy and regulatory frameworks: national experiences

For the 17 African countries that are members of OAPI, the policy, law and administration of IP rights is governed at the regional level. The remaining African countries have diverse laws, regulations and rates of participation in international norm-setting processes. There are, however, certain common factors in African countries' experiences with IP rights. Most African countries rely on natural resources, agriculture, tourism and light industry. Consequently, their economic growth has depended on their respective factor endowments—primarily unskilled labour and natural resources. With such economic structures, countries may find it difficult to generate enough IP rights to be competitive. A comparison with other regions and countries demonstrates the practical challenges related to IP rights:

- African countries collectively have the lowest share of global applications for IP rights and the gap between Africa and other regions is very high. The total number of patents granted for residents in 2017 in the entire continent was 1,330. In the same year, patent offices in Latin America and the Caribbean granted 1,682 patents to residents, compared to 592,508 in Asia and 116,359 in Europe;

- The gap between resident and foreign applications is also significant.[29] Out of 747 patent applications received by the ARIPO in 2017, only 17 of them were filed by residents, which include foreign companies based within the region covered by the organization.[30] There is a smaller gap between resident and non-resident applicants in Africa in the case of trademarks. However, as shown in table 2, in all other regions the trademarks granted for residents exceed those granted for non-residents.

Many African countries, including least developed countries, are, however, outperforming similarly developed countries in terms of innovation outputs (Figure 4.1). Nevertheless, a considerable portion of the innovation that occurs in African countries is likely to take place in the informal sec-

Table 4.1:

Total patent grants (direct and Patent Cooperation Treaty national phase entries)

OFFICE	ORIGIN	2014	2015	2016	2017
Africa	Resident	1,286	1,380	1,178	1,330
	Non-resident	7,514	7,220	6,722	8,070
Asia	Resident	453,109	502,519	561,716	592,508
	Non-resident	183,791	197,881	210,584	210,592
Europe	Resident	102,724	104,835	116,733	116,359
	Non-resident	59,076	60,565	79,167	87,241
Latin America and the Caribbean	Resident	1,274	1,447	1,515	1,682
	Non-resident	16,626	16,253	17,385	18,618
North America	Resident	147,593	143,823	147,030	153,436
	Non-resident	176,807	176,777	182,470	189,464

Source: WIPO IP Statistics Data Centre.

Table 4.2:

Total trademark registrations (direct and via the Madrid system)

	ORIGIN	2014	2015	2016	2017
Africa	Resident	35,177	35,849	22,041	26,840
	Non-resident	57,315	61,800	52,888	56,192
Asia	Resident	1,644,092	422,543	574,187	687,619
	Non-resident	399,062	319,849	329,348	351,907
Europe	Resident	362,530	367,866	372,583	414,721
	Non-resident	201,203	214,237	194,224	233,132
Latin America and the Caribbean	Resident	270,569	249,310	264,707	292,754
	Non-resident	157,379	146,502	142,863	155,811
North America	Resident	176,652	183,890	192,051	193,220
	Non-resident	56,123	68,502	76,519	93,898

Source: WIPO IP Statistics Data Centre.

tor, and accordingly, remain unrecorded, given the large share of this sector in most African countries. In this section, the involvement of African countries' participation in the multilateral norm-setting of IP rights is described and assessed. This is followed by examples drawn from a series of country case studies to illustrate the often informal structure of IP in African countries, and the steps African countries are taking to improve their IP infrastructure.

Innovation output index, global innovation index score, 2018

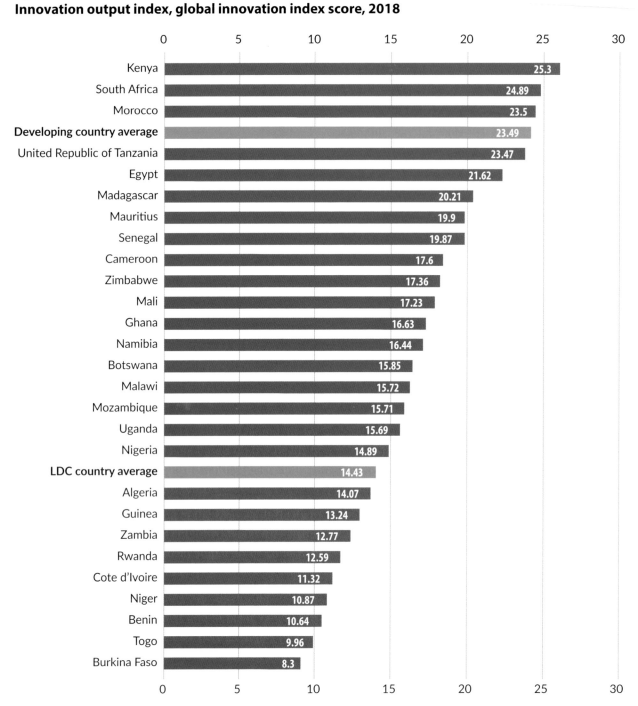

Source: Based on Cornell University, INSEAD and WIPO (2019).

Africa within the global Frameworks for intellectual property rights

African countries are party to several IP policy and regulatory frameworks. Most – but not all – African Union member States are members of the WTO. The WTO TRIPS Agreement is a key international harmonization tool because it establishes minimum standards for the protection of IP rights. Nevertheless, it is important to note that WTO member States have flexibility to, first, attach specific meanings to concepts, second, to decide on appropriate protection in some cases and, third, to set their own implementation agenda within the transition periods provided for in the TRIPS Agreement. For instance, while the TRIPS Agreement uses the concepts of "invention", "new", "inventive step" and "industrial application" as the criteria for patent protection in Article 27, it does not define them, and each country defines these internally in legislation or through case law.

The least developed countries' transition period permits them to delay TRIPS implementation (except for the principle of non-discrimination) until July 2021 or when they cease to fall into the category of least developed country. A separate transition period authorizes such countries to delay the implementation of obligations on patent and undisclosed information with respect to pharmaceutical products until 2033 or until a date on which they cease to be such a country, whichever is earlier.[31] To date, Angola, Bangladesh, Burundi, Cambodia, Madagascar, Rwanda, Uganda and Zanzibar (of the United Republic of Tanzania) have directly implemented this transition period under their respective patent laws. The Bangui Agreement Relating to the Creation of an OAPI was amended in 2016 to implement the transition period for the benefit of Benin, Burkina Faso, the Central African Republic, Chad, the Comoros, Equatorial Guinea, Guinea, Guinea-Bissau, Mali, Mauritania, Niger, Senegal and Togo.

Furthermore, Article 6 of the TRIPS Agreement leaves it to member States to decide what form of the principle of exhaustion of IP rights to use[32] and Article 22.2 allows countries to determine which form of protection would be appropriate for geographical indications. Countries are, accordingly, able to craft specific approaches to such matters depending on their level of economic development and the absorptive and innovative capacities of local firms (UNCTAD, 2018).

Most African Union member States are members of WIPO and party to its 27 IP treaties. Other important multilateral treaties administered by organizations other than the WTO and WIPO that are widely accepted by African countries are the following:

A Convention on Biological Diversity;

B Nagoya Protocol on Access to Genetic Resources and the Fair and Equitable Sharing of Benefits Arising from their Utilization to the Convention on the Biological Diversity;

C World Health Organization Framework Convention on Tobacco Control;

D Convention on the Rights of Persons with Disabilities;

E Convention on the Protection and Promotion of the Diversity of Cultural Expressions;

F Convention for the Safeguarding of the Intangible Cultural Heritage;

G International Treaty on Plant Genetic Resources for Food and Agriculture.

Of the above, the first and second treaties have had the most influence on IP regulation in Africa and globally. They have been the basis for the inclusion of a patent application requirement to disclose "the source and/or country of origin of biological resources, of associated traditional knowledge and of legal acquisition of such resources, if such resources and/or traditional knowledge are contained in an invention over which an applicant is seeking patent rights" (UNCTAD, 2014 p.47). Such disclosures ensure that the IP system supports the access and benefit sharing objectives of the Convention on Biological Diversity and benefits African traditional knowledge holders and sources by securing both acknowledgement and compensation for them.

Table 4.3 shows the level of participation in multilateral treaties of all countries in 1995 and 2015 while table 4.4 shows participation by African countries

Intellectual Property Treaties and Ratification Rates, 1995–2015 (listed alphabetically)

TREATY	REGIME	SOURCE	COUNTRIES RATIFIED	
			1995	2015
Beijing Treaty on Audiovisual Performances (2012)	Copyrights	WIPO		1
Berne Convention for The Protection for Literary and Artistic Works (1886)	Copyrights	WIPO	35	44
Brussels Convention Relating to the Distribution of Programme-Carrying Signals Transmitted by Satellite (1974)	Neighbouring rights	WIPO	2	4
Budapest Treaty on the International Recognition of the Deposit of Microorganisms for the Purposes of Patent Procedure (1977)	Patents	WIPO		3
International. Treaty on Plant Genetic Resources for Food and Agriculture (2001)	Plant genetic resources	WIPO		42
Hague Agreement Concerning the International Registration of Industrial Designs (1925)	Industrial designs	WIPO	6	15
Lisbon Agreement for the Protection of Appellations of Origin and their International Registration (1958)	Geographic indications	WIPO	6	6
Locarno Agreement Establishing an International Classification for Industrial Designs (1968)	Industrial designs	WIPO	1	2
Madrid Agreement for the Repression of False or Deceptive Indications of Sources of Goods (1891)	Trademarks	WIPO	4	4
Madrid Agreement Concerning International Registration of Marks (1891)	Trademarks	WIPO	5	11
Protocol Relating to the Madrid Agreement Concerning the International Registration of Marks (1989)	Trademarks	WIPO		21
Marrakesh Treaty to Facilitate Access to Published Works by Visually Impaired Persons and Persons with Print Disabilities, 2013 (Marrakesh VIP Treaty)	Copyrights	WIPO		1
Nagoya Protocol (2010)	Access and benefit sharing	CBD Secretariat		30
Nairobi Treaty on the Protection of the Olympic Symbol (1981)	Trademarks	WIPO	11	11
Nice Agreement Concerning the Intl. Classification of Goods and Services for the Purposes of the Registration of Marks (1957)	Trademarks	WIPO	5	9
Paris Convention for the Protection of Industrial Property (1883)	Patents and trademarks	WIPO	39	49
Patent Cooperation Treaty (1970)	Patents	WIPO	22	45
Convention for the Protection of Producers of Phonograms against Unauthorized Duplication of their Phonograms (1971)	Neighbouring rights	WIPO	4	6
Patent Law Treaty (2000)	Patents	WIPO		1
Rome Convention for the Protection of Performers, Producers of Phonographs and Broadcasting Organizations (1961)	Copyrights	WIPO	5	9
Singapore Treaty on the Law of Trademarks (2000)	Trademarks	WIPO		3
Strasbourg Agreement Concerning the Intl. Patent Classification (1971)	Patents	WIPO	2	3
Trademark Law Treaty (1994)	Trademarks	WIPO		4
TRIPS Agreement (1995)	Comprehensive	WIPO	33	43
Universal Copyright Convention (1952)	Copyrights	WIPO	14	15
Universal Copyright Convention (1971)	Copyrights	WIPO	9	10
Intl. Convention for the Protection of New Varieties of Plants (1961)	Plant varieties	UPOV	1	1
Intl. Convention for the Protection of New Varieties of Plants (1978)	Plant varieties	UPOV	1	2

TREATY	REGIME	SOURCE	COUNTRIES RATIFIED	
			1995	2015
Intl. Convention for the Protection of New Varieties of Plants (1991)	Plant varieties	UPOV		3
Vienna Agreement Establishing an Intl. Classification of the Figurative Elements of Marks (1973)	Trademarks	WIPO	1	2
Washington Treaty on Intellectual Property in Respect of Integrated Circuit (1989)	Computer chips	WIPO	1	1
WIPO Copyright Treaty (1996)	Copyrights	WIPO		12
UN Convention on WIPO (1967)	Copyrights	WIPO	43	53
WIPO Performances and Phonograms Treaty (1996)	Neighbouring rights	WIPO		12

Source: de Beer, and others (2017).

in 1995 and 2015. The Mediterranean countries (Algeria, Egypt, Morocco and Tunisia) bound by an association agreement with the European Union with the obligation to ratify treaties on IP rights have ratified the highest number of treaties. This group is followed by Kenya and six least developed countries (Benin, Burkina Faso, Guinea, Rwanda, Senegal and Togo).

National experiences: case study illustrations

Five national stories are explored from different angles of the IP system, beginning with the formulation of national IP policy in South Africa, highlighting the challenges posed by additional norm-setting processes, including at the AfCFTA. One of the outcomes of South African national IP policy is to introduce substantive patent examination, while in another case study, the lessons from Egyptian development of substantive patent examination is introduced. A case study on the trademark initiatives for coffee in Ethiopia demonstrates how Government can lead initiatives to use IP rights to improve commodities marketing. The case of the Nollywood film industry in Nigeria demonstrates how the private sector adjusts and develops within the prevailing copyright system. Finally, there is a case in which traditional knowledge and farming practices intersect with the IP rights system based on the case of patents concerning the preparation of products using teff in Ethiopia. These five illustrative case studies complement the two studies in boxes 4.2 and 4.3 on the development by Safaricom of M-PESA for money transfer in Kenya and the case of *Hoodia gordonii* that was used as a natural product by the San people of the Kalahari in South Africa, but which was later incorporated into patent claims abroad. A subsequent case study presented in the final section of this report demonstrates the efforts made by the Government of Zambia to link traditional knowledge systems with science.

The national IP policy of South Africa

The protection of IP rights is not an end in itself, but, as reflected under articles 7 and 8 of the TRIPS Agreement, a means to promote innovation and the dissemination of technology, to the mutual advantage of producers and users and in a manner conducive to social and economic welfare. The optimal level of protection sufficient to provide incentives and to promote social and economic welfare is likely to vary from country to country, based on the level of economic development, and from sector to sector, based on technological intensity and the nature of competition. As a result, countries implement national policies, laws and regulations, while complying with the international minimum standards for the protection of IP rights established by the TRIPS Agreement.

South Africa has been engaged in consultation on the development of an IP policy since 2013. The first phase was adopted in May 2018 after a series of public consultations conducted during open forums organized in partnership with UNCTAD and the United Nations Development Programme (UNDP), among others, and several submissions

Table 4.4:

Ratification status of African Countries, 1995 and 2015

COUNTRY	1995		2015	
	TREATIES RATIFIED	% TREATIES IN FORCE (26)	TREATIES RATIFIED	% TREATIES IN FORCE (34)
Algeria	9	34.6	16	47.1
Angola	1	3.8	5	14.7
Benin	6	23.1	12	35.3
Botswana	1	3.8	11	32.4
Burkina Faso	8	30.8	13	38.2
Burundi	3	11.5	5	14.7
Cameroon	7	26.9	8	23.5
Cabo Verde			4	11.8
Comoros			5	14.7
Central African Republic	5	19.2	5	14.7
Chad	4	15.4	6	17.6
Congo	7	26.9	10	29.4
Democratic Republic of the Congo	4	15.4	7	20.6
Djibouti	1	26.9	6	17.6
Egypt	11	15.4	17	50.0
Equatorial Guinea	1	3.8	5	14.7
Eritrea			2	5.9
Ethiopia	1	3.8	4	11.8
Gabon	6	23.1	11	32.4
Gambia	3	11.5	7	20.6
Ghana	5	19.2	11	32.4
Guinea-Bissau	4	15.4	7	20.6
Guinea	7	26.9	16	47.1
Côte d'Ivoire	6	23.1	8	23.5
Kenya	10	38.5	15	44.1
Lesotho	6	23.1	10	29.4
Liberia	6	23.1	11	32.4
Libya	3	11.5	5	14.7
Madagascar	5	19.2	10	29.4
Malawi	9	34.6	11	32.4

Source: de Beer, Baarbé, Ncube (2017).

COUNTRY (CONT.)	1995		2015	
	TREATIES RATIFIED	% TREATIES IN FORCE (26)	TREATIES RATIFIED	% TREATIES IN FORCE (34)
Mali	5	19.2	11	32.4
Mauritania	5	19.2	7	20.6
Mauritius	5	19.2	7	20.6
Morocco	12	46.2	20	58.8
Mozambique	1	3.8	9	26.5
Namibia	3	11.5	10	29.4
Niger	7	26.9	11	32.4
Nigeria	6	23.1	8	23.5
Rwanda	5	19.2	12	35.3
São Tome and Príncipe			5	14.7
Senegal	9	34.6	12	35.3
Seychelles			6	17.6
Sierra Leone	2	7.7	7	20.6
Somalia	1	3.8	1	2.9
South Africa	6	23.1	9	26.5
South Sudan		15.4		
Sudan	4	15.4	8	23.5
Swaziland	4	15.4	8	23.5
United Republic of Tanzania	4	26.9	8	23.5
Togo	7	46.2	15	44.1
Tunisia	12	19.2	17	50.0
Uganda	5	15.4	7	20.6
Zambia	4	15.4	7	20.6
Zimbabwe	4		7	20.6
Minimum	1		1	
Maximum	12		20	
Median	5		8	
Mean (standard deviation)	5.2 (2.8)		9.0 (4.0)	
Total signatory countries	48 countries	53 countries		

by stakeholders. Phase I of the final Intellectual Property Policy for the Republic of South Africa is aimed at aligning the IP regime with the national development plan and broad industrial policy to strike the balance between the rights of holders and the interests of users of knowledge and to foster investment and technology diffusion. During the first phase, the IP policy addresses key issues concerning the interface between IP and public health.

The policy adopted the introduction of substantive patent search and examination together with a robust patent disclosure obligation; procedures for the submission of third-party observations and post-grant oppositions concerning pending patent applications; the elaboration of the patentability criteria, parallel importation, the interface between IP and competition; and the adoption of a research exception. Phase I of the policy requires certain amendments to the South African domestic IP regime.

The importance of building capacity for patent examination: lessons from Egypt

In 2002, Egypt revised its IP law to implement the TRIPS Agreement. Two of the major changes were the introduction of pharmaceutical product patents (to be effective from 2005 upon the expiry of the transition period provided by WTO authorizing developing countries to delay the protection of pharmaceutical product patents) and the establishment of formal and substantive examination of patents and industrial designs.[33] Egypt also became a member of the Patent Cooperation Treaty in 2003. Accordingly, the Egyptian Patent office began to accept national and international patent filings. The Office started to invest in its patent examination capacity, taking into account the technical challenges of evaluating pharmaceutical and chemical product patents.

In 2009, the Egyptian Patent Office was accredited as an international searching authority and international preliminary examining authority under the Patent Cooperation Treaty. An international searching authority conducts prior art searches on patent claims and prepares an international search report, whereas an international preliminary

examining authority formulates "a preliminary and non-binding opinion on the question of whether the claimed invention appears to be novel, to involve an inventive step (to be non-obvious) and to be industrially applicable" (Patent Cooperation Treaty, Article 33).

Currently, 23 national patent offices are designated as an international searching authority and an international preliminary examining authority, including patent offices from several developing countries (Brazil, Chile, China, India and the Philippines) (WIPO, 2017). The achievement of this status of the Egyptian Patent Office demonstrates considerable investment in building technical competencies and infrastructure. To achieve international searching authority and international preliminary examining authority status, the Egyptian Patent Office had to meet the criteria under the Patent Cooperation Treaty and its regulations on sufficiency and competence of its personnel and technical experts, maintenance and use of patent, science and engineering databases, implementation of a quality control management system and achieving recognition by other patent offices. Building the capacity to achieve and maintain international searching authority and international preliminary examining authority status helps national patent offices to make high quality decisions, especially to prevent undue patenting of medicines.

As only a few developing countries have international searching authority and international preliminary examining authority status, prior art search and patent examination has been largely considered from the perspective of developed countries. For example, Egypt is among the few countries that had rejected part of the patent claims concerning Sofosbuvir (hepatitis C treatment), which is sold at very high prices. A competent national patent office also provides vital services to local industries, research centres and government agencies. Such services can involve the assessment of technical information contained in patent applications and scientific publications in the process of production, research and development and assisting competitive procurement of goods and services. The Egyptian Patent Office has made its expertise available to other developing country patent offices through capacity-building courses, especially in collaboration with UNCTAD.

Using trademarks for branding commodities: the case of the Ethiopian coffee branding initiative

About two thirds of the 135 developing countries are commodity dependent (UNCTAD, 2017); their economies suffer from volatility of prices and demand in international markets. Ethiopia is among the countries most dependent on only a very few commodities for its exports, coffee being one of its largest. For centuries, Ethiopian coffee producers, exporters, intermediaries and coffee roasters and to some extent consumers in importing countries, have differentiated Ethiopian coffee based on the geographical origin and the associated quality or reputation of the coffee. The Ethiopian Intellectual Property Office implemented an initiative for trademark protection of Ethiopian speciality coffee in collaboration with Light Years IP, a non-profit organization based in Washington, D.C. The initiative attracted worldwide attention when Starbucks Corporation, a United States-based multinational coffee enterprise, objected to the application for the registration of Sidamo coffee at the United States Patent and Trademark Office.

HARAR™
ETHIOPIAN
FINE COFFEE

YIRGACHEFFE™
ETHIOPIAN
FINE COFFEE

SIDAMO™
ETHIOPIAN
FINE COFFEE

In the process of securing the IP rights, the Ethiopian Intellectual Property Office needed to overcome serious legal hurdles and opposition from local coffee roasters in other countries as well. The Patent Office of Japan, for example, invalidated the trademarks held by Ethiopia for Sidamo and Yirgacheffe coffee based on an objection filed by the All Japan Coffee Association in 2009 arguing that the registration of the trademarks was merely indicating the place of production. Although the Intellectual Property High Court of Japan agreed with the Patent Office's ruling it preserved the

trademarks because of their recognition among dealers and consumers as indicating the distinctive brand or type of coffee or coffee bean rather than the place of production of the beans. The Intellectual Property high court of Japan took into account the quality control put in place by the Government of Ethiopia for coffee beans produced in Sidamo and Yirgacheffe (ILO, 2010).

The Ethiopian Intellectual Property Office has registered trademarks for Sidamo, Harar/Harrar and Yirgacheffe in more than 35 countries. To achieve the objectives of trademark registration, Ethiopia signed extensive licence agreements for the use of trademarks establishing a network of licensed exporters, importers, roasters and distributors.

Ethiopia and the patent for processing of teff flour

Teff, the staple grain in Ethiopia and Eritrea for millennia, is increasingly becoming the food of choice for well-heeled celebrities and health-conscious segments of Western society. With growing sophistication in the scientific understanding of its natural characteristics as a gluten-free and iron- and mineral-rich grain, teff is now often mentioned as a super-grain alongside, for example, quinoa. In February 2014, the Daily Mail (United Kingdom) described teff as "Hollywood's new favourite food".[34]

This development increases the commercial opportunities from teff that, under normal circumstances, should transform the livelihoods of the hard-working teff farmers for the better. However, in 2007, the European Patent Office granted a patent on "processing of teff flour" to a Dutch company called HPFI. All available evidence suggests that the patent was awarded on dubious legal grounds, as a patent is available only to products or processes that are new, not obvious and useful. The European Patent Office, however, awarded a patent for allegedly inventing "a method for baking a product comprising the steps of (a) preparing a dough or batter by mixing a flour according to the invention with a liquid (for instance water, milk, beer or oil) and optionally a leavening agent; (b) kneading this dough in a desired shape; and (c) heating the dough for some time."

In other words, the teff processing patent was given to a private company for "inventing" a method of how to produce baked food products from teff. Of course, most Ethiopians and Eritreans were brought up on injera and other food products made from teff, which they inherited from centuries of tradition. Nevertheless, the patent is now in place, and its scope is such that it effectively precludes these countries from exporting any teff-based products to Europe for the lifetime of the patent.

An attempt made to register "the patent" in the United States was unsuccessful. In a decision issued on 10 October 2012, the United States Patent and Trademark Office rejected all claims in the patent application on the grounds that the claimed invention "would have been obvious to one of ordinary skill in the art" and that many of the claims were in fact naturally occurring attributes of teff as gluten-free grain with naturally determined nutritional content and not an invention as such.[35] Although the United States Patent and Trademark Office did not assert lack of novelty per se, in response to the assertion that "the qualities and characteristics of teff traditionally have been unsuitable for baking", it remarked that injera is "a flat bread that is baked and has been baked for centuries in Ethiopia"[36] and that consequently baking with teff was known at the time of the claimed inventions.

Recently, the Ethiopian Intellectual Property Office launched a multi-pronged effort to reclaim teff through judicial as well as diplomatic means. Ethiopians and friends of Ethiopia are currently engaged in a campaign to disseminate information about what they believe to be an outright theft of the country's identity, traditional knowledge and cultural heritage by the Dutch company and its directors.[37] The teff patent was ruled invalid by a court in the Netherlands for lack of inventiveness in 2018 based on disputes between private parties.[38]

The Nigerian Film Industry

The growth and development of the Nigerian entertainment industry and its film industry, in particular may be traced to the early 1990s. This followed the establishment of the Nigerian Copyright Council in 1989, which was elevated to the status of the Nigerian Copyright Commission in 2004. The Nigerian entertainment industry consists of various creative industries, namely film, television, music, radio and video games. It is estimated to employ more than one million people and generate more than a billion dollars for the economy (Osinubi, 2017). The Nigerian film industry, popularly known as "Nollywood", is the largest film industry in Africa and the second largest globally after Bollywood. Although the industry has evolved from straight-to-video film to box office hits as well as online content, it remains largely informal.

Nevertheless, independent Nigerian filmmakers have emerged and attempted to formalize work in this environment with proper contracts, adherence to copyright law, especially in relation to the chain of title, and have had their films premiered in Nigerian cinemas as well as abroad. In April 2012, it was reported that Tiger Global Management, a United States hedge fund, had invested $8 million in one of the world's largest distributors of licensed Nigerian films, iROKOtv (Oyewole, 2014). Three years later, iROKOtv signed a partnership agreement with Netflix to provide Nigerian movies on the Netflix platform. This is testimony to the growing popularity of Nigerian films beyond Nigeria and the continent. Emerging technologies have made it easier for access and distribution of content, especially on online platforms, which, at the same time, raises challenges for its control.

Nollywood offers an excellent example of phenomenal growth not because but in spite of IP rights (Oguamanam, 2011). Notwithstanding mixed impressions on the role of IP in Nollywood, few deny that the lax IP regime in the industry has given rise to creative patterns of engagement between the industry and actors in the informal movie distribution networks in Nigeria. A more enforcement-oriented approach to IP would alienate and isolate members of such informal networks, criminalizing them as pirates. The industry continues to develop creative ways of leveraging the partnership and contractual potentials of these isolated actors who are now critical stakeholders in the Nollywood value chain. Some members of the industry recognize that while IP may be desirable, enforcement-centred implementation of IP policies often privileges a few in the industry and comes at the expense of the cultural contexts that favour collaborative creativity and the enduring desires of individual artists and creators for optimum exposure. Industry opinions suggest an acknowledgment fact that such exposure offers greater opportunities and potential for creators' independence through a universe of options for equitable economic benefits to all stakeholders in the industry. Nollywood continues to evolve, calling attention to the need for pragmatism and sensitivity to context in the making of IP policy, in rejection of the one-size-fits-all pattern.

The IP regime has been in place for a while and the 1989 Nigerian copyright law has been reviewed several times; it is again under review to ensure that it is in line with the latest developments at the national and international levels with respect to copyright and related rights, which include broadening exceptions and limitations as well as enhancing rights for performers and producers of sound recordings. The reform of the copyright law will go a long way towards enhancing the regulatory environment, which will, in turn, support, the growth of the film industry and the creative sector as a whole.

The Nigerian Copyright Commission was established not only to administer the rights provided for under the Copyright Act but also to enforce rights in the light of the increased unauthorized commercial use of copyright works. The Commission has a fully-fledged enforcement department that has the authority to search and seize alleged infringing material and arrest the infringers. It is important for Nigeria to have a clear IP Policy framework to capitalize on the ever-changing technological landscape for the benefit of the film industry and the creative economy as a whole. In this regard, it is important to acknowledge the need to enforce IP to help creators, but also that creativity depends on access to content, therefore demanding that a careful balance be maintained.

Nigeria recently ratified four WIPO Treaties on copyright and related rights, signifying readiness to develop the copyright industries in Nigeria. Providing for the protection of works in other countries, which are parties to the treaties, ratification

ensures that the rights holders get their due for the exploitation of their works in other countries.

Towards an intellectual property rights protocol for the African Continental Free Trade Area

The second phase of the AfCFTA negotiations contain an agenda to include an IP rights protocol. State parties have not yet determined the specific objectives and scope of the IP rights protocol. Taking into account the regional initiatives and the evaluation of the national experiences within Africa, this section includes an assessment of the rationale and justifications for such a protocol and its potential elements.

Why an intellectual property protocol in the AfCFTA?

The initial rationale for an IP rights protocol in the AfCFTA can be explained in the context of the continental agenda for increased intra-African trade and economic integration. The experience of the European Union provides an example of similar circumstances. The conflict between nationally limited IP rights and the promotion of regional trade and economic integration forced the European courts to develop norms for what is now called "regional exhaustion". IP rights allow the rights holders to prevent import and export of goods potentially leading to the fragmentation of a regional market. Over time, the European courts have acknowledged that IP rights should not be used to fragment the internal market, starting from the early stages of regional integration in 1960. Consequently, once a right holder has placed a product protected by IP rights into the European market, it cannot prevent the circulation of the product within the regional market. However, the right holder still maintains the right to prevent importation from or exportation to countries outside the regional market.[39] Following the decisions of the courts, the European Union incorporated regional exhaustion for all categories of IP rights under the respective IP laws.

Second, such a protocol is justified to avoid discrimination on protection of IP rights among States parties. Not all African States are WTO members and thereby benefit from the national treatment and most-favoured-nation treatment principles. Algeria, Ethiopia, Equatorial Guinea, Comoros, Libya, Sao Tome and Príncipe, Somalia, Sudan and South Sudan are not members of the WTO, although some are in the process of accession, while others have expressed an interest in joining. Furthermore, States parties have and will continue to have different levels of participation in multilateral IP treaties and may also engage in bilateral preferential trade agreements with IP provisions. Accordingly, an IP rights protocol in the AfCFTA is the key to establishing non-discrimination principles among States parties, irrespective of the status of their participation in international treaties.

A third justification for an IP rights protocol in the AfCFTA concerns the gaps in the TRIPS Agreement that require countries to develop norms at the national or regional level without any minimum standards to advance the approximation of laws and practices. For instance, Article 27(3) of the TRIPS Agreement requires countries to provide an effective level of plant variety protection either through patent protection or a system created specifically for the purpose (*sui generis*), or a combination of the two. As a result, most developing countries have developed their own national laws that respond to the specific nature of their national agriculture and seeds sectors. As noted in the previous section, some developing countries joined the 1991 UPOV Convention as part of free trade agreement deals with developed countries, while Kenya and the United Republic of Tanzania joined the 1991 UPOV Convention without any free trade agreement-related obligation.

The earlier versions of the UPOV Convention, especially the 1978 version, are more broadly accepted by developing countries, such as Argentina, Brazil, Chile, China, Colombia, Ecuador, Mexico, Nicaragua, Oman, Paraguay, the Plurinational State of Bolivia, South Africa, and Trinidad and Tobago, whereas the 1991 UPOV Convention has been criticized for not reflecting the priorities of developing countries. (Strba, 2017; Oguamanam, 2015; de Jonge and Munyi, 2016). Although alternative protection was envisaged and provided for in the African Model Legislation for the Protection of the Rights of Local Communities, Farmers and Breeders and for Regulations of Access to Biological Resources, 2000 (Strba, 2017), it had limited impact (Munyi, Mahop, du Plessis, Ekpere and Bavikatte, 2012).

Some African States have had no alternative but to adopt the 1991 UPOV Convention despite questions over its impact on traditional farming practices. OAPI became a member of the 1991 UPOV Convention in 2014 while ARIPO adopted the Arusha Protocol (2015) for the Protection of New Varieties of Plants compliant with the 1991 UPOV Convention. The ARIPO protocol will only come into force one year after four of its member States ratify it, and no State has ratified it to date, indicating countries' concern with emulating the 1991 UPOV Convention. Regional developments should also be considered in the light of the transition period for the large number of least developed countries in OAPI and ARIPO. An IP rights protocol in the

AfCFTA can provide substantive laws that reconcile the protection of plant varieties as envisaged in the 1978 UPOV Convention, with flexibilities for farmers and less-developed countries.[40]

An IP rights protocol in the AfCFTA can also address the gaps in the TRIPS Agreement on the relationship between IP rights and traditional knowledge, cultural expressions and biological resources, which are among the main issues that African countries have been advancing at WIPO and the WTO. The WIPO Intergovernmental Committee on Intellectual Property and Genetic Resources, Traditional Knowledge and Folklore has been negotiating a text for the protection of traditional knowledge, cultural expressions and biological resources for the past 19 years (Oguamanam, 2018). Although the substantive discussions can be left for multilateral processes, there are key issues on the relationship between the IP system and traditional knowledge, cultural expressions and biological resources that an IP rights protocol in the AfCFTA can take into consideration. The following example underscores the value of traditional medicinal knowledge in collaborative research and development efforts with the potential to develop technical solutions that can be protected by IP rights.

In summary, an IP rights protocol for the AfCFTA is necessary for the following reasons:

A To cover the trade aspects of IP rights that contribute to regional trade and value chain integration.

B To avoid the differential treatment of the AfCFTA countries compared to countries outside Africa arising from participation in different multilateral and bilateral IP rights treaties.

C To provide for harmonized approaches to key IP issues of interest for Africa that are not adequately covered under multilateral treaties, including plant variety protection and the protection of genetic resources, traditional knowledge and cultural expressions.

Objectives of an intellectual property rights protocol in the African Continental Free Trade Area

All the protocols in the AfCFTA are expected to advance the general objectives of the Agreement itself, which aim to liberalize the market for goods and services and facilitate movement of capital and natural persons with a view to creating a single market in accordance with the pan-African Vision of "an integrated, prosperous and peaceful Africa" as enshrined in Agenda 2063.[41] Trade liberalization is the immediate aim as a means to promote the ultimate objectives of the Agreement, which are the following:

- Sustainable and inclusive socioeconomic development, gender equality and structural transformation.

- Competitiveness of the economies of States parties within the continent and the global market.

- Industrial development through diversification and regional value chain development, agricultural development and food security;

The IP rights protocol in the AfCFTA needs to be developed within the Agreement's overall objectives. In the context of the Tripartite Free Trade Area, African countries have added the more specific objectives of protecting IP rights, promoting a balanced IP protection system, promoting cultural industries and utilizing flexibilities under international treaties (Tripartite Free Trade Area, 2015, Article 9). The regional economic communities have also advanced specific objectives similar to that of the Tripartite Free Trade Area. Taking into account the general objectives of the AfCFTA, the approaches taken by regional economic communities and the current negotiations under the Tripartite Free Trade Area, the objectives of the IP rights protocol in the AfCFTA can be defined to include the following areas:

A Supporting the African transformation agenda: In Agenda 2063, access to technology, opportunities and capital is identified as being critical to advancing the continent's political, social, cultural and economic transformation. Intellectual property rights are identified under the goal of achieving "transformed economies" with a tar-

get to operationalize PAIPO by 2023 under the overall goal of achieving a "united Africa" and with a view to promoting the role of Africa on the global stage in science and technology. In addition, the Science, Technology and Innovation Strategy for Africa and the Comprehensive African Agricultural Development Programme identify the importance of addressing IP rights and technology transfer.

B Promoting regional integration: regional exhaustion regimes for IP rights can help to promote regional trade and value chain integration and reduce discrimination between State Parties.

C Promoting policy coherence: the IP rights protocol in the AfCFTA would provide an opportunity to establish common rules on IP protection and the use of flexibilities in the global IP regimes, based on a common approach. It would also provide a framework for subregional cooperation and promote further cooperation at the continental level (ECA, African Union Commission and the African Development Bank, 2016, p. 75). The objective of promoting policy coherence should help Africa address the relationship between IP rights and other socioeconomic objectives, including innovation, environmental protection and traditional knowledge.

D Restoring, preserving and utilizing policy space: as indicated above, multilateral IP treaties include flexibilities (policy space) for States to nuance their IP frameworks to meet their national socioeconomic contexts, needs and priorities. Some of the regional economic communities' efforts have been directed at maximizing use of these flexibilities. Space for this should be explicitly recognized in the objectives of an IP rights protocol in the AfCFTA.

E Facilitating common approaches to multilateral norm-setting: by providing a platform for exchange of experiences, sharing of information and cooperation, an IP rights protocol in the AfCFTA can help African countries to promote common positions on multilateral norm-setting processes.

What approach should be taken in developing an intellectual property rights protocol in the African Continental Free Trade Area?

As discussed earlier, regional approaches to IP rights in Africa have followed three different models, arrangements for regional cooperation on IP rights, development of one substantive law for members of a regional economic community and regional filing systems for patents, trademark and industrial designs. Regional approaches to IP rights in other regions, especially those similarly involving developing countries, can also be informative.

The Andean Community, representing Colombia, Ecuador, Peru and the Plurinational State of Bolivia opted to develop a fully-fledged IP rights protection system, including common substantive laws, IP administration and enforcement mechanisms.[42] The Andean IP law system was credited with the successful and balanced implementation of the TRIPS Agreement, while at the same time safeguarding the interests of the participating countries on key issues, such as plant variety protection and traditional knowledge.[43] The system started to erode, however, when member States entered into bilateral free trade agreements. Peru requested authorization to opt out of the common IP laws to adapt its own IP laws to implement its obligations under an agreement it signed with the United States of America and later with the European Union.[44] Colombia also signed an agreement with the United States and the European Union. Ecuador joined Colombia and Peru in a comprehensive trade agreement with the European Union with provisions on IP rights independent from the Andean IP laws.[45] To implement their obligations under bilateral free trade agreements, Colombia, Ecuador and Peru have to adopt national laws that effectively derogate from some aspects of the Andean Community IP laws.[46] OAPI took an approach similar to the Andean Community by providing for common substantive laws. It has survived to date, but at the cost of losing some of the key flexibilities for least developed countries. Member countries of OAPI have been adopting their own national

copyright laws. In 2016, the organization initiated an amendment to implement some of the TRIPS flexibilities. Although its substantive IP laws are largely still in force, it may be difficult to show to what extent it has promoted regional integration, considering the fact that its member countries are also members of different regional blocs, such as the Economic Community of Central African States (ECCAS) and the Economic Community of West African States (ECOWAS).

The experience of the model followed by the Andean Community and OAPI demonstrates that this approach will not be appropriate for the AfCFTA for various reasons. First, at least in the Andean Community, a substantive regional IP law can be eroded through time as its member States engage in bilateral, regional and multilateral treaties. Second, it will be too ambitious, if not impractical, to harmonize IP laws for 55 African Union member States with significant cultural, geographical and economic differences. The model also carries its own risk of undermining the flexibilities that countries may need depending on their level of development or the need to observe their bilateral and multilateral commitments.

Although international instruments may provide substantive norms, the Association of Southeast Asian Nations (ASEAN) countries have adopted the operational aspect of IP rights management as their priority, opting to develop a regional cooperation scheme, which remains robust, instead of adding layers of substantive IP norms, based on the Framework Agreement on Intellectual Property Cooperation (1995).[47] The ASEAN Working Group on Intellectual Property Cooperation was formed in 1996, comprising the IP offices of the ASEAN member States. As the sectoral group responsible for IP issues in the region, this structure provides a platform for member States to discuss IP issues and formulate common positions. The Working Group's work is guided by ASEAN Intellectual Property Rights Action Plans that are periodically developed and implemented. The current programme of work for 2016–2025 is supported by other specific plans, such as the ASEAN Intellectual Property Rights Enforcement Action Plan, 2016. ASEAN maintains a regional online portal for exchange of information. The ASEAN Framework Agreement on Intellectual Property Cooperation has also created the ASEAN Intellectual Property Association, comprising individual and corporate members from ASEAN countries or with a business presence in ASEAN countries. The association provides a platform for non-States parties to engage with IP matters and accordingly presents an opportunity to frame common positions.[48] Furthermore, ASEAN has entered into cooperation arrangements with other countries, regional economic communities and organizations. These include the Japan-ASEAN Intellectual Property Rights Action Plan (Ministry of Economy, Trade and Industry, Japan, 2018), the European Union-ASEAN Project on the Protection of Intellectual Property Rights and WIPO-ASEAN Cooperation Programme in the Field of Intellectual Property.

The ASEAN model preserves policy space for States parties, addresses practical questions on administration and enforcement of IP rights and helps to facilitate the crafting of a common position for international engagement. The model, however, may not be sufficient to cover the overall objectives of the AfCFTA or those that would be related to the IP rights protocol in the AfCFTA proposed in the previous section.

A third model is provided by regional organizations specialized in the administration of the registration process for patents, trademarks and designs. The Eurasian Patent Organization, the Patent Office of the Cooperation Council for the Arab States of the Gulf and ARIPO are good examples. OAPI also carries out the registration of IP rights on behalf of its member States. Although the most important benefit of regional filing systems would be to pull together resources, especially for the examination of patents, ARIPO and OAPI seem to have generated very limited advantages to their member States. African countries generate the lowest number of IP rights compared to other regions; a regional filing system, if adopted, would prove very attractive to global enterprises, as they could file one patent, trademark or industrial application to cover 55 African Union member States. There would be many more filings to the AfCFTA IP registration system from outside the region than from within

the region. Accordingly, the regional registration model is more important for net IP exporting countries than for a region dominated by least developed countries and other low-income countries. It should be noted, in this context, that the mere filing of IP rights will not result in the transfer of foreign technology to African industries. Successful technology transfer depends on a much broader approach that embeds IP regimes within national innovation systems.[49] In any case, African countries, such as Egypt and South Africa, are building their own system of patent examination.

The three models can inform but do not answer the question of what should be the approach for the IP rights protocol for the AfCFTA, consequently needs to follow a selective approach, which allows it to do the following:

- To develop regional norms, following the model of the Andean Community, but only on issues strategically useful for regional integration, while preserving the policy space in other areas.

- To provide for a platform for cooperation on all IP rights following the example of ASEAN.

Potential elements of the intellectual property rights protocol in the African Continental Free Trade Area

In view of the diversity of national experiences and approaches to IP rights and the objectives for the IP rights protocol in the AfCFTA, the protocol could provide guiding principles for national IP law and policy and engagement of African countries in international treaties. These principles should consider the following:

- Stakeholder engagement and using empirical cost-benefit assessments and related research in developing national laws and policies and adhering to international treaties.

- Ensuring coherence between IP and other socioeconomic objectives.

- Striking the appropriate balance among stakeholders and promoting a robust public domain.

Guided by these objectives and principles, the IP rights protocol in the AfCFTA can include norms to safeguard African interests, in particular:

• Providing for non-discrimination among States parties on matters of IP rights.

• Establishing a regional IP exhaustion system in order to prevent fragmentation of the AfCFTA market and encouraging the development of regional value chain integration.

• Requiring the ratification of the protocol amending the TRIPS Agreement, 2005, in order to benefit from the facilitated production and exportation of pharmaceuticals for a regional trade agreement as 50 per cent or more of its members are least developed countries.

• Providing the minimum requirements to ensure the mutual supportiveness of the protection of IP rights and the protection of traditional knowledge, genetic resources and cultural expressions, with sufficient flexibility for domestic law and multilateral negotiations on the issue.

• Requiring the ratification of the Marrakesh Treaty, with the additional commitment to adhere to any other multilateral agreement that promote access to work for persons with other disabilities.

• Obliging countries to ensure the protection of geographical indications either through a *sui generis* system or certification and collective marks.

• Addressing the challenges of African countries concerning plant varieties protection by developing minimum standards on availability, scope of protection and exceptions to plant breeders' rights and the protection of traditional and new farmers' varieties.

• Developing guidelines to strike the appropriate balance under the procedures for enforcement of IP rights.

Considering the successes of the ASEAN regional framework, the IP rights protocol in the AfCFTA may also designate areas for regional cooperation, which may include the following:

• Sharing of experience, including on the protection of traditional knowledge and traditional cultural expressions and, where applicable, to identify areas for harmonization at continental level.

• Enhancing the use of open source licensing, research cooperation and other collaborative models as well as voluntary licensing to stimulate linkages and diffusion of knowledge;

• Strengthening the means for copyright holders to secure a fair share of the proceeds from commercial use of their work.

• Enhancing the use of geographical indications, collective marks and certification marks;

• Facilitating the use of flexibilities under international instruments for the protection of public health.

• Strengthening IP administration through exchange of experience and capacity- building and the creation of a continental database on IP registration.

As there are already specialized regional IP organizations in Africa and an initiative to create PAIPO, the IP Rights Protocol does not need to create new institutions. Following the protocols on goods and services in the AfCFTA agreement, the IP rights protocol should provide for a committee consisting of member States and give observer status to regional IP organizations and, where appropriate, also to regional economic communities and multilateral organizations. Finally, considering the rapid changes in technology and multilateral norm setting, the IP rights protocol should also be subject to periodic review.

Capacity-building for effective negotiations

As IP rights are among the most controversial of trade topics, the negotiations in the AfCFTA must be oriented towards ensuring balanced and widely supported policy through open, transparent, inclusive processes, such as public consultations and debates, including providing public access to draft documents and public hearings. Various forms of support to negotiations are required to ensure that there is adequate stakeholder engagement and effective consensus building. Some support has been extended to States by the African Union Commission, through its AfCFTA unit (UNCTAD, 2016 p.21). Effective capacity-building is iterative, so that it is constantly responsive to issues and challenges as they are presented during the negotiation process, and take various forms, taking into account informational, educational and procedural needs. For example, a training session may be needed to provide a negotiating team with subject-matter expertise, while policy discussions may help to apprise negotiators of the available policy options. Negotiations need to involve a broad range of stakeholders, given the varied interests in IP rights.

Key messages and policy recommendations

Key messages

- **As private rights used in the industrial and commercial context, IP rights function as policy tools to promote entrepreneurship, investment, competition and innovation. At the same time, IP regimes are essential in maintaining certain public policy objectives that relate to the dissemination of knowledge and indigenous learning. The AfCFTA provides an opportunity to advance a continental approach to a balanced IP rights system that responds to the aspirations contained in Agenda 2063.**

- **Membership of the WTO by 44 African Union member States has a significant influence on how the IP rights protocol in the African Continental Free Trade Area can be designed:** the WTO TRIPS Agreement does not provide exceptions for regional preferential agreements, which means that, unlike other the protocols in the AfCFTA, the benefits of an IP rights protocol must be extended to all WTO member States. African countries also differ significantly in their use of TRIPS flexibilities.

- **African countries have different levels of obligations in IP treaties beyond WTO:** including participation in multilateral IP treaties and commitments arising from bilateral trade agreements.

- **African countries have undergone extensive reforms in IP laws and regulations:** nevertheless, the use of IP rights, as demonstrated by patents and trademarks, is very limited in Africa compared to other regions and most patents and trademarks registered in Africa belong to non-residents. Considerable innovation is taking place in Africa, but without receiving protection from IP rights.

- **Three options may be identified in regional economic integration in IP rights:** (a) arrangements for regional cooperation and sharing of experiences on IP rights in general; (b) regional filing systems, usually for patents, but also for trademarks and industrial designs; and (c) development of one substantial law or unification of laws for members of a regional organization. Different parts of Africa have experience with all three of these models.

- **Developing one substantive IP regime for 55 African Union member States would be challenging:** (a) it may well prove over-ambitious to negotiate; (b) it may undermine existing flexibilities that African countries enjoy in their multilateral and bilateral IP commitments; and (c) it may conflict with obligations that African countries have committed to in international and bilateral agreements.

- **An African Continental Free Trade Area protocol involving only a cooperative framework for IP rights would fail to take advantage of many opportunities,** including developing tools for promoting regional integration, ensuring non-discrimination between countries with different international treaty membership and advancing the objectives of industrial diversification and value chain integration.

Policy recommendations

- **A viable IP rights protocol in the African Continental Free Trade Area could do the following:**

  a Provide guiding principles for national IP law and policy, as well as for engagement of African countries in international IP treaties.

  b Provide for non-discrimination among nationals of States parties on matters of IP rights.

  c Develop norms to safeguard African interests, including non-discrimination among African countries on matters pertaining to IP rights.

  d Establish a regional IP exhaustion system to prevent fragmentation of the AfCFTA market and encourage regional value chain development.

  e Provide the minimum requirements for the protection of traditional knowledge, genetic resources, and cultural expressions, but with

sufficient flexibility for domestic law and multilateral negotiations on these issues.

  f Require the ratification of the Marrakesh Treaty, with the additional commitment to adhere to any other multilateral agreement that promotes access to work for persons with disabilities.

  g Require the ratification of the protocol amending the TRIPS Agreement, 2005, in order to benefit from the facilitated production and exportation of pharmaceuticals for a regional trade agreement in which 50 per cent of the members are least developed countries.

  h Oblige the protection of geographic indications through either a sui generis system or certification and collection marks.

  i Develop minimum standards on plant variety protection, including on availability, scope of protection, and exceptions to plant breeders' rights and the protection of traditional and new farmers' varieties.

  j Develop guidelines on procedures for the enforcement of IP rights.

- **African regional organizations specializing in IP already exist (ARIPO and OAPI):** a protocol on IP rights, in its institutional arrangements, should accord observer status to these organizations.

- **Phase 2 of the Tripartite negotiations intends to include IP;** in view of the imminent negotiations related to the IP rights protocol for the AfCFTA, it would be prudent to consolidate these negotiations to avoid duplication and proceed from a single undertaking approach.

- **As a highly controversial negotiating topic, it is especially important for IP negotiations to be open, transparent and inclusive:** this should involve broad public consultations and debates and iterative capacity- building for key stakeholders, as well as training to ensure that negotiators are deeply engaged with subject-matter expertise and knowledgeable of available policy options.

References

Adachi, K. 2019. "Intellectual Property Provisions in Preferential Trade and Investment Agreements." Geneva and New York: UNCTAD.

African Regional Intellectual Property Organization. 1982. "Harare Protocol for the Protection of Patents, Industrial Designs and Utility Models." Harare, Zimbabwe.

———. 1993. "Banjul Protocol for the Protection of Trademarks."

———. 2004. "Lusaka Agreement on the Creation of the Industrial Property Organization for English-Speaking Africa."

———. 2010. Swakopmund Protocol for the Protection of Traditional Knowledge and Folklore."

———. 2015. "Arusha Protocol for the Protection of New Varieties of Plants."

———. 2016. "Guidelines for the Domestication of the Marrakesh Treaty."

African Union. 2014a. Common African Position (CAP) on the Post-2015 Development Agenda.

———. 2014b. Science, Technology and Innovation Strategy for Africa (STISA-2024).

———. 2016. "Decision on the Specialized Technical Committees." Assembly/AU/Dec.589(XXVI). Assembly of the Union, Twenty-Sixth Ordinary Session, 30–31 January 2016, Addis Ababa, Ethiopia.

———. 2017a. Second Ordinary Session of the Specialized Technical Committee (STC) on Agriculture, Rural Development, Water and Environment (Ministers' Session) 02–06 October 2017. Addis Ababa Report STC2/ARDWE/MIN.

———. 2017b. African Union Handbook 2017. Addis Ababa, Ethiopia: African Union Commission and New Zealand Ministry of Foreign Affairs and Trade.

———. 2017c. Continental Strategy for Geographical Indications in Africa.

———. 2018a. "The African Union Commission Hosted a Successful a High Level Stakeholders Engagement Round Table on the Accelerated Industrial Development for Africa (AIDA)" Press Release, 20 August. Available at: https://au.int/en/pressreleases/20180809/african-union-commission-hosted-successful-high-level-stakeholders-engagement.

———. 2018b. List of Countries which have Signed, Ratified/Acceded to the Statute of the Pan African Intellectual Property Organization (PAIPO). Available at: https://au.int/sites/default/files/treaties/32549- sl- statute_of_the_pan_african_intellectual_property_organization_paipo.pdf.

———. 2018c. "Agreement for the Establishment of the African Continental Free Trade Area." Kigali, Rwanda.

———. 2018d. Implementing the 2014 Malabo Declaration on Agriculture through Mutual Accountability African Union Commission hosts the 3rd CAADP PS Leadership Retreat. Available at: https://au.int/en/pressreleases/20180920/implementing-2014-malabo-declaration-agriculture-through-mutual 18 September.

Andean Community. 2000. "Decision No. 486 Establishing the Common Industrial Property Regime." Lima, Peru.

Andersen, R., and T. Winge. 2012. The Access and Benefit-Sharing Agreement on Teff Genetic Resources: Facts and Lessons (FNI Report 6/2012).

ASEAN (Association of Southeast Asian Nations). 1995. "Framework Agreement on Intellectual Property Cooperation."

———. 2015a. ASEAN Intellectual Property Rights Action Plan 2016–2025.

———. 2015b. ASEAN Intellectual Property Rights Enforcement Action Plan, 2015.

———. 2019. https://www.aseanip.org/.

AUC (African Union Commission). 2015. Agenda 2063: First Ten-Year Implementation Plan 2014–2023. Addis Ababa, Ethiopia: AUC. Available at: http://www.nepad.org/resource/agenda-2063-first-ten-year-implementation-plan-2014-2023.

Baldwin, R. 2013. "Lessons from the European Spaghetti Bowl." Trade Working Papers 23411, East Asian Bureau of Economic Research. Canberra, Australia.

Biadgleng, E. T., and J.-C. Maur. 2011. "The Influence of Preferential Trade Agreements on the Implementation of Intellectual Property Rights." In Developing Countries: A First Look, UNCTAD–ICTSD Project on Intellectual Property Rights and Sustainable Development.

Bilaterals.org. 2008. "Blow to the Intellectual Property Rules of the Andean Community." 15 August. Available at: www.bilaterals.org/.

Bouckley, B. 2010. "Phytopharm CEO insists hoodia still "interesting" despite patent disposal." NutraIngredients.com. 8 December 2010. Available at: www.nutraingredients.com/Industry/Phytopharm-CEO-insists-Hoodia-still-interesting-despite-patent-disposal.

Bramdeo, A. K. 2018. "The African Continental Free Trade Agreement: Its Potential Benefits and Impact: Building African Economic Resilience." Processed. Available at: http://www.intracen.org/uploadedFiles/intracenorg/Content/Publications/AfCFTA Business Guide_final_Low-res.pdf.

Branstetter, L., F. Foley, and K. Saggi. 2010. "Has the Shift to Stronger Intellectual Property Rights Promoted Technology Transfer, FDI, and Industrial Development?" WIPO Journal 2(1) 93–98.

Cliff, M. 2014. "Hollywood's new favourite food revealed: Victoria Beckham and Gwyneth Paltrow are fans of teff, an iron-rich Ethiopian grain that costs a whopping £7 a bag." Daily Mail, 3 February.

COMESA (Common Market for Eastern and Southern Africa). 2011. "Policy on Intellectual Property Rights and Cultural Industries." Council of Ministers, COMESA.

Communications Authority of Kenya. 2017. Sector Statistics Report Q3, 2017. Available at: https://ca.go.ke/wp-content/uploads/2018/07/Sector-Statistics-Report-Q3-2017-18-2.pdf.

Creative Commons. 2019. "About the License." Available at https://creativecommons.org/licenses/.

Dahlman C. J., and R. Nelson. 1995. "Social Absorption Capability, National Innovation Systems and Economic Development." In: Social Capability and Long-Term Economic Growth, edited by B.H. Koo and D.H. Perkins. London: Palgrave Macmillan.

De Beer, J., J. Baarbé, and C. Ncube. 2017. "The Intellectual Property Treaty Landscape in Africa, 1885 to 2015." OpenAIR Working Paper 4.

De Jonge, B., and P. Munyi. 2016. "A Differentiated Approach to Plant Variety Protection in Africa." World Intellectual Property 19: 28–52.

District Court, the Hague. 2018. "Ancientgrain B.V., v. Bakels Senior N.V." Case number ECLI:NL:RBDHA:2018:13960, 21 November.

East African Community Treaty for the Establishment of the East African Community. 1999. Adopted 30 November in Arusha, Tanzania.

ECA (United Nations Economic Commission for Africa). 2018a. "Synergies between the African Continental Free Trade Agreement and Tripartite Free Trade Agreement Will Benefit Africa's Traders and Consumers, Says ECA Chief." Press Release. Addis Ababa, Ethiopia. Available at: https://www.uneca.org/stories/synergies-between-afcfta-and-tripartite-fta-will-benefit-africa%E2%80%99s-traders-and-consumers-says.

———. 2018b. "African Continental Free Trade Area: Creating Fiscal Space for Jobs and Economic Diversification." Presentation on the theme of the fifty-first session of the Commission, 11–12 May 2018.

Economic Commission for Africa, African Union Commission and African Development Bank. 2016. Assessing Regional Integration in Africa VII: Innovation, Competitiveness and Regional Integration. Addis Ababa: ECA.

Fink, C., and P. Reichenmiller. 2006. "Tightening TRIPS: Intellectual Property Provisions of U.S. Free Trade Agreements." In Trade, Doha, and Development: A Window into the Issues, edited by R. Newfarmer, 289–303. Geneva: World Bank.

GIZ (German Society for International Cooperation). 2017. African Union: Continental Support for Agricultural Transformation in Africa. Eschborn, Germany: GIZ.

Helfer, L. R., and K. J. Alter. 2013. "The Influence of the Andean Intellectual Property Regime on Access to Medicines in Latin America." In Wealth and Health: Global Administrative Law and the Battle over Intellectual Property and Access to Medicines in Latin America, edited by Rochelle Dreyfuss and César Rodríguez-Garavito. Oxford, UK: Oxford University Press.

ILO (International Law Office). 2010. "Newsletter." London: ILO.

Isaac, A. G., and W. G. Park. 2004. "On Intellectual Property Rights: Patents versus Free and Open Development." Chapter 18 in The Elgar Companion to the Economics of Property Rights, edited by Enrico Colombatto. Cheltenham, UK: Edward Elgar Publishing.

Light Years IP. 2011. "Ethiopian Fine Coffee: Trademarking & Licensing Initiative." Available at http://www.lightyearsip.net/projects/ethiopiancoffee/.

Linsu, K. "Technology Transfer and Intellectual Property Rights. The Korean Experience." UNCTAD–ICTSD Project on Intellectual Property Rights and Sustainable Development, Geneva, June 2003. Available at: https://unctad.org/en/PublicationsLibrary/ictsd2003ipd2_en.pdf).

Makoni, M. 2010. San People's Cactus Drug Dropped by Phytopharm. SciDev.Net. December 20. Available at: www.scidev.net/en/news/san-people-s-cactus-drug-dropped-by-phytopharm-1.html.

Ministry of Economy, Trade and Industry, Japan. 2018. Japan–ASEAN IP Cooperation Programmes Enhanced: Outcomes of the 8th Japan-ASEAN Heads of Intellectual Property Offices Meeting, 6 September http://www.meti.go.jp/english/press/2018/0906_003.html.

Munyi, P., M. T. Mahop, P. Du Plessis, J. Ekpere, and K. Bavikatte. 2012. A Gap Analysis Report on The African Model Law on the Protection of the Rights of Local Communities. Addis Ababa, Ethiopia. African Union Commission.

Musungu, S. F. 2010. "The Potential Impact of the Proposed East African Community (EAC) Anti-Counterfeiting Policy and Bill on Access to Essential Medicines, UNDP BDP HIV Practice/March 2010 Discussion Paper.

Ncube, C. 2016. Intellectual Property Policy, Law and Administration in Africa: Exploring Continental and Sub-regional Co-operation. Routledge.

Ncube, C., T. Schonwetter, J. de Beer, and C. Oguamanam. 2017. Intellectual Property Rights and Innovation: Assessing Regional Integration in Africa (ARIA VIII). OpenAIR Working Paper 5. http://www.openair.org.za/wp-content/uploads/2017/05/WP-5-IPRs-and-Innovation-Assessing-ARIA-VIII.pdf.

Organization of African Unity. 2000. African Model Legislation for the Protection of the Rights of Local Communities, Farmers and Breeders, and for the Regulation of Access to Biological Resources. Model Law, Algeria.

Organization for Economic Cooperation and Development. 2015. Participation of Developing Countries in Global Value Chains: Implications for Trade and Trade-Related Policies: Summary Paper.

Oguamanam, C. 2018a. Breeding Apples for Oranges: Africa's Misplaced Priority over Plant Breeders' Rights. World Intellectual Property, 18: 165-195. doi:10.1111/jwip.12039, 2015.

———. 2018b. Tiered or Differentiated Approach to Traditional Knowledge and Traditional Cultural Expressions: The Evolution of a Concept. CIGI Papers No. 185, August 2018.

———. 2011. Beyond "Nollywood" and Piracy: In Search of an Intellectual Property Policy for Nigeria (2011) NJIP 3. Available at: https://papers.ssrn.com/sol3/papers.cfm?abstract_id=2291267. Accessed 16 June 2018.

Osinubi, F. 2017. The Business of Entertainment: Harnessing Growth Opportunities in Entertainment, Media, Arts and Lifestyle. https://www.pwc.com/ng/en/assets/pdf/the-business-of-entertainment-final.pdf.

Oyewole, S. 2014. "A Peek inside Nigeria's Film Industry." WIPO Magazine, April.

Regional Network for Equity in Health in East and Southern Africa (EQUINET). 2010. Anti-counterfeiting Laws and Access to Essential Medicines in East and Southern Africa, EQUINET Policy Brief, number 22.

Schwab, K. 2015. Global Competitiveness Report. Davos, Switzerland: World Economic Forum.

Štrba, S. I. 2017. Legal and Institutional Considerations for Plant Variety Protection and Food Security in African Development Agendas: Solutions from WIPO? Journal of Intellectual Property Law & Practice, 12(3), 191–205. Available at: https://doi.org/10.1093/jiplp/jpw209.

Tripartite Free Trade Agreement. 2017. Agreement Establishing a Tripartite Free Trade Area between COMESA, the East African Community and SADC.

Trade Law Centre (TRALAC). 2018a. The African Continental Free Trade Area (The African Continental Free Trade Agreement) and other African Union initiatives for economic integration. Available at: https://www.tralac.org/discussions/article/12790-the-african-continental-free-trade-area-the African Continental Free Trade Agreement-and-other-african-union-au-initiatives-for-economic-integration.html.

———. 2018b. The African Continental Free Trade Agreement Stakeholder Workshop, Cape Town 18–19 October 2018.

UNCTAD (United Nations Conference on Trade and Development). 2014. "Convention on Biological Diversity and the Nagoya Protocol: Intellectual Property Implications. A Handbook on the Interface between Global Access and Benefit Sharing Rules and Intellectual Property." Geneva: UNCTAD. Available at: https://unctad.org/en/PublicationsLibrary/diaepcb2014d3_en.pdf.

———. 2016a. African Continental Free Trade Area: Policy and Negotiation Options for Trade in Goods UNCTAD/WEB/DITC/2016/7.

———. 2016b. TRIPS Flexibilities and Anti-Counterfeit Legislation in Kenya and the East African Community: Implications for Generic Producers. An UNCTAD-UNIDO Discussion paper, New York and Geneva, 2016. Available at: https://unctad.org/en/PublicationsLibrary/diaepcb2015d6_en.pdf.

———. 2017. Intellectual Property Rights in the Tripartite Region, UNCTAD/DIAE/2018/1, Discussion Paper, Geneva.

———. 2018. Intellectual Property Rights in the Tripartite Region, Discussion Paper, UNCTAD/DIAE/2018/1, Geneva.

———. 2017 and 2018. The State of Commodity Dependence 2016, 2017, Geneva and New York.

UNCTAD, UNAIDS, African Union Commission, Ministry of Health, Kenya, and Department of Trade and Industry, South Africa, Nairobi Statement on Investment in Access to Medicines. 2016. Nairobi, 21 July. Available at: http://www.unaids.org/sites/default/files/media/documents/20160721_NairobiStmtAccessMedicines.pdf.

United States Department of Justice and Federal Trade Commission. 2007. Antitrust Enforcement and Intellectual Property Rights: Promoting Innovation and Competition.

UPOV International Union for the Protection of New Varieties of Plants. n.d. "Getting the Most out of your New Plant Variety" http://www.wipo.int/sme/en/documents/upov_plant_variety_fulltext.html.

———. 1978. *Union internationale pour la protection des obtentions végétales,* Geneva.

———. 1991. *Union internationale pour la protection des obtentions végétales,* Geneva, 1991.

———. 2018. Overview of UPOV Publication No. 437. April 13. Geneva.

———. 2019. Members of the International Union for the Protection of New Varieties of Plants International Convention for the Protection of New Varieties of Plants, UPOV Convention (1961), as revised at Geneva (1972, 1978 and 1991), Status on February 14. Available at: http://www.upov.int/export/sites/upov/members/en/pdf/pub423.pdf.

United States Patent and Trademark Office, Final Rejection, Application No. 10/565.375, 2012, Alexandria, Virginia-3. Retrieved from Global Dossier. Available at: https://globaldossier.uspto.gov/#/details/US/10565375/A/105349.

World Intellectual Property Organization (WIPO). n.d.

d. Statistical Country Profiles: Kenya http://www.wipo.int/ipstats/en/statistics/country_profile/profile.jsp?code=KE.

———. 2003. What is Intellectual Property? *WIPO Publication No. 450(E)*. Geneva: International Bureau, World Intellectual Property Organization.

———. 2005. "The African Proposal for the Establishment of a Development Agenda for WIPO", *IIM/3/2*, World Intellectual Property Organization. Available at: https://www.wipo.int/meetings/en/doc_details.jsp?doc_id=47470, last visited 7 March 2019.

———. 2008. Case Study: Hoodia Plant. Geneva.

———. 2011. Interface between Exhaustion of Intellectual Property Rights and Competition Law, *CDIP/8/inf/5 Rev*, Committee on Development and Intellectual Property (CDIP), Eighth Session, November 14–18, Geneva.

———. 2013. Marrakesh Treaty to Facilitate Access to Published Works by Visually Impaired Persons and Persons with Print Disabilities.

———. 2017. ISA and IPEA Agreements. Available at: http://www.wipo.int/pct/en/access/isa_ipea_agreements.html.

———. 2018. Approval of Agreements, Memorandum of Understanding between the World Intellectual Property Organization (WIPO), the African Regional Intellectual Property Organization (ARIPO) and the African Intellectual Property Organization (OAPI), WO/CC/75/1, Seventy-Fifth (49th Ordinary) Session Geneva, September 24 to October 2, 2018, WIPO, Geneva. Available at: https://inventa.com/uploads/5bb4edae02557_WIPO, %20AOPI%20 and%20ARIPO%20Agreement.pdf, last visited, 10 April 2019.

———. 2018. World Intellectual Property Indicators 2018. Geneva.

World Trade Organization (WTO). 1995. Agreement on Trade-related Aspects of Intellectual Property Rights (TRIPS). Geneva.

———. 2001. Doha Ministerial Declaration of WTO on TRIPS and Public Health, World Trade Organization, *WT/MIN(01)/DEC/2*, Ministerial Conference, Fourth Session, Doha, 9–14 November.

———. 2005a. Protocol Amending the TRIPS Agreement, WT/L/6418. Geneva.

———. 2005b. Draft Modalities for TRIPS-Related Issues–Communication from Albania, Brazil, China, Colombia, Croatia, Ecuador, the European Communities, Georgia, Iceland, India, Indonesia, the Kyrgyz Republic, Liechtenstein, the Former Yugoslav Republic of Macedonia, Moldova, Pakistan, Peru, Sri Lanka, Switzerland, Thailand, Turkey, the African, Caribbean and Pacific Group and the African Group (TN/C/W/52). Geneva.

———. 2013. Decision on the Extension of the Transition Period under Article 66.1 for Least-Developed Country Members, Decision of the Council for TRIPS, IP/C/64. Geneva

———. 2015. Extension of the Transition Period under Article 66.1 of the TRIPS Agreement for Least Developed Country Members for Certain Obligations with Respect to Pharmaceutical Products, Decision of the Council for TRIPS, IP/C/73. Geneva.

———. 2016b. TRIPS Flexibilities and Anti-Counterfeit Legislation in Kenya and the East African Community: Implications for Generic Producers. An UNCTAD-UNIDO Discussion Paper, New York and Geneva, 2016. Available at: https://unctad.org/en/PublicationsLibrary/diaepcb2015d6_en.pdf.

———. 2017. Intellectual Property Rights in the Tripartite Region, UNCTAD/DIAE/2018/1, Discussion Paper, Geneva.

———. 2018. Intellectual Property Rights in the Tripartite Region, Discussion Paper, UNCTAD/DIAE/2018/1, Geneva.

———. 2017 and 2018. The State of Commodity Dependence 2016, 2017, Geneva and New York.

UNCTAD, UNAIDS, African Union Commission, Ministry of Health, Kenya, and Department of Trade and Industry, South Africa, Nairobi Statement on Investment in Access to Medicines. 2016. Nairobi, 21 July. Available at: http://www.unaids.org/sites/default/files/media/documents/20160721_NairobiStmtAccessMedicines.pdf.

United States Department of Justice and Federal Trade Commission. 2007. Antitrust Enforcement and Intellectual Property Rights: Promoting Innovation and Competition.

UPOV International Union for the Protection of New Varieties of Plants. n.d. "Getting the Most out of your New Plant Variety" http://www.wipo.int/sme/en/documents/upov_plant_variety_fulltext.html.

———. 1978. *Union internationale pour la protection des obtentions végétales,* Geneva.

———. 1991. *Union internationale pour la protection des obtentions végétales,* Geneva, 1991.

———. 2018. Overview of UPOV Publication No. 437. April 13. Geneva.

———. 2019. Members of the International Union for the Protection of New Varieties of Plants International Convention for the Protection of New Varieties of Plants, UPOV Convention (1961), as revised at Geneva (1972, 1978 and 1991), Status on February 14. Available at: http://www.upov.int/export/sites/upov/members/en/pdf/pub423.pdf.

United States Patent and Trademark Office, Final Rejection, Application No. 10/565.375, 2012, Alexandria, Virginia-3. Retrieved from Global Dossier. Available at: https://globaldossier.uspto.gov/#/details/US/10565375/A/105349.

World Intellectual Property Organization (WIPO).

———. 2003. What is Intellectual Property? *WIPO Publication No. 450(E)*. Geneva: International Bureau, World Intellectual Property Organization.

———. 2005. "The African Proposal for the Establishment of a Development Agenda for WIPO", *IIM/3/2,* World Intellectual Property Organization. Available at: https://www.wipo.int/meetings/en/doc_details.jsp?doc_id=47470, last visited 7 March 2019.

———. 2008. Case Study: Hoodia Plant. Geneva.

———. 2011. Interface between Exhaustion of Intellectual Property Rights and Competition Law, *CDIP/8/inf/5 Rev*, Committee on Development and Intellectual Property (CDIP), Eighth Session, November 14–18, Geneva.

———. 2013. Marrakesh Treaty to Facilitate Access to Published Works by Visually Impaired Persons and Persons with Print Disabilities.

———. 2017. ISA and IPEA Agreements. Available at: http://www.wipo.int/pct/en/access/isa_ipea_agreements.html.

———. 2018. Approval of Agreements, Memorandum of Understanding between the World Intellectual Property Organization (WIPO), the African Regional Intellectual Property Organization (ARIPO) and the African Intellectual Property Organization (OAPI), WO/CC/75/1, Seventy-Fifth (49th Ordinary) Session Geneva, September 24 to October 2, 2018, WIPO, Geneva. Available at: https://inventa.com/uploads/5bb4edae02557_WIPO, %20AOPI%20 and%20ARIPO%20Agreement.pdf, last visited, 10 April 2019.

———. 2018. World Intellectual Property Indicators 2018. Geneva.

World Trade Organization (WTO). 1995. Agreement on Trade-related Aspects of Intellectual Property Rights (TRIPS). Geneva.

———. 2001. Doha Ministerial Declaration of WTO on TRIPS and Public Health, World Trade Organization, *WT/MIN(01)/DEC/2*, Ministerial Conference, Fourth Session, Doha, 9–14 November.

———. 2005a. Protocol Amending the TRIPS Agreement, WT/L/6418. Geneva.

———. 2005b. Draft Modalities for TRIPS-Related Issues–Communication from Albania, Brazil, China, Colombia, Croatia, Ecuador, the European Communities, Georgia, Iceland, India, Indonesia, the Kyrgyz Republic, Liechtenstein, the Former Yugoslav Republic of Macedonia, Moldova, Pakistan, Peru, Sri Lanka, Switzerland, Thailand, Turkey, the African, Caribbean and Pacific Group and the African Group (TN/C/W/52). Geneva.

———. 2013. Decision on the Extension of the Transition Period under Article 66.1 for Least-Developed Country Members, Decision of the Council for TRIPS, IP/C/64. Geneva

———. 2015. Extension of the Transition Period under Article 66.1 of the TRIPS Agreement for Least Developed Country Members for Certain Obligations with Respect to Pharmaceutical Products, Decision of the Council for TRIPS, IP/C/73. Geneva.

Endnotes

1   WIPO, What is Intellectual Property? WIPO Publication No. 450 (E), WIPO, International Bureau, World Intellectual Property Organization, Geneva, 2003.

2   African Union. Agenda 2063: The Africa We Want, Aspiration 1, 2015.

3   UNCTAD. World Investment Report, 2011.

4   See, for example, United States Department of Justice and Federal Trade Commission Antitrust Enforcement and Intellectual Property Rights: Promoting Innovation and Competition, 2007.

5   Creative Commons. About the License, 2019. Available at https://creativecommons.org/licenses/, last visited on 7 March 2019.

6   Isaac, Alan G. and Walter G. Park. "On Intellectual Property Rights: Patents versus Free and Open Development", Enrico Colombatto, (ed.), The Elgar Companion to the Economics of Property Rights, p.387, 2004.

7   WTO. TRIPS, preambular paragraph 5 and Article 8, 1995.

8   UNCTAD-ICTSD (International Centre for Trade and Development). Resource Book on TRIPS and Development, UNCTAD and ICTSD, Cambridge University Press, New York, p.4, 2005.

9   WTO. TRIPS Agreement, Article 4(d), 2004. According to the provision, international agreements relating to the protection of IP rights which entered into force prior to the entry into force of the WTO Agreement (1994) must be notified to the Council for TRIPS (WTO) in order to benefit from the exception as is the case for the European Community, the Andean Community, the North American Free Trade Agreement (NAFTA) and the Southern Common Market (Mercosur). UNCTAD-ICTSD. Resource Book on TRIPS and Development, UNCTAD and ICTSD, Cambridge University Press, New York, pp.80–82, 2005.

10   Kiyoshi Adachix. Intellectual Property Provisions in Preferential Trade and Investment Agreements, UNCTAD, United Nations, Geneva and New York, forthcoming, 2019.

11   Ibid.

12 See WIPO: "The African Proposal for the Establishment of a Development Agenda for WIPO", *IIM/3/2*, World Intellectual Property Organization, 2005. Available at https://www.wipo.int/meetings/en/doc_details. jsp?doc_id=47470, last visited 7 March 2019.

13 WTO. Doha Ministerial Declaration of WTO on TRIPS and Public Health, World Trade Organization, *WT/MIN(01)/DEC/2*, Ministerial Conference, Fourth Session, Doha, 9–14 November 2001.

14 WTO. Draft Modalities for TRIPS-Related Issues. Communication from Albania, Brazil, China, Colombia, Croatia, Ecuador, the European Communities, Georgia, Iceland, India, Indonesia, Kyrgyzstan, Liechtenstein, the Former Yugoslav Republic of Macedonia, Moldova, Pakistan, Peru, Sri Lanka, Switzerland, Thailand, Turkey, the African, Caribbean and Pacific Group of States and the African Group (TN/C/W/52 and Add.1, Add.2, Add.3), 2008.

15 Oguamanam, Chidi. Plant Breeders' Rights, Farmers' Rights and Food Security: Africa's Failure of Resolve and India's Wobbly Leadership (May 3, 2018). Indian Journal of Law and Technology, Forthcoming; Ottawa Faculty of Law Working Paper No. 2018-17. Available at SSRN: https://ssrn. com/abstract=3173268.

16 COMESA Policy on IP rights and Cultural Industries, 2011, Council of Ministers, Part A, para. 39 (d).

17 WTO. Decision on the Extension of the Transition Period under Article 66.1 for Least-Developed Country Members, Decision of the Council for TRIPS, IP/C/64, 2013.

18 WTO. Extension of the Transition Period under Article 66.1 of the TRIPS Agreement for Least Developed Country Members for Certain Obligations with Respect to Pharmaceutical Products, Decision of the Council for TRIPS, IP/C/73, 2015.

19 For the amended version of the TRIPS Agreement, see https://www.wto.org/english/ docs_e/legal_e/31bis_trips_01_e.htm.

20 See for example the Regional Network for Equity in Health in East and Southern Africa (EQUINET), 2010, Anti-counterfeiting laws and access to essential medicines in East and Southern Africa EQUINET Policy Brief number 22; Sisule F. Musungu "The Potential Impact of the Proposed East African Community (EAC) Anti-Counterfeiting Policy and Bill on Access to Essential Medicines" UNDP BDP HIV Practice/March 2010 Discussion Paper.

21 These are: Angola, Botswana, Democratic Republic of Congo (DRC), Lesotho, Madagascar, Malawi, Mauritius, Mozambique, Namibia, Seychelles, South Africa, Eswatini, United Republic of Tanzania, Zambia and Zimbabwe.

22 The Tripartite Agreement has been signed by 22 member countries namely Angola, Botswana, Burundi, the Comoros, Democratic Republic of Congo (DRC), Djibouti, Egypt, Kenya, State of Libya, Madagascar, Malawi, Mauritius, Namibia, Rwanda, Seychelles, Sudan, United Republic of Tanzania, Uganda, South Africa, Eswatini, Zambia and Zimbabwe.

23 UNCTAD. Intellectual Property Rights in the Tripartite Region, UNCTAD/DIAE/2018/1, Discussion Paper, Geneva, Annex I, 2017.

24 UNCTAD, UNAIDS, African Union Commission, Ministry of Health, Kenya, and Department of Trade and Industry, South Africa, Nairobi Statement on Investment in Access to Medicines, Nairobi, 21 July 2016. See http://www.unaids.org/sites/ default/files/media/documents/20160721_ NairobiStmtAccessMedicines.pdf.

25 Botswana, Eswatini, the Gambia, Ghana, Kenya, Lesotho, Liberia, Malawi, Mozambique, Namibia, Rwanda, Sao Tome and Principe, Sierra Leone, Somalia, Sudan, United Republic of Tanzania, Uganda, Zambia and Zimbabwe. The organization also has observer States: Angola, Burundi, Egypt, Ethiopia, Eritrea, Mauritius, Nigeria, Seychelles and South Africa.

26 Benin, Burkina Faso, Cameroon, Central African Republic, Comoros, the Congo, Ivory Coast, Gabon, Guinea, Guinea Bissau, Equatorial Guinea, Mali, Mauritania, Niger, Senegal, Chad and Togo.

27 African Union. Assembly/AU/Dec. 589(XXVI)), 2016.

28 See WIPO, 2018. https://inventa.com/uploads/5bb4edae02557_ WIPO,%20AOPI%20and%20ARIPO%20Agreement. pdf.

29 WIPO. World Intellectual Property Indicators 2018, pp. 43 and 101, 2018.

30 Ibid. p.73.

31 WTO, 2015, IP/C/73.

32 Article 6 reads: "For the purposes of dispute settlement under this Agreement, subject to the provisions of Articles 3 and 4 nothing in this Agreement shall be used to address the issue of the exhaustion of intellectual property rights".

33 Egypt, Law on the Protection of Intellectual Property Rights, Law no. 82 of 2002 and Council of Ministers Resolution no. 1366 of 2003, Regulations for Implementing Law no. 82 of 2002.

34 Cliff, Martin, "Hollywood's favourite food revealed: Victoria Beckham and Gwyneth Paltrow are fans of teff, an iron-rich Ethiopian grain that costs a whopping £7 a bag", Daily Mail, 3 February 2014.

35 United States Patent and Trademark Office, Final Rejection, Application No. 10/565.375, 2012, Alexandria, Virginia-3. Retrieved from Global Dossier, available at: https://globaldossier.uspto.gov/#/details/US/10565375/A/105349.

36 Ibid., p.23.

37 Further reading: Regine Andersen and Tone Winge, *The Access and Benefit-Sharing Agreement on Teff Genetic Resources: Facts and Lessons* (Fridtjof Nansens Institute Report 6/2012).

38 District Court, the Hague, Ancientgrain B.V. v. Bakels Senior N.V., case no. ECLI: NL: RBDHA:2018:13960, 21 November 2018.

39 WIPO. Interface between Exhaustion of Intellectual Property Rights and Competition Law *CDIP/8/inf/5 Rev*, Committee on Development and Intellectual Property (CDIP), Eighth Session, Geneva, November 14 to 18, 2011.

40 Countries with an international commitment to adhere to the 1991 UPOV Convention may require exemption from the Agreement Establishing the African Continental Free Trade Area.

41 African Union Commission. Agreement Establishing the African Continental Free Trade Area, , Article 3, 2018.

42 Andean Community. Decision No. 486 Establishing the Common Industrial Property Regime, 2000.

43 Helfer, Laurence R. and Karen J. Alter, The Influence of the Andean Intellectual Property Regime on Access to Medicines in Latin America, in Wealth and Health: Global Administrative Law and the Battle over Intellectual Property and Access To Medicines In Latin America (Rochelle Dreyfuss and César Rodríguez-Garavito, (eds.) 2013).

44 Biadgleng, E. T. J.-C. Maur. The Influence of Preferential Trade Agreements on the Implementation of Intellectual Property Rights in Developing Countries: A First Look, UNCTAD and ICTSD, Geneva, p.22, 2011.

45 Kiyoshi Adachi, Intellectual Property Provisions in Preferential Trade and Investment Agreements, UNCTAD, United Nations, Geneva and New York, forthcoming.

46 Bilaterals.org. (2008). "Blow to the Intellectual Property Rules of the Andean Community". 15 August, 2008. Available at: www.bilaterals.org/.

47 The ASEAN member States are Indonesia, Thailand, Singapore, Malaysia, Philippines, Viet Nam, Myanmar (Burma), Cambodia, Brunei, Laos.

48 See ASEAN, 2019, https://www.aseanip.org/.

49 Linsu Kim, *Technology Transfer and Intellectual Property Rights. The Korean Experience.* UNCTAD-ICTSD Project on Intellectual Property Rights and Sustainable Development, Geneva, June 2003 (available at https://unctad.org/en/PublicationsLibrary/ictsd2003ipd2_en.pdf).

Chapter 5
Competition Policy Protocol

Competition is at the heart of making market economies functional. As businesses seek to maximize profit, various practices (some anti-competitive) appear, including cartels, vertical restraints, mergers and acquisitions merger regulation and abuses of dominance. Some anti-competitive conduct crosses borders and affects multiple African countries, leading to power concentrations that create oligopolies and enterprises seen as too big to manage.

In the absence of safeguards regulating anti-competitive practices, businesses—both domestic and especially foreign—can abuse their dominant market positions through price fixing cartels, predatory behaviour that eliminates local competition and other market-sharing agreements. Such anti-competitive practices reduce choice and increase prices, thus denying consumers and excluding producers the benefits of trade liberalization. Anti-competitive practices are, therefore, a cancer in the bone marrow of free and fair trade, owing to their known abilities to restrict competition and deteriorate consumer welfare.

This chapter considers how an African Union–wide competition framework should be fashioned. In a continent where the absence of competition laws, policies and institutions typifies most countries, the opportunity presented by the African Union Summit decision to develop a continent-wide competition policy requires careful attention. Policy makers must consider how the competition protocol manages opportunities created in other parts of the African Continental Free Trade Area (AfCFTA) and how they can fast-track reforms. Their goal is to ensure that markets work fairly—for both business and consumers—by disciplining negative practices observed as businesses engage in trade, so that trade is brought to fruition for development. Ensuring that trade integration takes place in a marketplace of fair competition is the core objective of competition law and policy, here in the context of cross-border trade.

Why a competition protocol in the AfCFTA?

Background to cross-border competition policy

Competition policy aims to promote fair competition and ensure efficient market outcomes. Used effectively, competition policy ensures that consumers and producers get a "fair" price, products have good quality, markets employ conducive incentives, innovation achieves international competitiveness and consumer interests are safeguarded through increased choice. Competition policy nurtures and supports new industries, particularly small and medium-size enterprises. Establishing competition rules and competition-refereeing institutions to guard against anti-competitive conduct presents an important opportunity.

Although some developed countries have used competition policy as a central component of market regulation for over a century, for many developing economies the area is fairly new. Developing countries especially need international co-operation to overcome cross-border anti-competitive issues. They face the effect of international mergers and acquisitions and the anti-competitive practices of foreign firms in their domestic markets. But they often lack the information and capacity to address such challenges on their own and in many cases are limited by a lack of domestic competition laws. Africa, with few countries having competition policy and law regimes in place, must take care in managing matters of competition law and policy at the continental scale.

Some African countries have developed competition frameworks comprising laws, regulations and institutions. Examples include Algeria, Egypt, Morocco and Tunisia in the North; Benin, Côte d'Ivoire, The Gambia and Senegal in the West; Cameroon and Chad in Central Africa; Kenya and Tanzania in the East; Eswatini, Malawi, Namibia, South Africa, Zambia and Zimbabwe in the South; and the Indian Ocean islands of Mauritius, Mozambique and Seychelles. But other countries do not have legislation in place, although some are at various stages in the law drafting process. Even where there are laws, the record of implementation and enforcement remains unimpressive. An AfCFTA competition protocol could address these gaps.

Traditionally, competition policy concerned singular domestic markets. However, since modern investment, production and trade have spread production across regional and global value chains, competition policy solutions must address cross-border practices. Competition-related provisions have been adopted into more than 216 different free trade agreements (FTAs) (Laprevote, 2015). For Africa, the decision to launch a continental competition policy chapter in the AfCFTA portends well for leapfrogging domestic gaps by obliging national competition authorities to cooperatively address extra-territorial effects on anti-competitive firm behaviour.

Consumer protection interacts with competition policy. It provides information and rights awareness to consumers, enforces rules against unfair and misleading commercial practices, promotes product safety and integrates consumer interests across all economic sectors. It aims to balance the informational asymmetries between traders and consumers. Consumer protection occupies different legislative and institutional frameworks, with some countries having provisions in their competition laws (such as Botswana, Ethiopia, Kenya and Tanzania) and others having separate consumer protection laws and institutions (such as Egypt, Namibia and South Africa).

The revised United Nations Guidelines on Consumer Protection (adopted by the UN General Assembly in December 2015) includes recommen-

dations on national policies on consumer goods and services safety and quality standards, dispute resolution and redress, financial services and e-commerce. The guidelines affect development of an Africa-wide competition protocol in the AfCFTA.

To achieve its objectives, the economic liberalization to be achieved through the AfCFTA must benefit not only multinational corporations, but all AfCFTA State party economies, especially the small and medium-sized enterprises (SMEs) within them.

The first *Assessing Regional Integration in Africa* noted the need for "a common competition policy and law to protect and promote free competition and permit harmonization of trade and investment laws and regulations throughout the region" (ECA, 2004). It argued that the increased competition resulting from such a policy would stimulate productive efficiency, benefiting final consumers in Africa (ECA, 2004).

As Africa moves towards dismantling barriers to the combined continental market, continental rules and regulations should guide businesses so that that the benefits of opening the market are distributed fairly across consumers and economies. So, Africa requires functional national and regional competition and consumer protection laws and policies, anchored in continental rules and regulations embodied in the AfCFTA.

Cross-border anti-competitive practices in Africa

African countries face cross-border anti-competitive practices. Table 5.1, showing a selection of cases identified and addressed between 2015 and 2017 by the South African Competition Commission, highlights the breadth of products and countries affected.

The companies subject to cartel investigations in African countries have considerable presence in, or exports to, other African countries, creating cross-border anti-competitive effects, including substantially higher prices for consumers (Box 5.1). Such anti-competitive practices can burden sectors critical for development, such as agriculture (Box 5.2). In other cases, dominant positions are used

Table 5.1:

Cartels in southern Africa affecting regional competition, 2015–17

INDUSTRY	NUMBER OF COMPANIES IN THE CASE	COUNTRIES POSSIBLY AFFECTED	RAID, REFERRAL, OR SETTLEMENT	YEAR
Fruit processing	2	Botswana, Mozambique	Referral	2017
Bricks	6	Africa	Referral/settlement	2017
Fire protection services	29	Africa	Referral/settlement/raid	2017
Chemicals	2	Africa (including Botswana, Zimbabwe and others)	Settlement	2017
Meat	7	Africa	Raid	2017
Edible oils1	5	BLNSa	Raid	2016
Edible oils 2	2	Africa	Referral/Settlement	2016/2017
Cargo freight	6	Southern Africa	Raid	2016
Rail maintenance	3	Southern Africa	Raid	2016
Gear pumps	2	Southern Africa, Botswana, Zambia, Zimbabwe and others	Referral	2016
Security services	2	Africa	Settlement	2016
Packaging paper	2	Africa, excluding North African countries	Raid	2016
Telecom equipment	2	Angola	Referral	2016
Wooden products	2	Angola, Dem. Rep. of the Congo, Kenya, Malawi, Mozambique, Tanzania, Uganda, Zimbabwe, Zambia	Raid	2016
Glass fitment and repair services	2	Angola, Botswana, Dem. Rep. of the Congo, Eswatini, Lesotho, Malawi, Namibia	Raid	2016
Liquefied petroleum gas and cylinders	6	Angola, Botswana, Eswatini, Kenya, Lesotho, Malawi, Mozambique, Namibia Nigeria, Seychelles, Tanzania, Uganda, Zambia, Zimbabwe	Raid	2015
Plastic Pipes	4	Sub-Saharan Africa	Referral	2015

Source: Information adapted from CCRED Quarterly Review Analysis (Bosiu, 2017).

Notes: Settlement: Agreement to settle reached with the Competition Commission South Africa; Referral: Case referred to the Competition Tribunal for adjudication; Raid: Dawn raids conducted to obtain possible evidence on the existence of cartel conduct.

a. BLNS countries are Botswana, Eswatini (formerly Swaziland), Lesotho and Namibia.

to frustrate foreign direct investment (Box 5.3) or push out rivals (Box 5.4). Governments can themselves support anti-competitive behaviour through state aid (Box 5.5). The situation is worsened when a jurisdiction has weak capacities for investigation and prosecution, giving such companies the opportunity to replicate gains from cartel actions elsewhere in the region.

Cement cartels in Southern African Customs Union members

A cement cartel was uncovered after an investigation by the Competition Commission of South Africa (CCSA) began in 2008. The investigation targeted the southern African region's four main cement producers: PPC Ltd (PPC), AfriSam South Africa Pty Ltd (AfriSam), Lafarge Cement Company (Lafarge) and Natal Portland Cement Company Pty Ltd (NPC). The start of the investigation was based on research findings by the CCSA that cement prices had doubled since 2001, despite fluctuations in demand and input costs. PPC subsequently applied for leniency and confirmed the existence of a cartel among the four producers.

Afrisam also admitted that it had entered into agreements and arrangements with PPC, Lafarge and NPC to divide markets and indirectly fix the price of cement between 1996 and 2008.

From a historical perspective, the cartel operated as an official and legal cement cartel in South Africa from the 1940s until its disbandment in 1996. Following the disbandment, the cement producers agreed that each firm's market share should be proportional to its production capacities. Territorially, PPC agreed that it would not compete with Lafarge in KwaZulu–Natal (South Africa) in exchange for Lafarge not competing with PPC in Botswana, while Afrisam would supply Namibia.

The companies monitored the collusive agreement partly by sharing monthly sales data through the Concrete and Cement Institute of South Africa.

PPC received leniency in exchange for a complete disclosure of all cartel activities. Lafarge and Afrisam settled with the CCSA: Lafarge agreed to pay a penalty of 6 per cent of its annual turnover in cement sales in the Southern African Customs Union region in 2010, and Afrisam agreed to pay a penalty of 3 per cent of such sales. The CCSA has referred the case against NPC to the Competition Tribunal for prosecution.

Following this investigation, a joint report of the African Competition Forum and the World Bank Group (2016) reported that prices and margins have declined steadily since the breakup of the cartel. Using price data from cement producers, Govinda et al. (2014) estimated that the total savings to South African customers due to the breakup of the cartel—assuming an overcharge of 9.7 per cent—was in the range of 1.1–1.4 billion rand ($79–100 million) a year. Moreover, competition has been generally enhanced as firms have been penetrating regions where they were previously inactive. For example, prior to the investigation, the Western Cape of South Africa was solely allocated to PPC, but Afrisam has since entered that market. The Northern Cape of South Africa was split 75 per cent and 25 per cent between Afrisam and PPC during the cartel years, but Lafarge has since taken market share from them.

Source: Africa Competition Forum.

Anti-competitive telecommunications practices in Kenya, Mauritius and South Africa

Kenya—The Competition Authority of Kenya (CAK) ordered Kenya's Safaricom to open its mobile money transfer network and eliminate exclusive agreements with M-PESA agents. The CAK also prohibited the firm from levying extra charges on competitors to use its network. This followed a complaint from India-based Airtel, a rival telecom firm, which had been barred from doing business with the 85,000 agents Safaricom uses for its service.

Mauritius—Mauritius Telecom has been bundling its broadband Internet, international calling and pay-tv products. The firm has a monopoly in the broadband market, a 37 per cent share in the market for the retail supply of pay TV and a 3 per cent share in the market for the retail supply of premium content in pay TV. Since the firm has a monopoly in the broadband market and is using this power to gain share in the pay TV market, this behaviour could be considered an abuse of dominance, which leads to anti-competitive outcomes.

South Africa—During 2002 the South African Value-Added Network Service (VANS) Association and other Internet service providers (ISPs) complained, alleging that Telkom had abused its upstream dominance to create an unfair advantage for its downstream retail division in the VANS market. In 2004, the CCSA referred the case to the Tribunal following investigation and finding that Telkom:

- Unlawfully sought to extend its monopoly by refusing to supply essential facilities (its fixed-line network) to independent VANS providers.
- Induced VANS providers' customers not to deal with them by approaching the customers, claiming that the VANS model was illegal.
- Charged theVANS services customers excessive prices for access services.
- Discriminated in favour of its own customers by giving them a discount on distance-related charges that it did not advance to customers of the independent VANS providers.

Between 2005 and 2007, the Internet Service Providers' Association and three other ISPs submitted five separate complaints against Telkom. Following investigation, the CCSA found that Telkom had:

- Engaged in a margin squeeze against ISPs by charging excessive prices for inputs.
- Refused to lease essential facilities.
- Engaged in anti-competitive conditional selling of managed network services and Internet access services.

Telkom and the CCSA agreed to settle the case. As part of the settlement, Telkom admitted to contravening the Competition Act with the margin squeeze and anti-competitive bundling and tying of products.

Source: ACF Submission.

Box 5.3:
A fertilizer cartel in Zambia

Fertilizer, an important agricultural input, has been the subject of anticompetitive practices such as cartels. The anti-competitive practices raise production prices and reduce small farmers' ability to buy fertilizer, reducing their competitiveness with large scale farmers who are likely to enjoy economies of scale. In Africa, agriculture contributes a significant share of GDP, and the sector is usually dominated by small farmers.

In 2012, Zambia's Competition and Consumer Protection Commission received a complaint in relation to the Farmer Input Support Programme (FISP). Nyiombo Investments Limited and Omnia Fertiliser Zambia Limited had been supplying fertilizer under the FISP for 10 years. The complaint alleged that the companies were dividing the market for fertilizer tendered under the FISP. Based on documents seized from the two parties, the commission established that there was an agreement between them and imposed a fine of $20 million. The parties appealed the matter to the Competition and Consumer Protection Tribunal, which ruled in their favour. The commission then appealed to the High Court, which also ruled in favour of the parties. The commission has further appealed to the Supreme Court against the judgement of the High Court, and the matter is currently pending. Govinda et al. (2014) estimated that savings from ending the potential cartel would have been around $21 million.

Source: Africa Competition Forum.

Exclusive agreement on content, sports coverage and broadcasting rights.

In 2017 the Competition Authority of Kenya initiated an investigation into the conduct of South African company Multichoice Africa Limited (MAL) in the pay TV subsector. The investigation was triggered by the exit of two pay TV market players shortly after entering, to the detriment of Kenyan consumers. The authority's investigation established that MAL infracted against the Kenyan Competition Act through various exclusive agreements on contents, sports coverage and broadcasting rights. MAL entered into exclusive agreements with free-to-air broadcasters that the authority viewed to be anticompetitive.

The authority's decisions required MAL, among other things, to unequivocally undertake to comply with the Act and compete fairly with the other TV subsector player. MAL agreed with the authority, in consideration of the economic effects of such exclusive agreements, to: (1) desist from entering into agreements that foreclose competition in the relevant segment of the market, (2) not enter into exclusive vertical agreements that may dampen competition by effect and (3) comply with competition law and compete fairly with other sector players in the market.

Source: Competition Authority of Kenya.

Palm oil and State aid in WAEMU

Senegal was found in violation of the West African Economic and Monetary Union (WAEMU) regional competition law for taking actions that foreclosed its national market to competition from another member State, Côte d'Ivoire. The case, decided by the WAEMU Competition Commission, addressed indirect protectionist measures by the government of Senegal that blocked palm oil products from Côte d'Ivoire from entry into the Senegalese market.

In 2008, the Senegalese government adopted regulation NS 03-072 on palm oil enriched with vitamin A, following WAEMU regulations on consumable oils. In 2009, it unilaterally revised the regulation to require a maximum of 30 per cent content of fat acid in the refined palm oil. This measure was taken without consultation or approval by WAEMU, which had created the framework for accrediting, certifying and normalizing products. The measure prevented the importation and commercialization of palm oil products that did not meet the requirement. As a consequence, the Senegalese authorities blocked the commercialization of a quantity of refined palm oil, which the company West Africa Commodities had imported from Côte d'Ivoire, on the ground that it violated the new regulation. In reaction, the government of Côte d'Ivoire and the firm West Africa Commodities challenged the regulation on the ground that it affected trade between member States and was therefore anti-competitive.

The commission argued that although public health reasons may justify temporary measures by the member States, they should be coordinated at the regional level. In addition, if an intervention by member States affects inter-States trade, the community competition law, which forbids States from taking measures that affect regional trade, is applicable. So, for the commission, public health considerations should not provide an indirect means to foreclose a national market from competition.

The commission directed the government of Senegal to suspend the application of the regulation, since it violated the regional competition rules, especially regulation 02/2002/CM/UEMOA on anti-competitive practices. The Senegalese government was therefore requested to retract the regulation of refined palm oil.

A closer look at competition regimes in Africa

Diversity of national and regional competition laws and frameworks

The AfCFTA competition protocol will have to address competition regimes among African countries that are diverse in their provisions and in the types of institutions they are supported by. African Union member States' competition laws and institutions can be classified into four categories:

- 23 countries with a competition law in force and an operational competition authority: Algeria, Botswana, Burkina Faso, Cameroon, Côte d'Ivoire, Democratic Republic of the Congo, Egypt, Eswatini, Ethiopia, Gambia, Kenya, Liberia, Madagascar, Malawi, Mauritius, Morocco, Namibia, Senegal, Seychelles, South Africa, Tanzania, Zambia and Zimbabwe.

- 10 countries with a competition law but no competition authority yet: Angola, Burundi, Comoros, Cabo Verde, Djibouti, Gabon, Mali, Mozambique, Rwanda and Sudan.

- 4 countries where the preparation of competition legislation has reached a very advanced stage: Lesotho, Niger, Nigeria and Togo.

- 17 countries with no competition law or still in the early stages of preparing one: Benin, Central African Republic, Chad, Congo, Equatorial Guinea, Eritrea, Ghana, Guinea, Guinea Bissau, Libya, Mauritania, São Tomé and Príncipe, Sierra Leone, Somalia, South Sudan, Uganda and Western Sahara.

Although there is interest in competition law enforcement in Africa, most countries are still building their expertise, and new advances in the digital economy will bring more challenges. Of the 23 countries with an active competition law and an independent competition authority to administer it (Lipimile, 2018), only 15 have comprehensive competition laws that are strictly enforced (World Bank, 2016). So, more than 72 per cent of African countries face capacity challenges in competition enforcement. Capacity building is needed.

Countries widely converge in their substantive provisions on cartel offences but differ on applying public interest to merger control and on regulating dominant positions.

For merger control, one can distinguish between two categories of countries. Some apply pure competition considerations, looking for the effects of the merger on competition in the market, evaluating the likelihood of reduced competition and the creation of a dominant firm that may in the future abuse its dominance (Mauritius is an example.) Others incorporate a public interest filter in their assessment, considering public welfare factors such as job creation, promotion of exports and raising standards of living for disadvantaged groups (Oxenham, 2012) (Malawi, South Africa and Zambia are examples.) The incorporation of public interest issues has been a topic of much debate.[1] It has typically been received sceptically in developed jurisdictions, partly because of its potential to open competition assessments to external influences. But it has also allowed African countries to consider their distinct historical legacy and social and economic characteristics in adopting laws, rather than merely transplanting foreign competition laws.

Likewise, different national laws employ different thresholds for identifying a dominant position, and different definitions of what amounts to abusive practice.

Regional competition laws and authorities

REGIONAL ENTITY	COMMON MARKET FOR EASTERN AND SOUTHERN AFRICA (COMESA)	EAST AFRICAN COMMUNITY (EAC)	SOUTHERN AFRICAN DEVELOPMENT COMMUNITY (SADC)
Member countries	Republic of Burundi, Comoros, Democratic Republic of the Congo, Djibouti, Egypt, Eritrea, Eswatini, Ethiopia, Kenya, Libya, Madagascar, Malawi, Mauritius, Rwanda, Seychelles, Somalia, Sudan, Tunisia, Uganda, Zambia and Zimbabwe	Burundi, Kenya, Rwanda, South Sudan, Tanzania and Uganda	Angola, Botswana, Democratic Republic of the Congo, Eswatini, Lesotho, Madagascar, Malawi, Mauritius, Mozambique, Namibia, Seychelles, South Africa, Tanzania, Zambia and Zimbabwe
Competition articles in the treaty	Article 55 of the treaty says that any agreement between undertakings or concerted practice which has as its object or effect the prevention, restriction or distortion of competition within the common market shall be prohibited	Article 21 of the Protocol on the Establishment of an EAC Customs Union, signed in March 2004, contains competition provisions	Article 25 of the SADC Trade Protocol ("Competition Policy") requires member States to implement measures within the community that prohibit unfair business practices and promote competition. Further, all SADC member States are bound by the Declaration on Regional Cooperation and Consumer Policies, signed in September 2009, which provides that to make cooperation effective, member States shall take the necessary steps to adopt, strengthen and implement the necessary competition and consumer protection laws in their respective countries
Competition law adopted	In 2004, the COMESA Competition Regulations and Competition Rules were adopted to prohibit anti-competitive practices within the common market, to establish a merger control regime for cross-border cases and to address other competition law and consumer protection matters	EAC Competition Act of 2006	9 countries signed a memorandum of understanding on inter-agency cooperation in competition policy, law and enforcement to ensure cooperation between competition authorities and to strengthen enforcement, which came into effect on 26 May 2016 and is valid for three years, with the option of renewal
Competition authority	The regulations established the COMESA Competition Commission and the Board of Commissioners	The EACCA was set up in 2016, with its commissioners sworn in November. It is the most recent regional competition authority in Africa. The authority is an independent organ of the EAC but subject to judicial review by the East African Court of Justice (as provided for in Sections 44 and 46 of the EAC Competition Act, 2006). It is not yet operational	Cooperation approach adopted by SADC and working groups since 2015
Type of authority (supranational or cooperation)	Supranational	Nascent (supranational)	Cooperation
Regulations	Mergers, prohibition of anti-competitive agreements, prohibition against abuse of dominant position		Mergers and cartels
Consumer protection	Yes	Yes	Yes

SOUTHERN AFRICAN CUSTOMS UNION (SACU)	ECONOMIC COMMUNITY OF WEST AFRICAN STATES (ECOWAS)	WEST AFRICAN ECONOMIC AND MONETARY UNION (WAEMU)	ECONOMIC COMMUNITY OF CENTRAL AFRICAN STATES (ECCAS)	CENTRAL AFRICAN ECONOMIC AND MONETARY UNION (CEMAC)
Botswana, Eswatini, Lesotho, Namibia and South Africa	Benin, Burkina Faso, Cabo Verde, Côte d'Ivoire, Gambia, Ghana, Guinea, Guinea Bissau, Liberia, Mali, Niger, Nigeria, Senegal, Sierra Leone and Togo	Benin, Burkina Faso, Côte d'Ivoire, Guinea-Bissau, Mali, Niger, Senegal and Togo	Angola, Burundi, Cameroon, Central African Republic, Chad, Congo, Democratic Republic of the Congo, Equatorial Guinea, Gabon, Rwanda, São Tomé and Príncipe.	Cameroon, Central African Republic, Chad, Congo, Equatorial Guinea and Gabon
Article 40 ("Competition Policy") expresses the agreement of member States that there should be competition policies in each member State and obliges them to co-operate with each other on enforcement of competition laws and regulations. Article 41 ("Unfair Trade Practices") obliges the Council of SACU (acting on the advice of the SACU Commission) to develop policies and instruments to address unfair trade practices between member States. Such policies and measures are to be annexed to the SACU agreement	ECOWAS Regional Competition Policy Framework of 2007	Articles 88–90. Article 88 identifies the prohibited practices, and Article 90 gives power to WAEMU to apply the rules subject to control by a court of justice. Article 89 confers to the Council of Ministers the power to set rules	ECCAS Strategic Vision at the Horizon 2025 aims at building a competitive regional environment to attract private investments in growth areas	Article 28(5) of the Treaty establishing the Economic and Customs Union of Central Africa addresses finding solutions to phase out restrictive business practices between member States
	ECOWAS Supplementary Act A/SA.1/06/08 of 19 Dec 2008 on "Adoption of Community Competition Rules and the modalities of their application within ECOWAS"	Adopted May 2002 and operative January 2003.		Regulation 1/99-UEAC-CM-639 of 1999
	On 13 July 2018, the ECOWAS Regional Competition Authority was established	2002 WAEMU adopted regulations on anti-competitive practices giving the WAEMU Commission the effective powers of a competition authority		Three institutions: CEMAC Commission, CEMAC Court of Justice and Regional Competition Council
Cooperation	Nascent (supranational)	Supranational		Supranational
		Mergers, prohibition of anti-competitive agreements, prohibition against abuse of dominant position and State aid		Cartels, abuse of dominance, concentrations

REGIONAL ENTITY	COMMON MARKET FOR EASTERN AND SOUTHERN AFRICA (COMESA)	EAST AFRICAN COMMUNITY (EAC)	SOUTHERN AFRICAN DEVELOPMENT COMMUNITY (SADC)
Enforcement	Investigations and adjudication and policy elaboration	Investigate and impose sanctions and remedies	Evidence gathering and remedy design and implementation when conducting merger reviews. Legal frameworks and investigative techniques
Cooperation between member States	Notification, exchange of information, coordination of actions and consultations	Competition advocacy and consultations as well as cooperation with regional and international organizations and foreign competition authorities	The memorandum of understanding allows members to collaborate in evidence gathering and remedy design and implementation when conducting merger reviews. A Cartels Working Group has been in place since June 2015 with sub-groups on legal frameworks and investigative techniques
Countries without national competition laws	Burundi, Comoros, Eritrea, Libya, Somalia, Sudan and Uganda	Burundi and South Sudan	Lesotho
Countries without national competition authorities	Same as above	Same as above	Lesotho and Mozambique

Source: Compilation adopted from COMESA submission

Countries divergence in the level of effective enforcement of competition laws. Only a handful of competition authorities are fully operational, reflecting the need for training, capacity building and advocacy. The operational authorities do not have the same levels of finances, enforcement capabilities and case law. So, programmes must be tailored for different countries on the basis of exchanged experiences and best practices from the region.

Divergences are not fatal to the agenda of regional and continental integration. To the contrary: a one-size-fits-all competition policy would be hugely unsuccessful in Africa, given each country's distinct economic and political needs.

The multi-layered competition regulation landscape in Africa includes both national and sub-regional frameworks. In addition, most African countries have overlapping memberships in multiple subregional economic blocs. With deepening regional and continental integration, these arrangements deserve cautious examination if competition laws are to be effectively and successfully implemented. The AfCFTA protocol can provide a continental framework for connecting the layers and addressing substantive shortfalls or gaps.

Reconciling overlapping regimes: Competition laws at the regional level

Since the 1990s, the number of regional and international initiatives to promote competitive markets has grown. Most regional trade agreements make provisions for protecting against unfair competition.

Such provisions aim to ensure that the benefits of trade and liberalization are not compromised by cross-border anticompetitive behaviour. The full benefits of free trade can only be realized where regulatory trade barriers, once removed, are not replaced by artificial trade barriers erected by firms operating in the market. Regional integration schemes, by encouraging the free movement of goods and services across national borders, increased the likelihood of cross-border anti-competitive practices. These include cross-border mergers, international cartels and abuse of dominant positions (see Boxes 5.1–5.5). The challenge results from the disjunction between national laws and international markets. For market integration to succeed, it was therefore necessary for the regional trade agreements to adopt common measures to protect the competitive process.

SOUTHERN AFRICAN CUSTOMS UNION (SACU)	ECONOMIC COMMUNITY OF WEST AFRICAN STATES (ECOWAS)	WEST AFRICAN ECONOMIC AND MONETARY UNION (WAEMU)	ECONOMIC COMMUNITY OF CENTRAL AFRICAN STATES (ECCAS)	CENTRAL AFRICAN ECONOMIC AND MONETARY UNION (CEMAC)
		Article 90 gives powers to the WAEMU to apply competition rules, subject to control of the Court of Justice		Has started accepting notifications
		A directive was adopted on cooperation between the WAEMU Commission and the competition bodies of member States		Yes through the CEMAC Council of Ministers
Lesotho	Benin, Ghana, Guinea, Guinea Bissau, Niger, Nigeria, Sierra Leone and Togo	Benin and Guinea Bissau. In Niger, the law was validated but never operationalized	Central African Republic, Chad, Congo, Equatorial Guinea, São Tomé and Príncipe	
Lesotho	Same as above plus Mali	Same as above	Same as above plus Rwanda and Gabon	

In Africa, the founding documents of the major regional economic communities (RECs) include competition policy or laws, creating regional competition frameworks. The competition provisions differ institutionally, with some RECs, such as the Common Market for the Eastern and Southern Africa (COMESA) and the East African Community (EAC) establishing supra-national regional competition authorities, while others, such as the Southern African Customs Union (SACU) and the Southern African Development Community (SADC) operating through a cooperation framework. In a supra-national institution, negotiated power is delegated to an authority by governments of member States. The European Union (EU) is an example of such an arrangement. In the case of COMESA and EAC, competencies are shared concerning the handling of cross-border and domestic cases. The SACU and SADC arrangement entails exchanging non-confidential case information, capacity building activities and sharing experiences but no mandate to deal directly with cross-border cases. Irrespective of how they appear, competition provisions at the regional level can act as a major instrument to develop an open, rule-based, predictable, non-discriminatory trading system, with a fair distribution of benefits. Such transparency also helps to encourage foreign direct investment in the region, which in turn helps to improve allocative efficiency and reduce consumer prices.

Table 5.2 describes the treatment of competition in the RECs, displaying the overlapping memberships in most regions, existence of supranational competition authorities and authorities using a cooperation approach. It also highlights similarities. The next phase of AfCFTA negotiations should consider these issues and how to harmonize approaches as Africa moves to a continental framework.

Some existing RECs, such as COMESA, have established systems for competition law and dealing with cross-border anticompetitive practices, while others, such as EAC, ECOWAS and WAEMU, are setting them up. SADC and SACU's enforcement cooperation framework complicates the situation since some members are also members of COMESA. Those countries that are members of both COMESA and SACU or SADC have the option of applying the COMESA rules, making uniformity difficult. Since EAC and ECOWAS competition authorities have recently been established, working jurisdictional practices between EAC (within COMESA) and WAEMU (within ECOWAS) will need to be defined. So, the AfCFTA negotiations would need to deliberate on the following issues:

- Coordinating national, subregional and regional efforts on cross-border anti-competitive conduct.

- Building on the regional efforts already undertaken and leveraging existing competences and comparative advantages.

- Establishing an inclusive approach to building that capacity of member States without national competition laws, including such options as special and differential treatment.

- Establishing mechanisms to review competition cases and exchange experiences and best practices.

- Exploring establishing continental institutions.

Consumer protection in the AfCFTA

Consumer protection policies and laws guard consumer welfare. They set minimum quality specifications and safety standards for both goods and services and establish mechanisms to redress consumers' grievances. They allow consumers to select from the options presented by market competition unaffected by deception or the withholding of material information (Averitt and Lande, 1998).

The AfCFTA Protocol on Trade in Services recognizes consumer protection as a legitimate national policy objective that parties can consider in liberalizing services. The AfCFTA phase II negotiations present an opportunity to incorporate competition policy in addressing unfair trade practices to protect consumers.

The stated goal of legislation determines, to some extent, the importance of competition regulation. In Kenya, the competition authority has a statutory mandate to enhance welfare by promoting and protecting effective competition in markets and preventing unfair and misleading market conduct. In addition, regional competition agencies provide for consumer welfare under the objective of enhancing trade and advocating for the implementation of the competition law.

The inclusion of consumer protection in the competition protocol requires coordinated implemen-

tation to avoid challenges in jurisdictions where interagency collaboration is lacking. Yet, competition and consumer protection are interlinked; interventions by authorities enhancing competition lead to consumer welfare. If players in a market are found to be pricing too high and an intervention by the competition authority leads to reduced prices and healthy competition, the consumer benefits.

Consumer protection institutions across Africa differ considerably (Table 5.3). The supremacy of a continental treaty containing consumer protection stands to play a key role in addressing cross-border violations.

Emerging competition issues and challenges for the AfCFTA

Digital economy

Digital economy innovations disrupt traditional economic systems and challenge general thinking on production and goods and service delivery strategies. Artificial intelligence (AI), data fusion, app-based transactions, algorithmic business intelligence and other digital platforms are examples of advances in digital technologies (Ireland, 2017).

The new, technologically driven digital economy, operating alongside traditional commerce, often generates a competition landscape different from the one traditional competition policies are based on. Firms using traditional methods, often at a disadvantage compared with their digitally competitive counterparts, may accuse them of anticompetitive practices. This generally takes place because digital economic advances enable innovators and early adopters to increase efficiency, market share and competitiveness, mostly due to reduced costs and better and more innovative products and services for customers.

The digital economy has distinct features enabling digitalized firms to become more competitive than their non-digital counterparts (Pierre & Romain, 2017). It enables more efficient connection between offer and demand, resulting in higher consumption of goods and services. It facilitates

Table 5.3:

Institutions for consumer protection in selected African countries

COUNTRY/REC	CONSUMER PROTECTION LAW	INSTITUTION: INDEPENDENT INSTITUTION OR MINISTRY DEPARTMENT
Algeria	Law no. 89-02 of 7 February 1989 on the general rules of consumer protection	Under Ministry of Economy
Botswana	Chapter 42:07 on consumer protection	Consumer Protection Unit, Department of Trade and Consumer Protection
Burkina Faso	National Competition Law, no. 15/84/ADP, 1994	National Commission of Competition and Consumption
Cameroon	The National Assembly of Cameroon, law no. 2011/012	National Competition Committee
Egypt	Law no. 67 of 2006 on consumer protection	Consumer Protection Agency of Egypt
Eswatini	Competition Act, 2007	Swaziland Competition Commission
Gambia	Consumer Protection Act, 2014	Gambia Competition and Consumer Protection Commission
Kenya	Competition Act no. 12 of 2010—part VI, Consumer Welfare	Competition Authority of Kenya
Madagascar		Competition Council Directorate for Competition and Market Regulation
Malawi	Competition and Fair-Trade Act, 2000. The law has provisions for protection of consumer welfare)	Competition and Fair-Trading Commission
Mozambique		Competition Regulatory Authority
Namibia	Consumer Protection Act, 2008 (act no. 68 of 2008)	
Regulations	Namibia Consumer Protection Commission, Ministry of Trade and Industry	
Nigeria	The Consumer Protection Council Act, provided for under chapter C25, Laws of the Federation of Nigeria 2004	Consumer Protection Council
Rwanda	Competition and Consumer Protection Law	Rwanda Competition and Consumer Protection Unit—Under Ministry of Trade
South Africa	The Consumer Protection Act, 2008 (no. 68 of 2008)	National Consumer Commission
Tanzania	Fair Competition Act 2003	Fair Competition Commission
Zambia	The Competition and Consumer Protection Act, 2010	Zambia Competition and Consumer Protection Commission

Source: Author's compilation.

increased transparency and better flow of information, helping consumers make more informed choices. It lowers barriers to entry and to expansion, because with generally lower fixed and sunk costs and lower informational barriers, it increases market competitiveness. Most digital economies result in two-sided markets as two or more user groups at different levels of the value chain interact and create network effects. This also complicates analysis, because the two markets can be affected differently by transactions.

Competition law enforcement issues

Actors in the digital economy including intermediaries that can boost or hinder competitiveness, so competition authorities need to take note of them. Some players try to stay competitive by constantly innovating and adopting digital technology, thus creating a comparative advantage over their slower counterparts and over those leveraging technology for anti-competitive practices. In this arena, regulators have to recognize that duplicating a service or product can be over a thousand times cheaper than developing it, causing a mismatch between price and production cost in traditional terms.

The fast innovators can price products or services more competitively than slower ones, which normally struggle to match their pricing. They are quick to introduce a new range or variety of the product. The non-innovating firms may allege violation of competition law, especially predation. The competition authority's investigation and analysis then faces the challenge of distinguishing innovation-driven price reduction from predatory pricing and establishing the link between intellectual property rights, royalties and piracy.

This is like many international cases, where "dumping" is alleged when international firms become more competitive than local companies using obsolete technologies. The opposite happens in new industries such as ride sharing, when the use of technology that goes beyond the traditional phone call or taxi flagging and introducing digital payments has caused an avalanche of cases for competition authorities around the world and disrupted the transport industry. This disruption is expected to increase as driverless cars are introduced.

The challenge of the digital economy

The digital economy imperils the ability of competition policy, laws and regulation enforcement to remain relevant in dealing with anti-competitive practices. In the developing world, many economies are still characterized by competition laws that assume a one-way causal relationship from structure to performance (developed countries move more quickly into new areas of market change). The authorities need a clear understanding of the entire value chain or value network, especially of the players, their business models and, therefore, the competitiveness of the markets. The role of the Internet in intermediation and disintermediation is critical in the digital economy as well as the different classes of intermediaries.

Some assumptions underpinning traditional competition law may become irrelevant or fail to adequately capture the grounds for ability to engage in anti-competitive practices in the Internet-enabled economy. For example, assets, size of fleet or number of outlets may be seen as reflecting market share. But in the digital economy, a firm with very few assets and a small fleet may enjoy more buyer patronage than a firm with a very large fleet. In this case, measuring market shares by fleet size does not reflect the nature of competition in the market. So, competition laws defining market shares by assets may mis-measure competition.

Defining a market in the digital economy can also be a challenge. Some markets might appear to be the same even though they differ due to some added digital innovation at play. Because defining the relevant market is key in competition enforcement, complaining firms would try to narrow the market as much as possible, while the respondents would try to broaden the definition. Consequently, competition authorities in different jurisdictions have adopted different market definitions. A good example is again the ride sharing industry, which has seen complaints against Uber raised in different jurisdictions citing differing reasons (Box 5.6).

Although competition authorities produce regulations to adjust enforcement tools without sending them through parliament, they are often challenged by the way thresholds for dominance and ability to engage in predatory pricing are set. The average or marginal costs of production, often used as a yardstick in determining predation, is problematic when a more innovative digital firm with small costs introduces a product like one made by a firm with huge overhead. In such a case, the average cost of production needs to be firm specific rather than sector specific, since each firm uses its own production systems.

Competition law should, however, be able to punish a firm that is not yet dominant but is deliberately taking advantage of the digital economy to sell below its own marginal costs to gain a foothold in the industry. A competition authority needs to be able to investigate under various scenarios and to consider both traditional and digital causes of an advantage.

Other important digital economy issues, such as two-sided markets, algorithmic price fixing, user feedback loops, network effects, data and digital

Defining the market for Uber and taxi services in different jurisdictions

Uruguay- In 2014, the Uruguay Competition Authority categorized taxi services in two parts: intermediation and non-intermediation taxi services, based on the method used to get the taxi. Intermediation services were booked by radio dispatch, through a text message or a smartphone application. Non-intermediation services were hired by hailing a taxi in the street or hiring one from a taxi rank.

But in 2015, the Uruguayan Competition Authority received a complaint from Asociación de Taxis against Uber for abuse of a dominant position. This time, the competition authority changed its market definition—initially a narrow definition was used, later expanded due to both demand and supply substitution considerations. Eventually, the market was defined as "private transport of persons in return for payment," and it included all licensed taxi drivers and Uber drivers.

India- The Competition Commission of India, a case involving Uber was filed by the radio taxi operator, Meru, alleging abuse of dominance. The commission appeared to give more weight to the supply side substitutability effects than to the demand side: the product market was defined as "radio taxi services," so the means of communicating to get a taxi, "radio"—which include mobile apps—was identified as the basis for defining the market.

Complainants have also tried to narrow the market to create a higher market share for Uber. In the Flywheel vs. Uber case in 2016 in San Francisco, presided over by the US Federal Trade Commission, the complainant defined the relevant product market as a "mobile app-generated ride sharing service market." This definition would make Uber dominant in the market, meeting a prerequisite for an abuse of dominance case. This also happened in the Spencer Meyer vs. Travis Kalanick case, where the relevant market was defined as a "mobile app-generated ride sharing services market, excluding traditional taxis and delivery car services." A competition authority would have to be adequately versed in the operation of the industry to identify the relevant market.

Source: Consumer Unity and Trust Society (CUTS) submission.

monopolization, also present relevant implications for competition authorities.

How do digital economy issues affect competition in the AfCFTA?

Competition authorities in Africa face both externally and internally influenced challenges. Externally, the digital economy needs to be underpinned by connectivity. If access to locally relevant digital content is limited, if citizens lack digital literacy or access to appropriate devices or the government has not built the relevant infrastructure (GSMA, 2016), then authority's ability to keep pace with digital economy competition challenges will be below standard. In addition, the extent to which the regulatory system in the country promotes digital innovation would also affect the ability of the competition enforcement institutions to adopt and

adapt to digital economy advances. A regulatory system that embraces and supports change will help the digital economy thrive (GSMA, 2016). This is where payment and data security infrastructure become critical for monitoring transactions, offering data security and applying check points for fair trade.

Internally, Africa is acutely short of information and communications technology (ICT) skills for developing and managing the Internet. Challenges include limited efficacy of law-making bodies, poor ICT-related laws and slow enforcement of contracts. About two-thirds of African countries are in the bottom quartile of countries on indicators assessing these features (Rumana & Richard, 2018).

The AfCFTA can only be as strong as its ability to manage competition in the digital economy affecting trade in goods and services. This requires infrastructure for e-commerce as well as for intellectual property rights, especially as they relate to industrialization and the development of intra-Africa trade. It also requires increasing the capacity of competition authorities to identify markets, players and business models in the digital economy.

Trends in corporate conduct: Abuse of buyer power in Africa

Buyer power is an emerging concern. It describes a single buyer or a group of buyers dictating or influencing the terms of purchase for upstream suppliers—in general, the upstream firm exerts more market power if it faces many dispersed buyers than if it faces one or a few strong buyers (see Motta, 2003). The ability of a firm therefore to charge higher prices largely depends on the dispersion of the buyers.

Broadly speaking, monopsony and bargaining buyer power are the two types of buyer powers. A firm has monopsony power if its share of purchases in the upstream input market is big enough that it can cause the market price to fall by purchasing less and cause it to rise by purchasing more. Bargaining buyer power, on the other hand, refers to the bargaining strength that a buyer has with its suppliers. Both types of buyer power result in lower input prices, though the lower price obtained from monopsony power is achieved through purchasing less, whereas the lower price obtained from bargaining power is achieved through the threat of purchasing less.

In many African countries, dominant agricultural sector producers face increasingly concentrated demand and more power buyers of fast-moving and time-sensitive perishable consumer commodities. A few buyers of large quantities command enough economic power to negotiate for lower prices, lessening the profitability of competing sellers of agricultural produce. The bargaining power of the buyers is likely to be high when buyers are concentrated where it is difficult to switch to competing brands (of commodities or products) or to substitutes.

Powerful customers may have, in some circumstances, the incentive and ability to manipulate markets (Motta, 2003). The most powerful buyer has a disciplinary effect on a supplier if there is a credible threat that the buyer could switch sufficiently to other suppliers.

A strong buyer can use its bargaining power to stimulate competition among sellers—for example, by threatening to withdraw orders from one seller to give them to another (Motta, 2003). And evidence shows that buyer concentration often reduces the market power of sellers (Scherer and Ross, 1990). Regulators' decisions can be guided by recognition of buyer power in a market. In the European Union (EU), for instance, competition agencies have cleared mergers that would otherwise be blocked due to the role of buyer power in constraining suppliers or sellers (see EC case IV/M.1225, 1999).[2] One was cleared on grounds that buyer power in the packaging industry has a large market position in the relevant market and only limited competition with the common market. Similar argument was used to clear the EC ABB and Daimler-Benz merger case (EC No. IV/M.580, 1995).[3]

Abuse of buyer power has on occasion been raised as an issue. This can happen if a buyer's actions, intended to gain a competitive advantage likely to reduce suppliers' incentives to invest in new capacity, products and production processes, are detrimental to the interests of consumers. Delayed payments and related unfair trading practices of a buyer can affect contractual agreements between buyer/retailers (such as supermarkets) and suppliers (such as farmers and producers). Such events raise regulatory concerns and therefore require the attention of competition authorities and the enforcement of competition law.

A 2017 market inquiry by the Competition Authority of Kenya revealed that buyer power affects markets in the retail sector (Box 5.7). Buyer power was exerted through delayed payments to suppliers, shelf allocation and retailers selling their own brands. This grossly harmed small and medium-sized enterprises (SMEs) due to their inability to make purchases or pay for inputs.

Abuse of buyer power in Kenya

Abuse of buyer power recently affected the Kenyan economy when buyers failed to honour their contractual obligations to suppliers. The Competition Authority of Kenya received numerous complaints from suppliers in the retail sector, especially those who supply supermarket chains. Suppliers complained that they were exposed to unfair contractual terms with the supermarkets, were issued dishonoured cheques, received payments delayed beyond the agreed contractual period (even for perishable goods) and were unable to service loans due to continuous non-payments by the supermarkets. Suppliers claimed also to be threatened with de-listing if they challenged the supermarkets on this unfavourable behaviour. The authority also learned that supermarkets were using the money owed to the suppliers to aggressively open new branches country-wide and to expand into neighbouring countries. Some supermarkets were even tricking suppliers into packaging such goods as flour under the supermarket's brand name and then underselling other suppliers.

To address this problem, the Kenyan Competition Act No. 12 of 2010 ("the Act") was amended in January 2017, and provisions prohibiting abuse of buyer power in the Kenyan market or substantial part of it were included under Section 24. Provisions set criteria for determining whether there has been abuse of buyer power, defined buyer power and provided that rules be developed to tackle the issue. Several supermarket outlets collapsed recently, including Nakumatt Supermarket—one of the largest retailers in Kenya. Nakumatt stores, a wholly Kenyan family owned retailer, had more than 60 stores in the East Africa region (EA Regional Retail Study, 2018); more than 5,500 employees and a gross annual revenue of more than $450 million in 2014. The chain had stores not only in Kenya but also in other East African partner States, some of which were shut down (in Uganda and Tanzania, for example) as the retailer struggled to stay in business. By December 2017, only nine stores (six in Kenya and three in Rwanda) were operating. Court documents further showed that Nakumatt owed creditors 2.57 billion Kenyan shillings (about $25 million) in June 2017 and that its total liabilities stood at 36 billion shillings (about $354 million) and had not settled large debts to suppliers. Another big retailer, Uchumi Supermarket, was not spared by this worrying trend, either, and shut down several stores (only eight remaining today of over 35 in 2014), as many of its suppliers went unpaid.

Source: Competition Authority of Kenya.

The Kenyan Authority has developed rules and guidelines on buyer power, which are currently under consideration for approval by the legislature. In addition, the industry's key stakeholders (suppliers, the authority and other government agencies) have collaborated on a code of conduct to guide contracts between the suppliers and the supermarkets and overcome the challenges that retail sector suppliers are currently experiencing.

Public procurement

Issues and challenges

Public procurement will be an important channel for trade under the African Continental Free Trade Area (AfCFTA). The global public procurement market is estimated to make up 10–15 per cent of developed countries' GDP and 30–40 per cent of developing countries' GDP (Kirton, 2013). Global public procurement spending is estimated to be as much as 30 per cent of global government spending (World Bank Group, 2017). So, regional regulatory institutions, including competition authorities, should be synchronized on issues of public procurement to ensure uniform treatment of the regional players in all the countries.

In general, the objectives of public procurement policy centre on creating an efficient and transparent system under which governments efficiently procure goods and services to facilitate the day-to-day running of government business (Kirton,

2013). Ensuring that procurement is competitive and transparent is critical. Studies in the European Union by the World Bank and the Organisation for Economic Co-operation and Development established that an overall cost saving of 30 per cent is achieved by avoiding wasteful, incompetent or corrupt purchasing of goods and services (Kirton, 2013).

Public procurement is important for international trade. The accessibility of the public procurement market to all players helps shape international trade. However, given the large market, governments also use the public procurement market to enhance socio-economic welfare, tailoring policies to favour certain groups as a way of reducing inequality or pursuing other policy objectives. They often do so through preferential procurement policies.

Preferential policies under public procurement

Preferential policies are often differently designed across different countries, making for different access to public procurement. In general, preferential policies on procurement range from the least intrusive to the most intrusive, for example, from policies that seek to level the playing field to those that specifically target some firm characteristic (World Bank Group, 2017).

Preferential policies on public procurement mostly target two groups. The first, often mentioned, is small and medium-sized enterprises (SMEs). SMEs make up the bulk of businesses, especially in the developing world. But they often do not qualify for public procurement business for several reasons— including capital constraints, inadequate information, limited scale, fewer resources and limited capacity—which make uncompetitive with bigger enterprises. But since they are a large part of businesses, helping them benefit from the public procurement system creates immediate benefits for livelihoods and poverty relief. Engaging SMEs in public procurement increases competition, improves value, increases innovation, increases job creation, improves social and economic equity and de-concentrates industry (World Bank Group, 2017).

Countries in Africa have therefore deliberately promoted SMEs through public procurement policies and laws. Examples include Botswana (Briscoe, 1999), Ghana (Normanyo, Ansah and Asante, 2016), Kenya (Njuguna, 2015), South Africa (World Bank Group, 2017) and Tanzania (Panga and Kazungu, 2015). Although such reforms aim to enhance livelihoods, they also tilt the playing field against local and regional firms that will not partner with local SMEs in seeking government tenders.

Government procurement may also have stringent requirements that exclude SMEs. In Namibia, the tender amount should be above the threshold of 10,000 Namibian dollars for one to qualify (Kuugongelwa, 2015). In Zambia, SMEs are more suitable to participate in "simplified" bidding, which is used for low-value purchases of up to 500 million Zambian kwacha, while "open" bidding is only used for high-value procurements of above 500 million kwacha.[4] In Nigeria, one study showed, an arduous and stringent process prevents SMEs from participating fully in public procurement (Akenroye and Aju, 2013). In Egypt, the 2004 Small and Medium-Sized Enterprises Development Law actually impeded SME access by capping the proportion of government contracts awarded to SMEs at 10 per cent (Kaspar and Puddephatt, 2012). Performance guarantee requirements—in which a financial institution warrants that the agreed terms of the contract between the government and the SME will be completed successfully—also make it difficult for SMEs to participate in public procurement (International Trade Centre, 2003).

The second group often targeted by public procurement policies is marginalized and vulnerable groups, especially youth and women. Public procurement policies are used as an empowerment strategy for such groups. For example, using a public procurement law passed in 2015, the government of Kenya reserved 30 per cent of government tenders for youth, women and persons with disabilities, while in South Africa in 2013, a provincial government in Gauteng set a target for 10 per cent of all procurement contracts to be allocated to youth-owned enterprises (Kim, 2019). Other countries in Africa and beyond also use this strategy to support groups that would otherwise struggle to benefit from procurement opportunities.

Challenges with public procurement policies

The implications of the public procurement regulations for competition, and for regional integration, are apparent. A firm may need to be more than just competitive to win government tenders. While the appreciably safeguarding public interest, procurement policies also affect fair competition, since firms that might not be giving the best terms of trade can win tenders based on other socio-economic criteria. Competition policy must thus be accommodative under such a scenario, and so most competition laws in Africa embrace public interest issues. A transaction can be accommodated on public interest grounds even with some inherent anticompetitive tendencies. Regional integration initiatives under the AfCFTA should also accommodate this leeway to use public procurement as a poverty alleviation tool and a measure to reduce inequality.

Since each country has discretion to have its own procurement policies, some regional integration gains could be threatened if markets become inaccessible due to these safeguards. Procurement regulations and policies in a region should be predictable and transparent for investors and all the parties that might seek to bid. Harmonization of public procurement policies is a necessary topic in the AfCFTA discussion.

Harmonization of public procurement policies

Being harmonized is the most critical way to make public procurement policies in Africa predictable. AfCFTA would have benefited if the already existing RECs had protocols on public procurement in place. In the Caribbean Community (CARICOM), for example, the Revised Treaty of Chaguaramas provides for the establishment and implementation of a regional public procurement regime. Article 239 of that treaty specifically calls upon member States to establish a protocol relating to government procurement (CARICOM, 2015).

But in Africa, many differences in public procurement regimes could hinder the attainment of some

envisaged benefits of the AfCFTA. A study focusing on four countries—Angola, Botswana, Namibia and South Africa—found challenges to implementing procurement policies and procedures across them (British High Commission Pretoria, 2015). In some countries, public procurement regimes are not well developed, which will impede meeting the public procurement goals of fairness, integrity, transparency, competition, value for money and cost effectiveness at the regional level (Harpe, 2015). Harmonization is not well developed at the regional level, either.

In 2002, COMESA produced a public procurement strategy, which included basic requirements for reforming national public procurement laws and practices. This was followed by establishing a Regional Public Procurement Centre to build capacity for member States (Harpe, 2015). The EAC, ECOWAS and SADC do not have a regional procurement protocol or a regional procurement strategy. However, the EAC region can leverage the East African Procurement Forum, an annual event hosted on a rotating basis by the EAC's public procurement regulatory authorities. The forum brings together all stakeholders, including the public and private sector, in the East African partner States, to discuss challenges and best practices on public procurement.

It therefore follows that Africa needs a continental procurement policy to ensure that procurement policies are in harmony. The continental policy needs to be discussed and debated along with all the accompanying policy tools that will be introduced in the AfCFTA discourse. Procurement can also be harmonized by introducing a model policy, which countries can domesticate. The model policy is likely to gain traction if all the members have an input in its design. At the regional level, this has already been tried through the United Nations Commission on International Trade Law (UNCITRAL), which developed a model law for the procurement of goods, services and construction in 1994. UNCITRAL aimed for countries to use the model law as a template for reforming their public procurement systems. Eleven countries in Africa—Gambia, Ghana, Kenya, Madagascar, Malawi, Mauritius, Nigeria, Rwanda, Uganda, Tanzania and

Zambia—based their public procurement reforms on the model law (Harpe, 2015). That success makes the UNCITRAL model law a useful basis for discussion.

Under the AfCFTA, competition policy institutions should collaborate with public procurement institutions to combat anti-competitive practices, such as bid-rigging and collusive tendering, in procurement.

Towards an AfCFTA competition policy protocol

Designing a suitable protocol on competition in Africa that supports sustainable development requires an approach that considers the nature of firms in Africa.

While the operative elements of such a protocol are its fundamental substance, these provisions are similar across regional or national competition instruments. Given that a continental protocol will subsume national and sub-regional competition regimes, demarcating the coverage of the con-

tinental regime will be a particularly important issue. Perhaps most important will be the design of the enforcement modalities that will determine how ambitious Africa is about a competition regime. Negotiators will have to decide between a continental competition authority with supranational powers (similar to the CEMAC, COMESA, EAC, ECOWAS and WAEMU approach), a cooperation framework (as is the approach in SADC), or a sequential approach incorporating both a cooperation network and a supranational authority (as is done in the EU) (Figure 5.1).

Objectives of an AfCFTA competition policy protocol

Though the protocol on competition policy will derive from, and advance, the overarching objectives of the AfCFTA framework agreement, no specific objectives have yet been specified for competition. Clarifying these objectives is a critical first step for the protocol.

To begin with, the objectives of the protocol should encourage the contribution that competition can make to the growth, development and structural

Figure 5.1:
Schematic overview of AfCFTA competition protocol options

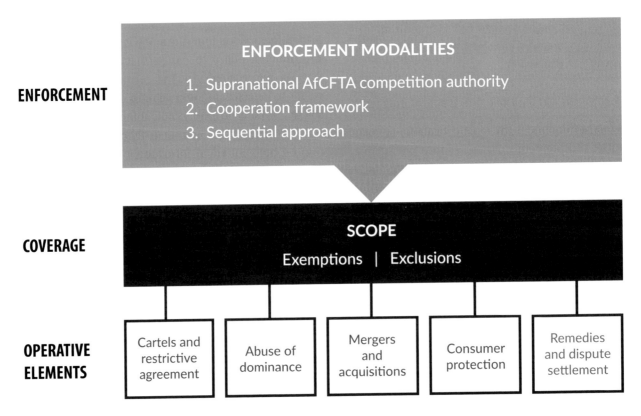

transformation of the African economies. The protocol should clearly specify the need to promote and preserve competition by enhancing market efficiency and ensure that the gains from liberalization are not undone by anti-competitive practices.

Negotiators might wish to specifically address cross-border anti-competitive practices, as discussed above, emerging trends in corporate conduct, and transparency in public policy, including that of public procurement. And given the overlap between the existing regional and national competition regimes, and the overlaps of country membership in those regimes, the continental protocol should seek to manage explicitly the interrelationships between competition regimes.

The following template offers basic objectives for the competition protocol:

1 Enhance competition on the African market for improved market efficiency, inclusive growth and the transformation of the African economies.

2 Safeguard gains from AfCFTA liberalization by ensuring they are not undermined by anti-competitive conduct.

3 Strengthen the capacity to deal with anti-competitive practices having international and cross-border implications.

4 Harmonize minimum standards of corporate conduct.

5 Provide a continental platform for consulting, cooperating and coordinating on competition policy and law and their evolution.

6 Enhance governance and transparency over [industrial and] competition policy in Africa.

7 Manage the interrelationships of competition regimes and sectoral regulatory laws at the national, regional and continental levels.

Objectives 1 and 2 address the contribution of competition to the overarching goal of the AfCFTA promoting the growth and development of the African economies, 3–6 consider specific substantive areas that could be addressed by the protocol, and 7 on overlap between competition regimes, and the membership of countries in those regimes.

Coverage of an AfCFTA competition policy protocol

I   Scope of application and exemptions

Scope of application both clarifies the types of economic activities to be covered and would demarcate the distribution of jurisdiction over applying competition rules between national, regional and continental levels.

The protocol should apply to all economic activities, whether conducted by private or public persons, within the AfCFTA or having an effect within it. Some standard provisions that capture this provide that the protocol applies to practices "affecting trade between the members" or "affecting a substantial portion of the region." However, negotiators may wish to designate a threshold of effect, so that the protocol focuses resources on the most important cases of anti-competitive conduct. Typical language for this would qualify the protocol as applying to competition or trade having an "appreciable effect in the market or a substantial part of it."

The protocol should clearly define the boundaries of its jurisdiction to avoid conflicts with national and regional laws. This is particularly important for the AfCFTA competition protocol because it will subsume both national and subregional competition jurisdictions. Again, thresholds offer a way to specify this, directing that the protocol consider only anti-competitive conduct that is "appreciable" at the continental level, leaving that what is appreciable at the subregional and national levels to the competition authorities at those levels. This would be similar to the approach adopted by the EU. Another approach would be to clarify that a "regional case" would be one affecting more than two countries within a regional block, while a "continental case" would be one touching on more than one regional block.

Even with clear guidance over jurisdiction in the scope of the protocol, overlap and contested jurisdictions may still occur because the continental competition issues necessarily include subregional and national issues as subsets. A network mechanism for consultation between various competition authorities over this delicate issue would provide for a nuanced instrument to assist with jurisdictional issues. The EU has adopted this approach with the European Competition Network—it is elaborated on below in the African context in the section on implementation modalities.

Negotiators may wish to exclude certain situations from the scope. Here negotiators can consider a careful balance between outright "exceptions" to the protocol and practices which may, upon application, be granted "exemption." *Exceptions* are typically excluded entirely and unconditionally. *Exemptions*, on the other hand, though incompatible with the protocol, may be the subject of consideration if they benefit the public or the development of the market. Exceptions can include activities that could be better handled at the national or sometimes regional level than at the continental level.

Providing for both exceptions and exemptions can help negotiators to keep outright exceptions relatively limited and narrow, and thereby reduce the risk of the protocol being watered down with broad and numerous exceptions. Common exceptions from the scope of such a competition protocol would be labour-related issues, collective bargaining agreements between employers and employees and standard setting by professional bodies necessary for consumer protection. Activities more suitable to exemption would include those necessary to pursue legitimate goals such as cooperation on research and development and joint ventures to achieve economic development or the economic development, growth, transformation or stability of any industry.

It is further recommended that State actors in commercial markets not be given a blanket exemption but be held to the same standards as private actors to encourage a level playing field and trust in the institutions.

Finally, consumer protection needs to be included in the scope. As yet, the protocol on competition policy has not been directed to consider consumer protection issues, but negotiators could introduce them under the provisions on scope. This is not without precedent: the COMESA competition regulations include scope for consumer protection.

While efficiencies and innovation are protected, consumer welfare should also be protected.

Operative elements of an AfCFTA competition policy protocol

II **Provisions dealing with cartels and other restrictive agreements**

The protocol should prohibit all agreements between undertakings, decisions by associations of undertakings and concerted practices that may affect trade between member States and have as their object or effect the prevention, restriction or distortion of competition within the AfCFTA.

Similarly, the protocol should have clarity on practices that can be authorized, when properly notified to the enforcement institutions, if the competition officials determine that there is a net public benefit.

III **Provisions dealing with abuse of dominance**

The protocol should clearly prohibit abuse of a dominant position—as when an enterprise, either by itself or acting together with other enterprises, occupies such a position of economic strength that it can operate in the market without effective constraints from its competitors or potential competitors. Included are situations where the behaviours of a dominant enterprise affects trade between member States. Among examples are behaviour that: restricts, or is likely to restrict, the entry of any undertaking into a market; prevents or deters, or is likely to prevent or deter, any undertaking from engaging in competition in a market; eliminates or removes, or is likely to eliminate or remove, any undertaking from a market; directly or indirectly imposes unfair purchase or selling prices or other restrictive practices; limits the production of goods or services for a market to the prejudice of consumers and so on.

IV **Provisions dealing with mergers and acquisitions**

It is recommended that the protocol institute a mandatory merger control regime and provide the thresholds at which notification obligations will be triggered. Only transactions that can appreciably affect trade within the AfCFTA should be captured, and no duplication of notifications at national and regional levels should occur.

Another issue is the assessment standard used in merger determinations: whether competition is the only factor to be considered, or public interest issues such as employment, and competitiveness of small and medium-sized enterprises will be recognized.

V Provisions dealing with consumer protection

Three of the REC competition regimes—COMESA, EAC and SADC—have explicit provisions dedicated to consumer protection. Others have articles that touch upon consumer protection, or aspects of consumer protection.

Consumer protection aims at safeguarding consumers' interest and promoting their economic and social welfare. The UN Guidelines for Consumer Protection provide the most comprehensive internationally recognized standards on consumer policy and the protection of consumer rights, including provisions on consumer education, protection of vulnerable consumers, protection in e-commerce and redress mechanisms, among others. The guidelines call upon UN Member States to develop, strengthen or maintain a strong consumer policy in line with international standards (UNCTAD, 2016).

Why include consumer protection in trade agreements? Substantively, integrating elements of consumer protection into trade policies can safeguard consumer empowerment while keeping consumer protection measures from becoming barriers to international trade and/or being inconsistent with international trade obligations (UNCTAD, 2005). Including consumer protection in these agreements can also reinforce the implementation of national consumer protection policies.

Different jurisdictions take different approaches in designing their consumer protection policies. In many instances, these policies are integrated with competition policies both substantively and institutionally. This integrated approach has advantages, particularly at the institutional level. Having a single agency cover both policy areas provides more centralized control, operational efficiencies and cross-fertilization (Huffman, n.d.). Also, combining the two could help leverage expertise that is usually similar in both fields. Pooling resources and expertise is especially beneficial to small economies (OECD, 2008). In countries where competition policy is fairly new, the public tends to be already more familiar with consumer policy and to view it more favourably, so combining the two could transfer good will to competition policy (OECD, 2008). Conversely, within government, consumer policy sometimes has fewer supporters than competition policy, resulting in an inadequate budget for consumer policy, and combining them could help to remedy that problem (OECD, 2008).

However, competition law is sometimes misperceived as adequate to cover consumer issues. Competition law optimizes consumer welfare through market regulation, while consumer protection optimizes consumer welfare through regulation transactions at the individual level.[5] Thus, competition law often addresses consumer welfare by protecting competition, which in turn maximizes consumer welfare. That approach may undermine any direct intervention on behalf of individual consumers, since the marketplace is to provide the solutions (Huffman, n.d.).

In addition, governments have multiple policy objectives. For example, a government may wish to ensure consumer protection welfare outcomes that will not be generated by competitive forces (COMESA, 2015). And some consumer regulation is too detailed or specialized to be included in a competition law of general application (COMESA, 2015).

So, although competition policy benefits consumer interests, the benefit depends on establishing an effective and complementary consumer policy (UNCTAD, 2005). An effective competition law does not eliminate the need for other consumer protections. Consumer organizations are pushing States globally to rethink the formulation of consumer protection policies in trade agreements. Modern trade agreements are dedicating chapters to other public good interests, such as labour rights and environmental protection, so why not consumer protection?[6] Negotiators of the AfCFTA may wish to align with these global efforts and recognize the importance of consumer protection policy by making dedicated provisions in the AfCFTA.

VI Provisions dealing with remedies and dispute settlement

At the international level, a series of possible remedies are available to redress competition violations, including public civil and criminal enforcement actions and private actions. Remedies aim to strike the right balance among deterring antitrust violations, punishing wrongful conduct and compensating injured parties.

Given the diverse legal rules across the African continent and the inexperience of most African courts and judges with competition violations, it is recommended that the competition protocol adopt a civil remedy option, as opposed to criminal remedies. Criminal sanctions require a thorough understanding by tribunals of the wrongs, effected by persons who engaged in anticompetitive practices, that would justify criminal sanctions usually reserved for other types of crimes such as theft or fraud. Without a critical mass of stakeholders on the continent who consider that competition violations are crimes, judges would be reluctant to apply criminal sanctions, so the provision of them under the protocol would be superficial. Civil remedies, however, would achieve the desired effects of deterrence and punishment and are the most common type of remedies on the continent.

Enforcement

Architecture

Implementation will depend on the institutional framework adopted for the enforcing the protocol. Two key models currently exist in Africa: the supranational competition authority (as adopted by CEMAC, ECOWAS, COMESA and EAC) and the cooperation framework adopted by SADC. The two structures exhibit some advantages and disadvantages, summarized below.

Scenario 1. A supranational AfCFTA competition authority

COMESA has based its regional competition policy on the EU model of economic union and has adopted a similar regional institutional structure. Under the COMESA framework, domestic and regional laws complement each other, each with defined and separate jurisdictions. The regional competition laws grant primary jurisdiction to the regional competition authority on cross-border matters, without encroaching on the rights of the national competition regulators on purely domestic matters. The regional regulations also recognize the benefits of subsidiarity as adopted in the EU, which allocates cases to the authority best placed for the investigation. So, national competition authorities may request the regional competition authority to cede jurisdiction under specific circumstances over a competition case regarding their respective markets.

The EAC model is closely modelled on COMESA, with the creation of a regional competition authority with jurisdiction on cross-border competition matters. The EAC Competition Act provides that the determination of any violation is within the exclusive original jurisdiction of the EAC Competition Authority (EACCA) and that the authority and the partner States shall mutually co-operate in the implementing the act. Like COMESA's, the EACCA's resolutions and decisions are legally binding on the partner States' authorities and subordinate courts.

Economies of scale and transaction cost savings result from the uniform application of common competition rules by supranational authorities acting as one-stop shops in dealing with anti-competitive cases. The widely recognized benefits of that framework include efficient allocation of already limited resources and reduced costs of business and regulatory compliance, leading to a more conducive environment for foreign direct investment, which in turn drives economic growth. A supranational regime also reduces the externalities of cross-border effects of decisions adopted by individual member States in the region.

Supranational AfCFTA competition regulations should not impose blanket, one-size-fits-all rules on the member countries and should be limited to cross-border matters. A decentralized structure, such as that adopted by COMESA and EAC, protects the sovereignty of States in their decision-making processes and policy space. Decentralization also addresses information asymmetries between competition agencies and enterprises. Enterprises may conceal or provide false information to authorities to protect their interests. It is often easier for the national competition authorities to obtain and verify information provided by firms operating in their markets than it is for supranational authorities. Institutional arrangements should be carefully thought through to be as inclusive as possible, extending to countries that do not have competition institutions and offering a platform for exchanging information and experiences, especially by experienced agencies.

Scenario 2. Competition cooperation framework between national authorities or RECs

The SADC model is markedly different from the COMESA and EAC structures. When the SADC Declaration on Regional Cooperation and Consumer Policies was adopted in 2009, only five member States had operational competition regimes, and SADC decided to adopt a cooperation model rather than a supranational competition authority. The cooperation model, as described above, requires that a critical mass of the member States adopt and enforce competition law in view of the integration agenda.

The cooperation model adopted by SADC could be extended to the other RECs as an alternative to the supranational competition authority model. This would require each REC to maintain its status on regional competition rules and to collaborate with other RECs on competition matters. Collaboration among national competition authorities enables them to tackle, at least to some extent, the national effects of cross-border anti-competitive conduct. The key advantage of this system is that member States retain complete sovereignty over their policy making. But the downside is that conflicts are more likely to arise when member States are suspected of defending their own national interests. Additional practical challenges are also likely to arise in:

- Different information protection standards in domestic laws.

- Reduced incentives for international players to cooperate in an investigation by one member State for fear of being prosecuted by other member countries.

- Limited admissibility of evidence.

- Lack of mutual understanding, trust and interaction between the competition authorities.

Further, the competition cooperation strategy does not eliminate the issues arising from the overlapping membership of countries across the various RECs in Africa. For example, eight SADC member States also belong to COMESA and are thus subject to the regional COMESA competition rules.

The conflicting obligations of members subject to more than one regional competition law will create a challenge. Negotiations on competition policy within the AfCFTA arrangement must therefore clearly delineate the jurisdiction of the regional authorities to avoid duplicating resources and creating political tensions and, for firms, raising business costs and spreading legal uncertainty on the outcomes of competition cases.

Scenario 3. A sequential approach

The third approach provides for a sequential combination of the supranational authority and the cooperation network. This would involve three steps:

- Require State parties to implement principles set out in the protocol in their national competition law.

- Establish an African Competition Network as a platform for cooperation and harmonized application and enforcement of competition laws and policies in the continental market.

- Establish a supranational competition authority.

The first step addresses the gaps or absence of competition laws in many African countries. It would require State parties that do not already have competition laws, to adopt one in line with fundamental competition principles, such as transparency, impartiality, procedural fairness and non-discrimination. And it would require them to designate a body for implementing competition laws, as a basis for the creation of a supranational competition authority.

The second step would establish a network to formally facilitate cooperation and consultation between national and sub-regional competition authorities. The African Competition Network would be a forum for discussion and cooperation in applying and enforcing competition laws and policies in the continental market. It would support sharing information and building continental competition rules for enforcing best practices.

An African Competition Forum already exists. An African Competition Network would upgrade and promote it within the broader AU structure and strengthen its ability to facilitate competition in the continent. The proposed model like the EU's, which has an EU-wide authority and also a network for cooperation between national authorities (Box 5.8). In fact, the EU network was created before the EU treaty when the member States recognized such a network's value.

In the third step, a continental competition commission would be established as a supranational enforcement entity, as elaborated in scenario 1.

Box 5.8:

The European Competition Network and the European Commission Directorate General of Competition

The European Commission Directorate General of Competition and the European Competition Network (ECN) offer a model. The European Commission and the national competition authorities in all EU member States cooperate with each other through the ECN. The network enables effective information exchange on cross-border anti-competitive practices. Competition authorities can engage and inform each other on upcoming decisions and receive comments from their counterparts. The ECN lets the authorities amalgamate their experiences and identify best practices.

Since the ECN is not itself an institution, it has no autonomous powers, competences or legal personality. Member State competition authorities and the European Commission, not the ECN, apply articles 81 and 82 of the community competition rules. The ECN operates under the framework for cooperation mechanisms provided under Council regulation 1/2003 and therefore does not deal with companies or individuals on cases—that falls in the jurisdiction of the competition authorities of member States.

In the case of the AfCFTA, the continental competition authority could act like the European Commission while an African Competition Network could perform the functions of the ECN. The only foreseen difference is the regional dimension of RECs, if it is decided to create regional competition authorities as part of the continental structure.

The African Competition Forum (ACF), which has enabled African countries to share information, learn from each other and engage in joint research and capacity building, offers an opportunity to leverage. The ACF now comprises 31 members and five regional competition agencies. It was established in 2011 in Nairobi, Kenya, by 19 founding members. As an informal network of African national and regional competition authorities, it promotes the adoption of competition principles in African national and regional economic policies; alleviates poverty and enhance inclusive economic growth, development and consumer welfare by fostering competition in markets and increases investment, innovation, productivity and entrepreneurship.

An African continental competition network could be an upgraded ACF, building on the work already accomplished, including information exchange on cross-border cases.

Relationship with national and regional institutions and capacity building

The continental protocol must take into consideration individual countries' needs, policy objectives and capacity building constraints and their experiences with competition problems. For countries without completed competition laws, the strategy of the continental policy should be to help them adopt competition and consumer laws and make necessary amendments in other legislation. The strategy for countries with competition laws but no competition authorities is to assist them in establishing their national competition authority, which would best fit in their administrative and bureaucratic structures. For countries with laws and competition authorities, the strategy is to strengthen their capacity to deal with anti-competitive cases and consumer affairs and to improve in areas where they feel weak or inefficient.

Countries acceding to the continental protocol should receive a grace period of approximately five years to implement national competition laws and establish competition authorities. Specific programs should be designed for countries needing assistance. If a country has not put the relevant laws in place within the prescribed period, the protocol could prescribe that the continental rules are applicable to it. Countries with competition laws and established institutions should be required to align them with the continental rules and institutions. The experience of the Organisation of Eastern Caribbean States (OECS), a sub-regional grouping in the Caribbean Region, is relevant.[7] Some islands in the region are too small in size and population to warrant a full-fledged competition authority, so they use the OECS as a national authority for cases in their jurisdictions.[8] OECS member States (with exception of Martinique) are either full or associate members of the Caribbean Community (CARICOM). The OECS countries, in the second group of countries that joined the CARICOM Single Market and Economy, face the issue of overlapping memberships, as well.

Financing competition institutions of the AfCFTA

The work and institutions of the AfCFTA can be financed through the AU's annual budget. National competition authorities are usually funded from their national treasury budgets to safeguard their independence. Fees from merger fillings and exemptions processing are additional funds for the authority but not a major source of income. REC authorities are funded from the main resources of the REC. For example, COMESA Competition Commission is funded by the COMESA secretariat in Lusaka (Lipimile, 2014). A continental authority can follow a similar model.

The AU should collaborate and coordinate activities with national, regional and international institutions dealing with competition and or consumer protection enforcement, especially in capacity building and technical assistance.

Key messages and policy recommendations

Key messages

- **Africa's competition regime remains patchy.** Only 23 countries have both competition laws in force and competition authorities to enforce them, a further 10 have laws but no authority, 4 have competition legislation in an advanced stage of preparation and 17 have no competition law.

- **Competition policy is a key driver of the growth of competitive markets in Africa.** Cross-border anti-competitive practices prevalent in Africa—such as cartels and abuse of dominance—constrain the growth of competitive markets and harm consumers. National, regional and continental enforcement of competition law will boost the fight against them.

- **The proliferation of competition regimes in Africa calls for a harmonization.** To consolidate the efforts of regional economic communities—such as the East African Community, the Economic Community of West African States, the Common Market for Eastern and Southern Africa, the Economic and Monetary Community of Central Africa and the West African Economic and Monetary Union—a continent-wide competition regime would be a timely and necessary next step, and countries not belonging to these communities could be included under the AfCFTA framework.

- **The African Competition Forum is a springboard for cooperation on competition matters at continental level.** The forum is an informal network established in 2011, comprised of 31 members and five regional competition agencies, promoting the adoption of competition principles in African countries to alleviate poverty and enhance inclusive economic growth, development and consumer welfare, by fostering competition in markets.

- **Consumer protection can be addressed in the AfCFTA protocol on competition.** Consumer protection is related to competition, and the protocol can ensure that the advantages of an integrated African market extend to consumer welfare.

Policy recommendations

- **The AfCFTA protocol on competition must cover the main substantive competition issues.** These include cartels, merger control, abuse of dominance and anti-competitive agreements.

- **The protocol should embrace consumer protection in a dedicated chapter.**

- **The protocol can be enforced through three arrangements:** (1) a supranational AfCFTA competition authority, (2) a competition cooperation framework or (3) a sequential approach in which a supranational authority follows a competition network.

- **A continental procurement policy can complement the competition protocol.** This would ensure predictability, transparency and harmony in procurement policies and produce competitively tendered government procurement, while preserving policy space for legitimate public policy objectives.

- **The AfCFTA may be used to provide a framework for rules and guidelines on buyer power.** Excessive buyer power in corporate conduct has emerged as an important issue that could affect many industries in Africa.

- **The advancing digital economy raises competition challenges.** The capacity of competition authorities will require investment so they can better identify new developments in digital markets, players and business models.

References

African Competition Forum and World Bank. 2016. *Breaking Down Barriers: Unlocking Africa's Potential through Vigorous Competition Policy.* Washington, D.C.: World Bank Group. Available at: http://documents.worldbank.org/curated/en/243171467232051787/Breaking-down-barriers-unlocking-Africas-potential-through-vigorous-competition-policy.

Akenroye, T. O., and O. Aju. 2013. "Barriers to SMEs Participation in Public Procurement in Nigeria: Some Preliminary Results." *International Journal of Entrepreneurship and Innovation Management* 17 (4/5/6): 314–328.

Averitt, Neil W., and Robert H. Lande. 1998. "Consumer Choice: The Practical Reason for Both Antitrust and Consumer Protection Law." *Loyola Consumer Law Review* 10 (1): 44–63.

Bakhoum, Mor. 2010. "The Competition Commission of the West African Economic and Monetary Union finds that Senegal infringes the regional competition law by taking actions that foreclose its national market to competition from Ivory Coast raising issues related to the integration process in West Africa." Article 52723, e-Competitions Bulletin, June 2010.

Brill, Julie. 2010. "Competition and Consumer Protection: Strange Bedfellows or Best Friends?" *The Antitrust Source* 2010 (December). Available at: https://www.ftc.gov/sites/default/files/documents/public_statements/competition-and-consumer-protection-strange-bedfellows-or-best-friends/1012abamasternewsletter.pdf.

Briscoe, A. 1999. *Review of Business Laws in Southern Africa.* Friedrich-Ebert-Stiftung.

British High Commission Pretoria. 2015. *Overview of Government Procurement Procedures in Sub-Saharan Africa: Angola, Botswana, Namibia and South Africa.* Pretoria, South Africa: British High Commission.

Bosiu, Teboho. 2017. "Cartels Investigated in South Africa: Possible Impact in the Region?" *CCRED Quarterly Review*, Centre for Competition, Regulation, and Economic Development, 20 December. Available at: https://www.competition.org.za/review/2017/12/20/cartels-investigated-in-south-africa-possible-impact-in-the-region.

CARICOM (Caribbean Community). 2015. *CARICOM Framework on Public Procurement.* Georgetown, Guyana: Caribbean Community.

COMESA (Common Market for Eastern and Southern Africa). 2015. *Consumer Guide to the COMESA Competition Regulations.* Lusaka, Zambia: COMESA. https://www.comesacompetition.org/wp-content/uploads/2014/05/COMESA-CONSUMER-GUIDE-2.pdf.

ECA (United Nations Economic Commission for Africa) 2004. *Assessing Regional Integration in Africa I: ECA Policy Research Report.* Addis Ababa, Ethiopia: ECA.

———. 2006. *Assessing Regional Integration in Africa: Rationalizing Regional Economic Communities.* Addis Ababa, Ethiopia: ECA. Available at: http://www.uneca.org/aria2/full_version.pdf.

GSMA. 2016. *Competition Policy in the Digital Age: Case Studies from Asia and Sub-Saharan Africa.* GSMA.

Govinda, Hariprasad, Junior Khumalo and Siphamandla Mkhwanazi. 2014. "On Measuring the Economic Impact: Savings to the Consumer Post Cement Cartel Burst." In *Competition Law, Economics and Policy Conference*, vol. 4. Available at: http://www.compcom.co.za/wp-content/uploads/2014/09/On-measuring-the-economic-impact-savings-to-the-consumer-post-cement-cartel-burst-CC-15-Year-Conference.pdf. Harpe, S. 2015. "Procurement under the Uncitral Model Law: A Southern Africa Perspective." *Potchefstroom Electronic Law Journal* 18 (5).

Huffman, Max. n.d. "Competition Law and Consumer Protection." Unpublished working paper, Indiana University School of Law, Indianapolis, IN. Available at: http://www.oecd.org/regreform/sectors/40898016.pdf.

Ireland, D. 2017. "Competition and Other Regulatory Challenges Posed by the Increasingly Crowded and Dynamic Digital Marketplace." Paper prepared for a conference on Disruptive Technologies and Regulation at the CUTS International/CIRC 5th Biennial Competition, Regulation and Development Conference Jaipur India on November 9–11.

International Trade Centre. 2003. *SME AND EXPORT-LED Growth: ARE THERE ROLES FOR PUBLIC PROCUREMENT Programmes? A Practical Guide for Assessing and Developing Public Procurement Programmes to Assist SMEs.* International Trade Centre UNCTAD/WTO.

Kaspar, L., and A. Puddephatt. 2012. *Benefits of Transparency in Public Procurement for SMEs: General Lessons for Egypt.* Global Partners and Associates.

Kim, Doyeun. 2019. "Public Procurement Opens Doors for Youth-led Firms." *AfricaRenewal*, April–July. Available at: https://www.un.org/africarenewal/magazine/special-edition-youth-2017/public-procurement-opens-doors-youth-led-firms.

Kirton, R. M. 2013. *Gender, Trade and Public Procurement Policy.* London: The Commonwealth Secretariat.

Kuugongelwa, E. N. 2015. *A Critical Analysis of Namibia's Public Procurement Supplier Remedies Regulatory Framework: Introducing the Standstill Period.* Stellenbosch University, Department of Public Law. Stellenbosch University.

Laprevote, François-Charles, Burcu Can and Sven Frisch. 2015. "Competition Policy within the Context of Free Trade Agreements." Think Piece, E15 Initiative, ICTSD (International Centre for Trade and Sustainable Development), Geneva.

Lipimile, G. K. 2014. "Interview with George Lipimile, Director of the COMESA Competition Commission." *The Antitrust Source* 2014 (June). Available at: https://www.americanbar.org/content/dam/aba/publishing/antitrust_source/jun14_lipimile_intrvw_6_17f.authcheckdam.pdf.

———. 2018. "Competition Law for the Tripartite Free Trade Area and the Africa Continental Free Trade Area." Paper prepared for a consultative meeting on 'Assessing Regional Integration in Africa (ARIA IX) focusing on 'Competition in The Next Steps for the African Continental Free Trade Area' held on 26–27 July in Nairobi, Kenya.

Motta, Massimo. 2003. "Market Definition and the Assessment of Market Power." Chapter 3 in *Competition Policy: Theory and Practice,* 1–34. London: Cambridge University Press.

Njuguna, H. K. 2015. *Factors Affecting Effective Participation of Micro and Small Enterprise in Public Procurement in Kenya.* Nairobi, Kenya: Jomo Kenyatta University of Agriculture and Technology.

Normanyo, S. S., J. Ansah, and D. Asante. 2016. "The Public Procurement Market as a Platform For SME and National Economic Growth." *European Journal of Logistics, Purchasing and Supply Chain Management* 4 (4): 26–43.

OECD (Organisation for Economic Co-operation and Development). 2008. "The Interface between Competition and Consumer Policies." Policy Roundtable, OECD Publishing, Paris. Available at: http://www.oecd.org/regreform/sectors/40898016.pdf.

Oxenham, John. 2012. "Balancing Public Interest Merger Consideratinos before Sub-Saharan African Competition Jurisdictions with the Quest for Multi-Jurisdictional Merger Control Certainty." *US–China Law Review* 9 (211). Available at: https://africanantitrust.files.wordpress.com/2013/11/2012072706196124.pdf.

Panga, F. P., and I. Kazungu. 2015. "Empowering Small and Medium Enterprises (SMES) to Harness Public Procurement Opportunities: Experience From Mwanza Tanzania." *International Journal of Economics, Commerce and Management* 3 (3).

Pierre, H., and V. Romain. 2017. "Competition Law in the Digital Economy: A French Perspective." *Italian Antitrust Review* 2 (2017).

Rumana, B., and H. Richard. 2018. *Development Implications of Digital Economies.* Manchester: Centre for Development Informatics, Global Development Institute.

Scherer, Frederic M., and David Ross. 1990. *Industrial Market Structure and Economic Performance.* New York: Houghton Mifflin.

Selle, Linn. 2017. "Consumer Rights in Trade Agreements: A Missing Element?" *Consumer Corner: The BEUC Blog,* 7 June. Available at: https://www.beuc.eu/blog/consumer-rights-in-trade-agreements-a-missing-element/.

Tavuyanago, Simbarashe. 2014. "Public Interest Considerations and their Impact on Merger Regulation in South Africa." University of Pretoria. Available at: https://repository.up.ac.za/bitstream/handle/2263/46006/Tavuyanago_Public_2015.pdf?sequence=1.

UNCTAD (United Nations Conference on Trade and Development) 2005. *Competition Provisions in Regional Trade Agreements: How to Assure Development Gains.* New York and Geneva: United Nations. Available at: https://unctad.org/en/docs/ditcclp20051_en.pdf.

Van Gorp, N., and O. Batura. 2015. *Challenges for Competition Policy in a Digitalised Economy.* European Union Parliament, Policy Department A: Economic and Scientific Policy. Brussels: European Union.

World Bank. 2015. *The Africa Competitiveness Report 2015.* Washington, DC: World Bank. Available at: http://documents.worldbank.org/curated/en/759341467995641147/The-Africa-competitiveness-report-2015.

———. 2016. *Breaking Down Barriers: Unlocking Africa's Potential through Vigorous Competition Policy.* Washington, DC: World Bank.

———. 2017. *Policies that Promote SME Participation in Public Procurement.* Business Environment Working Group (BEWG) of the Donor Committee for Enterprise Development (DCED). Washington, DC: World Bank.

Endnotes

1   Public interest is an integral part of South African competition law. See also Tavuyanago (2014).

2   See case information: https://publications.europa.eu/en/publication-detail/-/publication/94795e84-08d6-4bf6-82b1-c9a9bfcfbcc4/language-en.

3   See case information: https://publications.europa.eu/en/publication-detail/-/publication/2f12dbb1-ba35-4a17-be8a-6a62dd0ddf2b/language-en.

4   Tenders Zambia at http://tenderszambia.com/zambia_public_procurement_agency.php.

5   Huffman, n.d. However, the distinction is not always so neat. Occasionally, competition law addresses distortions that take place on the demand side and vice versa (Brill, 2010).

6   See also: Selle (2017).

7   Members of OECS: full members: Antigua and Barbuda, Dominica, Grenada, Montserrat, Saint Kitts and Nevis, Saint Lucia and Saint Vincent and the Grenadines; associate members: Anguilla, the British Virgin Islands and Martinique. See also: https://www.investopedia.com/terms/o/organisation-eastern-caribbean-states-oecs.asp.

8   Article 4(k) read with article 2 and 10 gives powers to the OECS Authority to deal with competition matters of member states. See also: https://www.gov.gd/egov/docs/other/OECS_draft_new_treaty.pdf.

Chapter 6
Investment

Investment, in particular intra-African investment, can drive regional integration, economic growth and poverty reduction. But Africa's investment policy landscape is fragmented, and a large number of vaguely drafted treaties can create uncertainty around, and encroach upon, the policy space needed for sustainable development. This chapter considers how an AfCFTA investment protocol could allow AU member States to revamp and unify investment policy on the continent and lead global discussions on investment policy reform. The investment protocol, drawing on the Pan-African Investment Code and other recent regional and bilateral initiatives, should balance the interests of private investors and the policy space promoting regional integration. Ultimately, it should provide countries with the tools necessary to attract investment and harness it for sustainable development.

This chapter reviews Africa's investment treaty environment and outlines some major challenges of traditional investment treaties often present on the continent. The chapter addresses four key issues: investment promotion and facilitation, investment protection, investor obligations and State commitments. Most investment treaties cover only investment protection, and recent ones have included investment promotion and facilitation. Legally binding investor obligations and specific State commitments would go beyond business as usual. An investment protocol built around these four pillars would represent a step change in investment treaties. The chapter also discusses the interrelation of investment with other phase I and phase II issues and the institutional questions of negotiations and implementation. The chapter concludes by considering how the investment protocol could fit into existing investment legal structures.

Setting the scene

The developmental ambitions set out in the global Agenda 2030 and the African Union's Agenda 2063 require foreign and domestic investment. Context-specific and robust laws and regulations backed by enforcement can channel and leverage responsible investment while minimizing adverse impacts (Sutton et al., 2016).

Investment will be negotiated together with the other phase II policy areas of the African Continental Free Trade Area. In accordance with the objectives of the Agreement Establishing the AfCFTA, an investment protocol was expected to pave the way towards a single market (article 3.a), contribute to the movement of capital and facilitation of investment (article 3.c) and foster cooperation on investment (article 4.c). The design of the investment protocol will be instrumental in harnessing the transformative potential of investment for structural transformation and industrialization to the benefit of all African citizens.

The investment policy landscape in Africa, and around the world, is characterized by a "spaghetti bowl" of overlapping bilateral and regional treaties with inconsistent provisions (ECA, 2017; UNCTAD, 2017b). The AfCFTA presents a unique opportunity to cohere a transparent and predictable regulatory environment that draws from the existing processes and institutions on the continent (Páez, 2017) and underpins dynamic investment possibilities that would boost intra-African investment flows (see Chapter 1 of this report) and promote the global attractiveness of African economies.

A common investment area can provide joint benefits of investment and trade (ECA, forthcoming a), enable economies of scale (Fofack, 2018), bolster regional and global value chains and trade diversification and ultimately lead to faster economic growth and poverty reduction.

The investment protocol can be underpinned by investment promotion and facilitation, and investment protection. African countries should collaborate and build institutions to reduce the transaction costs related to cross-border investment. And they must meticulously define the standards of investment protection to promote clarity for both investors and policy makers. Though the protocol should focus on dispute de-escalation and amicable solutions, it requires a credible dispute settlement mechanism of last resort, so African negotiators will need to weigh several options, ranging from a deep overhaul of the investor-State dispute settlement mechanism to the establishment of a permanent investment court.

African countries can also introduce legally binding obligations on investors to match their prerogatives with responsibilities oriented towards translating capital formation into tangible and sustainable development outcomes. With sustainable development as a guiding principle, countries may also want to prevent a regulatory race to the bottom in a bid to attract investments and help investors meet their additional obligations.

Conditions are propitious for African policy makers to rewrite the investment policy rulebook cater to investors' interests without imperiling the fulfillment of African peoples' needs, dreams and expectations . The Pan-African Investment Code (PAIC), adopted in 2017 by African ministers of economy, finance and integration as a non-binding instrument, reveals the growing assertiveness and penchant for innovation of African treaty drafters (Mbengue and Schacherer, 2017). The global investment regime is also undergoing a period of reflection, leading to new treaties that include sustainable development considerations (UNCTAD, 2018c). Countries as different as Bolivia, Indonesia and South Africa have distanced themselves from the prevailing regime and have terminated, or are about to terminate, some or all of their treaties (see Box 3). Prompted by Brazil's new investment treaty model in 2015, global attention is also shifting toward investment promotion and facilitation. So,

the AfCFTA investment protocol should consider including investment promotion and facilitation provisions to better respond to the day-to-day needs of investors.

To reduce the complexity and ambiguity of the treaty regime on the continent, bilateral investment should be terminated that would otherwise overlap with the investment protocol. Depending on the modalities of regional integration, regional treaties could also be terminated or subsumed within a continental treaty.

The investment protocol negotiations are taking place amid existing treaties, many of the problematic older generation, with partners outside the continent. The new investment rules will not modify them, and left as they are, companies may use them to circumvent the updated AfCFTA investment protocol.

Future investment negotiations with external partners can also follow from the new approach. The investment protocol can serve as a reference point for African negotiators by signalling the key priorities of African countries. Moreover, a pan-African approach reflecting a shared commitment and understanding among all the continent's countries would both lead towards a single African market and contribute to global making of investment treaties and shaping the ongoing reform of them. Collective, rather than bilateral negotiations, can be expected to promote coherence and yield results best aligned with the strategic interests of the African continent.

The investment landscape in Africa

The international legal framework governing foreign direct investment (FDI) flows in Africa is complex, consisting of bilateral investment treaties (BITs) and regional investment agreements. Since the 1960s, African countries have concluded 852 BITs, of which 515 are currently in force and 173 are intra-African (Figure 6.1) (UNCTAD, 2019). In line with global trends, the pace of concluding bilateral investment treaties picked up around the turn of century and slowed more recently. African BITs represent around 28 per cent of BITs worldwide.

Bilateral investment treaties in Africa

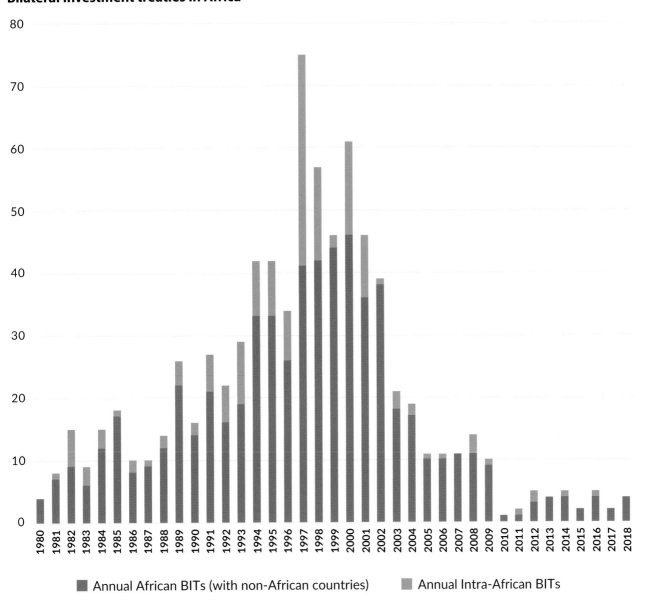

Annual African BITs (with non-African countries)   Annual Intra-African BITs

Source: UNCTAD (2019).

North African countries have proved the most active on the continent in concluding new investment treaties (Figure 6.2). Egypt boasts the biggest stock of signed BITs (100), followed by Morocco (68) and Tunisia (55). All African countries have signed at least one bilateral investment treaty—South Sudan, the youngest, signed its first, with Morocco, in 2017.

The majority of African BITs concluded between 1980 and 2012 are still in effect, with outdated and broad standards that limit the right of African host countries to regulate investment in their territories.

Only a few African countries have started to modernize their existing older generation BITs through renegotiation, amendment or termination. The unreformed BITs unduly expose African countries to investor–State dispute settlement (ISDS) with potentially costly consequences (UNCTAD, 2015a).

New bilateral treaties may be on the wane, but the number of ISDS cases continues to rise. By April 2019, African countries had been respondents in 106 known treaty-based disputes (UNCTAD, 2019). The African countries with the most cases are Egypt (29), Democratic Republic of the Congo (9) and

Figure 6.2:

The five African countries with the most bilateral investment treaties

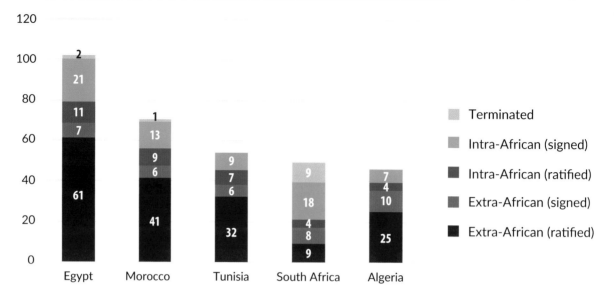

Source: UNCTAD (2019).

Guinea (7). The economic sectors most concerned by these disputes are oil and gas, and mining, which represent a third of all cases, followed by construction, with 10 per cent, and tourism, with 7 per cent. To date, the highest amount awarded in Africa was $935 million against Libya in 2011 in relation to a tourism project.

Africa has in recent years moved to the forefront of innovation in investment treaty-making. The PAIC was adopted by the Specialized Technical Committee on Finance, Monetary Affairs, Economic Planning and Integration of the African Union Commission in October 2017. It marked a step towards continental integration and reform of the international investment treaty system by emphasizing sustainable development through redefined State obligations and added investor obligations.[1] Although the fifth meeting of the AfCFTA Negotiating Forum in March 2017 declined to annex the PAIC to the AfCFTA agreement, because it was "not a binding agreement but a framework of cooperation," the PAIC can be expected to heavily influence the AfCFTA investment protocol. Reflecting a continental consensus, the PAIC can guide drafting and negotiation even if alterations can be expected for better alignment with the overall AfCFTA objectives and architecture as well as for further development, clarification and refinement of terms and concepts, conversion of the model into a binding legal document and integration of more investment promotion and facilitation features.

African countries have sped their regional and continental efforts to articulate common, and often innovative, approaches to rebalancing the international treaty regime, even if not all the treaties or their elements have been fully implemented (Muchlinski, 2010; Seatzu and Vargiu, 2015; Mbengue and Schacherer, 2017). Binding regional schemes on investment include the 2006 SADC Protocol on Finance and Investment and the 2008 ECOWAS Supplementary Act on Investments. The 2007 COMESA Investment Agreement, which has not yet been ratified, is currently under renegotiation. The EAC secretariat also developed in 2018 a new draft investment policy that would streamline and harmonize the existing investment regimes in the region. The 2006 EAC Model Investment Code is a guiding instrument whose features the EAC member States may incorporate in their national laws. A new ECOWAS Investment Code and Policy has also been drafted and is in the pipeline for adoption by the ECOWAS Council of Ministers. Among FTAs, the Tripartite COMESA–EAC–SADC agreement is scheduled to include investment in its second phase of negotiations, together with competition, trade in services and intellectual property rights (although these could be incorporated into the AfCFTA negotiations).

New-generation bilateral investment treaties negotiated by African countries include innovative provisions enhancing the development dimension and maintaining the right of host States to regulate. An example that has drawn a lot of international attention is the 2016 Morocco–Nigeria BIT.

African countries have also adopting new laws governing FDI recently to modernize their national investment frameworks. New or modernized investment laws or bills were introduced in 2017 in Egypt and in 2016 in Algeria, Namibia, Tunisia and South Africa. Several African countries, including Kenya, Madagascar and Nigeria, adopted new model BITs to guide them in future negotiations, while other countries, such as Burkina Faso, plan to undertake this practice.

Investment for development and responsible investment

Foreign investment, particularly FDI, can catalyse development if appropriate policy and regulatory frameworks fully use and internalize its potential for structural transformation while minimizing its potential negative externalities on communities, the environment and the economy. To support this, host countries must establish a transparent, broad and effective enabling environment for investment operation.

FDI can propel industrialization and structural transformation on the continent (Sandjong Tomi, 2015; Sutton et al., 2016), support economic growth (Zandile and Phiri, 2018) and drive down poverty (Fowowe and Shuaibu, 2014) by enabling technology transfers (Jude, 2016), facilitating export diversification (Fonchamnyo and Akame, 2017), enhancing the productivity of local enterprises (Alfaro et al. 2007; Abebe, McMillan and Serafinelli, 2018), establishing or reinforcing forward and backward linkages (Javorcik 2004; Newman et al. 2015) and supporting regional integration and insertion into regional and global value chains (UNCTAD, 2013b; ECA, 2018a). Intra-African investment can especially be expected to support regional integration

and the incorporation of African companies into regional and global value chains (ECA, forthcoming a). Alongside the accumulation of productive investment assets resulting in higher factor productivity and resource efficiency, investment provides an important source of development finance, as recognized in the Addis Ababa Action Agenda.

Growth in productive assets may similarly benefit the environment. For example, foreign investment could trigger the embrace and transfer of cleaner technologies and advanced managerial practices, leading to more socially responsible corporate policies (see Nyuur, Ofori and Debrah, 2015 for Ghana; Zhang, Shang and Li, 2018 for China; Manasakis, Mitrokostas and Petrakis, 2017 for a comparison of FDI with trade). Host economies therefore should address how best to institutionalize domestic policies in order to maximize the benefits of FDI.

Foreign investment may also have drawbacks (Zarsky, 2006; Bonnitcha, 2015). Human rights abuses, sometimes in complicity with the State apparatus, can occur in connection with investment projects (Human Rights Council, 2008; George and Thomas, 2018). Foreign investments can contribute to heightened inequality (Basu and Guariglia, 2007). Since multinational corporations may prefer flexible labour markets (Duanmu, 2014; Oliveira and Forte, 2017), host economies vying for additional capital could be tempted to lower labour standards (Olney, 2013). Similarly, countries have been under pressure to readjust their fiscal regimes, and particularly corporate taxes. African countries, notably, have done so by establishing and expanding special economic zones (Abbas and Klemm, 2013).

Some foreign companies may be attracted by the prospect of moving polluting activities to developing countries with weak legal frameworks and regulation infrastructure to drive down production costs (Gray, 2002). Investments, particularly in the extractives and heavy industry sectors, may cause the pollution of water resources, destruction of fauna and flora, increase of health hazards and deterioration of health quality, growth of air and noise pollution and destruction of traditional economic infrastructures within communities (Baghebo and Apere, 2014).

Funds transfers resulting from investments can cause macroeconomic turbulence. Balance-of-payments difficulties can burden host economies due to repatriation of capital and investment proceeds. Increases in illicit financial flows, including tax avoidance, pose a challenge to public finances (AU and ECA, 2015). Foreign investment can also crowd out domestic investments (Agosin and Machado, 2005), particularly if enjoying more favourable conditions than domestic investments (Stiglitz, 2007).

Countries must make deliberate policy and regulatory efforts to gain FDI benefits. However, policy makers need to also consider potential downsides of FDI and develop policy guidelines and actions to address them. Strong political commitment, clear priorities, stakeholder engagement and, crucially, robust and transparent enforcement mechanisms are key to aligning private initiative with broader developmental objectives. The investment protocol, alongside regional and national policies and frameworks, may prove an appropriate means of investment regulation.

A critical assessment of the investment treaty regime

What are international investment agreements?

International investment agreements (IAAs), primarily bilateral investment treaties but also free trade agreements with investment chapters, feature prominently in African countries' toolbox to raise investment inflows (ECA, 2017; Box 6.1). They are intended to reduce risks resulting from political changes detrimental to investors, including nationalization and conduct of the State authorities, by providing an additional layer of protection above national law (Salacuse and Sullivan, 2005; Sprenger and Boesma, 2014). Investment treaties ordinarily provide investors with access to international arbitration in the form of the investor–State dispute settlement (ISDS)—meant as an alternative to domestic courts, which may not be perceived as efficient or independent, and to diplomatic protection, which depends on the willingness of the investor's home State to pursue the case (Shihata, 1992; Ginsburg, 2005; Schwebel, 2014).[2]

If the conduct of the host State is found in breach of the investment treaty—for instance, if an investor's assets were expropriated—the injured investor can be awarded compensation determined by the arbitration tribunal. Tribunals' awards are final and binding and, if rendered as per the International Center for the Settlement of Investment Disputes Convention, automatically recognized in the defending country. Otherwise they are recog-

Box 6.1:
Do investment treaties boost investment?

Empirical evidence on the impact of investment treaties on investment inflows remains contested. Recent econometric studies tend to suggest that investment inflows into developing countries increase on the back of investment treaties (for example, Bankole and Adewuyi, 2013; Falvey and McGregor, 2017). However, measuring the corollary impact of those investments is challenging because of both data problems (Kerner, 2018) and methodological ones (Gazzini, 2014; Bonnitcha, Poulsen and Waibel, 2017). Many factors in addition to investment treaties always affect that impact, such as the country's economic size and structure, labour market, infrastructure and institutions. Current research also does not clearly answer whether investment treaties effectively decrease political risk associated with weak institutions (see ECA, forthcoming a). Further research into which particular sectors might be most responsive to investment treaties is also warranted.

nized domestically, which can be facilitated by the New York Convention (Box 6.2). The usual remedy ordered by investment tribunals is financial compensation for damages.

The origin of international investment agreements

The international investment treaty regime emerged after World War II so that Western economies could protect the capital exported by their companies to less developed countries, many of which, at that time, were pursuing economic eman-cipation, sometimes at the expense of those companies (Vandevelde, 2005; Sonrajah, 2018).[3] Up to now, all attempts at reaching a multilateral investment treaty have failed, not least due to opposition from developing countries and non-governmental organizations, resulting in a network of disparate but overlapping bilateral and regional treaties. In recent years, South–South investment treaties have become more widespread, with certain countries, including Brazil, China and Turkey, active in concluding new treaties with African countries.

Box 6.2:
Enforcement of arbitral awards in Africa

Legal instruments that provide for structures for enforcement of arbitral awards exist at the international, regional and national level.

At the international level, three major instruments prescribe enforcement structures for arbitration awards. First, the 1958 Convention on the Recognition and Enforcement of Foreign Arbitral Awards (New York Convention), which provides for procedures of enforcement and grounds for challenge. This convention has been ratified by 157 countries worldwide, including 36 countries in Africa (NYAC, 2019). Second, the UNCITRAL Model Law, prepared for countries to adopt as is or with minimal amendments, containing the same provisions as the New York Convention. It has been adopted by 80 States around the world, including eleven African countries (UNCITRAL, 2019). Thirdly, the Convention on the International Centre for the Settlement of Investment Disputes (ICSID). These conventions also set out the very limited grounds on which national courts may refuse to recognize and enforce awards.

Outside the annulment process available within the ICSID structure, the convention establishes that all ICSID awards are automatically enforceable. The awards do not need to be validated by local courts, explaining in part the successes of ICSID as compared with the UNCITRAL rules (Pupolizio, 2015). The ICSID convention has been ratified by 153 countries worldwide, including 45 African countries.

At the regional level, the 17 member States of the Organisation pour l'harmonisation en Afrique du droit des affaires (Organisation for the Harmonization of Corporate Law in Africa) have agreed to use a uniform arbitration act, which is mainly based on the UNCITRAL model law, especially the articles on enforcement.

At the national level, every African country has legislation governing arbitration and enforcement of arbitral awards, although some are much more intricate than others (i-ARB, 2018). So, 42 African countries have adhered to international standards of enforcement of arbitral awards (Onyema, 2018).

But African courts are fairly inexperienced at implementing these rules. During research for the collection of international arbitral awards with at least one African party declared enforceable by the Paris Court, an interview with a judge from that court revealed that on average 900 to 1,000 applications a year for enforcement of international awards come before this court alone. This is a stark contrast to the number of applications made before African courts, where some jurisdictions have not received a single application for enforcement of a foreign award, although they have adhered to all the international instruments and standards of enforcement (i-ARB, 2018). Of 36 applications for enforcement of arbitral awards, whether final or interim, made in 11 jurisdictions in Africa, the courts declined to enforce only four.

Most historical African BITs with the rest of the world, as well as a few recent ones, contain strict investment protection provisions. Developing countries, including many in Africa, rarely entered investment treaties on the basis of a careful cost–benefit analysis weighing the investment–policy space trade-off. Desire for recognition of newly independent states (ECA, 2017), competition for investment (Elkins, Guzman and Simmons, 2006; Jandhyala, 2011; Neumayer, Nunnenkamp and Roy, 2016), financial conditions (Betz and Kerner, 2015), structural adjustment loans (Kaushal, 2009), pressure from businesses and international organisations (Vandevelde, 2010), search for a commitment device to prevent policy reversal (Echandi, 2011), asymmetrical distribution of negotiating power (Salacuse and Sullivan, 2005; Trakman, 2009; Allee and Peinhardt, 2014) and expertise (Berge and Stiansen, 2016), fear of sending a negative signal by failing to sign a treaty (Vandevelde, 1998) and a lack of oversight and appreciation for the potential future repercussions (Poulsen, 2015) affected the spread and the content of investment treaties. Facing a prisoner's dilemma, countries may have agreed to more stringent conditions than would be the case in multilateral negotiations (Guzman, 1998).

IIAs and their discontents

The international investment regime has been said to be suffering from a "legitimacy crisis" due to restricted policy space, but also to the related issues of inconsistent and suspect arbitration tribunals, the lop-sidedness of the investment regime and the opportunistic behaviour of some investors (Franck, 2005; García-Bolívar, 2015). Investment treaties do not distribute rights and obligations equally: they usually contain legally binding obligations for host States but not for the home State or the investors (the last not being signatory parties to the treaty). IIAs usually lack substantive investor obligations and formal mechanisms host States could use to file claims or even counterclaims against transgressing investors.

Fears about investment treaties' impact on policy space have been stoked by investors claims against host country measures related to human rights (Box 6.3) (Bohoslavsky and Justo, 2011; Bodea and Ye,

2018), health (Box 6.4) (Tobin, 2018), environment (Tienhaara, 2006), taxation (ECA, forthcoming b), responses to economic crises (Burke-White, 2008) and measures taken to give effect to international commitments (Tienhaara, 2018). The prospect of costly arbitration with a result difficult to predict may induce governments to reconsider measures promoting legitimate public policy objectives, a phenomenon dubbed "regulatory chill" (see Box 6.4) (Pelc, 2016). Some authors, however, question this impact and point out how difficult it is to observe from the outside and to disentangle from other factors influencing policy making (Brower and Blanchard, 2014). Some investment treaties, however, go one further, with performance requirements stricter than those found in trade treaties.

Key standards of treatment offered to investors have often been vaguely defined, providing insufficient guidance on how they should be interpreted. The interpretations of individual arbitration panels, which are not bound by precedents, can vary, and so can the threshold for State liability. The result is a restriction of, or at least uncertainty about, the policy space available to host countries. In extreme cases, outright contradictory awards on the same set of facts can be yielded. The incentives of arbitrators have also been questioned—they do not enjoy secure tenure and may participate in different capacities, such as arbitrators and counsels, in parallel or subsequent proceedings.

Arbitrators have also been found to be rather homogenous in gender, origin, type of education and professional background (UNCTAD, 2018c). African nationals are underrepresented in important arbitration positions, including on the part of the defending African States. Though Africa and the Middle East account for 26 per cent of State parties involved in cases registered by ICSID until the end of June 2017, nationals from this region account only for 6 per cent of appointed arbitrators, conciliators and ad hoc committee members (ICSID, 2017).[4]

Arbitration is not always swift or economical (see Box 6.4). In its 2015 annual report, ICSID stated that the average length of proceedings in the 2014–15 fiscal year was more than three years (ICSID, 2015).[5]

Foresti v. South Africa

In November 2006, the Luxembourg-incorporated company Finstone, together with a group of its Italian owners, filed for arbitration to claim more than $340 million in compensation from South Africa over changes to mining rights and the affirmative action section of the new mining legislation (Case No ARB(AF)/07/1). The legal challenge garnered considerable attention because it was "the first time international investment laws [would] be used to directly confront State regulation linked to fundamental human rights norms" (Aguirre, 2008, 166) and because it raised fears of copycat action by other mining companies if the investors prevailed (Wythes, 2010). Although the proceedings were ultimately discontinued and the decisions of the tribunal positively accepted, the high-stakes case occasioned a comprehensive examination of South Africa's investment policy and a shift in it.

The claimants declared that the new mining legislation was in breach of the expropriation provisions of the 1997 Italy–South Africa and 1998 Belgium/Luxemburg–South Africa investment treaties by extinguishing mineral rights, obtained in conformity with the previous rules, due to the 2004 Mineral and Petroleum Resources Development Act (MPRDA) and the compulsory divestment prescribed by the new mining charter introduced the same year. The claimants also alleged breaches of fair and equitable treatment and national treatment, but the details are not publicly known.

Formerly, private companies owned both the land and the resources contained therein, but the MPRDA vested the rights to resources with the government in a bid to increase the role of the government in the industry. Previous rights owners could reapply for new licenses, but many private companies complained that the new rights were less valuable (Vis-Dunbar, 2009), since they were only valid to up to 30 years, subject to a five-year renewal process and compliance with the mining charter (Chow, 2009; Friedman, 2010).

Under the black economic empowerment (BEE) aspect of the mining charter, at least 26 per cent of the equity of mining companies had to be owned by historically disadvantaged South Africans by the end of 2014. The claimants maintained that it was not possible to sell the shares at fair market value, which the mining charter allowed. Though later criticized as "benefit[ting] a lucky few who got preferential access to equity in large firms" (*Economist*, 2019, 4-5; Tangri and Southall 2008), the BEE policies were adopted by the South African government to reduce entrenched income disparity along ethnic lines bequeathed from the apartheid era and centuries of racialized oppression.

Commentators worried that the international investment regime could be used as a wrecking ball against affirmative action in South Africa. Chow (2009, 315) noted that the two legal regimes were governed by a widely different logic because "under South African law, equality entails a positive duty to promote the advancement of disadvantaged groups of people, whereas international [investment] law's concept of equality is a negative duty to refrain from discrimination" and that the former focuses on the end result, while the latter is rather concerned with the means.

In assessing the claim, the ICSID tribunal allowed the submission of a joint petition by two local and two international non-governmental organizations and a separate petition by the Geneva-based International Commission of Jurists. These amici curiae highlighted the socio-economic inequality in the country and called on the tribunal to take into consideration the international human rights law and the constitution, which allows for positive affirmation measures to "advance persons or categories of persons disadvantaged by unfair discrimination." The "unprecedented level of participation of non-disputing parties" was welcomed by the expert community for promoting transparency (Leibhold, 2015, 7) and understanding of the "on-the-ground realities" (Friedman, 2010, 45) and, hence, could facilitate reconciliation of the investment law and human rights law, even though the tribunal did not articulate clear principles on the participation of non-disputing parties (Brickhill and Du Plessis, 2011).

The tribunal case did not reach the merits phase. In January 2010 the claimant asked for the discontinuance of the proceedings "with an award dismissing their claims with res judicata [already judged] effect" (ICSID award). The respondent had obtained a "partial relief" when, in place of the ownership requirements under the mining charter, it committed to a 21 per cent beneficiation offset and 5 per cent ownership programme for employees in the operating companies. Brickhill and Du Plessis (2011, 164–165) wrote that this outcome may highlight a temptation of defending governments to reach a "settlement of sorts" instead of "defend[ing] a case on human rights grounds… which could ultimately have a regulatory chilling effect on government human rights measures." At the same time, settlements may allow investors not having to disclose pleadings that would reveal those claims against human rights legislation and so avoid the reputational costs associated with such claims (Brickhill and Du Plessis, 2011, 164–165)

The tribunal ordered the claimant to pay 400,000 euros to the South African government for the fees and costs. Like the allowance of non-disputing parties, the decision to shift a portion of the costs on the claimant even though the merits stage had not been reached was perceived as a legitimacy-enhancing step and meaningful counter to frivolous claims (Leibhold, 2015). However, the partial award on costs does not spell out how the amount was determined or what portion of South Africa's costs associated with the claim it represented.

The Foresti case prompted South African officials to assess the country's stock of BITs, which had been concluded after the fall of apartheid amid the objectives of promotion of equality, economic independence and capital imports for economic development (George and Thomas, 2018, 420). As in many other countries, the level of potential liability arising from BITs had been underestimated until the first claim was filed against South Africa (Poulsen, 2015). Insufficient capacities, poor coordination and continuity, lack of clear strategy (Poulsen, 2015), a lack of parliamentary oversight (Chow, 2009; Schlemmer, 2018) as well as eagerness for foreign capital (Chow, 2009) have all been suggested as having a role in the final outcome of the South Africa's BIT programme.

Having concluded that the BITs "extend far into developing countries' policy space" (DTI, 2009, 38), the South African government has opted for a relatively radical departure from the international investment regime (Kidane, 2018a). Since 2010, South Africa has started terminating some BITs or allowing them to lapse, mostly with EU countries. Nonetheless, many of its still-valid treaties, such as those with Russia, Senegal, Sweden and Zimbabwe, still include vaguely defined standards of treatment and access to ISDS.

The government has instead refocused its efforts to rebalance the investment regime on domestic legislation (Schlemmer, 2016). In July 2018, a new Protection of Investment Act came into effect in spite of concerns of the investor community over reduced protection (Sicetsha, 2018). Fair and equitable treatment is replaced with "fair and administrative treatment" providing protection against arbitrary administrative, legislative and judicial processes and denial of administrative and judicial justice. National and most-favoured nation treatment are tempered by exception. The new law also establishes the right to regulate, for instance in relation to redress of social-economic inequalities and injustices, constitutional rights, economic development and environmental protection. The act does not offer recourse to ISDS, but only mediation and domestic litigation and State–State dispute settlement (SSDS) conditioned on the government's consent. The complementary draft bill to govern expropriation, spelling out conditions under which expropriation, including uncompensated expropriation, may take place, was presented in December 2018. However, some authors have raised concerns over a lack of clarity over its interaction with international law, to which the act refers (Schlemmer, 2018). Efforts are currently under way on a new national model BIT aligned with the investment act.

The average legal and expert costs amount to $6 million for claimants and $5 million for respondents, with mean tribunal costs hovering around $900,000 (Hodgson and Campbell, 2017).

A lost investment case can substantively affect the finances of developing countries. The median award for successful investors stands at $20 million, with the average rising to $504 million due to several with very high costs (UNCTAD, 2018c). The main financial beneficiaries tend to be companies with revenue exceeding $10 billion, which turn out to be very successful in their claims, and high net-worth individuals (Van Harten and Malysheuski, 2016).

The ISDS system is sometimes accused of bias in favour of investors, but publicly available cases do not paint a clear picture. Defending States have won 35.7 per cent of treaty cases, and investors, 28.7 per cent of awards, but nearly a quarter of cases end up settled, which often entails compensation for the investor (Figure 6.3). Nearly 11 per cent of the claims were discontinued at the behest of the investor. Of cases not dismissed on procedural grounds, claimants won 61 per cent (UNCTAD, 2018c).

Modelled on commercial arbitration, the prevailing dispute settlement system has also often been criticized for a lack of transparency. The mere existence of claims can be hidden from the public eye under some arbitration rules. However, substantive strides at both the institutional and the treaty level have been made. Transparency in international investment arbitration encompasses public access to materials, including the oral and written statements by both parties to the dispute and the possible participation by other interested parties, such as civil organizations, in the proceedings (see Box 6.3). Funding of claimants by third parties has become increasingly contested due to concerns that they could fuel unmeritorious claims (see Guven and Johnso, 2019 for discussion) and blunt the incentives to find common ground and settle (Van Boom, 2012). While increased transparency is meant to enhance procedural fairness and promote predictability and harmonization with other legal regimes (Fry, 2007; Coe, 2006), some authors argue that participation of non-disputing parties in particular may engender higher costs and delays (Bjorklund, 2009).

Figure 6.3:
Outcomes of concluded investor–State dispute settlement proceedings

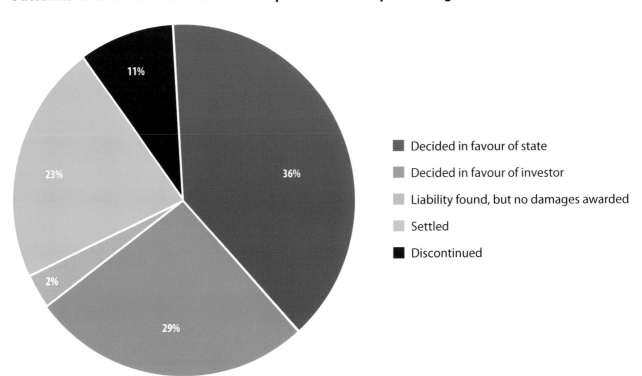

- Decided in favour of state
- Decided in favour of investor
- Liability found, but no damages awarded
- Settled
- Discontinued

Transparency provisions in investment treaties have become increasingly common (UNCTAD, 2012d), and further changes have also been taking place at the institutional level. The 2014 UNCITRAL rules on transparency that came into force in October 2017 address many of the transparency issues. The new UNCITRAL rules apply to all new treaties but can also be applied to those concluded before January 2014 if both parties have ratified the Mauritius Convention on Transparency. The ICSID arbitration rules dating to 2006 are currently under review.

Companies, including domestic ones, may also engage in opportunistic corporate restructuring to obtain treaty protection for their investments.[6] As a result, countries may face a higher potential for liability than they initially consented to, with further possible cramping of policy space (Skinner, Miles and Luttrell, 2010, Van Os and Knottnerus 2011). Foreign companies not covered by an investment treaty have in some cases attempted to change their nationality to gain additional treaty protection after their initial investment. Current case law suggests that "there is currently no universal rule against [t]reaty [s]hopping or nationality planning" (Skinner, Miles and Luttrell, 2010: 283). Arbitration practitioners appear inclined to accept changes in nationality unless they are made at a time when an investment dispute is already foreseeable (Kirtley, 2009; see Box 6.4).

Investors may be able to launch simultaneous proceedings, which can increase pressure on the host government and may raise the chance of winning compensation (Van Harten, 2016). Parallel claims,

Box 6.4:

Philip Morris v. Australia

On 21 November 2011, the Australian parliament approved new plain packaging legislation compelling tobacco manufactures to discontinue branding on packages and expand the space dedicated to health warnings. The public health measure was designed to reduce smoking and give effect to recommendations of the World Health Organization Framework Convention on Tobacco Control. On the very same day, Philip Morris, a major tobacco products manufacturer based in the United States, filed a notice of arbitration against the legislation on the plain packaging laws on the basis of the 1993 Hong Kong–Australia BIT (PCA Case No. 2012-12). The investor invoked several treaty breaches, including fair and equitable treatment (FET) and expropriation due to the deprivation of value derived from its intellectual property and goodwill. The umbrella clause, which can extend treaty protection to other types of claims, typically those arising from contract breaches, was also invoked to bring in the Agreement on Trade-Related Aspects of Intellectual Property Rights (TRIPS), the Paris Convention for the Protection of Industrial Property and the Agreement on Technical Barriers to Trade, all parts of the World Trade Organization law. The company demanded that either the plain packaging laws be rescinded or it be paid $4.2 billion in compensation.

The Australian arm of the corporation was initially manged by Philip Morris Brands Sàrl, a Swiss entity that was acquired by Philip Morris PM Asia incorporated in Hong Kong PM only on 23 February 2011. However, the Australian government had publicly announced its intention to enact plain packaging measures already at the end of April 2010. Commentators have noted that the claimant previously lacked access to international arbitration. There was no investment treaty between Switzerland and Australia (Fukunaga, 2018) and the US–Australia FTA did not contain an investor–State dispute settlement mechanism (Chaisse, 2015).

In December 2015, the arbitral tribunal dismissed the claim as it refrained from exercising its jurisdiction on admissibility grounds. The panel found that to commence arbitration after corporate restructuring undertaken with the aim of obtaining treaty protection "at a point in time where a dispute was foreseeable" amounted to "an abuse of right (or abuse of process)." The arbitral panel went on to if allowed to proceed, may yield inconsistent or outright contradictory results. There are currently no universally applied rules or approaches on how to deal with multiple claims (see, for example, Attanasio, 2018).

Although developing countries have usually led opposition to traditional investment protection, unease with the current system has also been growing in industrialized countries (Van Harten, 2005; see Ames, 2015, and Emmott and Blenkinsop, 2014, for public outcry in the European Union galvanized by the now shelved Transatlantic Trade and Investment Partnership negotiations with the United States). The recently concluded Comprehensive Economic and Trade Agreement between the European Union and Canada (CETA) and the renegotiated 1994 North American Free Trade Agreement (NAFTA) concluded among Canada, Mexico and the United States (the United States–Mexico–Canada Agreement—UMSCA) bear testimony to the reform trend in the developed world.

The AfCFTA phase II negotiations provide a unique opportunity to rewrite the investment rules in Africa and carefully design an effective and balanced investment dispute mechanism (Box 6.5). The investment protocol of the AfCFTA ought to reflect the current discussions and find a new balance between investor and State obligations to better align the treaty with sustainable development considerations and help level the playing field across countries seeking investment. At the same time, the new continental rules on investment should enhance investment promotion and

explain that "a dispute is foreseeable when there is [a] reasonable prospect… that a measure which may give rise to a treaty claim will materialise."

The Philip Morris case marks a wider trend of recourse to the "foreseeability test," which consists of analyzing the time and objectives or intentions of the investor engaging in nationality planning after the initial investment, underpinned by the notion of "abuse of rights" or "abuse of process" (Ascensio, 2014; Linderfalk, 2017). Arbitral tribunals have tended to order the claimant whose claims were found to amount to an abuse of process to pay most or all the costs of arbitration (Gaffney, 2010; Ascensio, 2014).

The foreseeability test, though not applied by tribunals in an entirely consistent manner, marks a positive development in assessing treaty abuse in international investment arbitration. However, clear treaty drafting provides a more reliable and predictable avenue for blocking opportunistic treaty shopping. Options for treaty refinement include provisions on denial of benefits, stricter definitions of investors and clauses against abuse of rights (Feldman, 2012; Zhang, 2013, Lee, 2015; Fukunaga, 2018). It is noteworthy that about a year before filing for arbitration against Australia, Philip Morris challenged plain packaging legislation in Uruguay (ICSID Case No. ARB/10/7). In that instance, the host country prevailed, as the tribunal upheld its right to regulate (see e.g. Foster, 2017; Hartmann, 2017).

Further challenges to the Australian plain packaging legislation indicate the inherent overlap between the investment and trade regimes. It was challenged on the basis of the TRIPS at the WTO level, following lobbying from Philip Morris, by Cuba, the Dominican Republic, Indonesia, Honduras and Ukraine in five separate proceedings. The trade restriction claims by these countries related to trademarks, geographic indications and the impact of the policy on value chains. As of February 2019, two of these claims had been struck down by the WTO panel, one was abandoned by the claimant and two were still ongoing. These parallel proceedings indicate that investors who deem injury may be incentivized to pursue all the avenues at their disposal to defend their rights and that the same company may re-litigate the same issue in various countries as they adopt similar legislation (Alford, 2013).

Tools to enhance treaty interpretation

Interpretation has been at the heart of investor–State dispute. States have therefore taken several steps to minimize interpretational issues by using tools to enhance clarity and reduce room for expansive interpretations threatening controversy and raising concerns over possible constriction of policy space. These tools include:

Clearly written exceptions to the treaty's protections. For example, the 2009 ASEAN Comprehensive Investment Agreement states, "Non-discriminatory measures of a Member State that are designated and applied to protect legitimate public welfare objectives, such as public health, safety and the environment, do not constitute an expropriation of the type referred to in sub-paragraph 2(b) (indirect expropriation).." This clause, by outlining a clear exception, limits the purview of expropriation. Another example can be found in the 2016 Argentina–Qatar BIT, which prohibits the use of the most-favoured nation clause to import fair and equitable treatment and dispute settlement clauses from a BIT signed with any third country before the entry into force of the base treaty. This exception would be most useful to countries that previously signed BITs containing expansive protections and have adopted a new model or have a new policy on BITs. Negotiators may also use exceptions to carve out specific policy areas from the scope of the treaty, such as taxation. However, case law indicates that measures taken in bad faith can constitute a treaty breach even if they fall within a policy area that has been carved out.

Definitions of terms as agreed upon by both parties provided in the legal instruments themselves. The Comprehensive Economic and Trade Agreement between the European Union and Canada (CETA), which provisionally came into force on 21 September 2017, lists measures that constitute fair and equitable treatment, effectively defining and limiting the agreement's scope. These measures are denial of justice, fundamental breach of due process, manifest arbitrariness, target discrimination, abusive treatments of investors or any other grounds that the parties agree to add to this list. A joint committee is set up with experts from all member States, which regularly meets and discusses additional measures or definitions to be added. The committee also provides guidelines on the definitions and measures for arbitral tribunals.

Increased institutionalization of the dispute resolution mechanism in international arbitration. The two main options raised are the creation of an appellate body and the establishment of a permanent ISDS court (Schill, 2017). The appellate court would review cases specifically focused on whether there is an error of law. A permanent court would establish legal certainty by having a two-tier system: a first instance and an appellate body. Both mechanisms would contribute to the emergence of a strong jurisprudence and create legal precedents, further increasing certainty and transparency in ISDS cases. Although such institutions do not yet exist in the world of ISDS, in 2018, the European Union Council approved the European Commission negotiating on behalf of EU member States "a convention establishing a multilateral court for the settlement of investment disputes set up a permanent body to settle investment disputes" (European Council, 2018). This court would effectively replace the ad hoc investment arbitration system (European Commission, 2017). This court is already envisaged in the most recent EU FTAs, starting with CETA.

rationalize the current fragmented and overlapping investment treaty regime on the continent. Policy makers embarking on international investment agreement (IIA) reform must determine the most effective means to safeguard the right to regulate while providing for the protection and facilitation of investment. In doing so, they need to consider the compound effect of options. Some combinations of reform options may "overshoot" the goal and result in a treaty that is largely deprived of its investment protection rationale.

Figure 6.4:
Schematic overview of AfCFTA investment protocol options

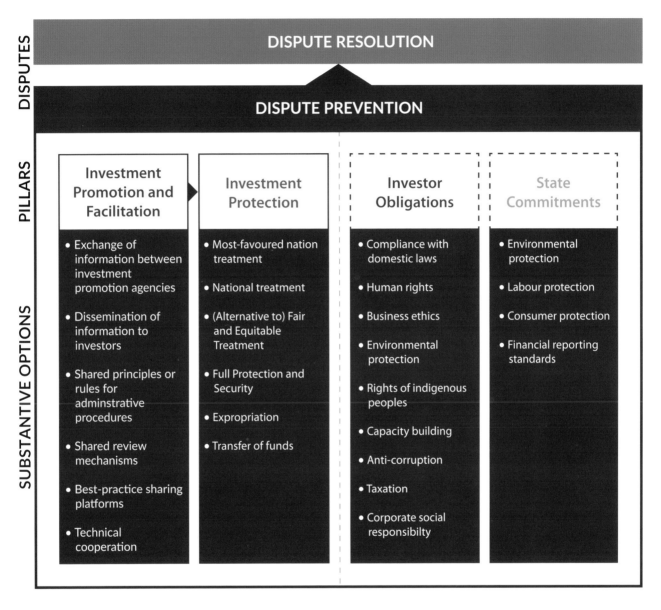

Source: Authors.

Investment promotion and facilitation

National approaches to investment promotion and facilitation

The ease of setting up, running and expanding business may be as important for foreign investors as investment protection, if not more so (Kusek and Silva, 2018; see Box 6.6). Investment promotion and facilitation has become a more frequent topic at such international forums as the G20, WTO and OECD. African countries may profit from the trend by increasing investment promotion and facilitation as a complement to investment protection. The addition of the investment promotion and facilitation pillar would make the investment protocol within the AfCFTA more comprehensive and progressive, to the benefit of domestic, regional and foreign investors.

Investment promotion and investment facilitation are related but distinct strategies. Investment promotion comprises activities to reduce the transaction costs of finding investment opportunities. It denotes marketing and public relations activities designed at attract domestic and foreign investors to the host economy by highlighting investment opportunities there (OECD, 2015). The marketing and public relations activities are typically undertaken by specialized investment promotion agencies (IPAs) or ministries of economy or trade. IPA activities in developing and emerging economies can prove cost-effective in increasing investment inflows, particularly in economies marked by high transaction costs for entry due to information asymmetry and burdensome administrative procedures (Harding and Javorcik, 2011).

Investment facilitation is a comparatively vague concept but is generally concerned with lowering the transaction costs at the point of entry and in day-to-day operations associated with seizing these investment opportunities (Ghiotto, 2018; Zhang, 2018). Investment facilitation encompasses "policies and actions aimed at making it easier for investors to establish and expand their investments, as well as to conduct their day-to-day business in host countries" while maximizing the benefits of investment for the host country (Sauvant, 2016; UNCTAD, 2017a, 3, see Box 6.6).

Investment facilitation concerns the entire business environment. Its key principles include transparency of the regulatory regime, timely sharing of relevant information with investors, streamlining and rendering more efficient the administrative processes for investors and ensuring consistency and predictability in the application of rules (UNCTAD, 2017a).

In practice, investment promotion and investment facilitation overlap, since some actors and activities may assume both roles. IPAs and dedicated ministries may play an important part in guiding and accompanying investors. But investment facilitation requires collaboration and cooperation among a wide array of public institutions and other stakeholders, ranging from immigration offices to environmental regulators to tax authorities.

REC approaches to investment promotion and facilitation

In step with global developments, regional treaties and initiatives are shifting from investment protection towards investment promotion and facilitation. Individual approaches, sometimes expressed in treaties and strategies, differ (Baruti, 2017) and may overlap with investment protection.

Under the COMESA treaty, member States agreed to a number of decisions promoting intra-regional investment, including harmonization of macroeconomic policies, provision of fair and equitable treatment to investors, creation and maintenance of a "predictable, transparent and secure investment climate," acceleration of investment deregulation and the conclusion of double taxation treaties to keep individuals from having to pay taxes twice on the same asset or activity in two different jurisdictions. Article 8 of the COMESA Common Investment Area (CCIA), which requires member States to develop and implement a co-operation and facilitation programme, emphasizes transparency and simplification of investment rules. Member States are compelled, for instance, to collectively manage a database on intra-regional investment flows, share information on investment opportunities and promote public–private linkages. Many of the objectives have been adopted by the COMESA Regional Investment Agency launched in 2006. The CCIA also requires member States to promote awareness through trainings, joint promotions, regular consultations among national investment agencies, exchange of information on priority investment sectors and examination of opportunities for encouraging investments in other member States.

The non-binding EAC treaty envisages member States establishing national IPAs, which would coordinate, encourage, promote and facilitate investment. The IPAs would be one-stop centres for facilitating investment and would also advise the government on investment policy matters while considering the view of the private sector and other stakeholders. They would enhance investment by providing investors with pertinent information and identifying potential partners for joint ventures. For individual investors, the IPAs should co-ordinate and facilitate establishing new companies and assist with registering the company, securing tax registration (such as a tax identification number and VAT) and obtaining necessary approvals, environmental impact assessments, security permits from the immigration authorities and other types of support and assistance.

The revised ECOWAS treaty encourages a regional approach to investment promotion. It envisages, among other objectives, a regional agreement on cross-border investment, an enabling legal environment and a regional investment code (Box 6.7). The Industry and Private Sector Promotion Department at the ECOWAS Commission, set up to mainstream private sector investment, collaborates with private and public stakeholders and development partners on facilitating investment flows into the region and a coordinating investment promotion. Regional business associations, for their part, facilitate a public–private dialogue with policy makers to identify and address business and investment bottlenecks. The dialogue feeds business reforms. They are monitored and benchmarked with the "ECOWAS investment climate scorecard tool" under the "improved investment climate in West Africa" project, which seeks to reduce investment entry barriers and simplify administrative processes for investors.

The SADC Protocol on Finance and Investment compels member States to devise and implement strategies to attract investment and foster entrepreneurship. It encourages States to build a favourable business environment and stresses the role of investment promotion agencies in facilitating investment flows into SADC countries. IPAs are to promote investment in accordance with national and regional developmental priorities; advise governments, the private sector and other stakeholders on formulating and reviewing policies and procedures affecting investment and trade and regularly exchange information to raise awareness about investment opportunities, incentives, legislation and events. A dedicated website lists all SADC IPAs and features pages on individual investment regimes.

The 2016 SADC Investment Policy Framework, using the OECD's Policy Framework for Investment as a reference point (OECD, undated), provides a non-binding template with specific actions for investment policy reform across a number of dimensions, including transparency and coherence of the investment environment and regional and international cooperation (Brauch, Mann and Bernasconi-Osterwalder, 2019). The framework's activities concern disseminating information, using e-government, realigning trade and investment and other areas.

Investment promotion and facilitation in IIAs

Internationally, Brazil has pioneered investment promotion and facilitation as an alternative to investment protection. So far, four African countries have signed Cooperation and Facilitation Investment Agreements with Brazil, one of which has already entered into force (Box 6.6).

Unlike national and bilateral efforts, multilateral efforts on rules for investment promotion have created controversy. Such initiatives have been taking place most prominently at the WTO, where member States remain divided over investment facilitation. At the 11th Ministerial Conference of the WTO in Buenos Aires in December 2017, 70 countries, including the EU, Russia and Singapore as well as the five African countries Benin, Guinea, Liberia, Nigeria and Togo issued a "Joint Ministerial Statement on Investment Facilitation for Development," which called for "structured discussions with the aim of developing a multilateral framework on investment facilitation." The other countries—more than 90—did not endorse the motion, and many, including India, South Africa and the United States, do not appear to favour binding rules on investment facilitation. Since March 2017, at least six proposals were advanced by WTO members, but none contained a specific definition of investment facilitation (Zhang, 2018).

The political division coincides with a lack of consensus among experts. Several argue in favour of agreeing binding principles for investment facilitation under the WTO (Novik and de Crombrugghe, 2018), possibly completed with international support (Sauvant and Hamdani, 2015). Other commentators warn that the WTO is not well suited to discuss investment facilitation, since cumbersome

Brazil's Cooperation and Facilitation Investment Agreements

Brazil is the largest recipient of FDI in the Latin American region, largely due to the size of its economy. In the 1990s, Brazil negotiated 14 BITs but never ratified any of them, in part because the National Congress has been wary of their future impact on the right to regulate and unequal treatment for local businesses (Viera Martins, 2017).

In 2015, the Brazilian government unveiled a new model "Cooperation and Facilitation Investment Agreement" (CFIA), which gained immediate attention in the region and beyond. The model shifts from investment protection towards investment facilitation and risk mitigation. It was developed in consultation with the private sector, which had been increasing its foreign investments, particularly in other Latin American countries and Africa. For investing capital abroad, investors showed more interest in facilitation of daily operations than dispute resolution (Morosini and Badin, 2015; Hees, Mendonca and Paranhos, 2018).

Brazil's CFIAs cover only direct investment. They grant lower standards of protection to foreign investors than either traditional BITs or the investment chapters of the most recent Latin American FTAs. For example, CFIAs exclude portfolio investment and pre-establishment commitments. They also omit protection against indirect expropriation, fair and equitable treatment, the umbrella clause, prohibition of performance requirements and recourse to ISDS. Subject to exceptions, national treatment and most-favoured nation treatment remain. The investors are expected to display best efforts to contribute to the sustainable development of the host economy by complying with specific principles and standards (Bernasconi-Osterwalder and Brauch, 2015).

To facilitate investments, each party commits to designate a ministry or other agency as an investment ombudsperson, whose main function is supporting foreign investors in its territory. The ombudsperson is akin to a single-window intermediary between investors and relevant agencies. It aims to improve the investment climate and to prevent controversies from escalating by processing information requests, suggestions and complaints from foreign investors. The CFIA also touches on information exchange, processing visa applications and assisting with environmental permits, among other issues.

Under the CFIAs, investment disputes must be first addressed through consultations and negotiation and examined by a joint committee set up by the contracting States. Multiple references to "affected investors" have led some commentators to suggest that the focus is on concerns affecting multiple investors, rather than individual situations (Muniz, Duggal and Peretti, 2017). Only if these consultations fail, the treaty allows for State-to-State arbitration.

By May 2019, Brazil had signed 10 bilateral CFIAs with Chile, Colombia, Guyana, Mexico, Peru and Suriname in Latin America and with Angola, Ethiopia, Malawi and Mozambique in Africa. The CFIA model became the basis for the 2017 Intra-MERCOSUR Investment Facilitation Protocol among Argentina, Brazil, Paraguay and Uruguay. But as of April 2019, only the agreement with Angola was in force, so more time will be needed to assess the practical effectiveness of the CFIA model. The text of the Brazil–Chile CFIA, signed in November 2015, was included as chapter 8 ("Investment Cooperation and Facilitation") of the Brazil–Chile Free Trade Agreement, signed in November 2018. It remains to be seen whether Brazil will replicate this practice with other CFIA partners, especially in Latin America.

binding obligations could result with insufficient focus on sustainable development (Brauch, 2017a). This could create pressure on countries with stricter regulations to lower their standards (Ghiotto, 2018) and limit their policy space (Singh, 2018) by fostering investment liberalization by stealth (ECA, 2018). On balance, given the lack of clarity on the precise scope and meaning of investment facilitation, African countries should engage in global discussions on general principles and ensure that investment facilitation is "first and foremost about attracting quality investment" (Mbengue, 2018: 3) but apply caution in agreeing to binding rules.

Investment promotion and facilitation need to be separated from market access and investment protection to avoid investment protection obligations to private investors (Sauvant, 2018). Transparency should also be understood simply as informing the investor community and other stakeholders in a timely mannner about the existing and applicable legislation, standards, regulations and judicial decisions and ensuring consistent application of rules and procedures eliminating scope for undue administrative discretion (UNCTAD, 2017a).

The AfCFTA can serve as a springboard for investment facilitation and promotion. The investment protocol can go beyond the PAIC and establish a robust investment architecture centred on investment promotion and facilitation and dispute prevention and de-escalation. Investment promotion and facilitation should become fundamental pillars of the AfCFTA investment architecture, while associated commitments, however, should be removed from the scope of obligations towards private investors to avoid increasing liability. Building on continental best practices, the AfCFTA protocol should allow institutions to emerge that enable smooth flowing of investments across African economies.

The tasks associated with these two distinct but complementary roles of informing investors and seeking amicable solutions may be performed by the same authority or agency, such as the IPA, or be split between two different agencies, depending on the preferences of national negotiators and the overall domestic institutional structure. These agencies would serve as a multidimensional link connecting the investor, the local communities, the host economy and the other AfCFTA economies.

The designated focal points could collaborate with the AfCFTA secretariat on implementing the investment promotion and facilitation agreement and liaise with other agencies in the network. Their role would be to provide investors with information on legal, regulatory and administrative matters, including customs and tax procedures, relevant international treaties and public programmes and incentives. The agencies could also maintain and provide statistics about investment flows and investigate and seek to resolve concerns or conflicts raised by stakeholders or interested parties concerning the conduct of foreign investors.

Given the ambitious single market logic underpinning the AfCFTA, negotiators may also explore the desire for a common understanding on the rules or principles, including guidelines, for facilitating investment flows among AfCFTA member States. A joint review mechanism could be established to monitor implementation and progress. Such rules could affect market access, so caution is warranted. For instance, the PAIC already contains a provision on visas and work permits and a framework for cooperation of central banks to manage risks, integrate payment systems and combat criminal activities. Member States may also consider establishing best-practice sharing platforms or building joint technical capacity for providing accompanying services to investors and maintaining services once investors have established themselves in the economy (see OECD and IDB, 2018, for example) and image building (see, for example, Ghouri, 2018). As African economies become integrated, policy makers may consider developing a continental brand for investors and African products.

However, resource constraints may hamper efforts to promote and facilitate investment (Singh, 2018). The different capacities among countries discourage strict and uniform rules for investment facilitation and bringing it under the umbrella of investment protection. Many African countries would therefore profit from targeted and coordinated technical assistance to help them fully harness the potential benefits of investment facilitation.

Investment protection

The key investment protection clauses that need to be considered in the AfCFTA include:

Preamble

The preamble does not create enforceable rights and obligations, but international arbitrators take heed of it when interpreting the treaty. Following the recent treaty practice on the continent and globally, including in the PAIC, treaty negotiators are encouraged to spell out the objectives they expect the investment protocol to achieve. They may go beyond the promotion of "economic cooperation" typical of older treaties and raise sustainable development, human rights, the State's right to regulate and investor responsibilities, for example. References to specific documents, such as Agenda 2063 and the Sustainable Development Goals, can promote the harmonization of the treaty with continental policy objectives and ambitions.

Definition of investor

The definition of investor determines which entities enjoy treaty protection, both natural and legal persons. The nationality criterion is used to regulate treaty coverage for natural persons, though double nationality may raise issues of determination. For companies, constitution under the laws of one of the contracting parties has traditionally been the condition they had to meet, but this condition, on its own, has proved insufficient to stem treaty shopping. The investment protocol ought to be immunized against treaty abuse through companies opportunistically restructuring themselves, although investment treaties are increasingly likely to face claims by mailbox companies, entities controlled by a domestic entity or entities created in anticipation of a claim ("time-sensitive restructuring"—see Box 6.4). The investment protocol should benefit only investors who are intended to be covered by it.

The treaty can add criteria for companies, such as the jurisdiction of incorporation, the management seat of the company and nationality of the people controlling the company (McLachlan, Shore and Weiniger, 2017). It should protect only companies that engage in "substantial business activities" in the host economy, to avoid speculative claims. To enhance clarity of the concept of "substantial business activities," treaty negotiators may consider adding specific criteria to assess the economic contribution of investment to the development of the host country. In a similar vein, spelling out the content of "effective control" would bring more clarity.

Definition of investment

The investment definition delineates the classes of assets that enjoy treaty protection. The broader the definitions, the more investments and investors enjoy treaty protection, but also the more host States can be exposed to treaty claims and higher valuations of potential damages. Since investment treaties are meant to promote productive assets conducive to sustainable development, the key challenge is to cover exactly those investments (Malik, 2009).

Two broad approaches to the conceptualizing investment have emerged: they can be assets-based or enterprise-based. Investment treaties have traditionally employed the former approach by including open-ended indicative lists of covered assets (UNCTAD, 2012c). Though this approach grants the highest level of protection, it may lead to unexpected liabilities for host States. Assets such as contracts, intellectual property rights, non-equity investments and public concessions have, for instance, been found to fall under the scope of treaty protection.

Some recent texts, including those of PAIC and SADC, and India's model BIT, favour the enterprise-based approach, which aligns investment protection with FDI based on the ownership and control of an enterprise. The definition should also be clear on whether indirectly owned investments (including investments controlled through entities registered outside African countries) were covered by the investment protocol.

Regardless of which approach is ultimately adopted, the treaty should specify the assets protected through the use of positive and/or negative lists (UNCTAD, 2015a). For instance, short-term, portfolio investment represents an additional, yet volatile, source of financing (Razin, Sadka and Yuen, 2001; Albuquerque, 2003; UNCTAD, 2015a) that may do little to advance the developmental agenda compared with greenfield investments (Dunning and Lundan, 2011). Based on recent treaty practices, negotiators may consider excluding debt securities; claims to money based on commercial contracts and domestic financing of such contracts and orders; and judgements and awards, which do not appear essential to long-term development. Treaty drafters should also consider to what extent intellectual property rights should be protected and how the investment protocol and intellectual property rights protocol should relate to each other.

More recent treaty practice has also added criteria for assets to be covered, such as that investments be only of "a certain duration" (2016 CETA), establish "lasting economic relations" (2011 Nigeria–Turkey BIT) and make a significant contribution to the host State's economic development (2016 Nigeria–Morocco BIT; 2017 Burundi–Turkey BIT).

Denial of benefits

Host States may wish to deny the benefits of the investment treaty to prevent aggressive nationality planning or to exclude investors from countries that do not have diplomatic relations with the host State or face measures forbidding them to have economic transactions with the home State as happens, for instance, in the US and SADC model BITs. As noted above, nationality planning can be addressed in the definitional section, though denial of benefits may still be useful for specific cases of corporate restructuring (see above and Box 6.4). The question whether to include the right to prevent investors from counties that maintain diplomatic relations with the host economy pits realpolitik instincts against regional integration ideals.

A denial-of-benefits clause needs to define the time when the clause can be employed. The clause should explicitly state that access to arbitration can be denied when a dispute had already arisen or was foreseeable, since several tribunals have held that denial of benefits cannot be effectively invoked against an investor after they have filed claim, which severely limits the use of the clause in countering "time-sensitive restructuring" (Feldman, 2012; Lee, 2015).

Most-favoured nation treatment

The most-favoured nation (MFN) clause is ubiquitous in investment treaties (Figure 6.5). It is designed to prevent nationality-based discrimination and to ensure a level playing field for investors from the IIA home country and comparable investors from a third country (UNCTAD, 2010b). But investors have proved more likely to use the MFN to "import" more favourable provisions from parallel investment treaties with third countries, a practice that has been allowed in many cases, than to use it in its original reading. A failure to address this use can challenge the balance of the treaty and the considerations underlying its other standards of treatment (UNCTAD, 2018b). Following the intentions of the PAIC, the draft investment protocol explicitly closes the avenue for using the MFN clause to import provisions from parallel treaties that may contain broader standards of treatment and access to arbitration.[7]

In addition, as with all standards of treatment, consideration ought to be given to policy flexibility. The treaty may contain exceptions for regulatory measures taken with the aim of promoting legitimate public welfare objectives followed by an indicative list of such objectives. Like national treatment, the MFN may also apply during the pre-establishment phase, but there is impact on policy space should be smaller and requires a choice of a comparator. The approach to MFN and national treatment (NT), in particular regarding the exceptions should be aligned to promote clarity.

National treatment

The national treatment principle protects investors against nationality-based discrimination and guarantees covered investors and their investments a level playing field with comparable domestic investors. De facto discrimination, as opposed to discrimination prescribed by the law, is also cov-

Frequency of provisions in international investment agreements

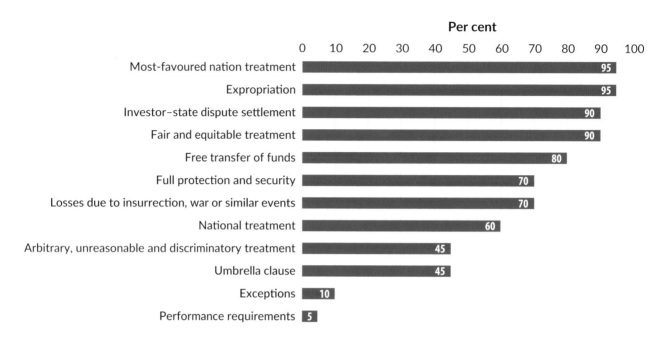

Source: Bonnitcha, Poulsen and Waibel (2017).

ered, and this type of violation is more likely to be claimed by investors.

The three-step application of national treatment is case-specific. It requires choosing a comparator, finding whether differentiated treatment has arisen and, if so, assessing whether the differentiation is justified (Dolzer and Schreuer, 2012). Assessments by tribunals of treaty-based claims of violations of the national treatment principle have not been consistent, particularly on choosing a comparator and assessing justification for differentiated treatment (Sornarajah, 2018). The treaty, to ensure greater certainty, should specify what aspects should be considered when seeking a comparator—which may include the aim of the measure, the particular economic sector, the regulatory processes that are generally applied and the effects of the investment on the community and environment.

Countries, particularly developing countries, may have an interest in limiting the scope of the national treatment clause to retain a higher level of sovereignty to pursue domestic development goals. For legitimate public welfare objectives to protect the regulatory space, exceptions to the general rule are advisable. The policy exceptions may include public health, taxation measures, safety and the environment, national developmental objectives and affirmative action for previously disadvantaged groups. Treaty negotiators may add further factors or consider whether they should be tempered by principles of good faith or lack of arbitrariness.

National treatment usually applies after an investment has been made, but a growing number of IIAs, especially free trade agreements with investment chapters, extend the application of national treatment to the pre-establishment phase. Pre-establishment national treatment, sometimes removed from the scope of ISDS, promotes economic liberalization at the cost of a lower degree of discretion in regulating entry matters domestically (UNCTAD, 2015a). Treaty negotiators would have to ponder the ultimately political decision of whether the standard should only apply to the post-establishment phase or also to the pre-establishment phase, considering the trade-off between sovereignty over policy space, and market liberalisation enabling deeper integration.

To further refine the scope of the national treatment provision, the States may exempt specific policy areas, measures or economic sectors or industries from the scope of the obligation (UNCTAD, 2015a). The exclusions may take the form of a positive or negative list that would apply to the post-establishment phase, the pre-establishment phase or both. However, application of exceptions to the post-establishment phase in particular need to be weighed against the loss in protective power. While the negative list approach arguably propels more forcefully the overall AfCFTA liberalization agenda, it is more demanding on the resources of countries to properly establish the list of exclusions (Cotula, 2014).

Fair and equitable treatment

Fair and equitable treatment (FET) lies at the centre of controversy over the international investment regime. Often seen as catch-all standards meant to

Figure 6.6:
Alleged claims and found breaches

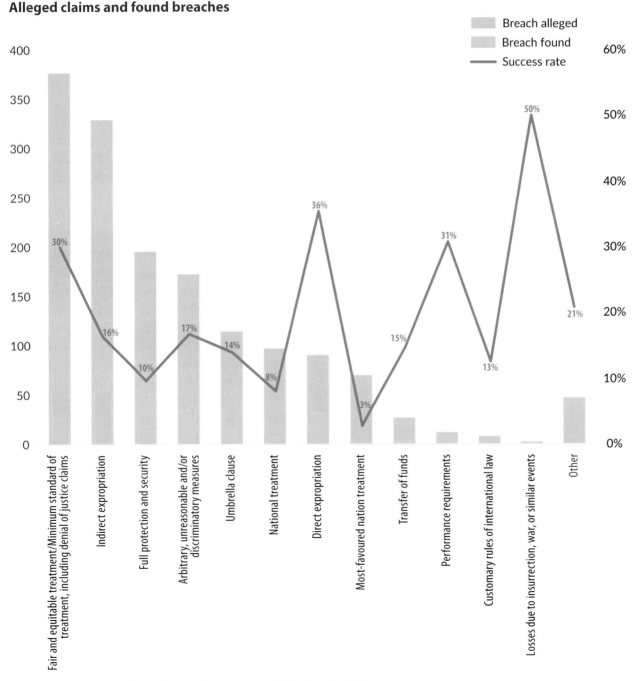

Source: UNCTAD (2019), figures based on ISDS cases concluded by December 2018.

attract foreign investors through a stable and predictable policy and regulatory environment in the host State (Dolzer, 2005), it has been interpreted in a highly inconsistent manner, potentially posing limits that are also difficult to evaluate ex-ante on a State's right to regulate, raising exposure to foreign investors' claims and the resulting financial liabilities (Sornarajah, 2018; UNCTAD, 2012b; Yannaca-Small, 2008). Virtually all recent claims brought by investors against States have included an allegation of a breach of fair and equitable treatment (Figure 6.6).

Given its prominence in investment claims, the fair and equitable treatment standard ought to be approached with utmost care in the investment protocol. Negotiators can consider several options, and the final choice of the dispute settlement mechanism may influence their respective pros and cons—for instance, the risk of excessive interpretation would be smaller in a court that commonly follows precedent (the principle of stare decisis) than in an ad-hoc tribunal.

An unqualified fair and equitable treatment standard is not recommended. It could seriously imperil the investment treaty reform efforts being undertaken on the continent. Some treaties anchor the standard on customary international law, but arbitration tribunals have expanded the scope of customary international law so that the difference between it and FET has become blurred (Barrera, 2017; Marshall, 2007; Mercurio, 2012). The PAIC, reflecting the controversies around the concept of fair and equitable treatment, remains silent on the issue. Such an approach would arguably maximize the latitude of State power within the limits set by the other provisions of the protocol, but the investors could see the protective power of the treaty as thin (UNCTAD, 2015a), heightening the dilemmas in relation to non-African investors (see section on extra-African treaties).

An alternative would be to replace traditional FET with a different standard of treatment that clearly delineates what State actions amount to violation. It might either set out a new standard or draw on some of the approaches that have already been pioneered on the continent, including the "fair administrative treatment" in the SADC model treaty. The standards of treatment that decision makers may want to guarantee to foreign investors could include, for instance, protection against denial of justice, due process in administrative proceedings and discrimination on wrongful grounds. Arbitrary decisions and measures by the State apparatus are hurtful to investors and their projects, and arbitrariness could lead to interpretive issues.

Full protection and security

The full protection and security (FPS) standard compels the host State to protect the investor against harm. Its often open-ended wording has created questions over the legal liability threshold for States and the nature of injury. Some tribunals have also suggested that FPS includes not only physical security for investors and their investments but also legal protection and even commercial security, thus creating an overlap with fair and equitable treatment (Junngam, 2017; Malik, 2011). The failure to prevent harm, rather than the issue of whether it has been caused by State actors or third parties, constitutes the breach of the standard (McLachlan, Shore and Weiniger, 2017). While interpreters have usually seen the standard as requiring due diligence as opposed to absolute liability, they have not shown consistency in accounting for the capacities of the host State (Junngam, 2017; Schreurer, 2010).

Due to anxiety over the impact of the FPS on policy space, the standard is missing in the SADC and COMESA treaties (Malik, 2011). The subsequent PAIC does not contain it, either. FPS features, in contrast, in the 2009 ASEAN treaty, 2018 EU–Vietnam treaty and recent bilateral treaties involving African countries, including the 2017 Kenya–Japan BIT and 2018 Morocco–Congo BIT.

A cautious approach to this provision is warranted. Negotiators may follow the path taken at the regional level by not including it in the treaty. To assure investors about physical security, they could alternatively subject the provision to certain limitations, such as State capacity to engage in its best efforts to prevent harm. Negotiators may also consider providing a further qualification by levelling treatment under the standard to that provided to domestic investors. In the light of the uncertainty around the scope of the standard and the general drive to promote clarity, it does not appear advisable to introduce an unqualified FPS clause.

Expropriation

International investment agreements regulate the conditions for lawful expropriation and typically protect investors against uncompensated expropriations, contributing to a stable and predictable legal framework. Expropriation provisions usually cover both direct forms of expropriation, notably nationalization, and indirect forms, which involve total or substantial deprivation of an investment or destruction of its value but without a formal transfer of title to the State or outright seizure, for example through changes in legislation or administrative malpractice.

Case law indicates a convergence around a relatively high threshold for State wrongdoing in the case of indirect expropriation (McLachlan, Shore and Weiniger, 2017). However, the relationship between regulatory and expropriatory measures in policy making may not always be clear (UNCTAD, 2012a; Radi, 2018), stoking concerns over a lack of predictability.

The investment protocol negotiators should carefully consider their approach to expropriation, including whether to cover indirect expropriation. If indirect expropriation is to be included, an expansive interpretation should be avoided by establishing criteria for it and defining what measures that do not constitute it (UNCTAD, 2015a), an approach taken, for instance, in the PAIC. While leaving out indirect expropriation might expand the State's policy latitude (for example, in the 2013 Serbia–Morocco BIT and the post-2015 Brazilian BITs – see box 6.6), it may also increase investors' perception of country risk and susceptibility to opportunistic regulatory behaviour. To prevent a tribunal reading that would encroach on the State's regulatory power, treaty drafters have provided more guidance as well as exceptions in more recent treaties than in earlier ones (Ewing-Chow, 2017).

The conditions for lawful expropriation, such as the public purpose of the measure, adequate and effective compensation (prompt, or without undue delay to allow for more temporary space) and observance of due processes, can be specified. Treaty interpreters can provide additional guidance by indicating that during the examination of expropriation, both the substantiality of the impact of the measure (for example, permanent or near complete deprivation of investment) and the character of the measure (including the public objective behind it) ought to be taken into account.

The standard of compensation for unlawful expropriation, when the standard is found to have been violated, also warrants attention. States may find it beneficial to provide further guidance to treaty interpreters on how to calculate compensation and clarify what factors should be taken into account, such as whether compensation should reflect the market value at the time the expropriation became known or was effectuated, or the duration and history of acquisition of the investment. Host States may also reserve the right to pay over a longer period of time (for instance, three years, as is the preference of the SADC model treaty) in case the payment would be burdensome on their finances.

Right to regulate

The right to regulate is a concept designed to safeguard policy space for promoting legitimate public policy objectives. It may encompass both legal and regulatory measures and relate not only to introducing them but also applying and enforcing them. Furthermore, it can also link investment law and other parts of international law, such as compliance with obligations arising out of other international treaties.

Contracting States can establish the right to regulate for sustainable development through limitations to standards of treatment (and general exceptions) or by integrating a specific clause into the agreement. These two approaches are not mutually exclusive (IISD and UN Environment, 2016) but should they be pursued simultaneously their wording needs to be precise so their combined interpretation would not raise questions over their scope or applicability. A specific provision may send a powerful signal to policy makers, the business community and other stakeholders about the commitment to investment treaty reform that supports sustainable development. However, the right to regulate will come at the price of treaty protection for investors, so its scope must be balanced and clear.

Investor obligations

The international investment regime historically imposed obligations only on host States, not on private investors (Paulsson, 1995). However, as underscored by the PAIC, IIAs may serve as vehicles for investor rights and also for their obligations, which could rebalance the regime. Investor obligations can be a source for claims against transgressing investors and for counterclaims by defending States. The right to initiate proceeding may be bestowed upon the home State, its nationals or both (Amado, Kern and Rodriguez, 2017).

Three cumulative conditions need to be met if an international investment treaty, such as the AfCFTA protocol, is to introduce investor rights effectively (Laborde, 2010). First, the treaty needs to formally confer such a right to the State or other actors. Second, investors must consent to arbitration since they, unlike the contracting States, are not party to the treaty. Investors' consent could be voluntary or could be made compulsory—for example, by predicating the issuance of an investment permit on the consent to comply with the AfCFTA treaty. Voluntary consent could be a tool to promote best practices on the continent. Compulsory consent could prove onerous to administer, which in turn would run counter to the investment facilitation goal but would cover all investors and investments.

African policy makers must choose substantive standards that foreign investors must comply with. The sources of these obligations can be national law, national or international corporate social responsibility standards, the treaty itself or any combination of these three. If they choose the national law as one of the sources of obligations, host States effectively give themselves the option to pursue investors through arbitration for breaches of domestic laws. But since domestic legislation can be unilaterally changed by governments, investors would be anxious to know what the possible sanctions for a failure to comply could entail. International corporate social responsibility standards, such as the UN Guiding Principles for Business and Human Rights and the OECD Guidelines for Multinational Enterprises, may be considered but should be examined carefully to ensure practicability, since they were devised as non-binding guidelines.

The treaty itself may spell out expected standards of conduct. Compared with national law, this source standardizes the nature and content of the investor obligations across countries. Careful and clear drafting is needed.

Effective investment facilitation can increase investors' confidence in the system of obligations. Clear information on rules and procedures and dynamic and reliable communication channels with the relevant public sector institutions to provide clarification can help investors avoid unintentional transgressions and so disputes with the host State.

Treaty negotiators should consider the possible consequences for the violations of these obligations.[8] They should also establish how international legal processes would interplay with parallel legal processes, including criminal proceedings, in the home or host economies.

As the PAIC demonstrates, a whole gamut of obligations can be envisaged. As with State obligations, the objective of sustainable development should guide the selections. Obligations can relate to economic, social and political elements, including business ethics, human rights, the rights of indigenous people, labour standards, environmental protection, corruption, taxation evasion and tax avoidance and interference in internal political affairs and intergovernmental relations.

State commitments

In addition to redrafted State obligations and added investor obligations, the new grand bargain could encompass specific commitments the States want to take upon themselves to best leverage investment for sustainable development (as, for example, in the 2016 Nigeria-Morocco BIT), while helping companies to meet the additional commit-

Highlights of sustainable development provisions in the draft ECOWAS investment code

The new draft ECOWAS investment code seeks to strengthen the investment regime in the region to promote investment for development. It provides policy space for host economies, introduces specific obligations for investors and also introduces commitments of ECOWAS member States to each other.

The code covers only investment with "considerable potential to contribute to economic development of the host economy". It provides exceptions from national treatment and most-favoured nation treatment to protect legitimate public interests such as health, safety and the environment and allows member States to grant preferential treatment to investment and investors during the first five years to achieve development objectives. Such measures may include positive discrimination in favour of regions affected by structural or historical imbalances and performance requirements to advance the objectives of building productive, human and physical capacities

All member States can establish their own level of environmental protection. They commit to not encourage investment by relaxing national health, safety or environmental standards and to uphold commitments to multilateral environmental agreements. Domestic laws and policies on the environment do not constitute protectionist measures. National environmental governance of member States is expected to be reinforced through flexible and voluntary mechanisms and market-based incentives.

Both member States and investors must comply with labour standards, employment policy and the highest level of labour and human rights protection. Investors must observe policies on equal opportunity and treatment in relation to wages, benefits and condition of work for both foreign and domestic staff and shall not discriminate on the basis of race, colour, gender or religion.

Under the draft code, investors must undertake pre-investment environmental and social impact assessment, applying the precautionary principle of resisting new activities with unknown impact and taking necessary actions to mitigate foreseen negative impacts. Such assessments are to be made public. Member State nationals and citizens can ask for investigation of alleged violations of environmental laws.

The use and transfer of environmentally sound technology and management practices, including recycling, waste discharge reduction and knowledge transfer, by affiliates of foreign companies in member States is required. Investors have to ensure that the transferred technology meets the policies and plans of the host State and contributes to the development of local and national innovative capacity.

Investors tapping traditional knowledge or folklore must protect this traditional knowledge under generally accepted international legal standards and best practices and adhere to minimum standards, including the local community's property rights in the innovations, practices, knowledge and technologies they have acquired through generations.

Finally, investors must respect all applicable tax laws and international standards relating to base erosion and profit shifting. They must also provide financial information required by member States.

ments placed upon them. Strategies underpinned by externalizing the costs of investment upon local communities by relaxing labour or environmental standards may produce immediate benefits but are obstructions to long-term benefits and anath-ema to the ideals of pan-Africanism. The investment protocol can promote two interconnected goals through State commitments. First, they can dissuade countries from sliding into a race to the bottom with one another to attract investment.

Second, they can create conditions enabling investors meet their own treaty obligations. Such State obligations would therefore be interrelated with investment facilitation.

African States may consider a number of specific commitments (Box 6.7). Some may be more relevant to the goal of avoiding a race to the bottom, such as obligations to adhere to minimum environment, labour and consumer protection standards and to refrain from relaxing such standards to attract investment. Others arguably lie at the intersection of the two goals, such as enforcing national laws and international obligations, notably in relation to human rights, labour rights, the environment, corruption and anti-bribery; measures to facilitate technology transfer; protection of indigenous populations; creation and maintenance of minimum financial reporting standards and work on a common strategy on fiscal incentives to promote and enhance strategic interests. Finally, some commitments, such as to national policies on developing human resources, are primarily for the benefit of the investors and local populations.

Creating State commitments entails deciding whom they should be owed to. Some can be primarily designed to help investors meet their own additional obligations and therefore create reciprocity between the host State and the investor. But expanding the scope of potential liability of the host State would be at loggerheads with the objective of protecting policy space. Many of these obligations fundamentally concern managing the relationship with other AfCFTA States, and a failure to live up to them may be expected to affect wide classes of companies. As a consequence, it may be appropriate to owe them to other AfCFTA State parties, mirroring trade dispute logic focusing on systemic issues rather than impacts on individual investors (see the section on trade in goods and services). States can also turn these commitments into unenforceable "soft" law, such as policy declarations or guidelines. They can opt for a middle way whereby a pan-African body, such as the AUC or the AfCFTA secretariat, could track and monitor progress. Finally, possibly depending on the choice of dispute settlement mechanism, States may com-

bine these various approaches, owing different commitments to different entities.

Transfer of funds

Unlike most other standards of treatment, the freedom to transfer funds in and out of the host country is primarily about liberalizing the capital account rather than protecting investment (Bonnitcha, Poulsen and Waibel, 2017). Capital movement across the African economies is a pre-requisite for regional economic integration. However, if unfettered, transfer of funds may pose an obstacle when countries are dealing with an emerging or actual macroeconomic or financial crisis, including capital flight (Waibel, 2009), balance-of-payment difficulties, enforcement of adjudicatory proceedings and upholding creditor rights.

Negotiators should therefore specify the conditions under which policy makers and regulators may obstruct the right to transfer funds. The exceptions should be underpinned by clear principles, such as good faith, equity and non-discrimination, to prevent abuse (UNCTAD, 2015a) and promote investors' confidence that the right to move funds across economies is fundamentally protected. State parties should be obliged to inform their peers about adopting safeguard measures derogating from the right to regulate and, as soon as possible, the schedule for removal.

In addition, treaty negotiators may consider subjecting the right to move funds out of the host country to domestic financial and tax laws. Instances may include cases of bankruptcy and insolvency, prevention of fraud and money laundering and measures necessary to ensure compliance with adjudicatory proceedings.

Dispute settlement

Effective enforcement is essential for credible investment protection. Negotiators for the investment protocol need to weigh carefully the respective merits and demerits of models of investment dispute settlement. General inspiration can be drawn from UNCTAD's five paths for ISDS reform: promoting alternative dispute resolution methods (very much in line with the investment promotion and facilitation agenda—see above), tailoring the existing system through international investment agreements, narrowing the access of investors to ISDS, establishing an appellate mechanism, and creating a standing international investment court (UNCTAD, 2015b).

The amicable resolution of conflicts and prevention of escalation into disputes should be emphasized to prevent a breakdown in the relations between the host State and the investor. Should these amicable methods fail to resolve a conflict, a credible and effective dispute settlement mechanism should be established to enforce the terms of the investment protocol.

Various approaches to managing and resolving disputes can be explored (see UNCTAD, 2010a). African countries can establish ombudspersons, which can be embodied in an IPA or a similar agency or can be hosted in others parts of the government. These agencies would be empowered to hear and register complaints of investors and to work in partnership with the relevant government agencies on clarifying and resolving the situation. Alternatives to adjudication also include fact-finding (submission of facts to a neutral committee), mediation (third-party assistance in facilitating and structuring communication between the parties) and conciliation (advisory activities by a conciliator or panel of conciliators, usually producing non-binding recommendations) (Smith and Martinez, 2009; UNCTAD, 2010a).

Four major options for the dispute settlement mechanism are a revamped ISDS, SSDS, a new permanent body and relegation to national courts. Several policy objectives and factors need to be considered by decision makers, including legitimacy, neutrality, effectiveness, cost and alignment with overall AfCFTA objectives and institutional architecture.

The ISDS is favoured by investors for giving them direct standing in an arena outside national courts. Conversely, it could be used by States for direct challenges against investors for transgressions of the investment protocol. Special provisions would have to be inserted to counter systemic flaws in the

system and ensure its acceptance and legitimacy. For instance, State parties might consider establishing a roster or pool from which arbitrators could be drawn, coming mostly or fully from the State parties. This would arguably further "Africanize" the system and bring it closer to the traditional judiciary system. Existing African dispute settlement venues could also be used to further build their capacity. At the same time, the protocol or its annex would have to contain rules on the conduct of arbitrators to foster trust among stakeholders.

Additional procedural rules would be needed to cover the dismissal of frivolous claims, third party funding (either an outright ban, regulation or an obligation to declare financial support), consolidation of claims, transparency, participation of non-disputing parties and security of costs. Small and medium-sized enterprises might additionally benefit from a streamlined ISDS featuring only one arbitrator. The institutional framework could also allow for the emergence of the use of precedence (stare decisis). The establishment of an appellate body could enhance clarity by allowing for the correction of misapplied law, though the loss of speed and finality could discourage investors (Nilsson and Englesson, 2013), so strategies would have to be deployed to minimize these risks.

The first alternative to ISDS would be SSDS as in WTO disputes, States would espouse claims on behalf of investors. The key advantage of the SSDS system would be States' likely reluctance to initiate claims against legitimate measures because some of their investors have been adversely affected (Bernasconi-Osterwalder, 2014), not least because such claims would wound diplomatic relations between the countries and heighten the prospect of facing similar counter-challenges in the future. But from the investors' perspectives, re-politicization of investment disputes (Schwebel, 2014) could turn home State discretion over taking up an investor's claim into reduced investor protection, since the decision whether to proceed would be informed by factors alien to the investors' circumstances. Smaller and medium-sized companies could be particularly disadvantaged, lacking the clout necessary to convince their home States to take up their claims or finding that their claims are not seen as worth a dispute with another country. Obstructed access to justice could engender discontent and fuel a trend towards restructuring investment via third countries offering higher levels of protection. Unless investor obligations were made enforceable through domestic courts, an additional mechanism to enforce them would also have to be established, since host States could lose the ability to launch claims directly against transgressing investors.

The SSDS would be the default option given AfCFTA institutional structure, because the Protocol on the Rules and Procedures of Disputes envisages a yet-to-be-established dispute settlement body (DSB), under whose supervision panels and an Appellate Body will adjudicate disputes under the various legal instruments of the AfCFTA, including the investment protocol.

The third, most ambitious and farthest-reaching option for settling disputes would be establishing a new mechanism, possibly backed by an appellate body. Creating a standing investment court would mark a radical departure from contemporary practice. It would serve as an alternative forum to venues based in the global West (Van Harten, 2016) and could go a long way towards addressing the issues of consistency, transparency and security of tenure and the related concerns over incentives (Nyombi, 2018). The predictability and legitimacy of the system could raise the commitment of key stakeholders. Rules governing the selection of judges, transparency and the participation of affected stakeholders would ensure impartiality.

The idea of a permanent court is not entirely new and is not as fanciful as it might have appeared a few years ago. The EU, in response to a public outcry over the ISDS, has started pushing for a two-tier, permanent institution. The most recent trade treaties with investment chapters concluded by the EU with Canada, Mexico, Singapore and Vietnam encompass the establishment of a permanent investment court with an appellate mechanism. Emboldened by this experience, the EU has also been promoting the idea of a global multilateral investment court.

The cost-effectiveness and distribution of costs for establishing and maintaining a permanent institution, compared with ISDS, would have to be analyzed. Considerable political commitment and alignment with the existing AfCFTA institutional structures would be necessary.

Another possibility is relegating the power to interpret and apply the investment protocol to the State parties' domestic courts. This option hinges on the capacity and reputation of the national judiciary systems, including their ability to interpret and apply international law. Investors would probably not receive this option well. The issue of consistency and use of precedents would arise. And a support or coordination mechanism would be needed lest the emerging African investment regime be fragmented impeding the journey towards a single market aspired to in the AfCFTA.

Relationship with other phase I and II areas

Trade in goods and services

Although the trade and investment policy regimes share a common history, they have grown apart and form two separate legal paradigms with different goals, rules and institutional structures (Dolzer and Schreurer, 2012). While the trade policy regime emphasizes liberalization, the investment policy regime focuses on investment protection (Broude, 2011). Their objectives are complementary, however (DiMascio and Pauwelyn, 2008), and related through governance and economic integration (Alford, 2013; Puig, 2016), with the goals of promoting economic efficiency (Broude, 2011; Puig, 2016) and seem to be converging (Alford, 2013; Lubambo, 2016; Puig, 2016).

Investment and competition policy have gained prominence as traditional trade barriers have been reduced (Puig, 2016). Following NAFTA, trade agreements with an investment chapter and even broader treaties on economic cooperation at the plurilateral level have proliferated (Dolzer and Schreurer, 2012; Bonnitcha, Poulsen and Waibel, 2017). FTAs with investment chapters tap the synergies between trade and investment exploited by modern, vertically integrated multinationals whose production may span many jurisdictions as they drive down trade costs along supply chains and seek security against political risks (Orefice and Rocha, 2011; Alford, 2013; Puig, 2016).

Companies and their projects that meet the definitions under both the investment protocol and the trade in services protocol will enjoy the coverage of both treaties. State obligations and the dispute settlement provisions contained in both treaties will be at the disposal of the investors. "[In the context of the trade and investment regimes the] exact same measure can fall within the jurisdictional reach of both systems, invoke a common legal norm and even be adjudicated simultaneously" (Kurtz, 2016: 13). For example, a ban on imports of goods and services may violate a quantitative restriction under the protocols on trade in goods and trade in services while also amounting to a violation of fair and equitable treatment or to an expropriation (see Alford, 2013 for WTO context).[9]

Disputes under the AfCFTA trade protocols are to be addressed through a State-to-State settlement mechanism, as happens under other free trade agreements and at the WTO level. The mechanism for enforcing the investment protocol is not yet clear—investment disputes may be dealt with in the dispute settlement body or in a stand-alone venue. If the stand-alone option is favoured, and in particular if investors have a direct standing in the body, the relationship between it and the two bodies and their legal regimes will need to be defined.

Under the trade regime, a remedy usually takes the form of compelling the State to resume compliance with its treaty obligations, but in ISDS it usually takes the form of monetary compensation (see Bagwell and Staiger, 2004; Bonnitcha, Poulsen and Waibel, 2017). Investors with a long-term commitment to a country may be interested in the WTO-like option, "ensur[ing] a competitive environment in the host state" (Ewing-Chow, 2007, 555), for instance when obligations, such as national treatment and most-favoured nation treatment, are in play, or when they concern industries with elevated entry costs, such as telecommunications (Molinuevo, 2006). Yet the direct standing, alleged

speed, flexibility and retrospective measures of ISDS can make it more appealing (Alford, 2013; Li, 2018). Investors who have seen their property annihilated through expropriation are likely to be more interested in compensation than in ex-post policy correction (Molinuevo, 2006).

The trade and investment regimes may therefore complement each other. Investors may find it attractive to seek remedies in both forums, if possible (see Allen and Soave, 2014; Ewing-Chow, 2007; Molinuevo, 2006). The global WTO and ISDS experience suggests that "investors (or their counsels) have realized that they can convert trade matters into investment disputes, with the potential of winning hefty damage awards, often appointing arbitrators with trade-law backgrounds" (Puig, 2016, 14). The number of parallel or consecutive WTO–ISDS proceedings has been rising, often in relation to TRIPS (see, for example, Box 6.4). The formulation, objectives and nature of provisions in the trade and investment regimes differ, which may lead to inconsistent interpretation (Allen and Soave, 2014) or even conflicts between bodies (Puig, 2016). The upshot is a loss of efficiency (resources are expended in multiple proceedings), undermined finality (Allen and Soave, 2014; Li, 2018; Shany, 2004) and lack of coherence and equality (since the same issue may be re-litigated). Such results jeopardize the sustainability of international adjudication and may contribute to "regulatory chill" (Puig, 2016).

Treaty negotiators will need to make important choices regarding the substantive and procedural rules that would apply to claims based on the same facts but governed simultaneously by the trade and investment rules. They may consider several different approaches to the relationship between the AfCFTA investment and trade treaties, which seem to involve a trade-off between consistency and scope of investment protection (Allen and Soave, 2014). The options include carve-outs for trade treaties, override rules in case of inconsistency and limits to the application of certain standards of treatment.

A trade and investment case related to the same set of facts or a dispute deemed by one party as related to both trade and investment rules could perhaps be entertained by one forum. The investment dispute settlement could consider both trade and investment law, with the dispute settlement body or a joint mechanism set up for these instances empowered to play such a role. This option could resolve the cost and consistency of the process and the finality of the decision but could pose appreciable practical challenges for treaty interpreters owing to the normative differences between the two regimes.

If treaty negotiators prefer both trade and investment claims to proceed through separate dispute settlements, they may consider introducing rules on information sharing between the two bodies to establish a common factual basis, prescribing ex-ante rules on the manner in which the proceedings should be sequenced or setting up a consultative body that could also decide the sequencing of the dispute (the DSB could play this role) (Allen and Soave, 2014).

Intellectual property rights

Investment treaty protection, unless subject to specific carve-outs, encompasses all policy areas influencing foreign investments in the contracting States. Intellectual property rights (IPR) come under the investment protection umbrella either through the definition of covered investments, which may explicitly mention various types of intellectual property rights, or through implicit coverage in open-ended definitions (Correa, 2004; UNCTAD, 2007).

At least some IPR holders push for including intellectual property (IP) in investment treaties to enhance the protection provided through national frameworks (Frankel, 2016). The investment protection and IP protection regimes are different, however. While investment protection was traditionally rooted in individual property rights protection, the IP regime seeks to balance wide societal values and public policy objectives, such as innovation, access to information, technology transfer and public health, reflecting them in flexibilities and exceptions. Bringing IP protection under investment protection represents a potentially momentous

shift from the IP regime, the mutual compromise between industrialized and developing countries reached under the TRIPS and other IP-related treaties (Correa, 2004; Dreyfuss and Frankel, 2015; Frankel, 2016; Gathii and Ho, 2017; Gervais, 2019; Ho, 2015; Okediji, 2014; Ruse-Khan, 2016; Upreti, 2016; Yu, 2017).

Some standards of treatment in the investment regime (such as national treatment and most-favoured nation treatment) are broader than those usually found in intellectual property treaties, and others (expropriation) are unknown there. The impact of some (for example, fair and equitable treatment) on IPR could be compounded by inconsistent interpretation (Jozwik, 2011). The domestic arena appears the most appropriate for setting IP laws in accordance with the local and evolving socio-economic context and within the agreed limits set by the TRIPS, AfCFTA investment protocol and related treaties.

The investment regime standards of treatment can endanger negotiated intellectual property flexibility, and investment treaties can be invoked to challenge policy and administrative measures and judicial rulings. The prospect of an expropriation claim, lying at the heart of then tension between public and private interests, may arise when investors deem their legitimate expectations quashed by the issuance of compulsory licenses (Gibson, 2010; Ho, 2015; Rutledge, 2012), patent invalidations (Upreti, 2016) or parallel imports (Correa, 2004).

Investors may prefer using ISDS, where they have direct standing, over the State-to-State trade regime mechanism designed for IP issues. Though IP-related ISDS cases can be traced back to at least the mid-1990s, they were brought into the spotlight in the 2010s by much-commented-on cases involving Philip Morris's challenges to plain packaging in Uruguay and Australia (see Box 6.4) and Eli Lilly's claims of expropriation against Canada (Box 6.8). All States prevailed—Australia on procedure, Uruguay and Canada on merits. Although the three investment panels took wider societal concerns into consideration, their different approaches rendered the "outcomes [of future IP-related ISDS cases] difficult, if not impossible, to predict"

(Gervais, 2019: 28). Canada ultimately changed the disputed policy. Colombia and Ukraine also shifted their policy to favour of patent holders at the expense of companies producing generic medications following a notice of arbitration (Colmbia) and a threat thereof (Ukraine), stoking fears of "regulatory chill" (Baker, 2017; Baker and Geddes, 2017; Gathii and Ho, 2017).

AfCFTA negotiators will need to ponder how best to reconcile the public and private interests across the different policy regimes. They will have to review the regimes' substantive provisions and dispute settlement mechanisms when they consider the policy linkages between the investment and intellectual property rights treaties. In one approach at the treaty level to undesirable contradictions between the two legal regimes, intellectual property could be left completely outside the scope of investment protection by removing it from covered definitions (Baker and Geddes, 2017). This would be viable if negotiators are confident that protection is fully treated under the intellectual property regime and investors do not need an additional avenue to defend IPR.

The linkage between the investment and intellectual property rights treaties could also be tweaked by reformulating the definitions or standards of treatment. For instance, only intellectual property rights recognized under the domestic regime in line with the IP protocol could be kept and protected against expropriation or other damage due to State action (or lack thereof), without recurring to intellectual property treaties. The expropriation provision in many recent treaties provides an exception for the "issuance of compulsory licenses" or to "the revocation, limitation or creation of intellectual property rights" to the extent that these actions are "consistent" with international investment agreements, such as TRIPS. However, this type of exception should be approached with caution, since it can paradoxically double as a gateway for the TRIPS law to be incorporated into investment law (Diependaele, Cockbain and Sterckx, 2017; Gibson, 2010) and could even constitute the most feasible way for investors to appeal IP law in investment arbitration (Ruse-Khan, 2016).

Box 6.8:

Eli Lilly v. Canada

Eli Lilly, a US pharmaceutical manufacturer, initiated in September 2013 arbitration proceedings against Canada under the UNCITRAL rules on the basis of NAFTA (Case No. UNCT/14/2). The company claimed that previous invalidation of two of its patents, Zyprexa for schizophrenia and Strattera for hyperactivity, by the Canadian courts amounted to indirect expropriation of its intellectual property, fell short of providing fair and equitable treatment and were arbitrary and discriminatory.

The patents were granted conditionally in the 1990s subject to prospective court review. Canadian courts decided to revoke them for failing the utility criterion—specifically, for failing to present support for all the claims of utility when filing for the patent. The company argued that it was only obliged to comply with a much lower standard requiring a "mere scintilla of utility" at the time of filing and that the threshold had since been raised. The change in rules was deemed to violate Eli Lilly's legitimate expectations, and its application was seen as "radically new, arbitrary, discriminatory" and unique to Canada. The retroactive application of the more radical test resulting in the invalidation of the patent was alleged to amount to expropriation.

Eli Lilly's claim was also in part based on an argument of legitimate expectations derived from TRIPS. NAFTA contains the TRIPS consistency exception, which is why the company sought to establish that the conduct of Canadian courts was out of step with it (Ruse-Khan, 2016). However, NAFTA and TRIPS only provide minimum standards and allow States to interpret patentability standards as they deem appropriate (Diependaele, Cockbain and Sterckx, 2017; Land, 2012; Okediji, 2014). Under NAFTA, IP issues are covered by SSDS not ISDS.

In 2017, the tribunal dismissed the case, finding that the utility doctrine had always been present in the Canadian law. It also reasoned that an "incremental and evolutionary" change had taken place, rather than a dramatic departure that could interfere with legitimate expectations, and that the company should have anticipated a shift towards the utility standards.

Reviewing the conduct of the courts, the panel admitted that judicial action (or inaction) could give rise to expropriation but explicitly accorded deference to the State and found that the conduct did not rise to being "egregious or shocking." The panel also dismissed the argument that the policy was arbitrary, given a rational link between the policy objectives and the law, and it found no evidence based on discrimination against the pharmaceutical sector or related to nationality. Eli Lilly was then requested to cover the full cost of the arbitration proceedings as well as three quarters of Canada's expenses related to arbitration and legal fees.

The ruling sent ripples through the expert community. Gervais (2019) noted that the tribunal had set the bar for review by the judiciary of the law that applies to the patent very high by applying the egregiousness test derived from international customary law and placing the evidence burden on the claimant. It also refused to assess the courts' interpretation of Canada's patent laws (Lipkus, 2017).

Other commentators, dismayed, saw the ruling "as extremely dangerous for public interest" (Howse, 2017). They noted that the tribunal left open the possibility that an investment tribunal can assess, and ultimately find in breach of a treaty, an invalidation of IP even if declared by courts in accordance with domestic law (Baker, 2017; Howse, 2017). The implication that judicial interpretation should not be marked by "dramatic, radical or fundamental changes," although no specific commitment was made, suggested that it could lead to a violation of fair and equitable treatment (Yackee and Ghosh, 2018) or even expropriation (Howse, 2017) and raised the prospect of regulatory inertia being the expectation of investors (Baker and Geddes, 2017).

Many experts also suggested that the tribunals should not use the egregiousness test on court decisions and should limit themselves to assessing denial of justice lest these tribunals become "supra-national Supreme Court[s]" (Ho, 2017; Liddell and Waibel, 2016, 36; Ruse-Khan, 2016). The fact that the tribunal had not outright dismissed as irrelevant the argument about "uniqueness" of Canadian law, allowed under TRIPS, was also met with criticism (Ho, 2017; Baker and Geddes, 2017, 502). Yackee and Ghosh, 2018 suggested that there was a risk that subsequent tribunals would give this argument even more currency. The question whether a frustration of legitimate expectations could have resulted in a treaty breach was left unanswered (Baker and Geddes, 2017). The tribunal also did not engage with the argument that IP issues covered by chapter 17 of NAFTA are meant to be dealt with through State-to-State dispute settlement (Flynn, 2015; Baker, 2017; Yackee and Ghosh, 2018) or the notion that validity of a patent is a pre-requisite to the patent qualifying as an asset (Diependaele, Cockbain and Sterckx, 2017) and by extension to expropriation claims (Upreti, 2016).

The company sought $500 million in compensation although some commentators were convinced the ultimate goal was to force a change in law (Okediji, 2014). Following the Eli Lilly case, the Canadian Supreme Court walked back on the utility doctrine and endorsed the lenient "mere scintilla" criterion, compounding fears of "regulatory chill" stemming from a confluence of ISDS, pressure from trade partners and private interests (Baker and Geddes, 2017).

Competition policy

International investment agreements may interact with competition policy and influence the substance and enforcement of competition law. Unless specified otherwise, the standards of treatment contained in the agreements also apply to competition policy.

Arbitral practice indicates that regulators' actions or inactions can be the subject of claims for breaches of investor protections (see Chapter 5 for discussion of competition policy). Heavily regulated sectors, such as energy or network services, could be particularly prone to such challenges. Investors who disagree with corrective remedies for anti-competitive behaviour imposed by a competition watchdog may seek redress not only in national courts but also through arbitration. A failure to stamp out anti-competitive practices by a local company, including a State-owned competitor, could also trigger treaty claims. Rather than assessing the State's authority in the competition area, investment tribunals seem likely to scrutinize whether political interference might have influenced the decision (Dolea, 2018).

While the fair and equitable standard and, possibly expropriation, can be expected to feature under the a dispute over corrective remedies, breaches of fair and equitable treatment or national treatment could probably be claimed in case of a failure of the State apparatus to act.[10] Investment, competition policy and intellectual property regimes can all interact in claims in a scenario whereby a competitor exploits a firm's trademarks or patents without authorization and the public watchdog fails to prevent this conduct.

Substantive provisions addressing competition law are uncommon in BITs, where they touch on a relatively discrete set of issues related to protecting the regulatory and investigatory policy space governing competition. Some BITs include an exemption imposed by a competition authority, court or tribunal from the prohibitions of performance standards requiring transfer of technology or knowledge for measures , carve-outs for information protected by competition law[11] and privileged or protected information withheld by a competition authority

from disclosure in the course of investor–State dispute settlement proceedings to correct anti-competitive conduct (for example, the 2018 Canada–Moldova BIT, not ratified). Some BITs also compel the contracting parties to "endeavour to maintain conditions of free competition for investments of investors of the other contracting state" (the 2001 Denmark–Kuwait BIT).

Regional and bilateral free trade agreements are also increasingly likely to include stand-alone chapters on competition law that require the parties to maintain and enforce competition laws, in accordance with certain principles (for example, CETA, UMSCA, the Comprehensive and Progressive Agreement for Trans-Pacific Partnership and the 2015 Japan–Mongolia and 2015 China–Korea free trade agreements). The competition chapters usually ensure that covered investors will have a fair and well-regulated market, without being subject to discriminatory and opaque actions by the competition regulator. On top of the wider competition-related provisions, some FTAs also contain provisions on competition in respect of specific sectors such as telecommunications (the 2008 Australia–Chile and the 2015 Japan–Mongolia free trade agreements) and competition with state-owned enterprises (CETA and USMCA).

The relationship between the AfCFTA investment and competition protocols needs to be considered. The PAIC already envisages a link to competition rules and provides for member States to "promote, maintain and encourage competition," prohibit "anti-competitive investment conduct" and "adopt clear and transparent competition rules." The most appropriate approach to the link with the Protocol on Competition Policy of the AfCFTA will be influenced by the protocol's final design. It may establish new rules backed by a dedicated enforcement mechanism only at the continental, or cross-border, level, leaving domestic competition issues within the purview of domestic authorities. While a wholesale exclusion of competition issues could damage investors' confidence that their investments are protected from anti-competitive threats, negotiators should consider the appropriate relationship between dispute settlement mechanisms for the two protocols. Will investors be allowed to use the investment dispute settlement mecha-nism as a check on the decisions of the continen-tal (or regional and national) competition author-ity—which would enhance investors' protection but could elevate the investment dispute body to being practically a de-facto appellate mechanism?

Negotiation and implementation

Negotiation and implementation of the investment protocol

Institutional framework for negotiation and implementation

The negotiation of the investment protocol is likely to follow the approach established during the phase I negotiations. A technical working group (TWG) on investment, comprising national experts, will generate a draft protocol, using national, regional and international best practices. The issues of the investment protocol—including investment promotion, facilitation and protection—are closely aligned, and so a single investment TWG, rather than several focusing on sub-areas, would be appropriate. The overlaps between investment and other policy areas call for close collaboration and coordination with the TWGs for other protocols.

TWG representatives and national negotiators should conduct national consultations with other key stakeholders, such as the private sector and civil society, to help inform the content of the protocol. Because investment issues overlap with those of trade in goods, services, competition and intellectual property rights, countries should establish coordination among policy specialists and negotiators across TWGs.

The two phase I protocols (trade in goods and trade in services) envisaged committees of national experts from each State party to oversee and moni-tor their implementation. Similarly, a committee on investment should be created as part of the institu-tional framework overseeing the implementation of the protocol on investment.

Support for negotiations, stakeholder engagement and consensus building

The ongoing bilateral, regional and continental policy initiatives, including those for the invest-ment protocol of the AfCFTA, highlight the deter-mination of African countries to reform the inter-national investment policy framework in Africa to be better balanced and more oriented towards sus-tainable development. However, disparate reform efforts risk overlap, potentially diluting efforts and creating a more complex regime instead of a har-monized and consolidated one (UNCTAD, 2015b). Synchronizing reform efforts at the different levels of policy making is crucial. Although the interna-tional and national dimensions of investment pol-icy may diverge, they must interact to maximize synergies, including those contributing to sustain-able development (UNCTAD, 2018c).

Internationally, consistency is needed between continental initiatives—including the AfCFTA—and regional projects—such as regional invest-ment protocols—to avoid policy overlaps, gaps and fragmentation. If investment policy is made in silos and instruments are formulated in a vac-uum, coordination may be inadequate between the authorities in charge of IIAs and those in charge of domestic investment rules. The African Union, regional economic communities and individual countries should set up a platform for informa-tion exchange and consensus building around key questions. RECs must ensure that all their member States are properly engaged. RECs can also act as conduits during the upcoming AfCFTA negotia-tions and facilitate formulation at the regional level of common approaches to continental negotia-tions (Nikièma, 2018).

Nationally, cooperation between the authorities in charge of the various dimensions of a country's investment policy framework is crucial for ensur-ing a coherent approach that reflects the country's overall strategy on investment for development. However, interaction is often insufficient between ministries in charge of investment and those in charge of related policies, especially in small, devel-oping countries that lack human resources and institutional or administrative capacities. African countries can consider establishing special agencies or inter-ministerial task forces with a specific mandate to coordinate the investment policy–related work of different ministries and other government units (including the negotiation of IIAs) (see Box 6.9).

Stakeholder consultations for informing the upcoming negotiations should take place. All voices should be given an opportunity to express their concerns and expectations about the AfCFTA negotiations. Among key are the national and international business community, trade unions, academia and non-governmental organizations. Stakeholders may be engaged at different levels, including by the African Union, RECs and individual countries. Publicly sharing with stakeholders the results of consultations with other participants in the negotiations will identify opinion trends and foster trust and transparency among the key actors.

Capacity building

Some African countries may benefit from technical assistance and building the capacity of decision makers and negotiators in investment policy, even as skill and capacity on the continent have increased rapidly in recent years. The investment protocol needs to be balanced and comprehensive and to reflect national developmental objectives. Investment promotion and facilitation need to be well designed and effective. The African Union, RECs and international organizations, including ECA and UNCTAD, can play important roles in developing national capacities. Both ECA and UNCTAD offer a range of tools and services to foster the ability of beneficiary country policy makers and other IIA stakeholders to negotiate sustainable development–friendly IIAs. Tailor-made and demand-driven technical assistance activities are provided upon the request of countries or regional organizations. They include national or regional training sessions for IIA negotiators and expert advisory services on key issues in IIAs. UNCTAD also assists African countries in reviewing their existing stock of IIAs and in drafting modern and sustainable development–oriented model BITs.[12]

For investment promotion and facilitation as well, resources and capacity need to be considered. International and regional organizations can build the capacities of public administration to tackle underfunding. UNCTAD has a number of tools and

Box 6.9:

Burkina Faso's inter-ministerial working group on international investment agreements

Burkina Faso established an inter-ministerial working group on IIAs during an UNCTAD technical assistance project focused on BITs reform. The inter-ministerial working group was composed of representatives of the ministries dealing directly with investment policies, namely:

- The Ministry of Trade and Industry.
- The Ministry of Economy, Finance and Development.
- The Ministry of Foreign Affairs and Cooperation.
- The Investment Promotion Agency of Burkina Faso.

The working group meets regularly to discuss progress on the recommendations UNCTAD made in its 2017 report on Burkina Faso's IIAs. The recommendations include modernizing Burkina Faso's BIT network, which comprises 17 treaties, and developing a new sustainable development–oriented model BIT.

Since then and in cooperation with UNCTAD, the working group has developed a roadmap for a gradual and comprehensive reform of IIAs concluded by Burkina Faso. The roadmap is being followed to amend existing outdated treaties and to finalize the new model BIT.

The working group has helped Burkina Faso coordinate better among the various ministries on issues related to IIAs and develop a coherent international investment reform strategy.

platforms that are available to all African countries, including the iGuides (implemented in Africa in collaboration with ECA), e-regulations, e-simplifications and e-registrations provided free of charge to the recipient countries.

Rationalizing existing treaties

Intra-African treaties

The African legal investment environment is fragmented across disparate and divergent bilateral treaties, sometimes overlapping with regional agreements and regional treaties. The investment protocol, reflecting a continental consensus, provides an unparalleled opportunity to gather the applicable rules under one treaty. The most straightforward way of rationalizing the legal environment is allowing the investment protocol to replace the continent's current investment treaties and, going forward, for African countries to refrain from concluding new treaties among themselves

(see Box 6.10 for a comparison of the experience of ASEAN, ECOWAS, and the EU).

The investment protocol should contain a mechanism that, once the treaty is ratified, would terminate all the treaties with which it would overlap and explicitly refer to any possible "sunset" or "survival" clauses on the basis of which investments realized during the applicable period benefit from treaty protection following a unilateral withdrawal (for example, 10 years in the 1996 Algeria–Mali BIT, 15 in the 2004 Mauritius–Madagascar BIT and 20 in the 1998 South Africa–Senegal BIT). This approach would be less taxing on African countries than their independently terminating the whole network of affected treaties through unilateral acts or by mutual consent.

If countries deem it necessary to maintain (at least some) of the already agreed treaties, for instance regional ones, they may consider elevating the investment protocol above them by introducing

---

Box 6.10:
EU, ASEAN and ECOWAS approaches

The status of existing and future BITs between member States of a regional organization (intra-regional BITs) and between members of a regional organization and other States (extra-regional BITs) poses a key challenge to regional integration in protecting cross-border investments. AU member States may learn from the approaches of three other regional organizations in the coming negotiation of the AfCFTA investment protocol: the European Union (EU), Association of Southeast Asian Nations (ASEAN) and the Economic Community of West African States (ECOWAS). The legal systems governing cross-border investments in each region differ.

Cross-border investments whithin the EU are subject to EU law, and there is no regional investment protection and promotion treaty or investor–State dispute settlement (ISDS) system. The EU Commission has had exclusive competence to negotiate investment treaties between the EU and third States on behalf of its member States since 2009, while the ASEAN secretariat and the ECOWAS Commission do not have such a power. The ASEAN and ECOWAS treaties co-exist with bilateral investment treaties among their members.

The EU prohibits the negotiation of new intra-regional BITs and requires the termination of pre-existing ones (mainly between older member States and newer ones that previously belonged to the Eastern bloc). In the aftermath of a March 2018 landmark ruling of the Court of Justice of the European Union that intra-EU BITs were not compatible with EU law, EU countries pledged to terminate their BITs—as the European Commission had long entreated. ASEAN and ECOWAS do not impose any rules on intra-regional BITs. Managing existing intra-regional BITs appears difficult in all three zones, as none opted for automatic termination following harmonization.

All three regions allow the maintenance of extra-regional instruments. Only the EU has set conditions for aligning extra-regional BITs and EU law. In all three organizations, member States can continue to negotiate new extra-regional BITs, but the European Commission imposes strict conditions on the choice of partners, the negotiation process and the content of the BIT and ultimately has to green-light the treaty. As a result, EU management of extra-regional BITs appears to be more organized than that of ASEAN or ECOWAS.

So, in evaluating approaches to intra- and extra-regional BITs, a region's level of integration, the legal system applicable to cross-border investments and the competences granted to regional institutions are important parameters.

ISSUE	EUROPEAN UNION	ASEAN	ECOWAS
REGIONAL LEGAL AND POLICY FRAMEWORK ON BITS			
Legal framework governing cross-border regional investments	**European Union law** (Different from investment protection treaties): EU internal market—free movement of goods and capital, freedom of establishment and freedom to provide services Charter of Fundamental Rights of the EU (for all citizens) Enforcement primarily through national courts Support to national courts through European Structural and Investment Fund System of preliminary rulings of the Court of Justice of the EU (CJEU)	**ASEAN Comprehensive Investment Agreement (CIA) (2009)**	**Supplementary Act A/SA.3/12/08 adopting community rules on investments and the modalities for their implementation with ECOWAS (2009) ECOWAS Energy Protocol A/P4/1/03 (2003)**
Regional organization has exclusive regional competence in BIT negotiations	**Yes, for extra-EU international investment agreements (IIAs)** European Commission has exclusive competence in IIA negotiations under Treaty on the Functioning of the European Union (TFEU), art. 3, para. 1, and art. 207 (2009)	**No** Note: Five Extra-ASEAN IIAs concluded by ASEAN after ASEAN CIA	**No**
Instrument on transitional arrangements	**Yes, for extra-EU BITs** Reg. 1219/2012 of the European Parliament and the Council of 12 December 2012 establishing transitional arrangements for bilateral investment agreements between member States and third countries	**No**	**No**
INTRA-REGIONAL BITS STATUS			
Automatic termination of intra-regional BITs	**No**	**No**	**No**
Possibility of maintaining existing intra-regional BITs·	**No** Requirement to terminate (unilaterally or bilaterally), because intra-EU BITs (including ISDS) are incompatible with EU law (see the 2018 Achmea decision). Member States subsequently declared their intent to terminate BITs among themselves. 22 EU countries also commited to withdraw from the Energy Charter Treaty, a multilateral compact applicable to projects in the energy sector in which partake, among others, all EU member States	**YES** (not regulated) Note: ASEAN CIA shall not derogate from other existing international agreements concluded by member States (art. 44)	**YES** (not regulated) Note: General obligation to ensure that other international trade agreements are compatible with the Supplementary Act (art. 32) Note: But see art. 31 on investment contracts
Possibility to negotiate future intra-regional BITs	**No**	**Yes** (not regulated) Note: One intra-ASEAN BIT concluded in 2018 (Indonesia–Singapore)	**Yes** (not regulated) Note: No intra-ECOWAS BIT concluded since 2009

ISSUE	EUROPEAN UNION	ASEAN	ECOWAS
EXTRA-REGIONAL BITS STATUS			
Possibility to maintain existing extra-regional BITs.	**YES, subject to conditions** Continues to be in force until an eventual IIA between EU and the third country enters into force Requirement to renegotiate existing BITs for compliance with EU law (for example: free transfer of funds without exceptions) All extra-regional BITs to be replaced by EU IIAs in the long run, but no specific time frame	**Yes** (not regulated) Note: Several existing extra-ASEAN BITs are still in force	**Yes** (not regulated) Note: Several existing extra-ECOWAS BITs are still in force.
Possibility to negotiate future extra-regional BITs.	**YES, subject to conditions (Reg. 1219/2012, art. 8 and 9)** Member States must obtain authorization from the European Commission European Commission can deny the authorization to negotiate an extra-regional BIT if: (1) there is a conflict with EU law; (2) there is an EU-led negotiation planned or ongoing; (3) there is inconsistency with EU principles and objectives; or (4) EU member State–led negotiations would pose a serious obstacle to an ongoing or planned EU-led negotiation Notification to the European Commission for final approval before signature Note: Many authorizations granted (member States remain active in negotiating extra-EU BITs)	**Yes** (not regulated) Note: Member States have been active in negotiating extra-ASEAN BITs since 2009	**Yes** (not regulated) Note: Member States have been active in negotiating extra-ECOWAS BITs since 2009

a rule that in cases of discrepancy, the investment protocol prevails. This would fall short of establishing a single set of rules and would require additional attention to manage the complexity that may materialize (for instance, to specify that an alternative standard of treatment, if accepted, effectively replaces the fair and equitable treatment standard usually found in intra-African treaties).

Extra-African treaties

The investment protocol is expected to apply to all 55 African Union member States. Investment treaties between African countries and the rest of the world, often belonging to the old generation, will remain unaffected. The protocol is likely to contain more flexible and clearly delineated standards of treatment. It will also contain obligations on investors that can be enforced in an international forum, which can entail additional business costs. As a result, there would be, at least in the short term, a substantive divergence between the protocol and existing extra-African BITs.

African investors would be subject to a different set of conditions, likely to include scaled-back standards of treatment and internationally enforceable obligations, compared with counterparts hailing from other parts of the world. This could create a sense of injustice, since African investors would bear the brunt of rebalancing an international investment protection system that was created and championed by developed countries. But in a bid to channel investment for sustainable development, African countries may end up giving superior treatment to investors from countries outside Africa than to those from within.

African investors, perhaps under pressure from shareholders, could be incentivized to restructure their operations in other African markets via third-country jurisdictions to expand their protection. That would undermine the impact of the investment protocol and dilute its intention to expedite intra-African investment flows.

Policy options to counter such restructuring are available both at the treaty and the national level. Negotiations with partner countries will be necessary to make the appropriate changes to treaties if they are to be maintained. To the extent that treaties specify that investments must conform to domestic law, policy makers can introduce legislation that would require full ownership disclosure before an investment is admitted; if an African company were trying to invest via a third country, administrators would have the prerogative of suspend the admission.[13] However, this approach would be rather unwieldy, could further alienate African investors and may prove legally problematic.

African policy makers are therefore advised to act at the root of the problem by aligning their internal and external investment rules. The investment protocol should guide all the future negotiations and renegotiations. A collective negotiation approach, possibly spearheaded by the African Union, would arguably prove more successful than efforts by individual countries at harmonizing the investment protocol treaties, since it would be easier to coordinate and enjoy more bargain power, in turn enabling a better final outcome.

Megaregional treaties, whether with economic blocks, as with ASEAN or with the EU following the expiry of the Cotonou agreement, or with major economic partners, including China, Japan and the United States, would replace scores of existing and prospective dyadic relationships. Because concerns over potential adverse effects of existing external treaties may dampen the appetite of some countries to establish a more ambitious investment protocol, a universal commitment to pursue external negotiations collectively could assuage their fears and reverse the prospect of a race to the bottom, enabled by bilateral relationships.

In addition to the substantive part of the protocol, the selection of the dispute settlement mechanism will be critical in future negotiations with external partners. Alignment is desirable. African countries, harnessing the AfCFTA experience, may project a single vision in talks on the ongoing UNCITRAL and ICSID reform. A common approach may be more effective and less costly for individual countries than promoting myriad related but not identical national positions. In the post-Cotonou negotiations and beyond, African negotiators will also have to consider their approach to the Multilateral Investment Court sponsored by the European Union and the Appellate Body as an alternative to the ISDS.

As the international investment regime goes through a period of introspection, the investment protocol is likely to shape its course by presenting a consensus of 55 developing countries. An ambitious project breaking from the orthodox models provides grounds for robust future negotiations and may influence the policy stance in other countries, both traditional and more recent economic partners.

Relationship with domestic legislation

The rights and obligations in the investment protocol, as in any international investment agreement, are grounded internationally. They will be independent of and take precedence over national laws by virtue of comprising an international treaty consented to by sovereign States (McLachlan, Shore and Weiniger, 2017). The hierarchical relationship between international and national law underlines the imperative to leave sufficient space for public policy whilst providing meaningful protection to investors. The failure of a country to enforce its own laws, such as providing subsidies and fiscal incentives, may result in successful treaty-based claims. Yet, even measures in line with national laws can be found in breach of treaty by adjudicators if they violate treaty standards. Investment treaties, and the fair and equitable treatment standard in particular, can be used to challenge changes in the domestic legal and regulatory environment.

The domestic legal framework co-determines access to treaty protection (Lim et al. 2018; Sornarajah, 2018). Investors must comply with the nationality requirements of the home economy to enjoy access to treaty benefits. Treaties often require that investments be made in conformity with national laws, and investments that do not meet all the registration requirements or are made through corrupt practices may therefore fail. Under customary international law national policy makers are usually free to set conditions for screening and admission of foreign investments, and treaty protection only applies once the investment has been made (Laviec, 2015). The denial-of-benefits clause often present in treaties also allows for a suspension of treaty protection when inter-governmental relations deteriorate to the point that diplomatic relations are not maintained. Arbitration awards, unless rendered under the New York Convention for arbitration awards, are enforced through domestic courts.

In recent years, however, a growing minority of treaties have extended the national treatment standard, and sometimes even the most-favoured nation standard, to the pre-establishment phase, as discussed earlier. Host countries are then required to provide equal conditions for access to domestic and foreign investors and to all eligible foreign investors. This approach embodies the liberalization logic dominant in trade policy, and it fits neatly with the single market aspirations of African countries. But it curtails the discretion enjoyed by domestic decision makers in setting investment policies. The protocol can include reservations to balance the liberalization logic with concerns over loss of sovereignty (UNCTAD, 2015b).

Unless treaties contain "fork-in-the-road" or "no-U-turn" clauses compelling investors to choose between domestic courts and investor–State arbitration, tribunals may seize claims that have already been taken up or even settled by the national judiciary (Lim, Ho and Paparinskis, 2018; McLachlan, Shore and Weiniger, 2017). Commentators are concerned that in claims related to judicial matters, adjudicators who are not necessarily well-versed in the domestic legal order of the respondent may go beyond a simple assessment of whether due process was observed to assess the application of law, thus further eroding the legal sovereignty of countries (see Box 6.8).

Some recent investment treaties, including the SADC protocol and the EAC model treaty, require the exhaustion of local remedies, compelling investors to bring their complaints to domestic courts before seeking redress through international mechanisms (Brauch, 2017b). However, some tribunals have allowed claimants to go around this conditions through the MFN provision in the base

treaty (Lim, Ho and Paparinskis, 2018). That route needs to be closed in the protocol if a mechanism with direct standing for investors requiring exhaustion of local remedies is envisaged.

Domestic laws and individual investor contracts can also provide an alternative path to investor–State arbitration independently of the investment protocol or other international investment agreements the country has entered into (Bonnitcha, Poulsen and Waibel, 2017). Some standards of treatment in national legislation may be akin to those traditionally found in international investment treaties (McLachlan, Shore and Weiniger, 2017).[14] To establish a coherent investment environment, the various levels of investment laws and regulations must be aligned (UNCTAD, 2018b).

Enforceable obligations of investors have been thus far contained in national laws. It is recommended that the AfCFTA investment protocol, inspired by the PAIC, elevate such obligations to the international plane. Investor obligations rooted in national legislation would further reinforce the link between treaty protection and domestic laws. Host States may then choose whether to pursue the misconduct of international investors through domestic courts or the relevant AfCFTA dispute resolution mechanisms.

Key messages and policy recommendations

Key messages

- **To channel investment for sustainable development, the investment protocol should foster flexible and robust regulatory frameworks supporting an attractive investment environment.** Capital formation can promote sustainable development, regional integration, and faster socio-economic advancement for African countries by enabling trade diversification and the emergence of regional and global value chains, but investments can also threaten human rights and entail social, environmental and economic costs.

- **The African investment policy landscape is fragmented, marked by 854 bilateral investment treaties (512 in force), of which 169 are intra-African (44 in force).** Binding regional treaties add further complexity to this entangled and overlapping investment regime.

- **Traditional investment treaties predominate on the continent, with major repercussions for the policy and regulatory space available to policy makers, but the AfCFTA investment protocol represents an unparalleled opportunity for AU member States to revamp the investment policy landscape.** Up to now, vaguely defined (and therefore potentially far-reaching) standards of treatment, inconsistent jurisprudence and vulnerability to treaty shopping have fuelled uncertainty since investors may challenge legitimate State action in international arbitration.

- **The AfCFTA protocol on investment should be informed by the Pan-African Investment Code (PAIC).** Although the PAIC guides investment treaty negotiations, the 5th Meeting of the AfCFTA Negotiating Forum in March 2017 declined to annex the PAIC to the AfCFTA since it was "not a binding agreement but a framework of cooperation"; however, the protocol should build on the PAIC's innovations in a binding investment treaty.

Policy recommendations

- **The investment protocol should feature new-generation investment treaty innovations for predictable, forward-looking and transparent rules to pave the way for further economic integration.** Among the features would be substantive obligations and dispute settlement provisions, development-oriented investor obligations and mutual commitments among African countries to an equilibrium between business activity and sustainable development.

- **The investment protocol can be built on four pillars: investment promotion and facilitation, investment protection, investor obligations and State commitments.** However, investment promotion and facilitation ought to remain separate from investment protection so as not to create additional obligations towards investors or lower regulatory standards, while investor obligations and State commitments represent novel features intended to harness investment for sustainable development.

- **A cross-thematic dialogue among specialists and negotiators needs to be established to align the investment protocol with the other AfCFTA protocols.** Parallel negotiations of the phase II protocols provide a unique opportunity for complementarities and minimizing undesirable overlaps.

- **Policy makers can use the protocol on investment as a reference point for future negotiations and renegotiations of treaties with external partners.** Adopting a common African approach ensure coherence and provide greater negotiating leverage than bilateral negotiations.

References

Abbas, Ali S. M., and Alexander Klemm. 2013. "A Partial Race to the Bottom: Corporate Tax Developments in Emerging and Developing Economies." *International Tax and Public Finance* 20 (4): 596–617.

Abebe, Girum, Margaret McMillan and Michel Serafinelli. 2018. "Foreign Direct Investment and Knowledge Diffusion in Poor Locations: Evidence from Ethiopia." Working Paper 24461, National Bureau of Economic Research, Cambridge, MA.

AUC (African Union Commission) and ECA (Economic Commission for Africa). 2016. *Track it! Stop it! Get it! Illicit Financial Flows: Report to the High Level Panel on Illicit Financial Flows from Africa*. Addis Ababa, Ethiopia: African Union Commission and ECA.

Agosin, Manuel R., and Roberto Machado. 2005. "Foreign Investment in Developing Countries: Does it Crowd in Domestic Investment?" *Oxford Development Studies* 33 (2): 142–162.

Aguirre, Daniel. 2008. *The Human Right to Development in a Globalized World*. Aldershot, UK: Ashgate Publishing Limited.

Albuquerque, Rui. 2003. "The Composition of International Capital Flows: Risk Sharing through Foreign Direct Investment." *Journal of International Economics* 61 (2): 353–383.

Alfaro, Laura, Areendam Chanda, Seblem Kalemli-Ozcan and Selin Sayek. 2007. "How Does Foreign Direct Investment Promote Economic Growth? Exploring the Effects of Financial Markets on Linkages." Working Paper 12522, National Bureau of Economic Research, Cambridge, MA.

Alford, Roger Paul. 2013. "The Convergence of International Trade and Investment Arbitration." *Santa Clara Journal of International Law* 12 (3).

Allee, Todd, and Clint Peinhardt. 2014. "Evaluating Three Explanations for the Design of Bilateral Investment Treaties." *World Politics* 66 (1): 47–87.

Allen, Brooks E. and Tommasso Soave. 2014. "Jurisdictional Overlap in WTO Dispute Settlement and Investment Arbitration." *Arbitration International* 30 (1): 1–58.

Amado, Jose Daniel, Jackson Shaw Kern and Martin Doe Rodriguez. 2017. *Arbitrating the Conduct of International Investors*. Cambridge, UK: Cambridge University Press.

Ames, Paul. 2015. "ISDS: The most toxic acronym in Europe". *Politico*. Available from: https://www.politico.eu/article/isds-the-most-toxic-acronym-in-europe/.

Ascensio, Hervé (2014). Abuse of Process in International Investment Arbitration. *Chinese Journal of International Law* 13 (4): 763–785.

Attanasio, David. 2018. "Controlling Chaos in Parallel Proceedings: A Report from the 30th Annual ITA Workshop." *Kluwer Arbitration Blog*. Available at: http://arbitrationblog.kluwerarbitration.com/2018/08/12/controlling-chaos-in-parallel-proceedings-a-report-from-the-30th-annual-ita-workshop/.

Baghebo, Michael, and Thankgod O. Apere. 2014. "Testing the "Pollution Havens Hypothesis (PHH)" in Nigeria from 1970–2013." *Mediterranean Journal of Social Sciences* 23 (5): 598–607.

Bagwell, Kyle, and Robert W. Staiger. 2004. *The Economics of the World Trading System*. Cambridge, MA: MIT Press.

Baker, Brook K. 2017. "Eli Lilly's ISDS Patent Claim against Canada Defeated." *Madhyam: Ideas and Action for a Better World*. Available at: http://www.madhyam.org.in/eli-lillys-isds-patent-claim-against-canada-defeated/.

Baker, Brook K., and Katrina Geddes. 2017. "The Incredible Shrinking Victory: Eli Lilly v. Canada, Success, Judicial Reversal, and Continuing Threats from Pharmaceutical ISDS." *Loyola University Chicago Law Journal* 49 (2): 479–514.

Bankole, Abiodun S., and Adeolu O. Adewuyi. 2013. "Have BITs driven FDI between ECOWAS countries and EU?" *Journal of International Trade Law and Policy* 12 (2): 130–153.

Barrera, Enrique Boone. 2017. "The Case for Removing the Fair and Equitable Treatment Standard from NAFTA." Centre for International Governance Innovation Papers 128, Centre for International Governance Innovation, Waterloo, ON.

Baruti, Rukia. 2017. "Investment Facilitation in Regional Economic Integration in Africa: The Cases of COMESA, EAC and SADC." *Journal of World Investment and Trade* 18 (3): 493–529.

Basu, Parantap, and Allesandra Guariglia. 2007. "Foreign Direct Investment, Inequality, and Growth." *Journal of Macroeconomics* 29 (4): 824–839.

Berge, Tarald Laudal and Øyvind Stiansen. 2016. "Negotiating Bits with Models: The Power of Expertise." Available at: https://www.peio.me/wp-content/uploads/2016/12/PEIO10_paper_67.pdf.

Bernasconi-Osterwalder, Nathalie. 2014. "State–State Dispute Settlement in Investment Treaties." Best Practices Series, IISD, Winnipeg, MB.

Bernasconi-Osterwalder, Nathalie, and Martin Dietrich Brauch. 2015. "Brazil's Innovative Approach to International Investment Law." *IISD blog*. Available at: https://www.iisd.org/blog/brazils-innovative-approach-international-investment-law.

Betz, Timm, and Andrew Kerner. 2015. "The Influence of Interest: Real US Interest Rates and Bilateral Investment Treaties." *The Review of International Organizations* 11 (4): 419–448.

Bjorklund, Andrea K. 2009. "The Emerging Civilization of Investment Arbitration." *Penn State Law Review* 113 (4): 1269–1300.

Bodea, Cristina, and Fangjin Ye. 2018. "Investor Rights versus Human Rights: Do Bilateral Investment Treaties Tilt the Scale?" *British Journal of Political Science*.

Bohoslavsky, Juan Pablo, and Juan Bautista Justo. 2011. *Protección del derecho humano al agua y arbitrajes de inversión (Protection of the Human Right to Water and International Investment Arbitration)*. Santiago de Chile: ECLAC.

Bonnitcha, Jonathan. 2015. "Foreign Investment, Development and Governance." *Journal of International Dispute Settlement* 7 (1): 31–54.

Bonnitcha, Jonathan, Lauge N. Skovgaard Poulsen and Michael Waibel. 2017. *The Political Economy of the Investment Treaty Regime*. Oxford, UK: Oxford University Press.

Brauch, Martin Dietrich. 2017a. *A Risky Tango? Investment Facilitation and the WTO Ministerial Conference in Buenos Aires*. Winnipeg, MB: IISD. Available at: https://iisd.org/library/risky-tango-investment-facilitation-and-wto-ministerial-conference-buenos-aires

———. 2017b. "Exhaustion of Local Remedies in International Investment Law." Best Practices Series, IISD, Winnipeg, MB.

Brauch, Martin Dietrich, Howard Mann and Nathalie Bernasconi-Osterwalder. 2019. "SADC–IISD Investment Facilitation Workshop." Report of the meeting in Johannesburg, South Africa, 21–23 August.

Brickhill, Jason, and Max Du Plessis. 2011. "Two's Company, Three's a Crowd: Public Interest Intervention in Investor-State Arbitration (Piero Foresti v. South Africa)." *South African Journal on Human Rights* 27 (1): 152–166.

Broude, Tomer. 2011. "Investment and Trade: The 'Lottie and Lisa' of International Economic Law?" Legal Studies Research Paper 10-11, Hebrew University of Jerusalem, Jerusalem, Israel.

Brower, Charles N., and Sadie Blanchard. 2014. "What's in a Meme? The Truth about Investor-State Arbitration: Why It Need Not, and Must Not, Be Repossessed by States." *Columbia Journal of Transnational Law* 52 (3): 690–777.

Burke-White, William W. 2008. "The Argentine Financial Crisis: State Liability under BITs and the Legitimacy of the ICSID System." Faculty Scholarship Paper 193 University of Pennsylvania Law School, Philadelphia, PA.

Chaisse, Julien. 2015. "The Treaty Shopping Practice: Corporate Structuring and Restructuring to Gain Access to Investment Treaties and Arbitration." *Hastings Business Law Journal* 11 (2): 225–306.

Chow, Marianne W. 2009. "Discriminatory Equality v. Nondiscriminatory Inequality: The Legitimacy of South Africa's Affirmative Action Policies under International Law." *Connecticut Journal of International Law* 24 (2): 291–380.

Coe, Jack. 2006. "Transparency in the Resolution of Investor-State Disputes: Adoption, Adaptation, and NAFTA Leadership." *University of Kansas Law Review* 54 (5): 1339–1386.

Correa, Carlos M. 2004. "Bilateral Investment Agreements: Agents of New Global Standards for the Protection of Intellectual Property Rights?" Available at: https://www.ictsd.org/sites/default/files/downloads/2008/08/correa-bits-august-2004.pdf.

Cotula, Lorenzo. 2014. "Investment Treaties and Sustainable Development: An Overview." Briefing, IIED, London. Available from: http://pubs.iied.org/pdfs/17238IIED.pdf.

DTI (Department of Trade and Industry of South Africa). 2009. "Bilateral Investment Treaty Policy Framework Review." Government Position Paper, DTI, Pretoria, South Africa.

Diependaele, Lisa, Julian Cockbain and Sigrid Sterckx. 2017. "Eli Lilly v Canada: The Uncomfortable Liaison between Intellectual Property and International Investment Law." *Queen Mary Journal of Intellectual Property* 7 (3): 283–305.

DiMascio, Nicholas, and Joost Pauwelyn. 2008. "Nondiscrimination in Trade and Investment Treaties: Worlds Apart or Two Sides of the Same Coin?" *The American Journal of International Law* 102 (1): 48–89.

Dolea, Sorin. 2018. "Investment Claim against Ukraine Follows an Antimonopoly Fine Imposed on Gazprom." CIS Arbitration Forum. Available at: http://www.cisarbitration.com/2018/12/13/investment-claim-against-ukraine-following-an-antimonopoly-fine-imposed-to-gazprom/.

Dolzer, Rudolf. 2005. "Fair and Equitable Treatment: A Key Standard in Investment Treaties." *The International Lawyer* 39 (1): 87–106.

Dolzer, Rudolf, and Christoph Schreurer. 2012. *Principles of International Investment Law.* Oxford, UK: Oxford University Press.

Dreyfuss, Rochelle, and Susy Frankel. 2015. "From Incentive to Commodity to Asset: How International Law is Reconceptualizing Intellectual Property." *Michigan Journal of International Law* 36 (4): 557–602.

Duanmu, Jing-Lin. 2014. "A Race to Lower Standards? Labor Standards and Location Choice of Outward FDI from the BRIC Countries." *International Business Review* 23 (3).

Dunning, John H., and Sarianna M. Lundan. 2011. "The Changing Political Economy of Foreign Investment: Finding a Balance between Hard and Soft Forms of Regulation." In *The Evolving International Investment Regime: Expectations, Realities, Options,* edited by Jose E. Alvarez and Karl P. Sauvant. Oxford, UK: Oxford University Press.

ECA (United Nations Economic Commission for Africa), 2017. "Investment Policies and Bilateral Investment Treaties in Africa: Implications for Regional Integration." ECA, Addis Ababa.

ECA, 2018. "Assessing Regional Integration in Africa VIII: Bringing the Continental Free Trade Area About." ECA: Addis Ababa.

ECA, forthcoming a. "Drivers for Boosting Intra-African Investment flows towards Africa's Transformation." ECA: Addis Ababa.

ECA, forthcoming b. "Linkages between Double Taxation Treaties and Bilateral Investment Treaties." ECA: Addis Ababa.

Echandi, Roberto. 2011. "What Do Developing Countries Expect from the International Investment Regime?" In *The Evolving International Investment Regime: Expectations, Realities, Options,* edited by Jose E. Alvarez and Karl P. Sauvant. Oxford, UK: Oxford University Press.

Economist, The. 2019. "Saving the Nation." pp. 3–5, 17 April–3 May.

Elkins, Zachary, Andrew T. Guzman and Beth A. Simmons. 2006. "Competing for Capital: The Diffusion of Bilateral Investment Treaties, 1960–2000." *International Organization* 60 (4): 811–846.

Emmott, Robin and Philip Blenkinsop. 2014. "Exclusive: Online Protest Delays EU Plan to Resolve U.S. Trade Row." Reuters. Available from: https://www.reuters.com/article/us-eu-usa-trade/exclusive-online-protest-delays-eu-plan-to-resolve-u-s-trade-row-idUSKCN0JA0YA20141126.

European Commission. 2017. "Factsheet on the Multilateral Investment Court." Brussels: European Commission. Available at: http://trade.ec.europa.eu/doclib/docs/2017/september/tradoc_156042.pdf.

European Council, 2018. "Multilateral Investment Court: Council Gives Mandate to the Commission to Open Negotiation." Press release. Available from: https://www.consilium.europa.eu/en/press/press-releases/2018/03/20/multilateral-investment-court-council-gives-mandate-to-the-commission-to-open-negotiations/.

Ewing-Chow, Michael. 2007. "Thesis, Antithesis and Synthesis: Investor Protection in BITs, the WTO and FTAs." *University of New South Wales Law Journal* 30 (2): 548–571.

Falvey, Rod, and Neil Foster-McGregor. 2017. "North-South Foreign Direct Investment and Bilateral Investment Treaties." *The World Economy* 48 (1): 2–28.

Fowowe, Babajide and Mohammed Shuaibu (2014). Is Foreign Direct Investment Good for the Poor? New Evidence from African Countries. *Economic Change and Restructuring,* vol. 47, No. 4, pp. 321-339

Feldman, Mark. 2012. "Setting Limits on Corporate Nationality Planning in Investment Treaty Arbitration." *ICSID Review: Foreign Investment Law Journal* 27 (2): 281–302.

Flynn, Sean. 2015. "Inside Views: How The Leaked TPP ISDS Chapter Threatens Intellectual Property Limitations and Exceptions." *International IP Policy News.* Available at: https://www.ip-watch.org/2015/03/26/how-the-leaked-tpp-isds-chapter-threatens-intellectual-property-limitations-and-exceptions/.

Fofack, Hippolyte. 2018. "Economic Integration in Africa (AfCFTA)." *IMF Finance and Development Magazine* 55 (4): 48–51.

Fonchamnyo, Dobdinga Cletus, and Afuge Ramsy Akame. 2017. "Determinants of Export Diversification in Sub-Sahara African Region: A Fractionalized Logit Estimation Model." *Journal of Economic and Finance* 41 (2): 330–342.

Foster, Caroline E. 2017. "Respecting Regulatory Measures: Arbitral Method and Reasoning in the Philip Morris v Uruguay Tobacco Plain Packaging Case." *Review of European, Comparative & International Environmental Law* 26 (3): 287–297.

Franck, Susan D. 2005. "The Legitimacy Crisis in Investment Treaty Arbitration: Privatizing Public International Law through Inconsistent Decisions." *Fordham Law Review* 73 (4): 1521–1625.

Frankel, Susy. 2016. "Interpreting the Overlap of International Investment and Intellectual Property Law." *Journal of International Economic Law* 19 (1): 121–143.

Friedman, Andrew. 2010. "Flexible Arbitration for the Developing World: Piero Foresti and the Future of Bilateral Investment Treaties in the Global South." *International Law and Management Review* 7 (1): 41–51.

Fry, James D. 2007. "International Human Rights Law in Investment Arbitration: Evidence of International Law's Unity." *Duke Journal of Comparative & International Law* 18 (1): 77–150.

Fukunaga, Yuga. 2018. "Abuse of Process under International Law and Investment Arbitration." *ICSID Review- Foreign Investment Law Journal* 33 (1): 181–211.

Gaffney, John P. 2010. "'Abuse of Process' in Investment Treaty Arbitration." *Journal of World Investment and Trade* 11 (4): 515–538.

García-Bolívar, Omar E. 2015. "La Crisis del Derecho Internacional de Inversiones Extranjeras: Propuestas de Reforma (The Crisis of International Law for Foreign Investments: Reform Proposals)." *Revista de la Secretaría del Tribunal Permanente de Revisión* 3 (5): 137–163.

Gathii, James Thuo, and Cynthia M. Ho. 2017. "Regime Shift of IP Lawmaking and Enforcement from WTO to the International Investment Regime." *Minnesota Journal of Law, Science & Technology* 18 (2): 427–515.

Gazzini, Tarcisio. 2014. "Bilateral Investment Treaties and Sustainable Development." *Journal of World Investment and Trade* 15 (5–6): 929–963.

George, Erika, and Elizabeth Thomas. 2018. "Bringing Human Rights into Bilateral Investment Treaties: South Africa and a Different Approach to International Investment Disputes." *Transnational Law and Contemporary Problems* 27 (2): 403–450.

Gervais, Daniel J. 2019. "Intellectual Property: A Beacon for Reform of Investor-state Dispute Settlement." Research Paper 19-01, Vanderbilt University Law School, Nashville, TN.

Ghiotto, Luciana. 2018. "A Critical Review of the Debate on Investment Facilitation." *Investment Treaty News*.

Ghouri, Ahmad. 2018. "Served on a Silver Platter? A Review of the UNCTAD Global Action Menu for Investment Facilitation." *Indian Journal of International Law* 58 (1): 139–170.

Gibson, Christopher. 2010. "A Look at the Compulsory License in Investment Arbitration: The Case of Indirect Expropriation." *American University International Law Review* 25 (3): 357–422.

Ginsburg, Tom. 2005. "International Substitutes for Domestic Institutions: Bilateral Investment Treaties and Governance." *International Review of Law and Economics* 25 (1): 107–123.

Gray, Kevin R. 2002. "Foreign Direct Investment and Environmental Impacts: Is the Debate Over?" *Review of European, Comparative & International Environmental Law* 11 (3): 306–313.

Guven, Brooke and Lise Johnson. 2019. The Policy Implications of Third-Party Funding in Investor-State Dispute Settlement. CCSI Working Paper 2019. *Columbia Centre for Sustainable Development*

Guzman, Andrew. 1998. "Why LDCs Sign Treaties That Hurt Them: Explaining the Popularity of Bilateral Investment Treaties." *Virginia Journal of International Law* 38 (4): 639–688.

Harding, Torfinn, and Beata S. Javorcik. 2011. "Roll Out the Red Carpet and They Will Come: Investment Promotion and FDI Inflows." *The Economic Journal* 121 (557): 1445–1476.

Hartmann, Stephanie. 2017. "When Two International Regimes Collide: An Analysis of the Tobacco Plain Packaging Disputes and Why Overlapping Jurisdiction of the WTO and Investment Tribunals Does Not Result in Convergence of Norms." *UCLA Journal of International Law and Foreign Affairs* 21 (2): 204–245.

Hees, Felipe, Pedro Mendonca and Pedro Paranhos. 2018. "The Cooperation and Facilitation Investment Agreement (CFIA) in the Context of the Discussions on the Reform of the ISDS System." South Centre Investment Policy Brief 8, South Centre, Geneva.

Ho, Cynthia M. 2015. "Sovereignty Under Siege: Corporate Challenges to Domestic Intellectual Property Decisions." *Berkeley Technology Law Journal* 30 (1): 213–304.

Ho, Cynthia M. 2017. "Inside Views: TRIPS Flexibilities under Threat from Investment Disputes: A Closer Look at Canada's 'Win' against Eli Lilly." *International IP News*. Available at: https://www.ip-watch.org/2017/04/27/trips-flexibilities-threat-investment-disputes-closer-look-canadas-win-eli-lilly/.

Hodgson, Matthew and Alastair Campbell 2017. "Damages and Costs in Investment Treaty Arbitration Revisited." *Global Arbitration Review*. Available from: http://www.allenovery.com/SiteCollectionDocuments/14-12-17_Damages_and_costs_in_investment_treaty_arbitration_revisited_.pdf

Howse, Rob. 2017. "Eli Lilly v Canada: A Pyrrhic Victory against Big Pharma." *International Economic Law and Policy Blog*. Available at: https://worldtradelaw.typepad.com/ielpblog/2017/03/eli-lilly-v-canada-a-pyrrhic-victory-against-big-pharma-.html.

Human Rights Council. 2008. "Promotion and Protection of All Human Rights, Civil, Political, Economic, Social and Cultural Rights, Including The Right to Development Report of the Special Representative of the Secretary-General on the Issue of Human Rights and Transnational Corporations and Other Business Enterprises." A/HRC/8/5/Add.2, United Nations Human Rights Council, Geneva.

I-ARB. 2018. Various country profiles. Available at: https://www.iarbafrica.com/en/resources/country-profile.

ICSID (International Centre for Settlement of Investment Disputes). 2015. *ICSID 2015 Annual Report*. Washington, DC: ICSID.

———. 2017. *The ICSID Caseload: Statistics (Special Focus – Africa)*. Washington, DC: ICSID.

ICCA (International Council for Commercial Arbitration) and Queen Mary, University of London. 2018. *Report of the ICCA-Queen Mary Task Force on Third-Party Funding in International Arbitration*. London: ICCA and Queen Mary, University of London.

IISD (International Institute for Sustainable Development) and UN Environment. 2016. *A Sustainability Toolkit for Trade Negotiators: Trade and Investment as Vehicles for Achieving the 2030 Sustainable Development Agenda*. Winnipeg, MB: IISD.

Jandhyala, Srividya. 2011. "Three Waves of BITs: The Global Diffusion of Foreign Investment Policy." *The Journal of Conflict Resolution* 55 (6): 1047–1073.

Javorcik, Beata Smarzynska. 2004. "Does Foreign Direct Investment Increase the Productivity of Domestic Firms? In Search of Spillovers through Backward Linkages." *The American Economic Review* 94 (3): 605–627.

Jozwik, Katarzyna. 2011.] "Investment Regulation and Intellectual Property." *Global Trade and Customs Journal* 6 (7–8): 351–359

Jude, Cristina. 2016. "Technology Spillovers from FDI. Evidence on the Intensity of Different Spillover Channels." *The World Economy* 39 (12): 1947–1973.

Junngam, Nartnirun. 2017. "The Full Protection and Security Standard in International Investment Law: What and Who is Investment Fully[?] Protected and Secured from?" *American University Business Law Review* 7 (1): 1–100.

Kaushal, Asha. 2009. "Revisiting History: How the Past Matters for the Present Backlash against the Foreign Investment Regime." *Harvard International Law Journal* 50 (2): 491–534.

Kerner, Andrew. 2018. "What Can We Really Know about BITs and FDI?" *ICSID Review: Foreign Investment Law Journal* 33 (1): 1–13.

Kidane, Won. 2018a. "Alternatives to Investor–State Dispute Settlement: An African Perspective." Global Economic Governance Discussion Paper, GEG Africa.

———. 2018b. "Contemporary International Investment Law Trends and Africa's Dilemmas in The Draft Pan-African Investment Code." *The George Washington International Law Review* 50 (3): 523–579.

Kirtley, William Lawton. 2009. "The Transfer of Treaty Claims and Treaty-Shopping in Investor-State Disputes." *Journal of World Investment and Trade* 10 (3): 427–461.

Kurtz, Jürgen. 2016. *The WTO and International Investment Law: Converging Systems*. Cambridge, UK: Cambridge University Press.

Kusek, Peter, and Andrea Antonia Lim Silva. 2018. "What Investors Want: Perceptions and Experiences of Multinational Corporations in Developing Countries." Policy Research Working Paper WPS 8386, World Bank, Washington, DC.

Laborde, Gustavo. 2010. "The Case for Host State Claims in Investment Arbitration." *Journal of International Dispute Settlement* 1 (1): 97–122.

Land, Molly K. 2012. "Rebalancing TRIPS." *Michigan Journal of International Law* 33 (3): 433–480.

Laviec, Jean-Pierre. 2015. *Protection et promotion des investissements: Étude de droit international économique (Protection and Promotion of Investments: Study of international economic law)*. Geneva: Graduate Institute Publications.

Lee, John. 2015. "Resolving Concerns of Treaty Shopping in International Investment Arbitration." *Journal of International Dispute Settlement* 6 (2): 355–379.

Leibhold, Annalisa M. 2015. "The Friction between Investor Protection and Human Rights: Lessons from Foresti v. South Africa." *Houston Journal of International Law* 38 (1): 215–267.

Li, Siqing. 2018. "Convergence of WTO Dispute Settlement and Investor-State Arbitration: A Closer Look at Umbrella Clauses." *Chicago Journal of International Law* 19 (1): 189–232.

Liddell, Kathleen, and Michael Waibel. 2016. "Fair and Equitable Treatment and Judicial Patent Decisions." *Journal of International Economic Law* 19 (1): 145–174.

Lim, Chin Leng, Jean Ho and Martins Paparinskis. 2018. *International Investment Law and Arbitration: Commentary, Awards and Other Materials*. Cambridge, UK: Cambridge University Press.

Linderfalk, Ulf. 2017. "Philip Morris Asia Ltd. v. Australia: Abuse of Rights in Investor-State Arbitration." *Nordic Journal of International Law* 83 (3): 403–419.

Lipkus, Nathaniel. 2017. "Canada's NAFTA Victory a Win for Judicial Sovereignty." *Policy Options*. Available at: http://policyoptions.irpp.org/magazines/april-2017/canadas-nafta-victory-a-win-for-judicial-sovereignty/.

Lubambo, Murilo. 2016. "How Does International Economic Law Regulate the Right of Entry of Investments in Services?" Working Paper 2016/15, Society of International Economic Law.

Malik, Mahnaz. 2009. "Definition of Investment in International Investment Agreements." Best Practice Series, IISD, Winnipeg, MB.

———. 2011. "The Full Protection and Security Standard Comes of Age: Yet Another Challenge for States in Investment Treaty Arbitration?" Best Practices Series, IISD, Winnipeg, MB.

Manasakis, Constantine, Evangelos Mitrokostas and Emmanuel Petrakis. 2017. "Strategic Corporate Social Responsibility by a Multinational Firm." *Review of International Economics* 26 (3): 709–720.

Marshall, Fiona. 2007. "Fair and Equitable Treatment in International Investment Agreements." Issues in International Investment Law Background Papers for the Developing Country Investment Negotiators' Forum, IISD, Winnipeg, MB.

Mbengue, Makane Moïse. 2018. "Facilitating Investment for Sustainable Development: It Matters for Africa." Columbia FDI Perspectives on Topical Foreign Direct Investment Issues 222, Columbia Center on Sustainable Investment, New York.

Mbengue, Makane Moïse, and Stefanie Schacherer. 2017. "The 'Africanization' of International Investment Law: The Pan-African Investment Code and the Reform of the International Investment Regime." *Journal of World Investment and Trade* 18 (3): 414–448.

McLachlan, Campbell, Lawrence Shore and Matthew Weiniger. 2017. *International Investment Arbitration: Substantive Principles*. Oxford, UK: Oxford University Press.

Mercurio, Bryan. 2012. "Awakening the Sleeping Giant: Intellectual Property Rights in International Investment Agreements." *Journal of International Economic Law* 15 (3): 871–915.

Molinuevo, Martin. 2006. "Can Foreign Investors in Services Benefit from WTO Dispute Settlement? Legal Standing and Remedies in WTO and International Arbitration." NCCR Trade Regulation Working Paper No. 2006/17, National Centre of Competence in Research, Switzerland.

Morosini, Fabio, and Michelle Ratton Sanchez Badin. 2015. "The Brazilian Agreement on Cooperation and Facilitation of Investments (ACFI): A New Formula for International Investment Agreements?" *Investment Treaty News* 6 (3): 3–5.

Muchlinski, Peter. 2010. "The COMESA Common Investment Area: Substantive Standards and Procedural Problems in Dispute Settlement." Research Paper No. 11/2010, SOAS School of Law, London.

Muniz, Joaquim P., Kabir Duggal and Luis Peretti. 2017. "The New Brazilian BIT on Cooperation and Facilitation of Investments: A New Approach in Times of Change." *ICSID Review: Foreign Investment Law Journal* 32 (2): 404–417.

Neumayer, Eric, Peter Nunnenkamp and Martin Roy. 2016. "Are Stricter Investment Rules Contagious? Host Country Competition for Foreign Direct Investment through International Agreements." *Review of World Economics* 152 (1): 117–213.

NYAC (New York Arbitration Convention). 2019. "Contracting States." New York. Available at: http://www.newyorkconvention.org/countries.

Newman, Carol et al., 2015. "Technology Transfers, Foreign Investments and Productivity Spillovers." *European Economic Review* 76: 168-187

Nikièma, Suzy H. 2013. "Compensation for Expropriation." Best Practices Series, IISD, Winnipeg, MB.

———. 2018. Presentation Delivered at *Promoting Transformative Investment in Africa through Regional Integration, 23 October 2018, ECA-UNCTAD Break-out Session at the World Investment Forum*

Nilsson, Anders, and Oscar Englesson. 2013. "Inconsistent Awards in Investment Treaty Arbitration: Is an Appeals Court Needed?" *Journal of International Arbitration* 30 (5): 561–579.

Novik, Ana, and Alexandre de Crombrugghe. 2018. "Towards an International Framework for Investment Facilitation." OECD Investment Insights, OECD Publishing, Paris.

Nyombi, Chrispas. 2018. "A Case for a Regional Investment Court for Africa." *North Carolina Journal of International Law* 43 (3): 66–109

Nyuur, Richard B., Daniel F. Ofori and Yaw A. Debrah. 2015. "The Impact of FDI Inflow on Domestic Firms' Uptake of CSR Activities: The Moderating Effects of Host Institutions." *Thunderbird International Business Review* 58 (2): 147–159.

OECD (Organisation for Economic Co-operation and Development). 2015. *Policy Framework for Investment*. Paris: OECD Publishing.

———. n.d. *Investment Policy Framework for the Southern African Development Community*. Paris: OECD Publishing. Available at: http://www.oecd.org/daf/inv/investment-policy/sadc-regional-investment-policy-framework.htm.

OECD and IDB (Inter-American Development Bank). 2018. *Mapping of Investment Promotion Agencies in OECD Countries*. Paris: OECD Publishing.

Okediji, Ruth L. 2014. "Is Intellectual Property 'Investment?' Eli Lilly v. Canada and the International Intellectual Property System." *University of Pennsylvania Journal of International Law* 35 (4): 1121–1138.

Oliveira, Pedro, and Rosa Forte. 2017. "Labour Market Flexibility and FDI Attraction: A Macroeconomic Analysis." *Panoeconomicus*.

Olney, William W. 2013. "A Race to the Bottom? Employment Protection and Foreign Direct Investment." *Journal of International Economics* 91 (2): 191–203.

Onyema, Emilia. 2018. "The Role of African Courts and Judges in Arbitration." In *Rethinking the Role of African National Courts in Arbitration*, edited by Onyema Emilia. Kluwer Law International: Amsterdam, Netherlands.

Orefice, Gianluca, and Nadia Rocha. 2011. "Deep Integration and Production Networks: An Empirical Analysis." Staff Working Paper ERSD-2011-11, World Trade Organization, Geneva.

Páez, Laura. 2017. "Bilateral Investment Treaties and Regional Investment Regulation in Africa: Towards a Continental Investment Area?" *Journal of World Investment and Trade* 18 (3): 379–413.

Paulsson, Jan. 1995. "Arbitration without Privity." *ICSID Review: Foreign Investment Law Journal* 10 (2): 232–257.

Pelc, Krzysztof. 2016. "Does the International Investment Regime Induce Frivolous Litigation?" Available at: http://dx.doi.org/10.2139/ssrn.2778056.

Poulsen, Lauge N. Skovegaard. 2015. *Bounded Rationality and Economic Diplomacy: The Politics of Investment Treaties in Developing Countries*. Cambridge, UK: Cambridge University Press.

Puig, Sergio. 2016. "The Merging of International Trade and Investment Law." Arizona Legal Studies Discussion Paper 16-43, The University of Arizona Rogers College of Law, Tucson, AZ.

Pupolizio, Ivan. 2015. "Il Diritto Ad Un Mondo Immutabile. L'esproprio Indiretto Negli Accordi Sulla Protezione Degli Investimenti E Il Concetto Di "Pubblico" Nel Diritto (The Right to an Immutable World. Indirect expropriation in investment protection agreements and the conept of "publicness" in law)." *Stato e Mercato* 104 (2): 309–340.

Radi, Yannick. 2018. "Philip Morris v Uruguay: Regulatory Measures in International Investment Law: To Be or Not to Be Compensated?" *ICSID Review: Foreign Investment Law Journal* 33 (1): 74–80.

Razin, Assaf, Efraim Sadka and Chi-Wa Yuen. 2001. "Social Benefits and Losses from FDI: Two Nontraditional Views." In *Regional and Global Capital Flows: Macroeconomic Causes and Consequences, NBER-EASE Volume 10*, edited by Ito Takatoshi and Anne O. Krueger. Chicago, IL: University of Chicago Press.

Ruse-Khan, Henning Gross. 2016. "Challenging Compliance with International Intellectual Property Norms in Investor–state Dispute Settlement." *Journal of International Economic Law* 19 (1): 241–277.

Rutledge, Peter B. 2012. "TRIPS and BITs: an essay on compulsory licenses, expropriation and international arbitration" *North Carolina Journal of Law & Technology Online* 13: 149-163

Salacuse, Jeswald W., and Nicholas P. Sullivan. 2005. "Do BITs Really Work: An Evaluation of Bilateral Investment Treaties and Their Grand Bargain." *Harvard International Law Journal* 46 (1): 67–130.

Sandjong Tomi, Diderot Guy D'Estaing. 2015. *Foreign Direct Investment, Economic Growth and Structural Transformation: The Case of West African Economies and Monetary Union Countries*. Munich, Germany: Munich Personal RePEc Archive. Available from: https://mpra.ub.uni-muenchen. de/62230/1/MPRA_paper_62230.pdf

Sauvant, Karl P. 2016. "Investment Promotion and Facilitation in a Broader Context." Presented at Good Practices in Investment Promotion and Facilitation, OECD, Paris. 18 October.

———. 2018. "Towards an Investment Facilitation Framework: Why? What? When?" Presented at "WTO: Paths Forward Towards a Shared Vision on Investment Facilitation Organized by the International Centre for Trade and Sustainable Development," Geneva, 5 March.

Sauvant, Karl P., and Khalil Hamdani. 2015. "An International Support Programme for Sustainable Investment Facilitation." E15 Task Force on Investment Policy, Think Piece, International Centre for Trade and Sustainable Development, Geneva.

Schill, Stephan W. 2017. "Reforming Investor–State Dispute Settlement: A (Comparative and International) Constitutional Law Framework." *Journal of International Economic Law* 20 (3): 649–671.

Schlemmer, Engela C. 2016. "An Overview of South Africa's Bilateral Investment Treaties and Investment Policy." *ICSID Review: Foreign Investment Law Journal* 31 (1): 167–93.

———. 2018. "Dispute Settlement in Investment-Related Matters: South Africa and the BRICS." *AJIL Unbound* 112: 212–216.

Schreurer, Christoph. 2010. "Full Protection and Security." *Journal of International Dispute Settlement* 1 (2): 353–369.

Schwebel, Stephen M. 2014. "In Defense of Bilateral Investment Treaties." Columbia FDI Perspectives on Topical Foreign Direct Investment Issues 135, Columbia Center on Sustainable Investment, New York.

Seatzu, Francesco, and Paolo Vargiu. 2015. "Africanizing Bilateral Investment Treaties (BITS): Some Case Studies and Future Prospects of a Pro-Active African Approach to International Investment." *Connecticut Journal of International Law* 30 (2): 143–170.

Shany, Yuval. 2004. *The Competing Jurisdictions of International Courts and Tribunals*. Oxford, UK: Oxford University Press.

Shihata, Ibrahim F. I. 1992. "Towards a Greater Depoliticization of Investment Disputes: The Roles of ICSID and MIGA." Washington, DC: World Bank.

Sicetsha, Andile. 2018. "South Africa's 'Protection of Investment Act' May Drive Foreign Investors Away." *The South African*. Available at: https://www. thesouthafrican.com/south-africas-protection-of-investment-act-may-drive-foreign-investors-away/.

Singh, Kavaljit. 2018. "Investment Facilitation: Another Fad in the Offing?" Columbia FDI Perspectives on Topical Foreign Direct Investment Issues 232 Columbia Center on Sustainable Investment, New York.

Skinner, Matthew, Cameron A. Miles and Sam Luttrell. 2010. "Access and Advantage in Investor-State Arbitration: The Law and Practice of Treaty Shopping." *Journal of World Energy Law and Business* 3 (3): 260–285.

Smith, Stephanie, and Janet Martinez. 2009. "An Analytic Framework for Dispute Systems Design." *Harvard Negotiation Law Review* 14 (1): 123–170.

Sornarajah, Muthucumaraswamy. 2018. *The International Law on Foreign Investment*. Cambridge, UK: Cambridge University Press.

Sprenger, Helena, and Bouke Boersma. 2014. "The Importance of Bilateral Investment Treaties (BITs) When Investing in Emerging Markets." *Business Law Today* 2014 (3): 1–4.

Stiglitz, Joseph E. 2007. "Regulating Multinational Corporations: Towards Principles of Cross-Border Legal Frameworks in a Globalized World Balancing Rights with Responsibilities." *American University International Law Review* 23 (3): 451–558.

Sutton, John, Amanda Jinhage, Jonathan Leape, Richard Newfarmer and John Page. 2016. "Harnessing FDI for Job Creation and Industrialisation in Africa." Growth Briefs, International Growth Centre, London. Available at: https://www.theigc.org/wp-content/uploads/2016/05/GrowthBrief_FDI-in-Africa-FINAL_WEB.pdf.

Tangri, Roger, and Roger Southall. 2008. "The Politics of Black Economic Empowerment in South Africa." *Journal of Southern African Studies* 34 (3): 699–716.

Tienhaara, Kyla. 2006. "Mineral Investment and the Regulation of the Environment in Developing Countries: Lessons from Ghana." *International Environmental Agreements: Politics, Law and Economics* 6 (4): 371–394.

———. 2018. "Regulatory Chill in a Warming World: The Threat to Climate Policy Posed by Investor-State Dispute Settlement." *Transnational Environmental Law* 7 (2): 229–250.

Tobin, Jennifer L. 2018. "The Social Cost of International Investment Agreements: The Case of Cigarette Packaging." *Ethics & International Affairs* 32 (2): 153–167.

Trakman, Leon. 2009. "Foreign Direct Investment: Hazard or Opportunity?" *George Washington International Law Review* 41 (1): 1–66.

UNCITRAL 2019. *Status—UNCITRAL Model Law on International Commercial Arbitration (1985), with amendments as adopted in 2006*. Accessed on 17 June 2019. Available at: https://www.uncitral.org/uncitral/en/uncitral_texts/arbitration/1985Model_arbitration_status.html .

UNCTAD (United Nations Conference on Trade and Development). 2007. *Bilateral Investment Treaties 1995-2006: Trends in Investment* Rulemaking. New York/Geneva: United Nation.

———. 2010a. *Investor–State Disputes: Prevention and Alternatives to Arbitration*. UNCTAD Series on Issues in International Investment Agreements II. Geneva: UNCTAD.

———. 2010b. *Most-Favoured Nation Treatment*. UNCTAD Series on Issues in International Investment Agreements II. Geneva: UNCTAD.

———. 2012a. *Expropriation: A Sequel*. UNCTAD Series on Issues in International Investment Agreements II. Geneva: UNCTAD.

———. 2012b. *Fair and Equitable Treatment: A Sequel*. UNCTAD Series on Issues in International Investment Agreements II. Geneva: UNCTAD.

———. 2012c. *Scope and Definition*. UNCTAD Series on Issues in International Investment Agreements II. Geneva: UNCTAD.

———. 2012d. *Transparency*. UNCTAD Series on Issues in International Investment Agreements II. Geneva: UNCTAD.

———2013a. UNCTAD Perspective Competition and Consumer Policy. New York/Geneva: United Nations.

———. 2013b. *World Investment Report 2013: Global Value Chains: Investment and Trade for Development*. Geneva: UNCTAD.

———. 2015a. *Investment Policy Framework for Sustainable Development*. Geneva: UNCTAD.

———. 2015b. *World Investment Report 2015: Reforming International Investment Governance*. Geneva: UNCTAD.

———. 2016. *World Investment Report 2016: Investor Nationality: Policy Challenges*. Geneva: UNCTAD.

———. 2017a. *Global Action Menu for Investment Facilitation*. Geneva: UNCTAD.

———. 2017b. *World Investment Report 2017: Investment and the Digital Economy*. Geneva: UNCTAD.

———. 2018a. *Migration for Structural Transformation, Economic Development in Africa Report 2018*. Geneva: UNCTAD.

———. 2018b. *UNCTAD's Reform Package for the International Investment Regime 2018*. Geneva: UNCTAD.

———. 2018c. *World Investment Report: Investment and New Industrial Policies*. Geneva: UNCTAD.

———. 2019. *Investment Policy Hub*. Geneva: UNCTAD. Available at: https://investmentpolicyhub.unctad.org/.

Upreti, Pratyush Nath. 2016. "Enforcing IPRs through Investor-State Dispute Settlement: A Paradigm Shift in Global IP Practice." *The Journal of World Intellectual Property* 19 (1–2): 53–82.

Van Harten, Gus. 2005. "Private Authority and Transnational Governance: The Contours of the International System of Investor Protection." *Review of International Political Economy* 12 (4): 600–623.

———. 2016. "A Critique of Investment Treaties." In *Rethinking Bilateral Investment Treaties: Critical Issues and Policy Choices*, edited by Kavaljit Singh and Ilge Burghard. New Delhi and Amsterdam: Both Ends/Madhyam/Somo.

Van Boom, Willem H (2012). *Third-Party Financing in International Investment Arbitration*. Available from: https://papers.ssrn.com/sol3/papers.cfm?abstract_id=2027114.

Van Harten, Gus, and Pavel Malysheuski. 2016. "Who Has Benefited Financially from Investment Treaty Arbitration? An Evaluation of the Size and Wealth of Claimants." Osgoode Legal Studies Research Paper Series, Paper No. 14.

Van Os, Roos, and Roeline Knottnerus. 2011. *Dutch Bilateral Investment Treaties: A Gateway to 'Treaty Shopping' for Investment Protection by Multinational Companies.* Amsterdam, Netherlands: SOMO.

Vandevelde, Kenneth J. 1998. "Investment Liberalization and Economic Development: The Role of Bilateral Investment Treaties." *Columbia Journal of Transnational Law* 36 (3): 501–528.

———. 2005. "A Brief History of International Investment Agreements." *U.C. Davis Journal of International Law & Policy* 12: 157–194.

———. 2010. "A Unified Theory of Fair and Equitable Treatment." *New York University Journal of International Law and Politics* 43 (1): 43–106.

Viera Martins, José Henrique. 2017. Brazil's Cooperation and Facilitation Investment Agreements (CFIA) and Recent Developments. *Investment Treaty News.*

Vis-Dunbar, Damon. 2009. "South African Court Judgment Bolsters Expropriation Charge over Black Economic Empowerment Legislation in the Mining Sector." *Investment Treaty News.*

Waibel, Michael. 2009. "BIT by BIT: The Silent Liberalization of the Capital Account." In *International Investment Law for the 21st Century: Essays in Honour of Christoph Schreuer*, edited by Christina Binder, Ursula Kriebaum, August Reinisch and Stephan Wittich. New York: Oxford University Press.

Wythes, Annika. 2010. "Investor-State Arbitrations: Can the Fair and Equitable Treatment Clause Consider International Human Rights Obligations?" *Leiden Journal of International Law* 23 (1): 241–256.

Yannacka-Small, Katia. 2008. "Fair and Equitable Treatment Standard: Recent Developments." In *Standards of Investment Protection*, edited by August Reinisch, 111–130. Oxford, UK: Oxford University Press.

Yackee, Jason Webb, and Shubha Ghosh. 2018. "Eli Lilly and the International Investment Law Challenge to a Neo-Federal IP Regime." *Vanderbilt Journal of Entertainment & Technology Law* 21 (2): 517–548.

Yu, Peter K. 2017. "Crossfertilizing ISDS with TRIPS." *Loyola University Chicago Law Journal* 49 (2): 321–59.

Zandile, Zezethu, and Andrew Phiri. 2018. *FDI as a Contributing Factor to Economic Growth in Burkina Faso: How True is this?* Available at: https://mpra.ub.uni-muenchen.de/87282/1/MPRA_paper_87282.pdf.

Zarsky, Lyuba. 2006. "From Regulatory Chill to Deepfreeze?" *International Environmental Agreements: Politics, Law and Economics* 6 (4): 395–399.

Zhang, Joe. 2018. *Investment Facilitation: Making Sense of Concepts, Discussions and Processes.* Background Note to the IISD Investment Law and Policy Webinar on Investment Facilitation, IISD, Winnipeg, MB.

Zhang, Xiao-Jing. 2013. "Proper Interpretation of Corporate Nationality under International Investment Law to Prevent Treaty Shopping." *Contemporary Asia Arbitration Journal* 6 (1): 49–74.

Zhang, Yi, Qiangqian Shang and Chun Li. 2018. "FDI Spillovers on Corporate Social Responsibility: The Channel of Labor Mobility." *Sustainability* 10 (11). Available at: https://www.mdpi.com/2071-1050/10/11/4265/htm.

Endnotes

1   For assessments of the PAIC, see, for example, Mbengue and Schacherer (2017) and Kidane (2018b).

2   The first investment treaty to allow for ISDS was the 1969 Italy–Chad BIT (still in force).

3   Starting with the 1959 Germany–Pakistan bilateral investment treaty (still in force).

4   The ICSID statistics also includes claims based on contracts.

5   Information on the average length of ICSID arbitration proceedings does not appear in the more recent annual reports.

6   The existence of other favourable conditions and treaties, such as double taxation treaties, may also weigh on decisions on corporate restructuring (see ECA, forthcoming B).

7   For instance, the arbitration tribunal on RosInvestCo UK Ltd. v. the Russian Federation established under the procedural rules of the Stocholm Chamber of Commerce (SCC Case No. V079/2005) was set up on the basis of a claim of expropriation based on the 1989 UK–Soviet Union BIT, whose article 8 limited the jurisdiction of a subsequent tribunal to "any legal disputes…concerning the *amount or payment* of compensation under Articles 4 [compensation for losses] or 5 [expropriation] of this Agreement…" [emphasis added] and therefore left the question of whether expropriation occurred in the first place outside the scope. However, the tribunal allowed the claimant to "import" the wider article 8 of the 1993 Denmark–Russia BIT via the most-favoured nation provision in the base treaty and entertained the issue of expropriation. The tribunal found that unlawful expropriation had occurred. The claimant was awarded $3.5 million against the original claim of $232.7 million.

8   Jurisprudence also is not consistent over whether corruption, unless specifically regulated in the relevant treaty, automatically leads to case dismissal or a lower quantum of compensation when an award is rendered in favour of the claimant.

9   Another hypotethical scenario can involve a company that invests in a foreign economy in anticipation of a quota withdrawal. The host state is meant to withdraw quotas but does not. The home government takes the issue to the state-to-state dispute settlement, which takes years, and then wins the case. Even if the home government prevails, the investor gets no compensation for the time the quotas applied (Ewing-Chow, 2007).

10   Several recent arbitration cases relate to competition policy, including AES v. Kazakhstan (ICSID Case No. ARB/10/16), revolving around energy tariffs; Global Telecom Holdings v. Canada (ICSID Case No. ARB/16/16), for a failure to create a competitive environment for new entrants and Croatian Courier v. Croatia ((ICSID Case No. ARB/15/5), related to allegedly anti-competitive practices of the state-owned postal services.

11   Presumably, for example, commercially sensitive information submitted in the course of a merger assessment, or a whistle-blowers testimony against a cartel.

12   In 2017 for example, UNCTAD worked extensively with Algeria, Botswana, Libya, Madagascar and Nigeria on issues related to international investment agreements.

13   While the nationality criteria are co-determined by the home economy, rules on investment admission are within the prerogative of the host state.

14   For instance, an ISCID tribunal in Lahoud v. the Democratic Republic of the Congo (ICSID Case No. ARB/10/4) was constituted on the basis of the Congolese New Investment Code (NIC). In 2014, it found the host government in breach of the fair and equitable treatment and expropriation provisions contained in the NIC over an eviction from rented spaces and destruction of property of a company engaged in the energy and forestry business. For a lack of clarity in the domestic legal order, the tribunal interpreted the standard of fair and equitable treatment in the light of international case law.

Chapter 7

E-commerce and integration in a digitalizing Africa

Having started late, Africa is now digitalizing faster than anywhere else in the world. Modes of business and trade are changing, with potential implications for economic development, integration and structural transformation. This chapter deliberates on how African countries can prepare for the digital economy, and in particular whether policy makers should consider e-commerce as a negotiating topic in the AfCFTA. It defines the contours of e-commerce and outlines the main opportunities and challenges associated with digitalization alongside national and regional trends. It presents national and regional strategies and policies, emphasizing the imperative of regulatory coherence. It details the potential of the AfCFTA to build cooperation given the plurality of e-commerce related strategies, policies and regulations. The chapter highlights important developments related to e-commerce at the multilateral level that hold implications for Africa. Thereafter it moves on to discuss the treatment of e-commerce in regional and free trade agreements-to identify common and divergent approaches of relevance in the AfCFTA

context. The chapter concludes by presenting possible approaches for the treatment of e-commerce in the AfCFTA.

Africa's experience in e-commerce: technological changes and policy responses

The digitalization of economies creates both opportunities and challenges for African countries at various stages of development. E-commerce models of business and trade can reduce transaction costs, deliver goods and services remotely and present new opportunities for entrepreneurship, innovation and job creation. A well-known example is the emergence of mobile money solutions that have extended services to many of the previously unbanked. Enterprise productivity tends to increase with greater use of information and communications technology (ICT), and digitalization has led to innovative business financing alternatives, including crowd-funding. By using e-com-

---

Box 7.1:

Defining e-commerce and the digital economy

The term digitalization is used in this report to refer to the transformation of economic activities through the application of digital technologies. The phenomenon is occurring around the world, though the pace and depth of the transformation vary by country and region. The digital economy encompasses both the production and use of digital technologies, goods and services.

Trading in the digital economy occurs primarily in the form of e-commerce, which has been more narrowly defined by the OECD to refer to placing and receiving orders over computer networks, using multiple formats and devices, including the web and electronic data interchange and the use of personal computers, laptops, tablets and mobile phones of varying levels of sophistication (OECD, 2011). The term is used here to cover physical goods as well as intangible products and services that can be delivered digitally. Related payments and deliveries can be offline or online.

Note, however, that statistical estimates rarely distinguish between domestic and cross-border e-commerce. The exact contribution of e-commerce to international trade therefore remains uncertain.

Source: UNCTAD, 2017b.

Examples of businesses active in the different e-commerce business categories

	TRADE IN GOODS	TRADE IN SERVICES	TRADE IN GOODS AND SERVICES
Primarily e-commerce-based business model	Platforms for trade in goods, e.g., Jumia, Mall for Africa.	Platforms for trade in services, e.g., LittleCab (transportation), Tuteria (tutoring), Zest Concierge (cleaning services)	Platforms for trade in goods and services, e.g., Farmcrowdy and Livestockwealth (agriculture)
Primarily traditional business model	Online portal of physical stores, e.g., Woodin Fashion	Online portal of physical service providers, e.g., Zenith Bank and Serena Hotels & Resorts	Commodity and worker exchanges

merce platforms sellers can reach more customers, including in foreign markets. Consumers benefit from the greater options and increased convenience of accessing and comparing more products from a broader range of firms. Technological developments have also contributed to shorter clearance times and transit periods through customs and single window environments, enabling traders to submit required documents at a single electronic location.

The potential challenges are as varied as the opportunities. Foremost, the uneven access to ICTs—across and within countries—can lead to an inequitable distribution of the benefits from e-commerce. Particularly vulnerable to exclusion are those in rural areas, those with little education or literacy and micro, small and medium enterprises with limited ability or means to deploy technologies. Other challenges include unreliable and costly power supply, limited awareness and skills to use e-commerce, insufficient or inconsistent laws and regulations, and limited or deficient transport and logistics infrastructure, lack of online or alternative payment facilities, limited purchasing power, cultural preferences for face-to-face interaction and reliance on cash for payments. A constraint to even appreciating the challenges of cross-border e-commerce is the lack of official statistics in this area, limiting the ability of governments to take informed policy decisions. In the context of regional integration, policies and regulations at national and regional levels affect the degree to which e-commerce can drive trade across borders.[1]

As the breadth of opportunities and challenges suggests, digitalization and e-commerce can mean different things to different stakeholders, and nomenclatures are still maturing. Anchoring the analysis here is defining the digital economy as "the production and use of digital technologies, goods and services," and e-commerce as "placing and receiving orders over computer networks" (Box 7.1).

Status of e-commerce in a rapidly digitalizing Africa

E-commerce enables trade in goods, trade in services and the combined trade in goods and services (Table 7.1). Within these broad categories can be distinguished e-commerce for which the business model is primarily based on e-commerce, and those businesses which maintain e-commerce channels for the purposes of engagement and execution of business functions, such as traditional banks and media. E-commerce channels are varied, including proprietary websites and applications (mobile or web), as well as marketplaces which aggregate consumers and producers.

E-commerce also occurs through social media platforms, such as Facebook, WhatsApp and Instagram, as well as other country and industry specific platforms that traders use as channels for engagement with markets. The digital economy has naturally reduced many barriers to entry, and the dynamism and rapid technological change in the sector may mitigate market concentration costs. But a degree of market segregation remains due to the languages and the particular characteristics of different markets. For instance, African Courier Express in Lagos, Nigeria, follows a "tailor-made for Africa" approach to address the absence of consumer addresses, cash-based economy and unpredictable Lagosian traffic.

The existing and projected potential of e-commerce is evident in the proliferation of businesses and structured pathways, such as competitions and investment programs for the emergence of e-commerce businesses run by venture funds, corporations, technology business incubators, governments and multilateral institutions.[2] It is also evident in the expansion of locally focused e-commerce platforms in Africa (Box 7.2).

E-commerce businesses are transforming the structures of economies, value chains and the nature of economic activities in Africa. Governments are delivering services through e-commerce channels. Solutions such as single windows enable the completion of customs and related formalities for trade in goods. E-visa platforms allow the virtual processing of applications and issuing of visas to visitors. Some governments have commenced processes to integrate e-commerce such that civil registration, taxation, property registration, marriage licensing and business registration and licensing will be conducted on e-commerce platforms.[3]

According to UNCTAD estimates, worldwide e-commerce sales in 2016 reached almost $26 trillion, 90 per cent in business-to-business (B2B) e-commerce and 10 per cent in business-to-consumer (B2C)

sales. China leads the B2C segment and, with the United States, accounted for more than half of all B2C sales in 2016. Also noteworthy is India's entry to the top 10 e-commerce markets for the first time in 2016.[4] E-commerce is hard to measure, however, and few developing countries collect e-commerce data and statistics, especially in Africa.

Regional e-commerce policies and strategies in Africa

Cognizant of the growing importance of e-commerce for the future of their economies and societies, countries and regional groupings across the continent are at various stages of adopting strategies and policies relevant to or directly addressing e-commerce. In many countries, discussions relating to ICT and e-commerce date back to the 1990s. The African Information Society Initiative, launched by ECA in 1996, was instrumental in developing a comprehensive regional ICT-for-development framework for Africa. It contributed to the adoption by many countries of national information and communication infrastructure plans and strategies. While the purview of the plans extend beyond the single issue of e-commerce, they directly address many of the prerequisites for its development. This section highlights selected recent initiatives in the various African regional groups and countries that illustrate the diversity of approaches to increase

---

Box 7.2:
E-commerce platforms in Africa

Several locally focused e-commerce platforms are operating in Africa, including Jumia and Konga (Nigeria), Takealot and Bidorbuy (South Africa), and Kilimall (Kenya). These platforms bring together African consumers and entrepreneurs. Some also sell goods from outside the continent, including from China, which currently dominates cross-border sales. One Nigeria-based site focusing on U.K. and U.S. sellers is the Mall for Africa, which allows customers to buy from about 250 websites, including Amazon, Amazon U.K. and eBay.

Online platforms, whether they operate for third parties or offer their own inventories as well, provide African producers with a venue to sell their products. It is important that there be enough platforms across Africa to avoid having a small number of them limiting the diversity of the goods and services on offer. And the economies hosting these platforms should have adequate competition and consumer protection regulation in place to address practices potentially detrimental to customers.

Source: Kaplan (2018).

the use of digital means to promote trade and regional integration.

SADC has developed a comprehensive regional strategy on the back of most of its members having national ICT strategies. The SADC strategy was developed in 2010 after the six member States assessed the readiness of the region to engage in e-commerce. Based on four pillars, it addresses national e-commerce strategies, legislation, national and subregional infrastructure, skill development, payment solutions and data collection (Table 7.2), accompanied by a plan of action for its implementation.

In 2018, **COMESA** adopted a digital free trade area (DFTA) to use ICT to improve efficiency in cross-border trade. The three main components are:

- E-trade (a platform for online trade, an e-payment gateway and mobile apps for small-scale cross-border traders).

- E-logistics (or the use of ICT to improve logistics).

- E-legislation (legislation which allows countries in the region to carry out e-transactions and e-payments).

Also incorporated into the DFTA is an electronic certificate of origin ("e-CoO"), accessible to users through a web browser. Operationalizing the digital FTA involves a situational review in each country (including through questionnaires relating to the three components) and the parallel development of the trading platform and e-CoO. Individual member States would then be free to begin to trade using the new digital instruments as soon as they consider themselves ready to do so.

The digital FTA can best be described as COMESA gone digital, since the digital tools would promote trade among member States, including through e-commerce (Hope, 2018). Several of the tools (such as the e-CoO) were already developed but not yet implemented, and the COMESA FTA is similar in many ways to the digital free trade zone Malaysia launched in 2017. An important feature of the Malaysian free trade zone that the COMESA programme could consider emulating is its design—

Table 7.2:

Summary of the SADC e-commerce strategy framework

PILLAR	EXAMPLES OF PLANNED ACTIVITIES
Pillar 1: Enable e-commerce environment	• Develop country specific e-commerce strategies. • Harmonize cyber legislation through the identification of best practice legislation in the region. • Set up of a regional label to increase trust and confidence in websites used for e-commerce.
Pillar 2: Develop capacity for e-commerce in each member State	• Engage with various stakeholders including legislators, the financial sector, logistics actors, SMEs, IT companies and end users, including knowledge-sharing platforms that would allow member States to benefit from each other's experiences. • Conduct human development activities.
Pillar 3: Strengthen e-commerce subregional and national infrastructure	• Promote subregional broadband backbones and Internet access points. • Build cost-effective, affordable and secured ICT infrastructure and broadband network. • Deploy ICT infrastructure beyond major cities and towns. • Produce a PPP protocol to support local and external investment in ICT infrastructure. • Elaborate a universal access strategy to connect those who are unconnected. • Establish a regional electronic payment gateway and associated online and mobile payment banking services.
Pillar 4: Institutionalize a framework to implement, evolve and govern the current strategy at regional level	• Establish a SADC observatory for e-commerce with representatives from the various member States to undertake capacity building, support data collection and set up a database. • Establish a structure that would oversee regional dispute resolution relating to e-commerce.

Source: ECA (2010).

Table 7.3:

E-commerce strategies, instruments and initiatives in selected African RECs

REGIONAL GROUP	REGIONAL E-COMMERCE STRATEGY?	REGIONAL LEGISLATIONS/ REGULATIONS	OTHER E-COMMERCE RELATED TOOLS/INSTRUMENTS
COMESA	Yes (e-legislation, e-trade, e-logistics)	Proposed e-legislation Digital signatures etc. Electronic transactions act, Computer misuse Act, Cyber security Act,	Regional payment and settlement system (REPSS)
EAC	No	• Framework for Cyberlaws 2010 • Electronic transaction bill 2014	Operational • Website for reporting and resolving non-tariff barriers • Biometric passport • East African Payment System • Trade Information Portals (REC and countries) Proposed • East Africa Single Customs Territory
ECOWAS	No	Supplementary Acts • Harmonization of policies and the regulatory framework for the ICT sector (2007) • Access and interconnection for ICT sector networks and services (2007) • Legal regime applicable to network operators and service providers (2007) • Universal access/service (2007) • Personal data protection (2010) • Electronic transaction (2010) • Fighting cybercrime (2011)	Operational • Biometric passport Proposed • ECOWAS postal service master plan • ECOWAS customs code • Customs interconnectivity • Digital single windows (regional) • E-certificate ECOWAS rules of origin
SADC	Yes 2010 ICT development strategy and e-SADC strategy framework	Developed • E-commerce/e-transaction model law, data protection model law and the cybercrime model law	Operational • SADC integrated regional electronic settlement system

to be interoperable with similar systems in other countries and regions. This would allow COMESA to ultimately link its programme to similar initiatives in the TFTA, the AfCFTA or more globally.

In September 2017, the **WAEMU** subregion adopted a ministerial declaration recognizing the strategic importance of e-commerce and trade in services and recommended implementing a regional work plan on e-commerce. In November 2018, a ministerial declaration called on member States to identify activities carried out to capture the potential of the digital economy and e-commerce and to address challenges and constraints. It called on the commission to finalize an action plan for the development of e-commerce.

ECOWAS and **EAC** have not developed specific e-commerce strategies, but they have instruments and initiatives to coordinate the efforts of their member States in this area.

Not all regional economic communities have comprehensive digital economy strategies or frameworks, but many have other technology-related policies and tools that foster e-commerce across countries, such as biometric passports, telephone roaming free areas and regional payments systems to support cross-border payments and transfers (Table 7.3).

Goals and action plan in Egypt's national e-commerce strategy

SIX STRATEGIC GOALS	ACTION PLAN (IMPLEMENTATION, GOVERNANCE AND MONITORING)
• Empower businesses through e-commerce. • Leverage e-commerce to incentivize formalization of the informal sector. • Exploit strengths of the ICT sector for e-commerce. • Boost Egypt's logistics sector into a regional hub. • Stimulate growth of the payment sector. • Build Egypt's e-commerce market.	• Megaproject 1: Create an e-commerce hub. • Megaproject 2: Construct a national B2C e-marketplace. • Megaproject 3: Launch a rural e-commerce development initiative. • Megaproject 4: Empower youth and SMEs for e-commerce. • Megaproject 5: Activate and create additional e-commerce payment methods • Megaproject 6: Brand Egypt's BPO/ITES sector

National e-commerce policies and strategies

Similarly, at national levels, countries have undertaken assessments and reviews which have led to the formulation of e-commerce strategies and policies.

Launched at the end of 2017, Egypt's national e-commerce strategy aims to support Egypt in growing its digital economy and to achieve the implementation of its Sustainable Development Goals Vision 2030. It was developed by the Ministry for Communication and Information Technology and UNCTAD. Within its broader vision 2030 for GDP growth and greater prosperity of its citizens,

Egypt has identified specific objectives for e-commerce to boost domestic trade and regional and international exports, to provide a channel for consumers and businesses to buy and sell, and to create jobs and innovation in the e-commerce ecosystem. E-commerce products, services and applications are expected to contribute 2.35 per cent to the economy's GDP by 2020.

South Africa framed its policy debate on e-commerce in its 2000 green paper on electronic commerce. Not a policy document, the green paper was designed to serve as a consultative document and to raise questions on issues to be addressed during

---

Box 7.3:

UNCTAD's eTrade for all initiative in Burkina Faso, Liberia, Senegal and Togo

e-Trade readiness assessment and strategy formulation: The countries that undertook UNCTAD readiness assessments expressed strong interest in e-commerce and have embarked on strategic policy discussions at national level. Some countries have already produced a specific strategy document to guide developments in the sector (Senegal has its Digital Strategy 2025; it established an electronic commerce working group in 2017; and it plans to develop a national e-commerce strategy). Burkina Faso developed three sectoral e-strategies—e-commerce, e-government and e-education—during 2013–17, but the implementation has been mixed due to the lack of steering structures. Burkina Faso's interest in e-commerce is reflected in its new national policy for the development of the digital economy. In Liberia, there is increasing cognizance of e-commerce in policy and private circles, but a common vision is yet to emerge, and the ongoing revision of the telecommunications and ICT policy and strategy covers the area only in general terms. Similarly, Togo has placed ICT development at the centre of national priorities through two sectoral policy statements, but e-commerce has not yet had a dedicated policy.

ICT infrastructure and services: The trend across the four countries is to rely on mobile telephony and mobile broadband Internet rather than to fixed-line broadband Internet. Differences remain stark in reliability, affordability, speed and coverage of the Internet between cities and rural areas, particularly between Monrovia (Liberia) and Dakar (Senegal) and the rest of those countries. The continued importance of a few dominant operators keeps broadband prices high (Liberia, Senegal) or service quality low (Togo).

Trade logistics and trade facilitation: A major challenge to e-commerce is the weakness of physical addressing systems. The situation is slightly better in major cities such as Dakar and Monrovia. Also cited as constraints were inadequate road infrastructure (Burkina Faso, Liberia), the cost of delivery (Burkina Faso, Senegal, Togo), security issues relating to the transport of cash (Liberia) and delays due to inadequate logistics and customs handlings (Liberia, Senegal, Togo). By contrast, there has been important progress in enhancing the reliability of postal services, achieving universal service and facilitating trade, including the establishment of national trade facilitation committees.

Access to financing for digital entrepreneurs: While access to financing may be a challenge for many firms in African LDCs, e-commerce related businesses face challenges in accessing loans, because their business propositions are especially perceived to be unquantifiable and unassessable. In Liberia, venture capital and other sources of funding have not been successful thus far. In Togo, SME financial support institutions or venture capital firms specializing in technology start-ups and e-commerce are rare or nonexistent. In Burkina Faso, incubators and trade support institutions support fundraising, but credit through the banking sector and microfinance institutions remains prohibitively expensive. A State scheme to support start-up financing has just been put in place, but nonfinancial services are still very poorly equipped. In Senegal, the main sources of investment are venture capital companies, the seed fund supported by the Agence française de développement and the shared-cost fund launched by the Agency for Development and Supervision of Small and Medium Enterprises. Firms that have already proven themselves in the market are attracting foreign capital stakes. And the State has recently demonstrated a willingness to fill the gap in public funding for digital entrepreneurship

Payment solutions: In all four countries assessed, cash on delivery remained the main payment mode. Mobile money is gaining pace, while online payments with a credit card or with PayPal are the least used means. Regional efforts through the Banque Centrale des Etats de l'Afrique de l'Ouest are expected to improve the interoperability of financial services offered by different operators by 2020 for Burkina Faso, Senegal and Togo.

Legal and regulatory framework: Some countries have put in place regulations on electronic transactions, cybersecurity, cryptology and personal data protection to provide a legal basis for the development of e-government and e-commerce (Senegal, Togo). These efforts are sometimes linked to policy developments in regional economic communities (ECOWAS). Liberia lags behind regional and global standards with outdated laws or no legislation in key areas such as consumer/data protection and cybercrime. Even in countries with legal and regulatory frameworks, private sector actors are poorly informed about the legislation and its impact on their activity.

E-commerce skills development: At one end of the spectrum (Senegal), universities and training centres are multiplying, offering a range of varied programmes to foster e-commerce start-ups. The focus is on network engineering, web development and applications and to less extent marketing, management and content development. At the other end of the spectrum (Liberia, Togo), website development, content management and bank application interface specialists are largely missing, or the offer is limited or insufficient in quality. Moreover, weak feedback loops between the public sector, private training schools, academia and the private sector constrain e-commerce skills development and lead to skill mismatches. In Togo, however, the lack of skills was not cited as the main impediment to developing e-commerce. For now, consumers' limited knowledge of e-commerce may be a greater hindrance to the sector's development.

Source: UNCTAD (2018 a, 2018 c, 2018d, 2018e, 2018g, 2018h, 2018j).

Note: Findings for Madagascar, Uganda and Zambia are not included here as the assessments were finalized after the drafting of this section.

government policy formulation. Chapter 12 of the paper highlights the benefits from e-commerce with the implementation of successful strategies and the contribution of e-commerce to sustainable socio-economic growth. It identifies the following principles for South African e-commerce policy:

- Improve the quality of life of people through the optimal use and the exploitation of electronic commerce.

- Develop an e-commerce policy based on international trends and benchmarks while taking cognisance of South Africa's special requirements.

- Balance the interests of the broader spectrum of stakeholders.

- Establish flexible rules and regulations for governance.

- Be technologically neutral.

- Support private-sector-led and technology-based solutions.

- Establish PPPs that promote and encourage the development and use of e-commerce.

- Support micro, small and medium enterprises.

The green paper was to be followed by a white paper and legislation. While a white paper was never published, the Electronic Communications and Transactions Act was passed in 2002. Since then, taxation has been at the forefront in Africa of South African e-commerce policy. A review of taxation in the digital economy concluded the South African tax law provided an opportunity for foreign e-commerce suppliers to avoid taxation and in so doing deny South Africa tax revenue and create unfair competition to resident suppliers who had to pay taxes (Davis Tax Committee, 2014). In response to the recommendations, South Africa amended its VAT Act in 2014 to better capture the digital economy and foreign and local digital suppliers. The amendments require foreign suppliers of e-commerce services—such as music, electronic books, Internet games, electronic betting and software—to register as VAT vendors and account for output tax if their turnover in South Africa exceeds the threshold of South African rand 50,000.

An increasing number of African countries have been using the UNCTAD-led "eTrade for all" initiative, which supports countries as they prepare for e-commerce. The initiative has identified several policy areas as particularly important for assessing country readiness to engage in e-commerce: e-commerce readiness assessment and strategy formulation; ICT infrastructure and services; trade logistics and trade facilitation; payment solutions; legal and regulatory frameworks; e-commerce skills development; and access to financing. The assessments by UNCTAD in four African LDCs give a broad view of where these countries stand in their readiness to take advantage of the benefits associated with e-commerce (Box 7.3).

Enabling e-commerce in Africa

E-commerce incorporates a range of processes and activities that intersect with various policy and regulatory issues across multiple jurisdictions (Figure 7.1). A vendor and buyer may engage in an electronic transaction, which must then be paid for and delivered. Supporting this trade are the digital identities of both transacting parties and third party service providers, the technology backbone and the regulatory infrastructure.

Identity

Identity at several levels and of various types is both required to engage in and is generated by e-commerce transactions.

Formal identity emanates from civil registration and vital statistics, official systems and other formal sources—and is often a prerequisite for engaging in e-commerce. For example, e-commerce marketplaces and financial service providers may require evidence of formal identity for the use of services. These requirements are often based on the needs of businesses to comply with laws and regulations, for taxation, or to satisfy obligations related to know your customer and anti-money laundering laws. Similarly, formal identity may be a prerequisite for digital workers and consumers on some platforms (as for Tuteria and Uber). For individuals, this can be through formal identity documents, or through other means already verifying identity,

E-commerce transaction map, with policy engagement points

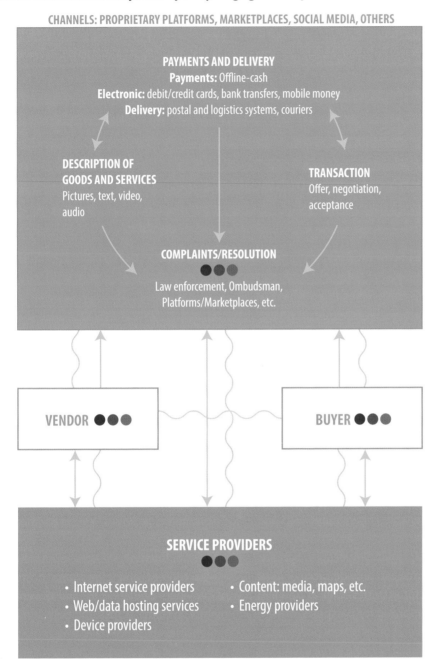

CHANNELS: PROPRIETARY PLATFORMS, MARKETPLACES, SOCIAL MEDIA, OTHERS

PAYMENTS AND DELIVERY
Payments: Offline-cash
Electronic: debit/credit cards, bank transfers, mobile money
Delivery: postal and logistics systems, couriers

DESCRIPTION OF GOODS AND SERVICES
Pictures, text, video, audio

TRANSACTION
Offer, negotiation, acceptance

COMPLAINTS/RESOLUTION
●●●
Law enforcement, Ombudsman, Platforms/Marketplaces, etc.

VENDOR ●●●

BUYER ●●●

SERVICE PROVIDERS
●●●

- Internet service providers
- Web/data hosting services
- Device providers
- Content: media, maps, etc.
- Energy providers

● **Identity:** Who trades
● **Technology and infrastructure:** internet access, energy access, data, transport, postal and logistics systems
● **Regulatory Infrastructure:** transactions, standards, laws and regulations (economy wide and sector-specific)
→ **Transactions**
∿ **Data Flows**

such as registered mobile telephone numbers. For businesses, formal and registered identities can determine whether and to what extent they can engage in e-commerce. In some countries, formal business registration requirements might serve as a prerequisite to engaging with e-commerce mar-ketplaces or service providers. But formal business identity can be a barrier to trading across borders where e-commerce platforms do not allow list-ing vendors or products on the basis of origin or geography.

Formal identity is more applicable with the use of platforms and marketplaces and is less relevant for e-commerce through social media or proprietary platforms. It is also more applicable for trade in goods, which intersects with formal systems including trade formalities and activities for managing supply chains, such as warehousing and delivery.

Digital identities can be created through email and platform-specific accounts and further developed through digital footprints or trails on a range of information including preferences, locations, interests, behaviours and transactions. They can also be created through the mechanisms of digital platforms, such as rating systems and reviews. Such digital identities can be enablers or inhibitors of the capacity of individuals and businesses to engage in e-commerce. For example, less than ideal ratings and reviews on an e-commerce platform can steer consumers away from service providers and vice versa. This type of digital identity includes targeted commercial advertising, political campaigns or screening candidates for employment.

Identity is particularly pertinent for Africa, since half the population has not been registered at birth. Digital identity (ID) systems and platforms that allow for establishing the legal identity of all individuals can help to enable engagement with and participation in e-commerce. The opportunities are manifold. Indeed, legal identification systems based in a digital format can provide proof of legal identity as required for activities such as opening bank accounts and applying for passports, driver's licences, voter's cards and other official documents. Full deployment of digital ID could serve a range of citizens, businesses and government.

Digital ID systems cater for the management and storage of large identification data in digital form, allowing its manipulation and authentication from virtually any location, if ICT platforms are adequate. Of relevance for trade in a digitalizing economy is the identification of buyers and sellers, currently one of the main impediments to the expansion of e-commerce in Africa. For instance, digital IDs provide a source of official identity authentication that FinTech enterprises can use to satisfy financing laws on anti-money laundering and anti-terrorism financing. Such systems must be underpinned by legal and regulatory frameworks and strong policies that promote trust, ensure data privacy and security, mitigate abuse and ensure provider accountability.

Some African countries, including Kenya, Nigeria, Rwanda and Togo have e-identity programs within or managed by the public sector. But digital identity has risks, particularly those associated with security and improper use by government and third parties. ECA has proposed principles of good digital identity covering governance (accountability, oversight, privacy, security and rights), inclusion (coverage, access, usage) and design (interoperability, open standards, sustainability, accuracy). These principles are part of the Digital Transformation Strategy for Africa that the policy organs of the African Union are considering.

Digital identity enables participating in regional and global production (Kagame, 2019). And its governance, management and use will be central to the AfCFTA, particularly the ability of individuals and businesses to trade within and across borders.

Technology and infrastructure

E-commerce activities are predicated on using technology including the devices, energy, mobile data and Internet services, application services, media/content and cloud/data hosting services of providers operating in, and governed by, regulatory systems across multiple jurisdictions. At regional levels, there have been efforts to coordinate regulations and policies for ICT infrastructure, and there is scope to broaden this cooperation at the continental level.

There is in addition the question of access to technology. Digital divides and uneven access to affordable ICTs can lead to an inequitable distribution of benefits from e-commerce, which may bypass people with little education and literacy; people in rural areas; people with limited capability or rights to connect; and micro, small and medium enterprises.

Figure 7.2:

Internet penetration rates in Africa (per cent of individuals using the Internet)

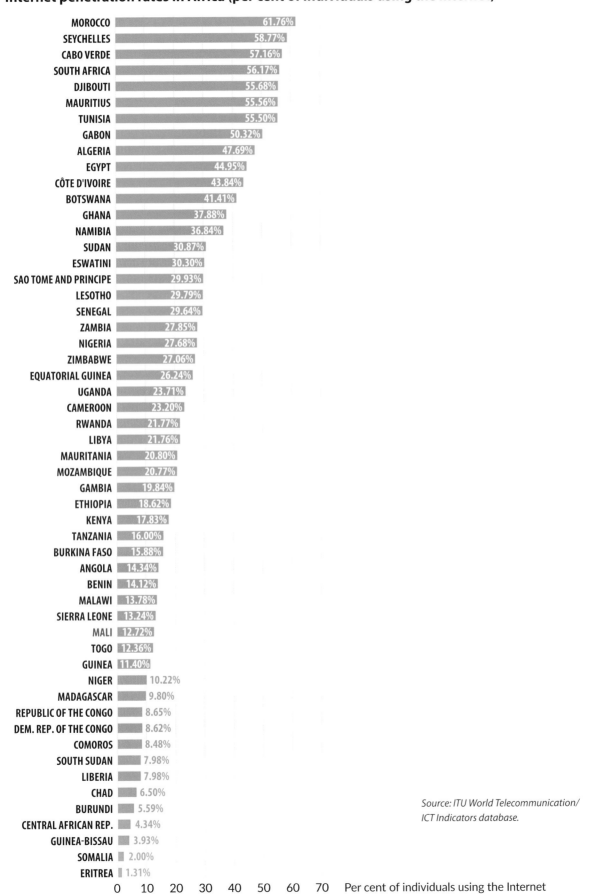

Source: ITU World Telecommunication/
ICT Indicators database.

Households with Internet access at home (2010–17) Per cent of total households

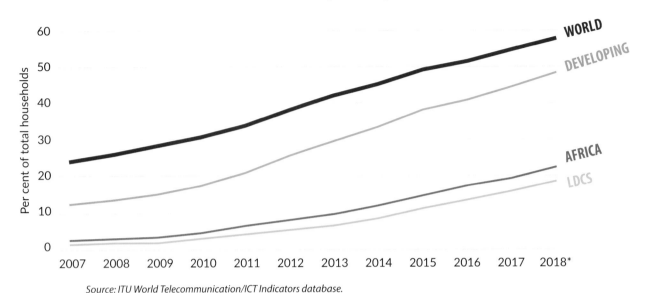

Source: ITU World Telecommunication/ICT Indicators database.

The top five performers in Internet use (Morocco, Seychelles, South Africa, Djibouti and Cabo Verde) reported more than 50 per cent of their population using the Internet in 2017. But the bottom five (Burundi, Central African Republic, Guinea-Bissau, Somalia and Eritrea) were at less than 6 per cent (Figure 7.2).

While the number of households with Internet access is increasing in Africa (Figure 7.3), Africa's digitalization is supported in the foremost by mobile-broadband (Figure 7.4). Africa still lags behind the world and developing country averages on both indicators.

Internet access is not the only factor explaining whether consumers can engage in e-commerce.

Figure 7.4:

Active mobile-broadband subscriptions, per 100 inhabitants (2010–17) Per cent of total households

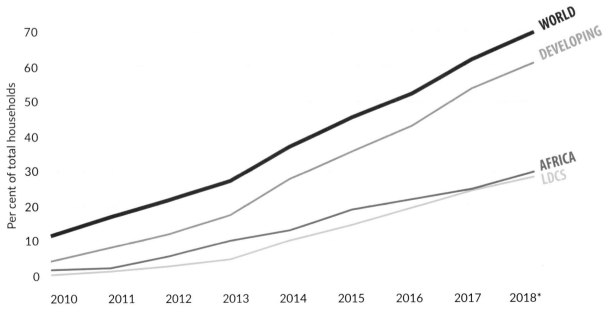

Source: ITU World Telecommunication/ICT Indicators database.

Proportion of Internet users purchasing online and participating in social networks, selected countries, 2015

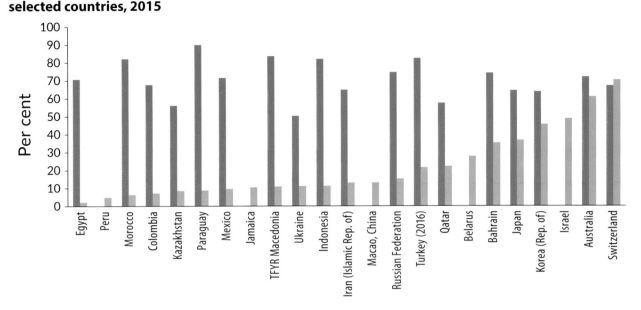

■ Participation rates on social networks   ■ Purchasing or ordering goods or services online

Source: Information provided by the ITU.

In many developing countries, the proportion of Internet users purchasing online can differ quite significantly from proportion of users which are active on social media (Figure 7.5). The two African countries included in the sample below (Egypt and Morocco) both follow this trend with less than 10 per cent of Internet users making online purchases, while 70 to 80 per cent among them participate in social media. Among the possible causes of the relatively small numbers of online shoppers are a lack of trust in the online environment, limited awareness of e-commerce, constraints with online payment options, challenges with delivery of goods associated with logistical challenges, including limited addressing systems, as well as cultural preferences.

Many factors can affect the evolution of access to and use of the Internet (Table 7.5). While Morocco surged from less than 1 per cent of individuals using the Internet in 2000 to the top of Africa's biggest economies in 2016, at close to 60 per cent, Nigeria and Angola achieved more modest rates of 26 and 13 per cent, respectively (Figure 7.6).

South Africa offers insights on what lies behind these figures. A 2017 study by UNIDO found that e-commerce in South Africa was still at a nascent stage compared to more advanced economies (UNIDO, 2017). Less than 10 per cent of South Africa's 33 million adults (20 years and above) were shopping online. And despite the growth of online retail, e-commerce constituted only 1 per cent of total retail sales in 2015 (compared with 8 per cent in the United States). The typical online shopper had Internet access for longer than five years and made purchasing decisions based on factors such as price, convenience and delivery cost and time. Finally, the vast majority of e-commerce transactions were over South African websites, possibly suggesting they may prefer first to feel comfortable with engaging in e-commerce and only later engage in websites based outside their national territory.

UNCTAD's B2C e-commerce Index reflects the processes in an online B2C shopping transaction and integrates elements relating to web presence of the seller, Internet access of users, availability of a payment method (credit card, mobile payment, or cash on delivery), and the delivery of the product to the customer's home or at a pickup point.[5] The only African country in the top 10 developing

Percentage of individuals using the Internet, five biggest African economies

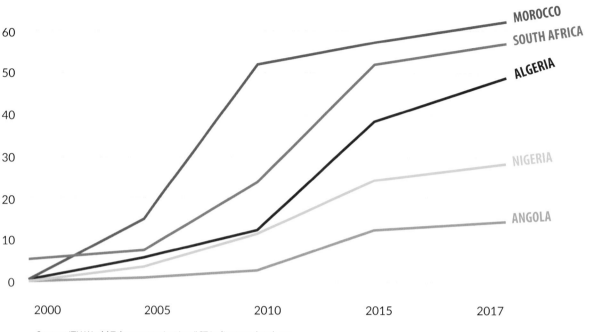

Source: ITU World Telecommunication/ICT Indicators database.

economies on the Index for 2017 was Mauritius, ranked 39th globally (UNCTAD, 2018i).

The UNCTAD B2C E-commerce Index 2018 confirms that Africa is lagging well behind other parts of the world. Two specific issues have featured as the main inhibitors of e-commerce: payments and logistics. To a significant extent, pay on delivery remains a prevailing feature of e-commerce in Africa, in contrast to other regions where payments tend to be completed electronically. Several reasons have been proffered, including low levels of trust and lower use of formal financial services. Cross-border payments are further inhibited by the cost of payments between countries. However, regional electronic payments systems can allow the interface of national banks, reducing the cost and time associated with cross-border payments.

A pan-African payments and settlement platform has been proposed by Afrexim Bank to enable intra-African trade. This continental platform will benefit from interoperability with other financial service providers, such as mobile money, payments platforms, service providers and e-commerce platforms to reach a wide range of users.

On logistics, e-commerce platforms have reported significant challenges with the delivery of goods due to the low availability and often high cost of logistic services, with Jumia, a leading e-commerce platform in Africa, choosing to integrate logistic services into their business model and service delivery (Jumia, 2019). Limited addressing systems and infrastructure deficits also reduce the ease and cost-effectiveness of the delivery of goods (Kaplan, 2018).

Within-country digital divides: e-commerce and disadvantaged groups

Traditionally disadvantaged groups, such as women, youth and persons with disabilities, could see their access to markets enhanced, as e-commerce helps to overcome barriers like physical distance, lack of access to networks, limited access to finance and other assets and, particularly for women, domestic responsibilities. However, without appropriate policies and interventions to ensure that these groups can access new digital opportunities, the digital economy may risk exacerbating existing inequalities.

The gender digital divide illustrates this. In 2017, the gender gap in Internet use was 11.7 percentage

Top 10 developing economies in the UNCTAD B2C e-commerce index, 2018

2018 RANK	ECONOMY	SHARE OF INDIVIDUALS USING THE INTERNET (2017 OR LATEST)	SHARE OF INDIVIDUALS WITH AN ACCOUNT (15+, 2017 OR LATEST)	SECURE INTERNET SERVERS (NORMALIZED) (2017)	UPU POSTAL RELIABILITY SCORE (2017 OR LATEST)	INDEX VALUE (2017 DATA)	INDEX VALUE CHANGE (2016–17 DATA)	2017 INDEX RANK
2	Singapore	84	98	98	100	95.2	1.7	18
15	Hong Kong (China)	89	95	84	92	90.2	1.1	16
21	Korea (Republic of)	95	95	66	100	89.0	0.6	5
33	United Arab Emirates	95	88	66	75	81.2	-4.6	23
34	Malaysia	80	85	78	80	80.8	2.2	39
43	Thailand	53	82	60	98	73.2	4.3	49
47	Turkey	65	69	74	76	71.1	4.5	60
49	Iran (Islamic Republic of)	60	94	52	77	70.9	0.8	47
50	Chile	82	74	81	44	70.4	-0.8	54
52	Saudi Arabia	80	72	49	74	68.7	0.7	46

Source: UNCTAD, 2018i.

Table 7.6:

Regional values for the UNCTAD B2C e-commerce index, 2018

REGION	SHARE OF INDIVIDUALS USING THE INTERNET (2017 OR LATEST)	SHARE OF INDIVIDUALS WITH AN ACCOUNT (15+, 2017 OR LATEST)	SECURE INTERNET SERVICES (NORMALIZED) (2017)	UPU POSTAL RELIABILITY SCORE (2017 OR LATEST)	INDEX VALUE (2017 DATA)
Africa	26	40	29	24	30
East, South & Southeast Asia	48	62	57	62	57
Latin America & the Caribbean	54	53	54	24	46
Western Asia	71	58	51	42	57
Transition economies	65	59	65	71	65
Developed	84	93	88	81	86
World	54	60	56	49	55

Source: UNCTAD, 2018i.

points worldwide. The Internet user gender gap is the largest in least-developed countries, increasing from 29.9 per cent in 2013 to 32.9 per cent in 2017 (ITU, 2017). Despite the increasing number of services available through mobile phones, including financial services, women in low and middle income countries are, on average, 10 percentage points less likely to own mobile phones than men. Among mobile phone owners, women are still 18 percentage points less likely to use mobile Internet, social media apps or SMS services compared with men. A gender digital divide is found in each

African country with gender-disaggregated data (Figure 7.7). The leading barriers to mobile ownership include cost, low literacy, low digital skills and safety and security concerns—all disproportionately affecting women more than men (ITU, 2017).

With such inequalities, the opportunities provided by e-commerce are not equally accessible to all entrepreneurs. Lack of access to digital facilities may also reduce access to opportunities in employment. The gender digital divide limits young women's ability to thrive in new categories of digital jobs. A 2015 study by Deloitte found that "digital know-how" will be the highest-priority skill for businesses of the future (Deloitte, 2015). Research by the World Economic Forum similarly predicts "particularly strong demand growth" for ICT skills in workplaces of the future.[6] Yet young women,

on the whole, remain underprepared for this shift in employer demand, which will be accompanied by automation of existing job categories and advances in artificial intelligence.

Therefore, measures will need to be introduced to support the engagement of less privileged groups with the digital economy. Some African countries have already taken steps to close the gender digital divide and enhance women's access to digital trade opportunities. In Rwanda, the eRwanda project, which trained more than 2,000 citizens, prioritized women. The project focused on having a minimum of 30 per cent female students in each of the classes it offered to young Rwandans to obtain the "ICT driving license". The eGhana initiative is credited with employing women in the IT industry and helping create strong ICT skills among

Figure 7.7:

Individuals using the Internet, by gender, for African countries with gender-disaggregated data, latest available year

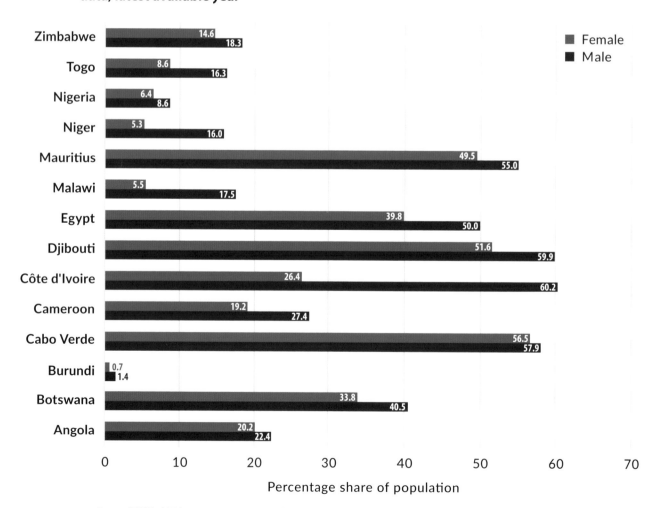

Source: ITU World Telecommunication/ICT Indicators database.

Traditional transaction pathway

| OFFER OF PRODUCT OR SERVICE | NEGOTIATION & ACCEPTANCE OF TERMS | PERFORMANCE OF AGREEMENT | COMPLAINTS & RESOLUTION |

women and young girls employed through the project. The follow-up operation included an eID component that for the first time allows women to be included in processes related to digital identity, credentials and authentication, all essential to online serve delivery, financial inclusion and social protection. In Kenya, the African Centre for Women in Information and Communications Technology implemented the Vusha Project, providing more than 19,000 youth with market relevant ICT skills. Program staff researched the ICT skills, which were most requested in local job postings, and reviewed studies showing skills in most demand.

The potential of e-commerce to contribute to Africa's development is in its ability to bring trade close to those who struggle to access traditional markets, trade information and trade finance. For e-commerce, it will be important to understand the local context and the enabling factors, and which groups are disadvantaged—beyond the remit of trade policy. For example, Nigeria's National Broadband Plan requires the Federal Ministry of Communications Technology to monitor the number of women without access to the Internet. Private educational centres and civil society organizations are also incentivized to train more women to use the Internet. And addressing the underlying inequalities will require interventions in the areas of education. The use of e-commerce to deliver inclusiveness thus has to be connected to a national commitment to gender equality and inclusive growth and development (ECA, FES and OHCHR, 2019).

Regulatory infrastructure

E-commerce transactions are executed through activities and processes mirroring traditional transactions (Figure 7.8):

E-commerce transactions have, however, added layers of complexity emanating from the virtual nature and opaque structure of interactions and relationships. A single transaction may be governed by several layers of agreements between multiple parties, across multiple jurisdictions, or without specification of terms between parties. In addition, inequality of negotiating power is a feature of e-commerce transactions as the party with the greater share of power can dictate the terms for access and use and thus restrict the freedom of choice available to other parties. For example, consumers, businesses and workers are obliged to accept the terms of use of e-commerce marketplaces to access products, services or work and business opportunities. Similarly, users do not necessarily have the opportunity to determine the ways their data collected by e-commerce platforms are stored or used. For example, a buyer making payments via a platform does not have the option to determine the payments processing service provider integrated into vendor's e-commerce platform, or the modalities for the storage of data by the e-commerce platform or its own service providers, such as cloud hosting services and data centres. There usually are several layers of interaction—between users and technology service providers, between users and e-commerce platforms, and between the e-commerce platform and its own service providers.

The new complexities of e-commerce require the support of new regulatory infrastructure to govern the particular data, cybercrime, consumer protec-

Adoption of e-commerce legislation by country

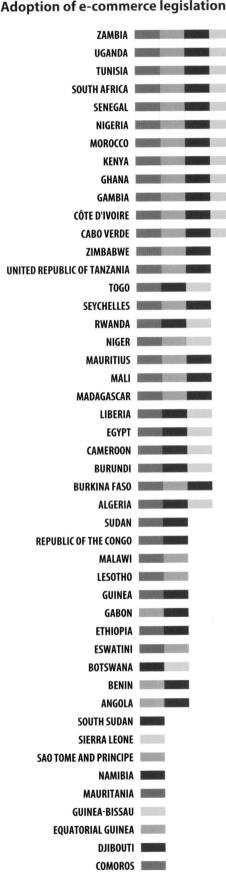

- ■ E-transaction legislation
- ■ Data protection and privacy legislation
- ■ Cybercrime laws
- ■ Consumer protection

0   1   2   3   4   Number of areas of legislation

Source: UNCTAD Global Cyberlaw Tracker, updated on 01.04.2018, https://unctad.org/en/Pages/DTL/STI_and_ICTs/ICT4D-Legislation/eCom-Global-Legislation.aspx.

Note: fields of legislation considered are E-Transaction Laws, Data Protection Privacy Laws, Cybercrime Laws, and Consumer Protection Laws.

tion, e-transaction and taxation aspects of e-commerce. As with physical Internet infrastructure,
there is also a digital divide in regulatory infrastructure in Africa (Figure 7.9).

Box 7.4:
The EU's General Data Protection Regulation

The regulation was developed to protect citizens from privacy and data breaches, whether in the EU or outside its territory. It focuses more specifically on the processing of personal data and the free movement of such data. Key principles are lawfulness, fairness and transparency in the processing of personal data. Data must inter alia be collected for specified, explicit and legitimate purposes (purpose limitation); collected in a manner which is adequate and necessary to the objective pursued (data minimization) and processed in a manner that ensures appropriate security of the personal data (integrity and confidentiality). The regulation applies to a natural or legal person, public authority, agency or other body that determines the purposes and means of the processing of personal data (referred to as controller) and a natural or legal person, public authority, agency or other body that processes personal data (referred to as processor) on behalf of the former. It also specifies remedies, liability and penalties for any infringement of the regulation.

The following rights of the data subject are preserved:

- The right to transparent information on how the personal data of a data subject are collected, the purposes of the processing for which the personal data are intended, the recipients or categories of recipients of the personal data and the period for which the personal data will be stored.

- The right to obtain from the controller confirmation as to whether or not personal data concerning him or her are being processed and, where that is the case, access to the data.

- The right to obtain the rectification of inaccurate personal data.

- The right to the erasure of personal data.

- The right to receive the personal data concerning him or her, in a structured, commonly used and machine-readable format as well as the right to transmit those data to another entity.

- The right not to be subject to a decision based solely on automated processing, including profiling.

Transferring data outside the EU therefore implies one of several cases. Either the European Commission has found that the country to which the data will be transferred has an adequate level of protection (which it has found for only five countries to date) or the transfer will be subject to a number of safeguards—such as binding corporate rules (when the data are moved between entities of the same conglomerate or group of enterprises of which one is based in the EU), standard contractual clauses (or a contract providing protection for individuals' data), codes of conduct or approval certification mechanisms (which ensure compliance with the regulation's standards). All of these approaches can be costly to implement for developing countries and their companies. Adopting a data protection regime equivalent to that of the EU in a country where the optimal level of privacy protection may be different could impose a burden on all actors, even those not doing business with the EU. Contracts and codes of conduct may be more relevant for large companies rather than micro, small and medium enterprises, since they can imply lengthy approval processes and require a data controller or processor that can be held liable and is established in the EU. This can be very costly for smaller firms.

Source: Regulation (EU) 2016/679 of the European Parliament and of the Council of 27 April 2016 on the protection of natural persons with regard to the processing of personal data and on the free movement of such data, and repealing Directive 95/46/EC (General Data Protection Regulation), Official Journal of the European Union, L 119; Mattoo and Meltzer (2018).

Data

E-commerce activities are underpinned by data exchanged by all parties and enablers to a transaction (see Figure 7.1). Given the concerns that have always existed regarding the use of personal data by others and the heightened stakes around privacy following the emergence of Big Data, the protection of data has become a key policy area for all governments. Vast amounts of information are transmitted, stored and collected online daily, and a growing number of data breaches call for adequate policy responses. Key international reference frameworks for privacy and data protection include the Asia–Pacific Economic Cooperation Privacy Framework, the OECD Guidelines and the European Union's General Data Protection Regulation (Box 7.4).

The principles in these frameworks tend to be similar, however. Some data protection regimes apply across the board to all those processing personal data while others opt for sector-specific rules (as for the health sector), rules applicable to the type of processing entity (as for public authorities) or to categories of data (as for data about children). In such cases, other sectors are not subject to regulatory controls. For enforcement, it is typical for countries to set up regulatory agencies, which can exercise ongoing oversight over the conduct of those that process personal data or to respond to actions brought by individuals, or their representative groups.

The African Union adopted the Convention on Cyber-security and Personal Data Protection (the Malabo Convention) in June 2014. The convention aims to establish regional and national legal frameworks for cyber-security, electronic transactions and personal data protection. For personal data protection, each party to the agreement commits to establish a regulatory framework aimed at strengthening data protection and to punish any violation of privacy without prejudice to the principle of free flow of personal data. Each party also commits to establish a regulatory authority in charge of protecting personal data. Only Mauritius and Senegal have so far ratified the convention.[7]

To facilitate the implementation of the Malabo Convention, the AU has also more recently published personal data protection guidelines for Africa (AUC and Internet Society, 2018). The guidelines offer guidance on how to help individuals take a more active part in protecting their personal data as well as specific recommendations for governments, policy makers, data protection authorities and data controllers and processors.

At the regional level, ECOWAS has a supplementary act on personal data protection. Like the Malabo Convention, the act requires the establishment at national level of a legal framework of protection for privacy of data and the establishment of national data protection agencies. Seven of the 15 ECOWAS member States have enacted legislation in compliance with the agreement. Other regional frameworks include the EAC Framework for Cyberlaws (adopted in 2010) and the SADC Model Law on Data Protection. The EAC framework recommends that each member State develop a regulatory regime for data protection but makes no specific recommendations on selection of the law (UNCTAD, 2016). The UNCTAD Global Cyberlaw Tracker finds that of 54 countries in Africa, 22 have legislation on data protection, 7 have a draft law and 13 have no legislation. No data were available for the remaining 12 countries (UNCTAD, n.d.). These figures suggest that African governments are faced not with a lack of information or knowledge on data protection issues, but with other hurdles. The absence of a regulator, even in countries that have data protection laws, points to insufficient resources as one of the causes for the suboptimal regulatory landscape.

But data issues associated with e-commerce and the data-driven economy go beyond the protection of privacy due to the economic value of data as an essential asset for a variety of economic activities including Big Data, AI, machine learning and the internet of things. Privileged access to and control over data are thus becoming key factors for competitiveness. With the increased importance of data in today's economy, the free flow of data across borders has become a central demand of firms engaged in e-commerce and has ultimately found its way into many trade agreements. On the other side, as data flows represent intangible capital assets, some consider that countries should not agree to provisions in trade agreements requiring data to flow freely. As these flows are not compensated in any way, countries lose the ability to exploit the data and to develop their own goods and services and participate in the industrial development of this era. In some cases, countries have opted to impose data localization requirements, requiring data to be processed and stored inside the country.

Data are the life-blood of e-commerce, so continental data policy related to e-commerce should incorporate perspectives that account for the range of actors and activities that underpin and enable e-commerce. In addition, the regulation of data should balance data protection and privacy with the necessity of accessible data for businesses operating in a continental market and the issues of storage, access and security. Data are already regulated at national and regional levels through broad and sectoral regulations and authorities, which will require harmonization.

Cybercrime

Another important challenge facing countries in developing domestic and cross-border e-commerce are concerns stemming from online fraud and data breaches. Addressing cybercrime requires adequate legal and regulatory responses, which are often difficult to establish and maintain due to rapidly evolving technologies and markets. According to the latest information available, of 54 African countries, 28 countries have cybercrime legislation, 11 have draft legislation and 15 have no legislation (UNCTAD, n.d.). The Malabo Convention encourages parties to the agreement to develop a national cyber security policy which is to be implemented by a host of measures such as legislation, sensitization and capacity-building initiatives, public-private partnerships and international cooperation. Other significant global instruments include the Council of Europe Convention on Cybercrime (2001) and the Commonwealth Model Law on Computer and Computer-related Crime (2002).

In addition to adequate legislation, efforts are needed to enforce laws and strengthen the capacity of computer emergency response teams. International coordination and cooperation are also important as they contribute to a safe business environment by promoting faster responses and the sharing of information, thus giving countries the opportunity to react quickly and efficiently in combatting cybercrime (UNCTAD, 2015). This is particularly crucial in light of the 2016 report by

---

Box 7.5:
The ECOWAS cybersecurity agenda

ECOWAS, in collaboration with various partners, has been working to promote the secure use of ICT services among its member States. A 2011 directive on the fight against cybercrime aims to adapt the substantive criminal law and criminal procedures of ECOWAS member States. Despite this directive, the ECOWAS region remains vulnerable to cybercrime activities, because of insufficient implementation of the adopted legal and regulatory frameworks at the national level, limited capacity of governments to deal with the complexity of cybercrime issues, limited technical and legal human capacity and expertise, and insufficient awareness among stakeholders of risks relating to cybersecurity. Among the additional factors limiting member States' ability to deal with these challenges: most countries had not yet set up Computer Emergency Response Teams and inadequate cooperation between member States and the global community on cybercrime (investigation, electronic evidence etc.). In this light, the ECOWAS Commission developed a cybersecurity agenda in 2015 titled "Enhancing Cybersecurity in ECOWAS region" to promote a collective approach by member States, based on partnerships with relevant partners (including the Council of Europe, ITU and UNCTAD) to encourage more public–private strategies as well as regional cooperation.

Source: GFCE (2016).

the AUC and Symantec which recalls that while some analysts have suggested that Africa's burgeoning e-commerce industry is poised to expand to an estimated $75 billion by 2025, this will come hand in hand with new risks and vulnerabilities, including a rise of cybercrime (AUC and Symantec, 2016). In 2013, 47 per cent of smartphone users in South Africa had experienced mobile cybercrime, and in 2016 one of every seven mobile devices in Nigeria was infected with mobile malware. Given that almost half of the countries on the continent have no legislation or legislation still in draft form, a continued push for legislation is essential, including regional initiatives accompanied by capacity building for law enforcement officials, prosecutors and the judiciary.

E-transaction laws and e-signatures

E-transaction laws guarantee legal equivalence between paper-based and electronic forms of exchange. Many countries that have such laws were influenced by the legislative standards prepared by the United Nations Commission on International Trade Law, including its model law on electronic commerce (1996), model law on electronic signature (2001) and convention on the use of electronic communications in international contracts. In Africa 29 countries have e-transaction legislation, 12 still have draft legislation and 4 have no legislation. No data were available for 9 countries (UNCTAD, n.d.). Among the key principles advanced by this category of laws are technology neutrality, nondiscrimination of electronic communications and functional equivalence.

When considering which laws to adopt in this area, some countries may opt to go beyond electronic signatures to incorporate other important contractual terms, such as time and place of dispatch and receipt, acknowledgment of receipt, party location and use of automated message systems. Two broad options can be considered: one is technology-neutral and another specifies which types of signature technologies are acceptable. For example, ECOWAS opted to enact technology-specific legislation based on key public infrastructure.

The adoption of e-transaction laws generally requires a national certification authority, which may be perceived as burdensome for some developing countries due to the human and financial costs. The absence of such an institution or delays in its formation can mean e-transactions lack legal recognition when the intervention of the national certification authority is required. An additional difficulty in some countries is the lack of capacity for enforcement, since judges and practitioners often have limited knowledge of and experience with e-transactions. In these countries, companies may be reluctant to embrace the use of electronic means.

A particular challenge of cross-border e-commerce is the absence in most e-transaction laws of references to the international aspects of e-commerce, such as choice of law, which is one of the potential issues of conflict. One regional grouping which has sought to address some of these implications is the EAC, which developed an electronic transaction bill (2014) to promote electronic transactions. In addition to this bill, EAC States adopted e-transaction policy recommendations to be domesticated by EAC countries through the development of regulatory frameworks (ITC, 2015).

Consumer protection

E-commerce presents challenges for consumers that differ from those encountered during traditional offline commercial transactions. Such challenges have given rise to the need to adapt existing legal and regulatory frameworks to the particular requirements of e-commerce, and they were the driving force behind the revision of the United Nations guidelines for consumer protection, adopted by the UN General Assembly in 2015. As the prevalence of e-commerce is extending globally, instances where the relevant transactions involve businesses and consumers from different jurisdictions are also increasing, potentially leading to transactions between actors governed by different regulations. Moreover, either the jurisdiction of the seller or that of the buyer may lack specific frameworks applicable to e-commerce.

Among the objectives of the revised United Nations guidelines for consumer protection is to ensure a level of protection for consumers using e-commerce that is not less than that afforded other forms of commerce. The guidelines call upon governments to establish national policies for consumer protection that encourage good practices applicable to all forms of commerce, including e-commerce in areas of information disclosure, contract terms, secure payment mechanisms, consumer privacy, data security and dispute resolution and redress. They also propose to include e-commerce in education programmes, encourage member States to enhance consumer confidence through transparent and effective policies and stress the need for awareness-raising among consumers and businesses of their rights and obligations relating to e-commerce. The UN Guidelines refer to other relevant international guidelines and standards on e-commerce, particularly the OECD guidelines for consumer protection in the context of electronic commerce.[8]

Consumer challenges in e-commerce can occur in any of the three stages of the consumer–business relationship in which e-commerce specific consumer protection issues arise: pre-purchase (deceptive information and marketing, misleading advertising, lack of clear and sufficient information on the identity and location of traders), purchase (data security and online scams, identity theft and fraud) and post-purchase (insufficient or non-existent customer care, denial of after-sales service). The protection of consumers from harmful and abusive practices is all the more complex due to the absence of a physical business, the cross-bor-

Box 7.6:
Consumer protection laws and e-commerce in Kenya

The countries of the East African Community are well-known as being among the most proactive in Africa in seeking to reap the benefits of technological innovations and of the digital revolution. However, governments in the region still need to develop their policy and regulatory frameworks in support of e-commerce. Consumer protection is still addressed piecemeal. In Kenya, for example, the Consumer Protection Act No 46 of 2012 is the principal act that lays down and guarantees rights to consumers. Other relevant laws include the Kenya Information and Communication Act 2009 and the Law of Contract Act.

However, several weaknesses of this legal arsenal have been identified. One shortcoming relates to a common practice of most online shopping portals that provide only two options "I agree" or "I disagree" in concluding a contract with customers. This implies that the customer has no other option, except to accept the terms of the contract in order to move forward with the transaction. But the consumer protection act provides that before a customer enters into an Internet agreement, the supplier shall disclose the prescribed information to the consumer with an opportunity to accept or decline or correct errors before entering into the agreement. Moreover, the act does not cover misuse of data made available by online transactions and jurisdiction in case of disputes.

Likewise, the Kenyan Information and Communication Act provides an avenue for the minister responsible for information to prescribe regulations providing for the manner and format in which electronic records shall be filled, created or used. However, this act mainly addresses transactions between the public and government rather than the business to consumer transactions common in online shopping, online banking and money transfers. Both the Consumer Protection Act and the Kenya Information and Communication Act provide legal recognition to the concept of electronic contracts, partially compensating for the silence of the Law of Contract Act on this matter. Even so, no method was developed for the implementation of the fundamental principles for formation of a valid contract like acceptance, revocation etc. to e-contracts. Though several acts are already applicable to e-commerce in Kenya, further development of the regulatory framework would be warranted, particularly as cross-border e-commerce continues to develop.

Source: Lunani (2017).

der nature of e-commerce transactions and insufficient Internet awareness in some jurisdictions and among some consumer groups. Among the key relevant laws for enhancing consumer confidence in e-commerce—such as electronic transactions, consumer protection, privacy, data protection and cybercrime—adoption levels are lowest for laws protecting consumers online. In Africa, only 19 countries have online consumer protection legislation, 6 have a draft law and 10 have no legislation. No data were available for 19 African countries (UNCTAD, n.d.).

Governments and civil society are not the only ones responsible for building trust in e-commerce. Businesses must also play a role, including better business practices to enhance consumer trust, especially in cross-border e-commerce. Businesses may respond to such needs by engaging in self-regulation, trust-marks, codes of conduct and best practices (UNCTAD, 2017a).

Taxation

Digitalization can increase productivity and income, and thus the opportunities for taxation. This includes different types of tax, such as corporation tax, value added/sales taxes from e-commerce, trade tariffs and taxation of users of platforms for economic activity. But policy makers in Africa face the challenge of taxing new activities appropriately. Reliance on digital platforms may weaken the international tax concept that allocates jurisdictional tax claims over profits of multinational companies based on physical presence. Traditional corporate tax systems are based on permanent residency and have not been adapted to be applicable to the digital economy. This raises issues such as enforcement, where to tax nonresident e-commerce businesses, how to assess intragroup transactions, how to classify digital goods, how to identify taxpayers and where and how to collect consumption tax. Concerns related to tax implications from e-commerce are likely to be more pronounced in countries where the uptake of e-commerce is high, but finding ways to address related concerns is of relevance to all countries.

In theory, the digital economy could enable global platform companies to engage more in tax optimization practices, through profit shifting towards locations with lower taxation, which may exacerbate tax base erosion in many African countries. In this context, coherently addressing taxation issues in e-commerce and the digital economy is crucial for African policy makers. However, given the global dimension of the digital economy and the importance of cross-border transactions, these issues cannot be solved from a purely domestic perspective and will require increased regional and international cooperation. At the national level, it is important to ensure that taxation of digital economy activities—for example, through social media or mobile taxes—does not affect economic growth by reducing incentives to engage in those activities, as would appear to be the case in some African countries.[9]

Global and regional approaches for regulating e-commerce

E-commerce in the United Nations General Assembly

The UN General Assembly has committed to harnessing the potential of ICTs to advance all 17 of the Sustainable Development Goals of Agenda 2030. In particular, the digitalization of trade is of direct relevance to several SDGs, including to:

- Promote the empowerment of women as entrepreneurs and traders (SDG Target 5b).

- Support productive activities, decent job creation, entrepreneurship, creativity and innovation.

- Encourage the formalization and growth of micro, small and medium enterprises in developing countries, including through access to ICT-enabled financial services such as online and mobile payments (SDG Target 8.3).

- Promote the integration of micro, small and medium enterprises into value chains and markets (as by leveraging virtual marketplaces) in support of SDG Target 9.3.

- Significantly increase the exports of developing countries (SDG Target 17.11; UNCTAD, 2017a).

The UN Secretary-General recently announced the establishment of a 20-member panel, repre-

E-commerce issues addressed by the different WTO bodies

WTO BODY	ISSUES ADDRESSED
General Council	Review of progress in the implementation of the work programme; Cross-cutting nature; Imposition of customs duties on electronic transmission
Council on Trade in Services	Scope (including modes of supply); Most Favoured Nation treatment; Transparency; Increasing participation of developing countries; Domestic regulation, standards and recognition; Competition; Protection of privacy and public morals; Market-access commitments on electronic supply of services (incl. on basic and value-added telecoms services and on distribution services); National treatment; Access to and use of public telecom; Customs duties; Classification issues
Council on Trade in Goods	Market access for and access to products related to electronic commerce; Valuation issues (relating to Agreement on Implementation of Article VII of the GATT 1994); Issues relating to the Agreement on Import Licensing Procedures; Customs duties and other duties and charges; Standards in relation to e-commerce; Rules of origin; Classification issues
TRIPS Council	Protection and enforcement of copyright and related rights; Protection and enforcement of trademarks; New technologies and access to technology
Committee on Trade and Development	Effects of e-commerce on the trade and economic prospects of developing countries, including their SMEs; Challenges to and ways of enhancing the participation of developing countries in e-commerce, incl. as exporters of electronically delivered products; Role of improved access to infrastructure and transfer of technology, and of movement of natural persons; Use of information technology in the integration of developing countries in the multilateral trading system; Possible impact of e-commerce on the traditional means of distribution of physical goods; Financial implications of e-commerce for developing countries

Source: WTO (2017a).

senting government, private industry, civil society, academia and the technical community, which is tasked to contribute to the broader public debate on the importance of cooperative and interdisciplinary approaches to ensure a safe and inclusive digital future for all taking into account relevant human rights norms. One of the premises for the creation of this panel is that technology is neither good nor bad, but is a powerful tool that should be used to improve the lives of all people, especially the poorest and most vulnerable.[10]

E-commerce in the World Trade Organization

The WTO is one among several international organizations involved in the policy discussions touching on e-commerce.[11] In 1998, WTO members agreed to undertake a comprehensive work programme to examine all trade-related issues relating to global electronic commerce (WTO, 1998). This programme was to be pursued in all the relevant bodies—Council on Trade in Goods, the Council on Trade in Services, the Trade-Related Intellectual Property Rights Council and the Committee on Trade and

Development—and to take into account work by other international organizations. The General Council was mandated to provide the membership with regular progress reports.

For the work programme, e-commerce was defined as the production, distribution, marketing, sale or delivery of goods and services by electronic means. It was also decided that the work programme would include consideration of issues relating to the development of the infrastructure for e-commerce (Table 7.7).

The work programme's activity was modest until 2016, when a number of members began introducing new issues relevant to e-commerce, including copyright, e-signatures and consumer protection in addition to a more general trade-related discussion.[12] Key issues failed to garner consensus from the entire membership: whether to make the moratorium on customs duties for electronic transmissions permanent, whether digital products traded electronically are goods (to which the GATT would apply), services (to which the GATS would apply) or products of another nature, and how to implement technological neutrality and the applicability of the likeness criteria to products available online and offline).[13]

In the run-up to the 11th WTO Ministerial Conference (MC11) in 2017, these discussions were organized around four themes: the future of the work programme, the moratorium, possible negotiations on e-commerce and setting up a working group or other institutional structure (WTO, 2017b). At MC11, members decided to continue the work under the work programme based on the existing mandate while seeking to reinvigorate their work, with a mandate for the general council to report to the next session of the ministerial conference. WTO members agreed to extend the moratorium until the 2019 ministerial conference. In addition to this outcome, 71 countries (including only Nigeria from Africa) issued a joint statement on electronic commerce, affirming their intention to initiate exploratory work towards future WTO negotiations on trade-related aspects of e-commerce. Participation would be open to all WTO members and without prejudice to participants' positions in future negotiations.[14] Over 2018, discussions continued under both the work programme and the joint statement, with informal meetings on a regular basis among participating members. In January 2019, 76 (with only Nigeria from Africa) members of the WTO issued a joint ministerial declaration stating their intentions to commence negotiations on e-commerce. In April 2019, these members started exchanging negotiating documents outlining their overall objectives or offering text-based proposals for discussion.

African positions on e-commerce in the WTO

The longstanding position of the African group in the WTO has been that they are not *demandeurs* for the work programme or for the moratorium on customs duties on e-commerce. The group recalled prior to MC11 that African ministers of trade, in their declaration in Addis Ababa in November 2016, had declared that in line with the Agenda 2063: The Africa We Want they would seek to ensure that the work they undertake in multilateral trade and

rule-making support Africa's continental integration agenda and, at a minimum, not undermine it. The group considers that the discussions under the work programme have not yet exhausted a number of questions, including a trade policy perspective, and that the time is not right for negotiations as many members were still coming to grips with the profound changes brought on by the digital transformation of which e-commerce is an integral part.

The group emphasized that the suggestion by some WTO members that e-commerce will allow micro, small and medium enterprises to leapfrog development was not very convincing. In its view, micro, small and medium enterprises were the least likely to compete with multinational corporations, which have become global digital leaders, decimated smaller companies and benefitted from digital industrial policies such as subsidies, ownership of technologies, economies of scale and government-sponsored infrastructure.

The group is concerned that WTO members already had undertaken enough rules. The multilateral rules as they currently existed were deemed to impose constraints on members' domestic policy space and ability to industrialize. In this regard, it preferred to maintain the focus on the Doha Development Agenda, which aimed at achieving development outcomes and to redress the imbalances inherited from GATT/WTO agreements. The "E-commerce for Development Agenda" was in the group's view a trade liberalization agenda. On the moratorium on customs duties on electronic transmissions, the group considers that it was still discussing this issue in view of the revenue implications of the current moratorium, particularly in the context of increasing digitization of goods and services. So, it does not support the automatic renewal of the moratorium (WTO, 2017c).

Only one African country (Nigeria) was among the 71 signatories of the joint statement on electronic commerce issued at MC11, and a few others have joined on an informal basis since the negotiations in 2019.

While the WTO cannot embark on multilateral negotiations as consensus is still lacking across the entire membership, the variable geometry approach currently being relied on reflects the inclusion by a number of countries of provisions and chapter pertaining to e-commerce or digital trade in their regional trade agreements.

E-commerce in regional trade agreements

Issues related to e-commerce have received growing attention in regional trade agreements (RTAs). Provisions on e-commerce are becoming an increasingly common feature and vary across the different RTAs in the type of provisions, their number and the issues addressed. Moreover, these provisions are in some instances scattered across the trade agreements under various chapters and not necessarily in e-commerce provisions. Examples include provisions relating to telecommunications services, which are found under the services chapters and tariff liberalization or IT products, found in goods schedules.

A review of these agreements may be useful for African countries to the extent that they consider adopting any similar approaches in agreements to which they are party. As of late 2018, however, only one African country was party to an RTA that includes e-commerce provisions: the Morocco–US free trade agreement. Several others are engaged in negotiations where such provisions are referred to in draft provisions or scheduled to be included in future negotiations (Box 7.7).

A simple listing of the main types of e-commerce provisions reveals the large number of issues (more than 30) that have been included in RTAs ranging from definitions, to general exceptions, and to cus-

---

Box 7.7:

Agreements Involving African countries and e-commerce provisions

The Morocco–US free trade agreement is the only FTA involving an African country with a standalone chapter on e-commerce. The chapter highlights the economic growth and opportunity that e-commerce provides, the importance of avoiding barriers to its use and development and the applicability of the WTO Agreement to measures affecting e-commerce. It states that the measures affecting the supply of services using electronic means are subject to the obligations contained in the relevant chapter of the FTA dealing with Investment, Cross-Border Trade in Services and Financial Services, subject to any exceptions or non-conforming measures that the Parties may have set out.

The agreement also states that the parties may not impose customs duties, fees, or other charges on or in connection with the import or export of digital products by electronic transmission, though they may continue to impose internal taxes. Further the agreement states that the customs value of an imported carrier medium bearing a digital product of the other party will be determined on the cost or value of the carrier medium alone, without regard to the cost or value of the digital product. Both MFN and national treatment are to be granted to like products of a party as compared with products of a non-party and of the other party, unless specified in the nonconforming measures. It clarifies that the product is to be provided treatment no-less favourable should it be created, produced, published, stored, transmitted, contracted for, commissioned or first made available on commercial terms in the territory of one of the parties. The agreement also provides a number of e-commerce-related definitions.

Several draft economic partnership agreements (EPAs) between the EU and individual African countries or groupings (Central Africa, ESA and SADC) include provisions on the protection of personal data; for dialogue or cooperation aimed at technical assistance and capacity building on regulatory issues raised by e-commerce (including recognition of electronic signatures; treatment of SPAM, consumer protection, etc.) or for future negotiations on trade in services and e-commerce.

Source: ECA (2018).

toms duties, online consumer protection, liability of intermediary services providers and access to and use of the Internet (Monteiro and Teh, 2017). This expanding list reflects the growing scope of what trade agreements cover and the shift from a narrower focus on e-commerce to a broader focus on digital trade. Several authors have attempted to group these provisions in categories. For example, the issues related to e-commerce in RTAs can be categorized into three broad groups: market access commitments, commitments relating to rules and regulation and facilitation commitments (Table 7.8).

A second approach uses the following categories: physical infrastructure (such as the telecommunication system); domestic regulatory system (such as consumer protection) support services systems (such as payments, logistics and express delivery) and border regulations (such as duties, trade procedures) (Monteiro and Teh, 2017).

A third approach distinguishes between general provisions, market access, enabling digital trade, protection of users of electronic commerce and other cutting-edge issues, which include cross-border information flows, data localization and treatment of source code (Wu, 2017).

A final approach seeks to categorize the issues that are included in trade negotiations pertaining to e-commerce in three categories: most contentious issues (such as cross-border data flows, localization measures and transfers of source code), moderately controversial issues (such as liberalization commitments on services and goods necessary for e-commerce) and less controversial issues (such as transparency in e-commerce related measures, measures enhancing consumer confidence)

(MacLeod, 2017). This distinction is pertinent as there has been at times a bid in the WTO to conclude negotiations on "low-hanging fruits" (or less controversial issues), but the inclusion of certain noncontroversial issues can also be a stratagem to create a mandate as well as an attempt to cloud the difficult issues with noncontroversial "easy wins."

The many attempts to develop analytical categories for e-commerce provisions in trade agreements point to the complexity of the e-commerce phenomenon as it relates to international trade, the difficulty in isolating trade-specific measures from more general measures aimed at promoting the digital economy, the differing weight or depth of different provisions in the obligations that they carry, as well as the fact that some of these provisions are being developed while there still is not a full understanding of their potential impact in a fast-evolving area of the economy.

Going back to the first classification proposed, possibly the one that is most closely modelled on the typical trade vernacular, a broader set of enabling issues may need to be addressed even before those related to facilitation, rules and regulations and market access. Figure 7.10 captures this point and illustrates the fact that the enabling issues are the foundations on which facilitation and then market access as well as rules and regulations can be built. It is noteworthy that all the categories, with the exception of market access issues, are commonly pursued outside of trade agreements, including through harmonization and cooperation, in non-trade fora. And even market access can be pursued through autonomous liberalization and outside of formal trade agreements.

Table 7.8:

Categories of E-commerce issues in RTAs

CATEGORY OF COMMITMENTS	EXAMPLES
Market access	Custom duties, valuation issues, movement of natural persons, access to data
Rules and regulations	Intellectual property rights, protection of personal information, consumer protection, unsolicited commercial messages
Facilitation	Paperless trade, e-signatures, digital authentication

Source: Adapted from Ebrahimi Darsinouei (2017).

Figure 7.10:

Pyramidal classification of e-commerce provisions in trade agreements

Source: Kaukab (2017) cited in Ebrahimi Darisinouei (2017).

General trends and issues in regulating e-commerce in trade agreements

Monteiro and Teh (2017) undertook a quantitative analysis of all RTAs notified to the WTO, which identified the 75 RTAs which explicitly addressed e-commerce among the 275 RTAs in force as of May 2017. A number of findings are of relevance for the analysis here.

The first RTAs to include a provision and a dedicated chapter on e-commerce date back to 2001 (provision on paperless trading in the RTA between New Zealand and Singapore) and 2003 (e-commerce chapter in the RTA between Australia and Singapore). Since then, the number of RTAs that address e-commerce has been regularly increasing and represented 27 per cent of all notified RTAs. While 47 per cent of North–South RTAs include such provisions, the figure drops to 33 per cent for South–South RTAs. Among countries that do include e-commerce provisions in their RTAs, the trend is also for the number of provisions in each RTA to increase over time. The average number of common e-commerce provision between RTAs was relatively low, with around six common provisions. Even in RTAs negotiated by the same country, provisions varied significantly, which points to the impact of the negotiating partner on the outcome.

The same study identified different approaches for addressing e-commerce issues in RTAs. Relevant provisions have been included in the main text of the RTAs in a non-specific article to e-commerce, in an article or chapter/section dedicated to e-commerce, or in side documents (joint statements, letters or annexes). The vast majority of notified RTAs (81 per cent) have opted to include them in a dedicated chapter/section. Among those standalone chapters, the most commonly cited objectives were the promotion of e-commerce between parties, cooperation on e-commerce and the promotion of e-commerce use globally.

Some 38 of the 75 agreements reviewed included a provision that referred to the applicability of WTO rules to e-commerce. As many as 66 of these agreements included provisions referring to the promotion and development of e-commerce. For provisions related to custom duties, 56 of the 75 RTAs analysed include at least one provision referring to the non-imposition of custom duties on electronic transmission or digital products. In some cases, the RTAs refer both to custom duties and other fees or charges. In contrast to the WTO's moratorium on the imposition of customs duties, to be renewed at each ministerial conference, several RTAs stipulate a permanent agreement not to impose duties.

Some RTAs seek specifically to prevent barriers to e-commerce. One type of provision states that trade by electronic means should not be treated more restrictively than trade by other means. The relevant provisions sometimes refer explicitly to the supply of services through electronic means. About one-third of the reviewed agreements (25) include provisions aimed at ensuring that digital products do not receive less favourable treatment. These provisions are sometimes drafted to imply that digital products of another party will receive national treatment or most-favoured nation treatment. A specific subset of nondiscriminatory treatment relates to provisions upholding the principle of technological neutrality.

Another category of provisions deals with the domestic legal framework and/or specific regulatory aspects. A first type of provision aimed to promote the adoption of a general framework such as the UNCITRAL model law on electronic commerce. Such a provision can take the form of a best endeavour engagement by the parties to adopt or maintain a legal framework. It can also involve a more binding commitment to take into account relevant international guidelines and standards. Alternatively, some parties of RTAs have committed to avoid imposing unnecessary regulations and restrictions on e-commerce or more positively to promote transparency and predictability. In this category of provisions are articles referring to the exchange of information and experience, research and training activities or assistance to developing countries.

Specific regulatory issues often included in RTAs relate to online consumer protection (49 agreements), electronic authentication and signatures (48), paperless trading administration (47), personal information protection (44), unsolicited commercial electronic messages (21), cross-border transfer of information (19) and liability of intermediary ser-

---

Box 7.8:

E-commerce provisions in mega-regional FTAs

The Comprehensive and Progressive Agreement for Trans-Pacific Partnership (CPTPP) (also known as TPP-11 after the exit of the United States from the agreement) creates a trading bloc that represents 495 million consumers and 13.5 per cent of global GDP. It dedicates a full chapter containing 18 articles to e-commerce. Eleven provisions are drafted as strong obligations (using the term "shall"), and seven as soft obligations (best endeavours or subject to national laws and regulations clauses). Notably, the agreement requires members to allow full cross-border data transfers, bans forced localization of computing facilities and services, prohibits requirements to transfer technology as a condition for conducting business and prohibits the imposition of customs duties or taxes on Internet traffic. There are exemptions in sensitive areas such as consumer protection, privacy and national security. The agreement entered into force on December 30, 2018 for the first six countries that ratified the agreement: Australia, Canada, Japan, Mexico, New Zealand and Singapore.

Currently under negotiation, the Regional Comprehensive Economic Partnership aims to build upon existing agreements between ASEAN and a number of its partners, with 16 countries involved in the negotiations, including the 10 ASEAN member States (Brunei Darussalam, Cambodia, Indonesia, Lao PDR, Malaysia, Myanmar, the Philippines, Singapore, Thailand and Viet Nam) in addition to Australia, China, India, Japan, Korea and New Zealand. The partnership would create an even larger trading bloc as the participating countries represent almost half the world's population and 30 per cent of global GDP. It is expected to include a standalone chapter on e-commerce, which is being developed through a separate working group on e-commerce. Given the presence of strong proponents of e-commerce provisions in the partnership, which are also parties to CPTPP (Australia, Japan, New Zealand), many provisions on the negotiating table are similar. However, the partnership includes a larger number of developing countries, including China and India, which may lead to different negotiated outcomes. As of late 2018, consensus had not yet been reached on the e-commerce and a few other chapters including competition and investment.

vice providers (8). Like the previous provisions, this group of articles have been drafted in both best endeavour language or as a firm commitment by the parties depending on the agreement.

Thus, within RTAs, the scope and extent to which e-commerce issues are included and the way they are addressed varies greatly. Should African countries wish to include certain e-commerce provisions in continental agreements, including the AfCFTA, they could look at this diversity of practices for inspiration and then develop trade rules as necessary in areas that reflect their specific interests and needs. As noted, only one African country (Morocco) is currently party to an RTA with e-commerce provisions and only on African country (Nigeria) is a signatory to the joint statement on e-commerce in the WTO though a few more have participated informally in the meetings in 2018.

Is there a role for e-commerce in the AfCFTA?

E-commerce is attracting growing attention from the private sector and policy makers alike. At a conference organized by the African Union in July 2018, e-commerce was showcased as having the potential to contribute towards increasing intra-African trade. It was also suggested that e-commerce could potentially contribute to the realization of the objectives of the AfCFTA, which itself seeks to contribute to Africa's Agenda 2063. The conference sought to enhance participants' understanding of recent developments in the digital economy, focusing on e-commerce; allow for the sharing of country and regional experiences in the area of e-commerce; explore the merits and scope of using the AfCFTA as a platform for advancing e-commerce in Africa and identify elements of a roadmap for the development of an African e-commerce strategy.

The premise for the conference was that the AfCFTA could be an opportunity to help reap the benefits of engaging in e-commerce (including allowing for economies of scale), that a comprehensive and holistic pan-African e-commerce strategy could be designed to tailor it to the continent's specifics and that such a strategy would support African countries and particularly the African private sector, and

notably the SMEs, in enhancing their readiness and maximizing their participation in e-commerce, thereby further enhancing intra-African trade as well as facilitating the integration of the continent into the global economy.

While the conference recognized that e-commerce presents opportunities for African countries, including in the AU's industrialization agenda, challenges were also identified. These included the fragmented nature of the African market, the nascent state of logistic chains and the inadequate trade-related infrastructure. Specific recommendations included the need for prioritization of investments in hard infrastructure; for enabling measures (such as establishment of national and continental electronic trade platforms, online access to government services and information and electronic single windows); for appropriate legal and regulatory framework to address issues such as intellectual property rights, data protection, consumer protection, cybersecurity, trust and privacy; the need for skill development and capacity building and for cooperation, collaboration and knowledge sharing among African countries. The conference concluded that skill development should target both the private sector and policy and law makers; that any future continental e-commerce strategy should build on RECs' initiatives and ensure coherence between national, regional and continental initiatives and that member States should endeavour to ensure that the necessary infrastructure to support e-commerce is put in place (including upgrading or enhancing telecommunications infrastructure to ensure broadband diffusion).

With respect to including e-commerce into the AfCFTA framework, there was no consensus. It was suggested that proper analysis of e-commerce in Africa should be a prerequisite and that a specific mandate of the ministers of trade was required to include e-commerce in the AfCFTA. Some expressed the view that African countries should be wary of e-commerce, but still seek to leverage its potential contribution to increasing intra-African trade and Africa's overall structural transformation through clear and comprehensive strategies.

The question remains: how, and whether, to handle e-commerce in the AfCFTA. Tangible issues remain around the digital divide—such as unreliable electricity supply, poor telecom networks, lack of broadband Internet availability, high costs of access to the Internet—and related issues pertaining to skills, logistics and trade facilitation. But e-commerce is fast being adopted and integrated into public and private spheres of African economies and rule-making may be premature. Increased intra-African will feature elements of e-commerce—such as digital payments, trade information portals, trade facilitation tools used by governments and logistics systems for transportation and monitoring goods in transit. E-commerce platforms have the capacity to radically transform trade in goods and services, thus reducing the fractured systems for intra-African trade. But would the second phase of AfCFTA negotiations be the right forum for developing an African approach on e-commerce? And in practical terms, what aspects of e-commerce might AfCFTA negotiations address?

Options for e-commerce in the AfCFTA

Africa could learn from regions that have established policy frameworks to support their member States and facilitate regional e-commerce. For example, the Association of Southeast Asian Nations (ASEAN) has a Blueprint 2025 to intensify cooperation on e-commerce, an ASEAN Agreement on e-commerce to facilitate cross-border e-commerce transactions and an ASEAN ICT Masterplan 2020 to transform ASEAN towards a digital economy by 2020. The EU has harmonized data protection with the 2018 general data protection regulation and continues working on an EU digital single market strategy.

When determining the exact route that African countries will take towards an integrated digital economy, they can consider three options.

Option 1: Countries could agree to negotiate a standalone protocol on e-commerce in the context of phase II of AfCFTA negotiations to take advantage of the momentum associated with these negotiations. The inclusion of e-commerce would aim to ensure that the AfCFTA ultimately offers a com-

prehensive set of trade rules that can steer African economies towards leveraging e-commerce as one of the components of the desired structural transformation in the coming years and decades.

Proponents of the inclusion of e-commerce in international trade negotiations point to the ever-increasing contribution of the digital economy to growth and development and the need to ensure that the dimension is adequately reflected in trade agreements. An e-commerce protocol in the AfCFTA would be a proactive, rather than a reactive approach to the evolution of the digital economy on the continent. Cross-border e-commerce is extremely limited in Africa, so such a protocol would be prospective.

Such a protocol could draw from experiences at national and regional levels in order to capitalize on gains achieved and to avoid the replication of strategies with limited success. Importantly, an AfCFTA e-commerce protocol could foster coherence between the institutional efforts such as REC strategies and policies the pan-African payments platform (Afrexim Bank) and the Africa e-commerce platform (African Union Commission), which anticipate and seek to facilitate the emergence of a continental digital economy.

While there are divergent positions among African countries, including at the WTO, the AfCFTA could provide an opportunity for convergence, clarity, and formulation of the policy responses to ensure that e-commerce is a driver of increased levels of intra-African trade and deeper integration. An e-commerce protocol would serve as the legal and regulatory framework to bring clarity to the issues surrounding multijurisdictional transactions. This is especially important in the absence of national legislation in different areas, such as privacy and e-transactions, and in the context of varying regulations between RECs and countries. Such a protocol would also reduce the potential for the erection of digital barriers and promote the interoperability of technology systems between countries and RECs.

The potential pitfalls of this approach would be to overburden the AfCFTA negotiating agenda at the risk of delaying the finalization of pending issues from phases I and II. This option also presupposes that enough AU member States feel comfortable embarking on such negotiations in the context of the overall AfCFTA objectives and principles and would agree on the scope and level of ambition for the negotiations. If one refers to the positions of the African group in the WTO, it appears that many African countries are more focused on maintaining a maximum of policy space to devise an industrial policy for the digital economy rather than on taking liberalization commitments (Foster and Azmeh, 2017). Also, the different routes chosen so far by RECs that have started addressing e-commerce would have to be compared in order to identify a common basis or *acquis* on which to move forward. The prevailing acquis suggests that African countries seem more comfortable undertaking e-commerce commitments in dedicated instruments, such the electronic transaction bill (EAC), personal data protection act (ECOWAS)) and cyber security act (COMESA) (see Table 7.3), or in using digitalization to improve trade facilitation (COMESA digital free trade area).

If this option is pursued, there are three important issues to consider:

1 *Locate e-commerce protocol in broader policy discourse:* E-commerce is enabled by a range of activities and processes, supervised by various regulatory structures at national and regional levels. Any e-commerce protocol in the AfCFTA should account for the multiple processes and layers of activities, interactions and supervisory structures.

2 *Distinguish between types of e-commerce:* There are important differences between types of businesses, platforms and mode of delivery. A blanket approach to an e-commerce protocol may be applicable to some types of e-commerce and limited or irrelevant to other types. A contextual approach is necessary to address the particular models, processes and elements within the main forms of e-commerce.

3 *Regulatory cooperation for cross-border e-commerce:* The complexities of e-commerce are amplified across borders. Standards, trade rules and formalities, consumer and worker protec-tion and identity take on a transnational dimension. Regulatory cooperation to cover the main enablers of e-commerce is necessary to prevent the erection of digital barriers and to foster a landscape to encourage use of e-commerce channels.

Option 2: Countries may choose to prioritize the development of a continental e-commerce strategy under the ongoing AU programmes given the option of eventually integrating e-commerce in the AfCFTA at a later stage. The comprehensive AU digital trade and digital economy development strategy that the African Union (AU) Executive Council (held on 7–8 February 2019) directed the AU Commission, ECA and other relevant stakeholders to develop with the expectation that it be adopted by the AU Summit in February 2020 could already provide guidance and a concrete roadmap to enable member States to fully benefit from the fourth industrial revolution. The strategy could be developed in such a manner as to facilitate the implementation of the AfCFTA, through recommendations to AU member States in favour of specific trade policy measures while stopping short of developing binding trade rules and obligations. A useful starting point could be to consider the treatment of e-commerce at national and regional levels. This would allow countries to develop their policy, regulatory and institutional frameworks and put in place cooperation initiatives before undertaking binding trade commitments in relation to e-commerce. This option in particular recognizes that African RECs and individual countries are still at very different levels in their readiness to engage in e-commerce.

Considering the pyramid of issues that have an impact on e-commerce, prime policy attention among African policy makers may still be required for issues at the base of the pyramid—those aimed at enabling and facilitating e-commerce. While some of these measures could be included in trade agreements, the specific provisions addressing them often relate to cooperation for information exchange, technical assistance and capacity building, which can all be—and in most cases already are—addressed and promoted outside of trade agreements through other mechanisms. Likewise, the development of rules and regulations can be achieved through cooperation among regulatory institutions, particularly in the context of groupings pursuing deep integration which may even develop regional institutions superseding national regulators. This leaves a relatively small set of market-access issues that may require attention by policy makers, but possibly at a later stage.

The risk associated with this approach is that it does not leverage the rigorous timelines, political visibility and momentum of the AfCFTA. AU instruments exist in this area, such the African Union convention on cyber security and personal data protection (or Malabo Convention), which have not attained the breadth of country coverage of the AfCFTA. Despite covering one of the key elements of the digital economy and offering an attractive alternative to the disparate implementations of data protection regulations across the continent, the Malabo Convention has been signed by only 10 countries, and ratified by 2 States, of the 55 AU member States.

Option 3: Countries may decide to integrate a focus on cross-border e-commerce in the AfCFTA aimed at facilitating the development of the e-commerce ecosystem in African economies while stopping short of a standalone protocol. This could involve, for example, identifying areas in the phase I implementation (as in liberalization packages relating to IT products and/or to communications and financial services which have been identified as priority liberalization sectors within the AfCFTA) and in phase II negotiations (with both negotiations on competition and intellectual property having the potential to deliver results on the activities of digital platforms) which could facilitate the emergence of e-commerce. This option may be a way to promote e-commerce through the AfCFTA negotiations and to promote active engagement by the trade communities and stakeholders in member States on these issues without requiring African countries to take on a whole negotiating area in the current round of negotiations.

The shortcoming of this approach is that it may result in more modest outcomes. It would involve a piecemeal approach across several negotiating area, rather than a broader multistakeholder approach that would likely be used in the context of a standalone protocol.

Perhaps more important than the option chosen by African policy makers for e-commerce in the AfCFTA is what they do alongside it. African countries will have to step up their capacity-building efforts, after careful needs evaluation from countries and in collaboration with development partners. The focus should be to develop capabilities for engaging in the digital economy and e-commerce, including e-readiness assessments and assistance for strengthening government capabilities to develop policies in support of and regulations for e-commerce and the digital economy. It will also be important to develop a research agenda that would guide the work of academics and think tanks and allow for evidenced-based policy discussions or negotiations. A priority focus should be the analysis of the existing barriers to intra-regional, cross-border e-commerce faced by exporters of goods and services, particularly those faced by micro, small and medium enterprises, and of the e-business models best suited to the African context. Technical assistance could also help to identify in more detail areas of policy and regulatory convergence among the RECs and to promote the common interests of African countries in the areas outlined in this chapter. Also important, the option chosen must not fracture the African position at the WTO, accounting for the diverse situations on the continent and enabling cooperation between countries.

Key messages and policy recommendations

Key messages

- **E-commerce is likely to be a significant driver and outcome of intra-African trade.** The public and private sectors are increasingly adopting e-commerce platforms—governments deliver services through them, electronic marketplaces aggregate consumer and producer demand as well as trade-related services, traditional businesses have incorporated e-commerce into their business models and operations and individual entrepreneurs and small businesses use social media platforms to engage with market opportunities.

- **Opportunities and challenges of e-commerce in Africa interplay with other policy issues.** These include the AfCFTA phase II issues and policy issues such as data, gender, inclusion, cybercrime, taxation, informal trade, consumer protection, the digital divide, digital identity and e-transaction laws.

- **The e-commerce policy landscape is evolving with policies and strategies at regional and national levels.** Cooperation between African countries can prevent barriers in digital space from being erected through varied regulatory approaches and can inhibit the fracturing of African countries by technology giants.

- **Consistent rules across the African continent could create an environment where firms (whether digital or not) can compete fairly and can simplify cross-border and national e-commerce.**

- **A gap in digital infrastructure and literacy and disparities in access to technologies and the cost of using them determine the extent to which e-commerce will be adopted and, by extension, enable intra-African trade.**

- **An important step for e-commerce development in Africa is the African Digital Trade and Digital Economy Strategy mandated by the AU Executive Council in January 2019.** This strategy seeks to enable AU member States to fully benefit from the fourth industrial revolution and facilitate the implementation of the African Continental Free Trade Area; it will be presented to the AU Assembly for adoption in February 2020.

Policy recommendations

Three policy options are identified for e-commerce in the AfCFTA:

- An e-commerce protocol as an instrument within the AfCFTA agreement.

- An African digital economy strategy covering the governance of cross-border e-commerce and related issues.

- E-commerce perspectives integrated into existing AU instruments.

Regardless of the approach taken for e-commerce in the AfCFTA, African countries can support the development of e-commerce through investing in digital policy capacities, e-readiness evaluations, research agendas for academics and researchers and technical assistance.

References

AUC (African Union Commission) and Internet Society. 2018. "Personal Data Protection Guidelines for Africa." Available at: https://www.Internetsociety.org/wp-content/uploads/2018/05/AUCPrivacyGuidelines_2018508_EN.pdf.

AUC and Symantec. 2016. "Cyber Crime and Cyber Security Trends in Africa." Available at: https://www.thehaguesecuritydelta.com/media/com_hsd/report/135/document/Cyber-security-trends-report-Africa-en.pdf.

Al-Azzam, Ala'a, and Emad A. Abu-Shanab. 2014. "E-Government: The Gate for Attracting Foreign Investments [online]." Paper presented at the 6th International Conference on Computer Science and Information Technology (CSIT). Available at: https://www.researchgate.net/publication/269308681_E-government_The_gate_for_attracting_foreign_investments.

Boateng, R., J. Budu, A. S. Mbrokoh, E. Ansong, S. L. Boateng and A. B. Anderson. 2017. "Digital Enterprises in Africa: A Synthesis of Current Evidence." Development Implications of Digital Economies Paper 2, Centre for Development Informatics, Global Development Institute, SEED, University of Manchester, Manchester, UK.

Burri, M. 2014. "Should There Be New Multilateral Rules for Digital Trade?" E15 Initiative. Geneva: International Centre for Trade and Sustainable Development (ICTSD) and World Economic Forum (WEF).

Casella, Bruno, and Lorenzo Formenti. 2018. "FDI in the Digital Economy: A Shift to Asset-light International Footprint." *Transnational Corporations* 25 (1): 101–130.

CERRE (Centre on Regulation in Europe). 2017. *Big Data and Competition Policy: Market Power, Personalised Pricing and Advertising*. Brussels: CERRE.

Davis Tax Committee. (2014). Addressing Base Erosion and Profit Shifting in South Africa

Deloitte. 2015. *From Brawn to Brains: The Impact of Technology on Jobs in the UK*. https://www2.deloitte.com/content/dam/Deloitte/uk/Documents/Growth/deloitte-uk-insights-from-brawns-to-brain.pdf.

ECA (United Nations Economic Commission for Africa). 2010. "E-Commerce in the SADC Sub-Region Strategy Framework." Addis Ababa, Ethiopia: SADC and UNECA. Available at: http://www1.uneca.org/Portals/6/CrossArticle/4/document/ict/SADC_e-commerce_Strategy_FINAL_Oct18-FINAL.pdf.

———. 2018. "Brief on E-commerce in Africa." Prepared by ATPC for the WAEMU/UNCTAD E-commerce Workshop, held on 9–11 October 2018 in Ouagadougou, Burkina Faso.

ECA, FES (Friedrich Ebert Stiftung) and OHCHR (Office of the United Nations High Commissioner for Human Rights). 2019. *Digital Trade in Africa: Implications for Inclusion and Human Rights*. Addis Ababa, Ethiopia: United Nations.

ECA and South Centre. 2017. "The WTO's Discussions on Electronic Commerce." Analytical Note SC/AN/ TDP/2017/2. Geneva: South Centre.

Ebrahimi Darsinouei, A., 2017. "Understanding E-Commerce Issues in Trade Agreements: A Development Perspective towards MC11 and Beyond." Geneva: CUTS International.

Foster, Christopher, and Shamek Azmeh. 2018. "Digital Technologies and Data Flows are Increasingly the Subject of Provision in Trade Negotiations. How Do African Countries Position Themselves in These Discussions in Order to Expand Their Digital Economies and Support Digital Industrialization?" *Bridges Africa* 7 (2).

GFCE (Global Forum on Cyber Expertise). 2016. "Cybersecurity and the Fight against Cybercrimes in West Africa: Current Status, Challenges and the Future." News item, 12 July.

Graham, Mark, Sanna Ojanperä, Mohammad Amir Anwar and Nicolas Friederici. 2017. "Digital Connectivity and African Knowledge Economies." *Questions de Communication* 32: 345–360.

Hope, Ashly. 2018. "What is COMESA's Digital Free Trade Area and Should SADC Have One Too?" TRALAC Trade Brief T18TB01/2018, TRALAC (Trade Law Centre), Stellenbosch, South Africa.

ITC (International Trade Centre). 2015. *International E-Commerce in Africa: The Way Forward*. Geneva: ITC.

ITU (International Telecommunications Union). 2017. "ICT Facts and Figures 2017." Geneva: ITU. Available at: https://www.itu.int/en/ITU-D/Statistics/Documents/facts/ICTFactsFigures2017.pdf.

Jumia. 2019. "Jumia Services." Retrieved from Jumia Corporation Website: https://services.jumia.com/.

Kagame, P. 2019. "Kagame Makes Case for African Digital Identity." 12 February. Available at: https://www.tralac.org/news/article/13901-kagame-makes-case-for-african-digital-identity.html.

Kaplan, M. 2018. "Africa: An Emerging Ecommerce Market with Many Challenges." 13 June. Available at: https://www.practicalecommerce.com/africa-emerging-ecommerce-market-many-challenges.

Lunani. S. 2017. "E-commerce and Consumer Rights: Applicability of Consumer Protection Laws in Online Transactions in East Africa." *International Journal of Scientific Research and Innovative Technology* 4 (1, January).

MacLeod, J. 2017. "E-Commerce and the WTO: A Developmental Agenda?" Discussion Paper, GEG Africa.

Mattoo, A., and J. P. Meltzer.. 2018. "International Data Flows and Privacy: The Conflict and its Resolution." Policy Research Working Paper 8431, World Bank, Washington, DC.

Meltzer, J. P.. 2016. "Maximizing the Opportunities of the Internet for International Trade." E15 Initiative. Geneva: ICTSD (International Centre for Trade and Sustainable Development) and WEF (World Economic Forum).

Monteiro, J-A., and R. Teh. 2017. "Provisions on Electronic Commerce in Regional Trade Agreements." Staff Working Paper N. ERSD-2017-11, WTO (World Trade Organization), Geneva.

OECD (Organisation for Economic Co-operation and Development). 2011. *OECD Guide to Measuring the Information Society 2011*. Paris. OECD Publishing.

———. 2018. *Implications of E-commerce for Competition Policy: Background Note*. Paris:: OECD Publishing.

Pires, Guilherme, John Stanton and Ioannis-Dionysios Salavrakos. 2010. "The Interaction of Foreign Direct Investment with Electronic Commerce in Less Developed Countries." *Forum for Social Economics* 39 (2): 127–143.

UNCTAD (United Nations Conference on Trade and Development). 2015. "Cyberlaws and Regulations for Enhancing E-commerce: Case Studies and Lessons Learned." Secretariat Note TD/B/C.II/EM.5/2, UNCTAD, Geneva.

———. 2016. *Data Protection Regulations and International Data Flows: Implications for Trade and Development*. Geneva: UNCTAD.

———. 2017a. "Consumer Protection in Electronic Commerce." Secretariat Note TD/B/C.I/CPLP/7, UNCTAD, Geneva.

———. 2017b. "Harnessing E-Commerce for Sustainable Development." In *Aid for Trade at a Glance 2017: Promoting Trade, Inclusiveness and Connectivity for Sustainable Development*. Paris: OECD Publishing; Geneva: WTO.

———. 2017c. *ICT Policy Review: National E-Commerce Strategy for Egypt*. New York and Geneva:: United Nations.

———. 2017d. *Information Economy Report 2017: Digitalization, Trade and Development*. New York and Geneva, United Nations.

———. 2017e. "Maximizing the Development Gains from E-commerce and the Digital Economy." Secretariat Note TD/B/EDE/1/2, UNCTAD, Geneva.

———. 2017f. *Trade and Development Report 2017: Beyond Austerity: Towards a Global New Deal*. Geneva: UNCTAD.

———. 2017g. *World Investment Report 2017: Investment and the Digital Economy*. Geneva: UNCTAD.

———. 2018a. Burkina Faso Rapid eTrade Readiness Assessment. Geneva: UNCTAD.

———. 2018b. "Globalization and Trade: A Holistic Policy Approach is Needed." Policy Brief 64, UNCTAD, Geneva.

———. 2018c. Liberia: Rapid eTrade Readiness Assessment.". Geneva: UNCTAD.

———. 2018d. Madagascar Rapid eTrade Readiness Assessment. Geneva: UNCTAD.

———. 2018e. Senegal Rapid eTrade Readiness Assessment. Geneva: UNCTAD.

———. 2018f. *South–South Digital Cooperation for Industrialization: A Regional Integration Agenda*. Geneva: UNCTAD.

———. 2018g. Togo Rapid eTrade Readiness Assessment. Geneva: UNCTAD.

———. 2018h. Uganda Rapid eTrade Readiness Assessment. Geneva: UNCTAD.

———. 2018i. "UNCTAD B2C E-Commerce Index 2018, Focus on Africa." Technical Notes on ICT for Development 12, UNCTAD, Geneva.

———. 2018j. Zambia Rapid eTrade Readiness Assessment. Geneva: UNCTAD.

———. 2019. "The Role and Value of Data in E-commerce and the Digital Economy and its Implications for Inclusive Trade and Development." UNCTAD Secretariat Note TD/B/EDE/2/2, UNCTAD, Geneva.

———. n.d. Global Cyberlaw Tracker [database]. Geneva: UNCTAD. Available at: https://unctad.org/en/Pages/DTL/STI_and_ICTs/ICT4D-Legislation/eCom-Global-Legislation.aspx.

UNIDO (United Nations Industrial Development Organization). 2017. "National Report on E-commerce Development in South Africa." Working Paper 18/2017, UNIDO, Vienna.

WEF (World Economic Forum).). 2016. "Future Workforce Strategy." Available at: http://reports.weforum.org/future-of-jobs-2016/future-workforce-strategy/.

WTO (World Trade Organization). 1998. "Declaration on Global Electronic Commerce." Adopted on 20 May 1998, WT/MIN(98)/DEC/2, WTO, Geneva.

———. 2017a. "Work Programme on Electronic Commerce," Adopted by the General Council on 25 September 1998." Document WT/L/274, WTO, Geneva.

———. 2017b. "Work Programme on Electronic Commerce: Report by the Chairman." Document WT/GC/W/739, WTO, Geneva.

———. 2017c. "The Work Programme on Electronic Commerce: Statement by the African Group." Document WT/MIN(17)/21, WTO, Geneva.

Wu, M.. 2017. "Digital Trade-related Provisions in Regional Trade Agreements: Existing Models and Lessons for the Multilateral Trade System." IDB (Inter-American Development Bank) and ICTSD International Centre for Trade and Sustainable Development).

Zekos, Georgios. 2005. "Foreign Direct Investment in a Digital Economy." *European Business Review* 17 (1): 52-–68.

Endnotes

1   As this report focuses on the integration of African economies, the emphasis will be on cross-border e-commerce though the existence of a vibrant national e-commerce environment within countries is a strong indicator of individual economy's readiness to engage in cross-border e-commerce.

2   See Aso Villa Demo Day (Presidency of Nigeria), MEST Africa Challenge, UNICEF Innovation Challenge, Mission Billion Challenge (World Bank), Ecobank FinTech Challenge.

3   See Kenya https://www.ecitizen.go.ke/ and Rwanda http://www.gov.rw/home/.

4   See https://unctad.org/en/pages/newsdetails.aspx?OriginalVersionID=1707.

5   The definition of the various components of the B2C index as well as the data sources used are available at: https://unctad.org/en/PublicationsLibrary/tn_unctad_ict4d09_en.pdf.

6   http://reports.weforum.org/future-of-jobs-2016/future-workforce-strategy/.

7   Status as of 10/05/2018 provided by the African Union Commission.

8   See UNCTAD (2017a) for a detailed description of the UN and OECD guidelines.

9   See, for instance, ICT sector taxes in Uganda, Unleash, not squeeze, the ICT sector. Research ICT Solutions, 22 August 2018, available at: https://researchictsolutions.com/unleash-not-squeeze-ugandas-ict-sector/.

10   Secretary-General Appoints High-Level Panel on Digital Cooperation, Press Release, SG/A/1817, 12 JulyJuly 2018.

11   Other organizations such as WIPO, ICANN, ITU, UNCITRAL and UNCTAD and others have developed agreements and solutions to specific issues arising from this particular form of trade and programmes to support the development of enabling conditions for e-commerce.

12   The WTO also provided opportunities for Members to exchange on their national and regional experiences, including in various workshops and seminars held over the last couple of years.

13   See Burri (2013) for a detailed listing of these issues.

14   Joint Statement on Electronic Commerce, communication, dated 13 December 2017, is being circulated at the request of the delegations of Albania; Argentina; Australia; Bahrain; Brazil; Brunei Darussalam; Cambodia; Canada; Chile; Colombia; Costa Rica; European Union; Guatemala; Hong Kong, China; Iceland; Israel; Japan; Kazakhstan; Korea, Republic of; Kuwait; Lao PDR; Liechtenstein; the former Yugoslav Republic of Macedonia; Malaysia; Mexico; Moldova, Republic of; Montenegro; Myanmar; New Zealand; Nigeria; Norway; Panama; Paraguay; Peru; Qatar; Russian Federation; Singapore; Switzerland; Separate Customs Territory of Taiwan, Penghu, Kinmen and Matsu; Turkey; Ukraine; United States and Uruguay; Document WT/MIN(17)/60 dated 13 December 2017.